GCC Financial Markets

The World's New Money Centers

The Gulf Region: Economic Development and Diversification

Edited by Giacomo Luciani, Steffen Hertog, Eckart Woertz, and Richard Youngs

4 Volume Set
Total No of Pages: 1,136

ISBN: 978-3-940924-00-1 (hardcover)
ISBN: 978-3-940924-05-6 (ebook)

The four volumes in this major research collection address the key economic issues which affect the future development and diversification of the member states of the Gulf Cooperation Council (GCC), namely Saudi Arabia, Kuwait, Bahrain, Qatar, UAE and Oman.

The work brings together state-of-the-art analysis by some 40 international scholars who participated in a major joint initiative by the EU and the GCC, the al-Jisr Gulf-Europe Research Program.

This collection will prove an essential reference work for policy makers and scholars on all the critical issues facing the Gulf countries as their economies develop beyond dependence on the oil and gas sector and forge new international alliances.

The GCC in the Global Economy

Edited by Richard Youngs (Director-General, FRIDE, Madrid)
184 pages
ISBN: 978-3-940924-01-8 (hardcover) ISBN: 978-3-940924-06-3 (ebook)

Changing geopolitical realities have seen the Gulf region turning to Asia and Africa to build new economic links, while strengthening old ones. This proactive internationalism is visible not just in economics and energy, but also in politics and security where a host of new agreements has been developed. This work provides an overview of the ways in which the GCC states now need to move ahead with reforms that will reflect issues such as raised expectations from a period of high revenues and the region's demographics.

Resources Blessed: Diversification and the Gulf Development Model

Edited by Giacomo Luciani (Paris School of International Affairs, Sciences-Po, and Princeton Global Scholar)
344 pages
ISBN: 978-3-940924-02-5 (hardcover) ISBN: 978-3-940924-07-0 (ebook)

The Gulf countries have adopted a unique combination of policies to encourage diversification with largely positive results, while there are significant distinctions between the individual cases. This work evaluates various examples to show the extent to which the Gulf economies have diversifed to date, and how results can be measured, taking into consideration factors such as composition of GDP or exports; government services; and the categorization of industrial activities downstream of resources extraction (oil refining, petrochemicals) and their availability (aluminium, phosphates, iron, steel, glass and other energy- and resource-intensive industries).

GCC Financial Markets: The World's New Money Centers

Edited by Eckart Woertz (Princeton Environmental Institute, Princeton University)
304 pages
ISBN: 978-3-940924-03-2 (hardcover) ISBN: 978-3-940924-08-7 (ebook)

Bond markets in the GCC countries are underdeveloped, and the capital mix is heavily skewed towards banks, while ambitious development plans in fields like petrochemicals and infrastructure, as well as a rapidly growing population, create an increased need for finance. This study outlines the structure of various segments of GCC financial markets and points to regulatory challenges and future developments, ranging from capital market structures to the planned GCC Monetary Union, Islamic banking, and sovereign wealth funds.

National Employment, Migration and Education in the GCC

Edited by Steffen Hertog (London School of Economics)
304 pages
ISBN: 978-3-940924-04-9 (hardcover) ISBN: 978-3-940924-09-4 (ebook)

This volume provides a cross-cutting analysis of the policy challenges related to GCC labor markets. It analyzes the different dimensions of segmentation of these markets, factors of change influencing labor supply such as trends in education and demography, as well as the impact of potential future reforms in areas such as immigration policy, labor sponsorship, taxation and minimum wages. The work therefore provides an overview of what arguably will be the core socio-economic challenge for the GCC in the coming years.

GCC Financial Markets

The World's New Money Centers

Edited by
Eckart Woertz

GerlachPress

First published 2012
by Gerlach Press
www.gerlach-press.de

Cover Design: www.brandnewdesign.de
Printed and bound in Germany by
Freiburger Graphische Betriebe
www.fgb.de

Bibliographic data available from German National Bibliography
http://www.dnb.de/EN

ISBN13: 978-3-940924-00-1 (4 vols hardcover set)
ISBN13: 978-3-940924-03-2 (this hardcover volume)
ISBN13: 978-3-940924-08-7 (eBook)

Contents

Introduction 1

Eckart Woertz

1. **Future Direction of the GCC Financial Sector a Specific Look at Banking and Asset Management** 7

Mandagolathur Raghu

2. **Do GCC Stock Markets Support Their Domestic Economies: An Analytical Overview** 31

Randa Alami

3. **GCC Bond Markets** 67

Michael P. Grifferty

4. **Prospects of the Banking and Finance Sector and the Development of Financial Centers** 87

Eckart Woertz

5. **The Determinants of Capital Structure Choice: the Case of GCC Listed Companies.** 111

Lamia A. Obay

6. **Repercussions of Dubai's Debt Crisis** 137

Eckart Woertz

7. **The Impact of Monetary Policy and Financial Sector Development on Economic Growth in GCC Countries** 165

Elias El-Achkar and Wassim Shahin

8. **The Establishment of a Monetary Union among the Member States of the Gulf Cooperation Council** 185

Erwin Nierop and Gabriela Lippe-Holst

9. **Approaches to Islamic Banking in the Gulf** 211

Rodney Wilson

10. **Gulf Sovereign Wealth Funds in International Comparison** 229

Eckart Woertz

11. **How Competitive are Gulf Economies?** 255

Kenneth Wilson

About the Contributors 289

Acknowledgements

This volume is one of a series of four that are the outcome of the research component of the Al-Jisr (the bridge) project, which the Gulf Research Center (GRC) undertook in 2008-10 with support from the European Commission under Grant Agreement no.Si2.501599 (EU-GCC Public Diplomacy/008/2007).

The project's main objective was threefold: Firstly, to enhance public and well as professional knowledge and understanding of the European Union, its policies and institutions, among GCC citizens; secondly, to strengthen reflection and debate about EU-GCC relations and contribute to the future of policy-making between the two regions; finally, to facilitate closer links between the EU and the GCC through the dissemination of information on the EU.

The project, whose overall director was Dr. Christian Koch, had several components, including policy-oriented joint meetings, training sessions about the EU, translation into Arabic of key texts about the EU – and a research component, of which I was overall responsible.

The Al Jisr project was undertaken by a consortium of 11 partners under the leadership of GRC, including:

- the Arab Reform Initiative
- the Bertelsmann Stiftung
- the Centre for European Policy Studies (CEPS)
- the National Technical University of Athens
- the Fundación para las Relaciones Internacionales y el Diálogo Exterior (FRIDE)
- the Istituto Affari Internazionali
- the Saudi Institute of Diplomatic Studies

- Kuwait University
- Sciences-Po (Paris)
- the Centre for Middle Eastern Studies (CMES), Lund University

The research component aimed at establishing the base for a better understanding of the process of economic transformation underway in the GCC and asserting the importance of the latter as a partner to the European Union. The research effort mobilized some 40 researchers and academics, who contributed papers or participated in intensive discussion of draft papers in three research workshops, which took place respectively in Dubai in February 2009; in Doha, in October 2009; and again in Dubai, in June 2010.

The outcome of this massive research effort are the four volumes that are now being published, namely:

- Resources Blessed: Diversification and the Gulf Development Model, edited by Giacomo Luciani
- The GCC in the Global Economy, edited by Richard Youngs
- National Employment, Migration and Education in the GCC, edited by Steffen Hertog
- GCC Financial Markets: the World's New Money Centers, edited by Eckart Woertz

Other papers presented in this book were discussed at a workshop on Gulf banking and finance at the first Gulf Research Meeting (GRM) at Cambridge University in July 2010, which was organized by GRC. This book has also benefitted from a contribution by a member of the Gulf Bond and Sukuk Association (GBSA) to whose foundation the GRC contributed an impetus when hosting a workshop about GCC bond markets in March 2008 with bankers from the UAE. Michael P. Grifferty who co-organized the event has become GBSA's Founder and President and GBSA is poised to play an important role in the development of GCC bond markets as a financial industry membership association that acts as a focal point for discussions within the industry, with regulators, with issuers and the general public. To all sponsors and participants who have contributed to these workshops and conferences and have made them possible a wholehearted thank you.

It goes without saying that in an undertaking of this magnitude very numerous debts of gratitude are incurred. I wish to thank Dr. Abdulaziz Sager, founder and chairman of the Gulf Research Center, for his vision and courage in establishing the center, promoting GCC integration and EU-GCC closer cooperation, material support to our work, and, last but certainly not least, the trust and friendship that he has extended to me. Thanks also to Christian Koch for taking responsibility of the overall organization of the project – a massive undertaking that has not deterred him from continuing with a new project, currently underway. My thanks to the colleagues of the Gulf Research Centre in Dubai, notably Dr. Oskar Ziemelis and Sanya Kapasi, who did miracles in smoothing the organization of all events. I am grateful also to Rachida Amsaghrou, who helped me in managing the research component out of the Gulf Research Centre Foundation in Geneva. Thanks also to all that wrote papers or participated in the discussions – too numerous to be mentioned individually: my intellectual debt to all is indeed very great.

Finally, an especially warm thanks to Dr. Eckart Woertz, my colleague at GRC first and then at Princeton, who took upon himself the task of editing this volume: not the first and certainly not the last project that we undertake in association; and to Radhika Menon, who undertook the task of editing all the individual paper manuscripts and bringing them to some coherent shape.

I was able to complete the preparation of this manuscript during my residence at Princeton thanks to being appointed a Princeton Global Scholar, with support from the Institute for the Transregional Study of the Contemporary Middle East, North Africa and Central Asia, the Department of Near Eastern Studies and the Woodrow Wilson School of Public and International Affairs. I am grateful for this support, which allowed me to make use of Princeton's world class library resources and inspiring environment.

Princeton, April 29, 2012

Giacomo Luciani

Introduction

Eckart Woertz

Spurred by high oil revenues, credit growth and economic diversification, real GDP growth rates in the GCC countries have been high in international comparison. They have been comparable to those of other emerging and developing markets and considerably higher than those of the world or the advanced economies on average (see Figure 1). Qatar and UAE, in particular, have witnessed breakneck development with growth rates in double digit territory until 2008. In 2009, only two GCC countries faced a mild recession (Kuwait and the UAE). While the IMF expects GCC growth to lag emerging and developing economies in the years to 2015, it will still remain at or above the world average. Together with growth in intra-GCC trade in the wake of the GCC customs union, this will inexorably lead to increased demand for financial services.

Figure 1: Real GDP Growth

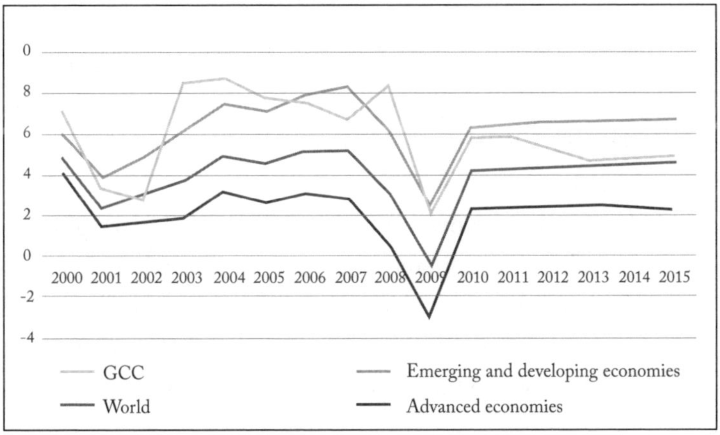

Source: IMF, World Economic Outlook Database, April 2010

Whether it is petrochemical plants, aluminum smelters, power plants, railway lines, housing programs, roads or airports, all these projects are in need of finance. Besides, a rapidly growing population in the GCC countries has provided business for a substantial retail banking market. This increased need for finance meets underdeveloped capital markets in the GCC. While world capital markets show on average a balanced capital structure of debt securities, stock market capitalization and bank assets, the capital mix in the GCC countries is heavily skewed towards bank assets, with a share of nearly 60 percent. Stock markets constitute a significant portion with around a third, but bond markets are underdeveloped. In the GCC, the percentage of corporate bonds issued in comparison to GDP equaled 3.2 percent in 2007. In the US, the ratio was 112 per cent and in China, it was 10 percent. An increase in the relative importance of bond markets in the overall capital structure of the GCC is certainly warranted. It could lead to better capital access, efficiency gains and improved price discovery and risk assessment. GCC stock markets have developed by leaps and bounds over the last decade, but there is room for improvement. Market capitalization and turnover still focus on a limited number of large-cap stocks from specific sectors like banking and real estate. Often these companies also have the state as a majority stakeholder, while most family enterprises in the GCC are not publicly listed. Derivatives have fallen from grace in the wake of the global financial crisis, yet the nearly complete lack of derivative markets in the GCC could prove to be a disadvantage. As banks in the MENA region show a strong bias towards large companies and access to bank credit for small and medium sized companies (SMEs) is more difficult than in other world regions according to the World Bank, the overreliance on bank finance is a particular handicap for this important segment of the economy. Finally, Islamic banking has proved to be a fast growing niche segment of global financial markets, and the GCC countries are in a unique position to capitalize on competitive advantages in this segment.

This book examines these aspects and challenges of GCC financial markets. As financial markets often witness rapid change they are a moving target to study. The papers in this book mostly reflect events as of October 2010.

Mandagolathur Raghu of Kuwait Financial Center (Markaz) gives an outline of the various segments of the GCC financial sector and relates them to macroeconomic figures such as GDP growth, money supply, fiscal balance and inflation. He gives particular attention to asset management practices and the structure of the banking sector and identifies areas where further institutionalization and professionalization are needed.

Randa Alami of the School of Oriental and African Studies (SOAS) in

London assesses the GCC stock markets, their peculiarities and their evolving role in supporting domestic Gulf economies. While growth rates have been considerable over the last decade, she sees major challenges in the regulatory structure, the one-sided sectoral composition and high volatility of these markets. Due to these structural limitations, she cautions that heightened growth expectations could be misguided at this stage.

Michael P. Grifferty, the President of the Gulf Bond and Sukuk Association (GBSA), then discusses the GCC bond markets from a practitioner's point of view. While they are still underrepresented important improvements have been made in this area such as the increased issuance of government bonds. They could someday provide a benchmark all across the yield curve for the growing corporate bond market sector. Grifferty argues that pension funds and other institutional investors could play an important role in the future development of bond markets and draws comparisons with other emerging markets. While he discusses persistent shortcomings, overall he is optimistic that debt market securities in the GCC could enter a phase of accelerated growth in the years ahead.

Eckart Woertz, a visiting fellow at Princeton University, sheds light on the strategy of Dubai, Qatar, Bahrain and Riyadh to develop international financial centers. While they aspire to adapt international norms and regulation to a Gulf context and carve out specific niches, there have been duplications of and competition with existing onshore market places. By comparing the different approaches, Woertz assesses how the various centers might be able to capitalize on existing strengths and brace themselves for the consolidation phase that lies ahead of them.

Lamia A. Obay of the University of Abu Dhabi has subjected the capital structure of publicly listed GCC companies to an extensive econometric analysis. By evaluating the data of 150 non-financial companies in the UAE, Bahrain, Qatar and Saudi Arabia she concludes that size and profitability are significant factors that affect the chosen capital structure, irrespective of the used leverage measure. She identifies a strong dominance of short-term debt and discusses how industry classifications could be added in future research.

Eckart Woertz deals with the Dubai debt crisis which sent shock waves through regional and international capital markets at the end of 2009 and put the viability of Dubai's model of economic diversification into the spotlight. He outlines the unfolding of the crisis and gives special attention to its impact on the market for Islamic bonds (*sukuks*), where Dubai Inc. entities have been major issuers. While he sees continuing problems in the real estate sector, he also highlights Dubai's success and traditional role as a trading hub.

As four of the GCC countries aim to establish a currency union, Elias El-Achkar of the Association of Banks in Lebanon and Wassim Shahin of the Lebanese American University in Byblos combine analysis of financial markets with developments on the macroeconomic level. By econometrically analyzing the effects of exchange rates policies on economic growth they discuss the pros and cons of different exchange rate regimes. They find that a depreciation in the value of the anchor currency tends to impede growth and argue that a flexible exchange rate regime could be beneficial for economic growth and should be gradually adopted in a unified GCC currency.

On a more theoretical plane, Erwin Nierop of the European Central Bank (ECB) and consultant Gabriela Lippe-Holst outline the prerequisites of a successful currency union and how this relates to developments on the GCC level. While Nierop does not write for his organization here, but in his capacity as researcher, he can draw on the experiences he has gained while advising GCC countries in the build-up to the GCC currency union. The authors conclude with a set of recommendations for a successful implementation of a future GCC currency union such as the operational requirements for a functional Gulf Monetary Council and the legal status of a Gulf Central Bank.

Rodney Wilson of the University of Durham compares the structures of the two largest Islamic banking markets in the Gulf, Saudi Arabia and Iran. While Iran has build its Islamic banking system on a state-led top down approach, Saudi Arabia's model is more of a market-driven bottom up approach that has included demand side driven innovation from its customer base and has the potential for international expansion. While he sees the chance for Saudi Islamic banks to succeed in a global market for Islamic banking, he sees the future prospects of Iranian Islamic banks as being closely tied to political developments and a questionable economic sustainability of the Islamic revolution in Iran.

Eckart Woertz deals with Gulf sovereign wealth funds (SWF), which were initially maligned by Western politicians for lack of transparency but later developed into most welcome white knights for struggling Western banks after the eruption of the global financial crisis. While they mostly manage offshore assets and are not part of GCC financial markets, strictly speaking, they influence available options of GCC governments in their roles as agents of development. By using a liability-based approach to their analysis and comparing their asset allocation policies with other SWFs in the world, he speculates that strategically-positioned, government-owned companies might play a larger role than SWFs in the future.

Ken Wilson of the National Research Foundation (NRF) in the UAE discusses a topic that does not seem to be financial on first sight; but the international competitiveness of Gulf economies is of course of paramount importance for GCC banks. Not only does it affect the future success and creditworthiness of their customers, it also impacts on the banks themselves as they require continuous qualification of their workforce and need to brace for international competition as GCC markets have become more open in the wake of the WTO process. By comparing the GCC countries' results in international competitiveness rankings, Wilson identifies lack of innovation and entrepreneurship and inadequate knowledge economy fundamentals as important constraints in the Gulf countries and concludes with a number of recommendations on how these shortcomings could be overcome.

1

Future Direction of the GCC Financial Sector – A Specific Look at Banking and Asset Management

Mandagolathur Raghu

1. The Macro Setting

The global financial crisis, triggered by the collapse of Lehman Bros., led to wholesale liquidity freeze, equity market collapse, volatility and spread spikes, and fall in industrial production all leading to loss of investor confidence. From that situation, we are now slowly limping back to normalcy even though smaller episodes such as in Greece keep the tension alive. The GCC region was believed to have avoided the recession due to certain factors such as weaker integration with the global economy, timely policy response and possession of adequate resources to sustain domestic demand.[1]

The GCC region enjoys one of the highest rates of economic growth backed by a surplus generated over the years thanks to high oil prices. Oil accounts for nearly 50 percent of GDP and 80 percent of export revenues of the region.[2] Hence, the boom in oil prices throughout the 2000s resulted in the swelling of surpluses both in current and fiscal accounts. While the previous oil boom in the 1970s generated similar surpluses, it was channeled more outside the region (predominantly in

1. G.T. Abed, "Impact of the Crisis on the Mena Region and the Road to Recovery," *Arab Banker*, no. 10 (Winter 2009).
2. Sven Behrendt, "When Money Talks. Arab Sovereign Wealth Funds in the Global Public Policy Disclosure," Carnegie Middle East Center, no. 12, October 2008.

treasury investments), while this time around it was channeled inward leading to high levels of credit growth which fuelled inflation and asset price bubbles (both in real estate and stock market) leading eventually to the bursts when the global financial crisis erupted. The immediate impact of the crisis was a steep fall in the oil price.[3] The rapid credit expansion during the boom years had been aided by the growth of external financing in certain markets like Dubai, which evaporated during the meltdown. This increased the risk perception of the region with CDS spreads widening as high as 830 bps for Dubai at one point in time, though it was more specific to defaults related to Dubai entities. In response, the GCC governments enacted various measures including deposit guarantees, provision of liquidity, and monetary easing to a large extent. According to a Booz & Co report, the Saudi plan was one of the largest worldwide relative to overall GDP, representing 10.3 percent of the country's 2008 GDP. The two successive UAE support packages, totaling Dh120 billion, exceeded 12 percent of 2008 GDP.[4]

Other smaller measures like deposit support, stock market support, and capital infusion were also implemented. The economic situation is slowly improving on the back of strong oil prices and a recovering global economy. This section reviews the overall economic scenario for the GCC region against this backdrop.

1.1 Real GDP Growth Forecast

According to the latest economic forecasts from IMF and other agencies (see Table 1), real GDP across the GCC is likely to show a contraction of 0.1 percent in 2009 due to negative growth rates in the three largest economies. Economic growth is expected to resume in 2010 with GCC real GDP growing at 4.2 percent. Following negative growth in 2009, Saudi Arabia, Kuwait and the UAE are expected to see real GDP growth of 3.4 percent, 3.2 percent and 2 percent, respectively, in 2010. For Saudi Arabia, this would mark a return to the average growth seen during 2000-2008; however, it remains sub-standard growth for both Kuwait and the UAE. Steadily increasing crude oil prices (IPE Brent was up nearly 77 percent for the year 2009) coupled with expansionary fiscal policies in many GCC economies are the main catalysts for the 2010 figures. Kuwait and the UAE are expected to have the lowest growth rates in 2010 while Qatar is expected to forge ahead with a 2010 real GDP growth of 13.9 percent following an estimated 8.6 percent growth in 2009.

3. From a peak of $147 in mid-2008, oil prices crashed to a low of $34 in December 2008 before recovering to about $70 later.
4. "One Year On: The GCC Region's Post-economic Crisis Prospects," Booz & Co website, July 10, 2009.

Table 1

Real GDP Growth	Saudi	Kuwait	UAE	Qatar	Oman	Bahrain
Real GDP Growth (2000-2008 Avg) % GDP	3.9	6.6	8.0	10.00	5.8	6.4
Real GDP Growth (2009 e) % GDP	-0.6	-2.4	-1.6	8.6	3.6	3.1
Real GDP Growth (2010 f) % GDP	3.4	3.2	2.0	13.9	5.1	3.7
Source	IIF	IIF	IMF	IIF	IMF	IMF
Inflation	Saudi	Kuwait	UAE	Qatar	Oman	Bahrain
Inflation (2000-2008 Avg) annual change	1.6	3.4	5.8	6.9	2.4	1.4
Inflation (2009 e) annual change	5.1	4.0	-1.0	-4.9	3.5	2.8
Inflation (2010 f) annual change	5.0	4.4	0.9	0.7	3.4	2.8
Source	IIF	IIF	IMF	IIF	IMF	IMF
Fiscal Balance	Saudi	Kuwait	UAE	Qatar	Oman	Bahrain
Fiscal Balance (2000-2008 Avg)-% to GDP	11	27	12	9	8	3
Fiscal Balance (2009 e)-% to GDP	-0.6	17.5	0.4	9.2	0.5	-5
Fiscal Balance (2010 f) - % to GDP	6.3	21.9	9.4	10.8	5	-1.6
Source	IIF	IIF	IIF	IIF	IIF	IIF
Current Account Balance	Saudi	Kuwait	UAE	Qatar	Oman	Bahrain
Current Account Balance (2000-2008 Avg) - % to GDP	18	30	13	23	10	8
Current Account Balance (2009 e) - % to GDP	2.6	28.7	-0.1	8.6	0.7	2.7
Current Account Balance (2010 f) - % to GDP	8.6	36	6.9	16.1	9.5	7.5
Source	IIF	IIF	IMF	IIF	IMF	IMF
Broad Money Growth	Saudi	Kuwait	UAE	Qatar	Oman	Bahrain
Average (1998-2002)-% change	7	5	13	8	6	10
Average (2003-2008)-% Change	15	14	25	30	18	18
2009	10.8	13.4	8.8	-1	4.7	3.3

Source: Central Banks

1.1.1 Inflation

The GCC countries experienced mild inflation in the 1980s and 1990s thanks to the dollar peg and soft commodity prices globally. However, during the period 2003-2007, the dollar peg turned inflationary as the monetary policy was divorced between the US and the GCC. As per an IMF analysis, a peg to the dollar brings macroeconomic stability only if two conditions are met: first, there is macroeconomic stability in the US; and second, the business cycles of the US and the GCC countries are synchronized. For years, these two conditions were met. However, post 2006 business cycles started to diverge as a result of the subprime crisis. Loosening monetary policy in the US contributed to inflationary pressures in the GCC. The authorities stuck with the peg as they judged the inflationary pressures to be transitory. The facts turned out in their favor.[5]

While the US reduced interest rates to prop up growth, the GCC was experiencing high growth but still had to follow the US due to the currency peg. This led to import of inflation. However, it was sharp increases in real estate and other asset prices that mainly contributed to domestic inflation. The onset of the financial crisis fortunately saw the synchronization of the monetary policies of the US and GCC, while commodity prices cooled off significantly. Also, the financial crisis reduced asset prices, including that of real estate. Inflation cooled off significantly in 2009 and is expected to continue to decline in 2010 for most of the GCC economies, except for the UAE, Qatar, and Kuwait where consumer prices are expected to increase 0.9 percent, 0.7 percent, and 4.4 percent, respectively (see Table 1).

1.1.2 Fiscal Balance

Over the last decade, the GCC countries have enjoyed significant fiscal surpluses thanks to rising oil prices and conservative budgets based on low oil price assumption (Table 1). Saudi Arabia, Kuwait and UAE all enjoyed double digit fiscal surpluses as a percentage of GDP during 2000-2008. However, due to contracting oil prices, the fiscal balance slowed down significantly during 2009. In Saudi Arabia, for example, the fiscal balance as a percentage of GDP declined to -0.6 percent during 2009 from an average of 11 percent seen during 2000-2008. In 2010, Bahrain is expected to post a fiscal deficit of -1.6 percent of GDP while the remaining GCC countries are expected to have another year of surpluses, the highest being Kuwait, where a decline in fiscal spending is expected to push the fiscal surplus to 21.9 percent of GDP.

5. "Global Financial Crisis: Gulf Countries Limit Fallout from Crisis," IMF Survey Online, March 12, 2010.

1.1.3 Current Account Balance

The GCC countries also enjoyed significant current account surpluses as a result of an improved trade balance (see Table 1). Current account balance as a percentage of GDP averaged 30 percent for Kuwait during 2000-2008 while the same was at 23 percent for Qatar. However, due to oil price declines as well as the generally inelastic nature of certain key imports, current account balance shrunk during 2009. In the case of Saudi Arabia, for example, it reduced to 2.6 percent during 2009 from an average of 18 percent experienced during 2000-2008. Current account balances as a percentage of GDP are expected to recover across the board during 2010. The largest gain is expected in Kuwait with a 2010 current account balance equal to 36 percent of GDP.

1.1.4 Broad Money Growth

The broad money growth, as measured by M3, is an indicator of economic liquidity. It is important to note that money supply growth was modest, mostly in single digits, during the period 1998-2003 when oil prices were placed at normal if not low levels. However, a significant increase in oil price since 2003 saw accelerated money supply growth during the period 2003-2008 (see Table 1). In the case of Qatar and UAE, it reached 30 percent and 25 percent, respectively during 2003 - 2008. The money supply growth cooled off during 2009 and is expected to be modest in 2010 as well.

In summary, it is believed that going forward GCC growth will be solid but not spectacular since the region has to live with anemic global growth (leading to a stable, if not weak oil price) along with sustained global and regional de-leveraging. In that respect, it is worth quoting the latest outlook for global growth from IMF.[6]

> "The global recovery is off to a stronger start than anticipated earlier but is proceeding at different speeds in the various regions. Following the deepest global downturn in recent history, economic growth solidified and broadened to advanced economies in the second half of 2009. In 2010, world output is expected to rise by 4 percent. In most advanced economies, the recovery is expected to remain sluggish by past standards, whereas in many emerging and developing economies, activity is expected to be relatively vigorous, largely driven by buoyant internal demand. Policies need to foster a rebalancing of global demand, remaining supportive where recoveries are not yet well sustained."

6. IMF, *World Economic Update*, Washington D. C., January 26, 2010.

2. GCC Financial Sector

The GCC financial sector has evolved over the period primarily as a banking centric structure. While other financial services are slowly changing this predominance, the fortunes and travails of the banking sector still determine the overall financial architecture for the GCC.

The GCC financial sector is primarily impacted by four forces:

- Size (defined as M3/GDP)
- Intermediation (defined as Claims on Private Sector/GDP)
- Cross Border Activity (Net Foreign Assets/GDP) and
- Capital Market representation (Market Capitalization/GDP)

2.1 Size

The size of the financial sector as measured by broad money/GDP averaged 58 percent for the period 2000-2009 (Table 2). However, for the year 2009 it shot up to 78 percent primarily due to 20 percent contraction in GDP, only the second time since 2000. Broad money growth averaged 17 percent during the period 2000-2009. However, it slowed down to 11 percent during 2009. Among the GCC countries, Qatar has been witnessing the highest growth rate in broad money at a CAGR of 25 percent between 2000- 2009 followed by UAE at 22 percent.

Table 2: Size of the Financial Sector (%) (M3/GDP)

Country	2000	2001	2002	2003	2004	2005	2006	2007	2008	2009E
Saudi	45	48	55	52	53	47	49	55	53	78
Kuwait	71	86	83	73	67	55	54	60	54	77
Qatar	44	62	61	53	48	51	53	59	50	63
Oman	31	34	36	35	32	31	32	38	33	38
Bahrain	72	79	81	75	68	69	68	81	82	109
UAE	49	62	64	62	64	63	64	78	70	94
GCC	48	56	60	56	56	52	53	61	56	78
Asset Intermediation (Claims on Private Sector/GDP) %										
Country	2000	2001	2002	2003	2004	2005	2006	2007	2008	2009E
Saudi	24	27	29	28	33	37	36	40	42	56

Kuwait	45	57	58	59	56	51	51	63	58	83
Qatar	27	35	29	30	29	35	39	47	47	52
Oman	37	39	39	37	34	31	31	38	38	44
Bahrain	46	47	50	48	51	52	52	62	75	79
UAE	48	53	55	53	55	60	67	80	91	103
GCC	33	37	39	38	41	44	45	54	57	71
Cross border Activity (Net Foreign Assets/GDP) %										
Country	2000	2001	2002	2003	2004	2005	2006	2007	2008	2009E
Saudi	31	32	30	33	40	50	67	81	96	124
Kuwait	25	33	27	19	22	17	19	18	19	38
Qatar	21	22	25	30	26	30	28	22	12	14
Oman	10	10	15	17	18	20	19	24	19	31
Bahrain	42	45	42	37	30	30	38	53	33	27
UAE	34	47	51	42	39	33	25	22	3	9
GCC	30	34	33	32	35	38	45	50	49	63
Capital Market Representation (M.Cap/GDP) (%)										
Country	2000	2001	2002	2003	2004	2005	2006	2007	2008	2009E
Saudi	36	40	40	73	123	205	92	135	53	91
Kuwait	55	77	91	127	127	176	143	181	81	86
Qatar	29	47	55	114	127	205	107	134	76	60
Oman	26	23	25	34	38	50	44	64	34	33
Bahrain	84	84	90	99	121	130	134	147	92	78
UAE	16	20	40	45	78	166	99	120	40	55

Source: Central Bank Websites and Markaz Research

2.2 Asset Intermediation

Claims on the private sector represent loans provided to the private sector. Its proportion to GDP indicates the extent of credit growth in the private sector relative to GDP. While the average was 46 percent for the period 2000-2009, it edged up during the recent years and is placed at 57 percent and 71 percent for the years 2008 and 2009, respectively. The value of claims on the private sector grew by 20 percent annually between 2000 and 2009. However, it contracted by 1 percent during 2009 indicating strain in the financial sector.

Among the GCC countries, Kuwait's intermediation levels shot up from 58 percent in 2008 to 83 percent in 2009 primarily due to contraction in GDP. Also, the average intermediation levels for UAE was placed at 66 percent much higher than the GCC average of 46 percent. In fact, the intermediation ratio shot up above 80 percent in 2007 to reach more than 100 percent during 2009.

2.3 Cross Border Activity

Cross border activity indicates the trend in outward investments from the GCC countries. Cross border activity as a percentage of the size of the economy provides a better perspective on relative quantum of assets which are held outside the home country. While the average ratio stood at 41 percent during the period 2000-2009, it stood at 63 percent during 2009 due to contraction in GDP. Due to high oil prices, the quantum of investments reaching foreign shores from the region grew at a CAGR rate of 20 percent between 2000 and 2009. The bulk of this growth has come in between 2004 and 2008 coinciding with the strong uptick in oil prices during that period. However, the growth slowed down to 3 percent during 2009 due to the financial crisis. Also, the majority of these net foreign assets in the GCC are from Saudi Arabia forming on an average 73 percent of the total GCC foreign assets.

2.4 Capital Market Representation

While the average capital market representation (Market cap/ Nominal GDP) stood at 85 percent for the period 2000-2009, it showed wide year-on-year variation. It stood at well above 100 for the period 2004-2007, a period of relatively strong stock market performance. However, it cooled off since then to 56 percent and 74 percent during 2008 and 2009, respectively. The GCC market capitalization, after hitting a peak of $1.1 trillion in 2007, cooled off to $624 billion at the end of 2009.

In summary, we can clearly see that the GCC financial sector has grown, in most cases doubling, between 2000 and 2009.

Table 3: GCC Financial Sector Metrics

	2000	2009
Size (M3/GDP)%	48	78
Asset Intermediation (Claims on private sector/GDP)%	33	71
Cross Border Activity (Net foreign assets/GDP) %	30	63
Capital Market Representation (Market Capitalization/GDP) %	34	74

3. GCC Banking Sector

The GCC banking sector is an important segment of the GCC financial sector. From a modest asset base of $314 billion at the end of 2003, the total assets for the industry grew to an astonishing $966 billion by the end of 2009, implying an annual growth of 20 percent (Table 4). The banking sector is dominated by domestic players due to regulatory protection. The sector enjoys a large market opportunity set primarily due to absence of non-bank finance companies. Hence, one can find banks actively pursuing asset management, investment banking, stock broking and the like. The GCC banking sector is inherently helped by certain fundamental advantages like benign demographics that is not only young but also rich. The region is still under-penetrated when benchmarked with Western banks. As per an AT Kearney study, loans to nominal GDP ratio for Saudi Arabia was 42.4 percent as against 151.1 for UK, 105.7 for France and 120.9 for Germany[7].

While the sector cruised along nicely all these years, a major brake occurred during the fourth quarter of 2008, after which the sector continued to witness tremendous challenges. While the sector was hit by the global financial crisis, the general assessment is that it has shown more resilience than expected.[8] As per an IMF assessment, regional banks withstood the onslaught better due to their low exposure to structured products and derivatives (both on and off balance sheet). On an average, banks in GCC held 18 percent of their portfolios in securities as of end-2008 of which exposure to equities/derivatives is just 1 percent. Also, regional banks enjoyed high capital and profit leading to larger buffers. In

7. "GCC Banks: On the Road to Maturity. The Laissez-faire Approach to Business Will No Longer Work," AT Kearney, 2010.
8. Abdullah Al-Hasan, May Khamis, and Nada Oulidi, "The GCC Banking Sector: Topography and Analysis," IMF Working Paper WP/10/87.

addition, timely help from central banks reduced the impact. According to a study, GCC governments invested nearly $350 billion in the form of facilities and liquidity windows to ease the pressure on banks.[9] However, their increased reliance on external financing over the period and high exposure to real estate and construction sectors and stock markets weakened them during the crisis. In the first section, the sector is analyzed from a macro perspective and towards the end policy challenges and actions that need to be taken for a sustainable growth are discussed.

Table 4: GCC Banking Sector

USD mn	31-Dec-03	31-Dec-04	31-Dec-05	31-Dec-06	31-Dec-07	31-Dec-08	31-Dec-09
Interest Income	11,940	14,064	22,004	32,329	41,610	47,775	43,647
Interest Expense	5,024	5,170	9,155	15,448	21,278	26,497	23,418
Net Interest Income	6,916	8,894	12,849	16,880	20,331	21,278	20,228
Loan Loss Provision	1,579	1,160	1,442	1,277	1,808	6,857	9,860
Net Interest Income After LLP	5,337	7,735	11,407	15,604	18,523	14,421	10,368
Non-Interest Income	3,773	4,663	8,929	10,748	12,275	12,200	11,262
Non-Interest Expense	3,394	3,895	6,290	9,170	11,637	10,475	6,354
PBT	5,716	8,503	14,046	17,181	19,162	16,145	15,277
Tax	0	0	0	0	0	0	0
Profit After Tax	5,716	8,503	14,046	17,181	19,162	16,145	15,277
Loans	168,697	191,539	253,673	320,556	443,645	593,751	589,773
Deposits	248,052	270,248	332,837	419,988	568,561	688,682	686,629
Equity	35,096	42,329	60,171	74,206	98,266	115,613	129,205
Assets	314,032	348,766	444,512	570,764	796,466	953,401	966,694
Total Revenues of Bank	15,713	18,728	30,932	43,076	53,885	59,975	54,909

9. "GCC Banks: On the Road to Maturity."

Provisions to loans %	0.94%	0.61%	0.57%	0.40%	0.41%	1.15%	1.67%
RoA %	2%	2%	3%	3%	2%	2%	2%
RoE %	16%	20%	23%	23%	20%	14%	12%
L/D	68%	71%	76%	76%	78%	86%	86%
Cost-to-income ratio	32%	29%	29%	33%	36%	31%	20%

Source: Markaz Research

3.1 Assets

As stated before, the assets of the banking sector witnessed a phenomenal growth. However, what is interesting to note is that the share of the largest segment viz., Saudi Arabia came down to benefit UAE and Qatar. While Saudi Arabian banking assets as a percentage of total assets came down from 36 percent in 2003 to 29 percent in 2009, that of UAE moved up from 19 percent (2003) to 33 percent (2009). The case of Qatar is also interesting where the share of assets improved from 6 percent (2003) to 11 percent (2009). Bahrain, considered to be the banking hub of the region, grew more modestly at an annual rate of only 9 percent against the sector average of 20 percent ceding market share.

3.2 Loans

The stupendous credit growth caused the asset price bubble (in real estate and stock markets) which later bust with wide implications. The GCC banking sector loans recorded an average annual growth rate of 23 percent between 2003 and 2009 (see Table 4). The years 2007 and 2008 were remarkable with loan growth averaging 38 percent and 34 percent, respectively. However, the growth contracted to -0.67 percent for 2009 implying considerable slowdown. In tune with asset growth, UAE and Qatar witnessed high growth levels in loans of 34 percent and 35 percent, respectively. This impacted the share of Saudi Arabia again to the benefit of UAE and Qatar. While Saudi Arabia's share fell from 35 percent (2003) to 30 percent (2009), the same for the UAE improved from 22 percent (2003) to 36 percent (2009). The high levels of credit growth were essentially supported by domestic deposits more than external financing. According to the IMF report, GCC banks have a relatively large concentration of credit to big family-owned business groups as well as high net worth individuals, which increases credit risk. In cases like Kuwait, in addition exposure to non-bank financial entities also adds to the risk.

3.3 Provisions

The impact of financial crisis can be directly assessed from this parameter. While provisions just averaged 0.58 percent of total loans during 2003-2007, it reached 1.15 percent during 2008 and 1.67 percent during 2009 nearly three times the long-term average. In absolute terms, provisions increased from $1.6 billion in 2003 to nearly $10 billion by 2009 (Table 4). Pivotal in moving the overall GCC provisions were that of over $1 billion from both Gulf Bank of Kuwait and Bahrain's Arab Banking Corporation, over $700 million from Kuwait Finance House and nearly $500 million from Emirates NBD. UAE and Kuwait lead the table in terms of provision. In UAE, provisions increased from $444 million in 2007 to $1.5 billion in 2008 and to $4 billion in 2009. In other words, between 2007 and 2009 provisions increased nearly nine times. In the case of Kuwait, the bulk of the increase happened during 2008 when provisions increased from $371 million in 2007 to $2.8 billion in 2008 implying a growth of 666 percent and stayed at that high level at $2.4 billion during 2009. On the whole, 2008 proved to be the nemesis with provisions clocking a threefold increase to $6.8 billion from $1.8 billion in 2007. Normally when economic growth slows and prices collapse, it takes time for these losses to materialize on bank's balance sheets, sometimes up to 2-3 years.[10] However, in the case of GCC countries they showed up immediately leading to very high levels of provisioning and recapitalization. The two GCC countries that have systemic nonbank financial institutions i.e., Kuwait (investment companies) and UAE (mortgage companies) topped the table in terms of this assessment. Assessing future write downs is rendered difficult in an atmosphere of weak transparency and disclosure along with poor corporate governance safeguards.[11]

3.4 Deposits

The loan growth discussed earlier is fuelled by deposit growth averaging 18 percent for the GCC during 2003-2009. However, UAE and Qatar witnessed a 30 percent growth while Oman registered an annual growth of 22 percent. Bahrain lagged

10. "Global Financial Crisis: Gulf Countries Limit Fallout from Crisis," IMF Survey Online, March 12, 2010.

11. *Arab Banker*, issue no.10.

significantly with an annualized growth of 5 percent. The deposit growth was placed at 0 percent for 2009 indicating the strain due to financial crisis. It should be noted that the loan growth exceeded that of deposit growth thereby pushing higher the loan to deposit ratio from 68 percent in 2003 to 86 percent by 2009. The ceilings on loan-to-deposit ratio are set by the respective central banks and vary from country to country.[12]

3.5 Net Income

While at the aggregate level, net income grew by an annualized 18 percent during the period 2003-2009, there is wide variation noticed among countries. Kuwait, for example, registered a 0 percent growth, the UAE registered an annualized growth of 24 percent and Qatar 41 percent. After witnessing consecutive growth up to 2007, the subsequent two years witnessed a fall in aggregate profits. From a high of $19 billion in 2007, aggregate net income dropped to $15 billion in 2009 (Table 4).

3.6 Suggested Measures

Globally, the rescue response has been taken three different ideological shapes. Firstly, there is government guarantee and insurance (the Britain model). Secondly, the notion of segregating toxic assets into one structure like a bad bank and dealing with them separately. Finally, there is the reemergence of nationalization. The verdict is far from clear on what is the best course of action for the GCC banking sector and a structured prescription is necessary to tackle the current crisis. Some of these broad policies have already been enacted by a few GCC countries and the rest are expected to follow suit.

3.6.1 Overt Economic Stimulus

The global response to the current financial crisis has been predominantly a rescue package initiated, launched and managed directly by the government in order to rescue local banks and financial institutions. The rescue efforts are even spreading to sectors other than banks and financial institutions. The merits and demerits of such an approach where governments become a dominant player (instead of being a referee) may be debated. The experience in the GCC countries has been very different. The government has been showing marginal interest in initiating and managing a direct rescue program. The only country where such efforts are in progress is Kuwait, but

12. Saudi Arabia and Kuwait 85 percent;UAE 100 percent; Bahrain 75 percent; Oman 88 percent; and Qatar 90 percent.

with little success. Given the scale of destruction in the GCC, overt banking rescue packages are no longer a policy option but a necessity. While GCC governments were hugely responsive in terms of fiscal measures (through increased government spending), they did not venture directly into rescuing banks or creating a "bad bank" to deal with toxic assets, thus leaving the issue unaddressed. The flip side of this issue is that we do not know how bad the balance sheets of banks are today and how long the provisioning for bad loans will last. As per analysis, banks have still not done with their provisioning even after two years of crisis.

3.6.2 Enhanced Fiscal Stimulus

Oil revenues (which form approximately 80 percent of the GCC government revenues) are expected to witness a significant fall in 2009. Despite this, a majority of the GCC governments have announced an increase in government expenditures to provide fiscal stimulus to their economies. Saudi Arabia has projected a 9 percent decline in revenues for 2009; however, government expenditure has been significantly increased by 16 percent. This is expected to result in a budget deficit of $17 billion as compared to a budget surplus of $11 billion in 2008. Dubai too has unveiled an 11 percent increase in government spending. This has resulted in a budget deficit for the first time in Dubai to an extent of 1.3 percent to Dubai's GDP. However, Kuwait posted a contraction in its budget both in revenues and expenditures. The government expenditures are expected to reduce by 36 percent and the revenues are budgeted to reduce by 39 percent. Analyst expectations on Qatar are also on the similar lines with expenditures expected to be same as that of 2008. An enhanced fiscal stimulus is a must in the current scenario and should be approached along with monetary easing.

3.6.3 Decrease Interest Rates on Loans

The benchmark interest rates vary from country to country (Table 5). However, since the currencies are pegged, the GCC countries follow the US Fed rates even though with a lag. For e.g., at the beginning of 2008 the differential rate between the US Fed and Saudi Arabia was only 25 basis points. However, towards the end of April 2010, the difference was placed at 175 basis points leaving lot of room for further rate cuts. Bahrain is totally aligned with US interest rate policy while Qatar's differential is placed at 57 basis points. The differences in the spread among GCC countries can be related to their specific monetary situation in hand, though in the medium term they need to align more closely with Fed funds rate.

Table 5: Key Interest Rates

Country	Key Interest Rate	Beginning 2008	End 2008	End 2009	2010
USA	Fed Funds Target Rate	4.25	0.25	0.25	0.25
Saudi	Repurchase rate	4.5	2.5	2	2
Kuwait	Repo Rate	4.5	2	1.75	1.5
Qatar	Deposit Rate	4	2.00	0.25	0.82
Oman	Repo Rate	5.87	1.53	2	2
Bahrain	One-week deposit rate	4	0.75	0.73	0.25
UAE	Over-night repurchase rate	4.5	1.5	1	1

Source: Central Bank Websites, Markaz Research

3.6.4 Cut Deposit Rates to Increase Exposure to Risky Assets

Deposit rates have already been cut in almost all the GCC countries except Kuwait. Kuwait is the only country in the GCC to witness an increase in the deposit rate in 2008 (Table 6). The upward move in interest rates in Kuwait can be attributed to the currency factor, wherein, the Kuwait Dinar has moved from a full peg to the USD to a basket of currencies with a strong bias towards USD in 2007. The deposit rates have been cut across the GCC mainly to deter speculators from taking advantage of the differential in interest rates between US and the GCC countries. While this is the primary motivation of Central banks behind the deposit rate cut, an unintended fallout of this action would be movement of liquidity to other asset classes, especially equities.

Table 6: Deposit Rates

Country	2008 Beginning	2008 End	2009 End	2008 Change (Bps)	2009 Change (Bps)	Current
US	4.69	1.54	1.34	-3.15	-0.20	1.34
Saudi	2.6	1.72	0.2	-0.88	-1.52	0.18
Kuwait	3	5.61	0.28	2.61	-5.33	0.77
UAE	3.99	3	0.44	-0.99	-2.56	0.27
Qatar	3.22	2.44	0.25	-0.78	-2.19	0.82
Oman	3.9	1.89	0.17	-2.01	-1.72	0.22
Bahrain	4.32	1.58	0.23	-2.74	-1.35	0.49

Source: Central Bank Websites, Markaz Research

3.6.5 Lend to Longer term Projects

The immediate fallout of the financial crisis on the GCC is the cancellation or putting on hold of projects. As per latest data available, projects worth nearly $570 billion have been put on hold/cancelled as of September 2009. Nearly 76 percent of this amount was in UAE with little impact on Saudi Arabia and rest of the region. As per the Booz & Co report, upstream projects are being rescheduled to benefit from lower input costs, the ease of inflationary pressure, and abundance in the supply of energy services and materials required to implement these projects.[13] Also, it is significant to mention that nearly 76 percent of these cancellations/on hold pertain to the real estate sector. However, the scenario has since changed for the better, wherein prices of commodities for projects and other input costs have declined drastically thereby enabling cancelled projects to come on stream. Financial institutions should take advantage of such a scenario by kick-starting lending to long-term projects.

3.6.6 Increase Government Deposit in Banks

Due to the decline in interest rates in banks, attracting retail and institutional investors towards bank deposits has become a challenge. Anecdotal evidence also points to a decline in lending activities by banks resulting in reluctance of banks to take in time deposits (Higher cost than demand deposits). This requires the governments to increase their participation in the banking sector by increasing deposits in banks. Some GCC governments have historically been active participants in a few banks e.g. Qatar National Bank, wherein the bulk of the deposits are from the government. Such an increase in deposits by the government also provides greater room for banks to increase their exposure to risky assets.

3.7 Future Direction

Banking constitutes the largest share of the segment (measured in market capitalization terms) and has been the worst hit in the financial crisis. Asset quality deterioration has led to very high level of provisioning during the last two years which dented profitability, especially that of Islamic banks. Exposure to troubled sectors (like real estate, construction and financial services) coupled with bad corporate governance can stand as the main reason. The days of easy money (through high spreads) are gone with a high level of risk aversion setting in among banks. This will lead to lower credit growth. With other avenues for capital deployment being weak, deposit growth will

13. "One Year on: the GCC Region's Post-economic Crisis Prospects."

continue to be strong adding further pressure. The potential for fee income has also been reduced. This will lead to consolidation and restructuring never seen before. Ambition to foray beyond borders will also be reviewed in this challenging time.

GCC banks were laid-back in the past in a protected environment leading to poor customer service and product offering. On an average, the ratio of product-per-customer ratio is two to three in the GCC compared to eight or nine in the western retail banks as per an AT Kearney study.[14] The banking sector is getting highly competitive with limited potential in the domestic market and the gradual relaxation of regulatory restrictions. Most banks operated within their country of operations and had limited branch network thereby keeping a control on infrastructure costs. Also, through expat hiring banks kept their costs low even in areas like information technology. All this enabled GCC banks to enjoy a low cost-to-income ratio compared to other banks in the western world.[15] Also, GCC banks enjoyed high capital cover and a stable shareholder base which in some countries could be the respective government providing cheap and stable capital and deposits. But going forward, GCC banks may have to face some change in paradigm leading to the vanishing of these advantages. The WTO would bring in more pressure on the local regulators to allow entry of foreign banks. Also, post financial crisis, regulators will lay more emphasis on encouraging the development of local capital markets as depending only on the banking sector could be dangerous. This is likely to reduce the overall dependence on and importance of banks as the main intermediary.

4. GCC Asset Management

From a modest $120 billion market capitalization in the year 2000, GCC market capitalization levels reached $1.1 trillion by the end of 2007, an annual growth of 37 percent though placed at $625 billion at the end of 2009. This probably sets the scene for the GCC asset management industry that is experiencing rapid growth. Dubai is now home to all the major names in the asset management and investment banking industry and so is the case with Saudi Arabia. Some of them wound up in response to the financial crisis but the bulk of them are holding up. Even though the GCC stock markets are yet to find their rightful place within the global family of indices, they are not far from it. Therefore, the GCC asset management industry is a very important component of the financial sector.

14. "GCC Banks: On the Road to Maturity."

15. As per the AT Kearney study, a typical cost-to-income ratio for leading European banks ranges from 60 to 75 per cent, while the same ratio for major GCC banks is less than 40 per cent.

The region enjoys an active retail investment culture aided by the performance of the GCC stock markets. In spite of high volatility, GCC stock markets have delivered superior risk-adjusted returns during the last few years. This has also been helped by low correlation to emerging markets and developed markets though that luxury is slowly closing down.

However, GCC stock markets lack both depth and breadth with low institutional participation. The GCC stock market is dominated by retail investors with very low levels of institutional participation, except in Kuwait. Sovereign wealth funds and other investment institutions have evinced little interest in the local markets due to perception of high risk as well as due to fear of stoking liquidity in an already speculative market. Asset management is a people's business and is critically dependent on the quality of fund managers, research analysts and the like. Most of the talents are home grown and are not required to carry certain credentials by regulation. It is only recently that we have witnessed the arrival of managers with professional credentials (like CFA, MBA). Even though stock markets have been in existence since the 1980s in some of the markets (like Saudi Arabia and Kuwait), mutual funds came into being only recently. Hence, there are very few funds that can claim a track record of say 5 or 10 years. Mutual funds continue to offer a narrow range of products with very little innovation. Most of the funds are direct country funds in what can be termed as "plain vanilla." Innovation at the maximum stretches to offering sharia-compliant versions.

4.1 Industry Overview

The GCC asset management industry is estimated to be worth $27.6 billion in size (Table 7). There are currently more than 100 asset management companies which manage money under 325 funds (Table 8). From a product structure point of view (elaborated subsequently), equities lead the pack with a 48 percent share followed very closely by debt at 42 percent. The rest of the asset classes like money market and *sukuk* have a negligible share. Geographically, Saudi Arabia accounts for 63 percent of the industry, distantly followed by Kuwait at 21 percent. The high share of Saudi Arabia and Kuwait can be traced to their early adoption of mutual funds as an investment vehicle. Besides, they have a stock exchange that dates well back in time. Others have a negligible share, especially UAE that had a late start in terms of stock exchange activity relative to Saudi Arabia and Kuwait. The market is very much concentrated among the top asset management companies, with the top 10 asset management companies having a share of 72 percent of the total fund management industry. NCB Capital and Riyad Capital (both of Saudi

Arabia) lead the list of asset management companies with a combined size of $10 billion approximately, which forms 35 percent of the market share. Therefore, the industry structure is skewed as more than 70 percent of asset managers manage less than $100 million. The asset management industry in GCC is composed of two parts viz., mutual funds and managed accounts. Due to the high net worth nature of the GCC market, more assets tend to be managed through discretionary/ non-discretionary (managed portfolios) than through the mutual funds route. A recent survey by McKinsey[16] estimates that assets under management for managed accounts could be twice as much as that managed under funds. It must be noted that Kuwait is the only market that discloses statistics pertaining to managed accounts. As of December 2009, Kuwait managed nearly $53 billion in managed accounts compared to $5.7 billion in funds, a factor of 9.3 times. Such a high ratio can be attributed to the presence of a large number of investment companies (over 100) as well as an active sovereign wealth fund in Kuwait Investment Authority (KIA). If we assume a factor of 2 x for other markets, then total assets managed, including managed funds, stand at an estimated $125 billion with Kuwait leading the list at 47 percent followed by Saudi Arabia at 40 percent. However, organized statistics is available only for mutual funds segment. The asset management industry must be reviewed keeping this limitation in mind. Throughout this report, the term "assets under management" refers to only the mutual fund segment.

Table 7: GCC Assets Under Management

	Equity			Debt			Money Market			Others			Total		
Country	Con	Isl	Total	Con	Isl	Total	Con	Isl	Total	Con	Isl	Total	Con	Isl	Total
Saudi	1,801	3,478	5,279	0	10,484	10,484	1,235	5	1,240	89	290	379	3,124	14,257	17,382
UAE	496	91	587	18	2	20	9	0	9	2	0	2	525	94	618
Kuwait	3,547	734	4,281	527	12	539	447	440	886	0	17	17	4,521	1,203	5,724
Qatar	272	18	290	0	0	0	0	0	0	0	0	0	272	18	290
Oman	106	0	106	0	0	0	0	0	0	0	0	0	106	0	106
Bahrain	20	0	20	0	0	0	0	0	0	0	0	0	20	0	20

16. McKinsey, *Asset Management Survey 2009*, January 2010.

GCC	887	781	1,669	149	429	578	0	0	0	0	6	6	1,036	1,216	2,252
MENA	956	66	1,023	91	2	93	0	10	10	49	107	156	1,097	185	1,282
Total	8,086	5,168	13,254	785	10,929	11,714	1,691	455	2,145	140	420	560	10,701	16,972	27,673
Share	61%	39%	100%	7%	93%	100%	79%	21%	100%	25%	75%	100%	39%	61%	100%
Con - Conventional funds Isl - Islamic funds															

Note: All data as of April 2010
Source: Markaz Research, Zawya and company websites

Table 8: GCC Number of Funds

	Equity			Debt			Money Market			Others			Total		
Country	Con	Isl	Total	Con	Isl	Total	Con	Isl	Total	Con	Isl	Total	Con	Isl	Total
Saudi	26	26	52	0	28	28	7	1	8	7	17	24	40	72	112
UAE	13	2	15	1	1	2	1	0	1	1	0	1	16	3	19
Kuwait	22	17	39	5	1	6	5	6	11	0	2	2	32	26	58
Qatar	6	1	7	0	0	0	0	0	0	0	0	0	6	1	7
Oman	5	0	5	0	0	0	0	0	0	0	0	0	5	0	5
Bahrain	1	0	1	0	0	0	0	0	0	0	0	0	1	0	1
GCC	23	27	50	2	2	4	0	0	0	0	4	4	25	33	58
MENA	32	7	39	8	4	12	0	3	3	4	7	11	44	21	65
Total	128	80	208	16	36	52	13	10	23	12	30	42	169	156	325
Share	62%	38%	100%	31%	69%	100%	57%	43%	100%	29%	71%	100%	52%	48%	100%
Con - Conventional funds Isl - Islamic funds															

Note: All data as of April 2010
Source: Markaz Research, Zawya and company websites

4.2 Product Focus

In the GCC countries, the skew of assets managed under funds is towards equity, which includes sector funds, diversified equity and index funds. At $13 billion, the share of equity funds as a percentage of the total assets managed under funds is at 48 percent spread over 208 funds yielding a per fund value of $63 million. The

Islamic segment of this constitutes 39 percent. Saudi Arabia leads the pack in the equity segment with $5.2 billion in assets under management, a market share of 40 percent, followed by Kuwait with a market share of 32 percent. However, in Saudi Arabia, 66 percent of equity funds are Islamic while in Kuwait it is only 17 percent. Within the various types of equity funds, a majority of the assets are managed under diversified equity funds.

At $10.9 billion, the debt segment enjoys a share of 40 percent. The debt mutual fund is composed of traditional fixed income, trade finance, balanced and capital guaranteed funds with 80 percent of them being trade finance predominantly from Saudi Arabia. Almost the entire debt segment is accounted for by Saudi Arabia and that too is fully Islamic. Others have a negligible share. Money market funds come a distant third with a share of just 8 percent coming mostly (80 percent) from conventional funds. Other categories like IPO, *sukuk* and fund of funds account for negligible share of 2 percent.

4.3 Geographic Focus

Saudi Arabia is the largest market in the GCC in terms of stock market capitalization at $320 billion as at the end of 2009. However, the size of the asset management industry in Saudi Arabia at $17 billion is only 5 percent of the market capitalization. However, in spite of such low institutional rate, Saudi Arabia is the largest market for asset management, managing $17 billion constituting 63 percent of the total. There were 112 funds under management. The bulk of the money is being managed under fixed income, especially trade finance, followed by equities. By virtue of being the largest market, Saudi Arabia enjoys highest allocation among GCC/Mena funds.[17] The top asset manager in Saudi Arabia is NCB Capital with assets at $6.9 billion, with an overall GCC market share of 33 percent. There is a significant gap between the first and the second in the order of quantum of assets managed. Riyad Capital holds the second position with assets of $2.7 billion with a market share of 9.7 percent.

Kuwait manages about $5.7 billion in about 58 funds mostly in equities (75 percent) and accounts for a market share of 20 percent and institutional rate of 6 percent. The high rate of institutionalization in Kuwait can be attributed to the presence of significantly large number of investment companies and the active

17. As per the Markaz report for Q1-10 "GCC Equity Funds", on an average fund managers had the following allocations in their portfolio: Saudi Arabia 43 percent, Qatar 16 percent, Kuwait 13 percent, UAE 11 percent, Oman 5 percent, Bahrain 1 percent, and other Mena countries 10 percent.

association of sovereign wealth funds like Kuwait Investment Authority nurturing and supporting the industry. Unlike Saudi Arabia, 75 percent of assets under management pertain to the equity segment. Between Saudi Arabia and Kuwait, they hold a market share of 80 percent. Even though the UAE market is larger in size in terms of market capitalization as compared to Kuwait, the fund management industry is hardly 11 percent of the size in Kuwait due to the late start of the industry in UAE. The total assets managed in funds in UAE is at $618 million, which is 1 percent of the market capitalization of UAE markets as compared to assets under management in funds to an extent of 6 percent in Kuwait and 5 percent in Saudi Arabia.

Nearly 88 percent of the equity segment is estimated to belong to managed accounts with the rest accruing to mutual funds. The significant share of managed portfolios in the industry is due to government surpluses in the form of sovereign wealth funds and pension funds, which get routed more towards managed accounts, and the significant presence of high net worth individuals. While the statistics pertaining to mutual funds can be corroborated to a large extent, the same is rendered extremely difficult for managed accounts.

4.4 Future Direction

Capital markets are quite nascent in most of the Gulf countries, providing for immense scope for growth going forward. Due to its short history, markets exhibit inefficiencies that can be successfully exploited by fund managers through superior fund performance relative to their benchmarks. The Gulf region has undergone tremendous economic expansion and is expected to remain strong in the years to come. This provides for a classic situation where companies can benefit immensely from this economic boom. High economic growth will directly result in very strong liquidity – a situation that is highly conducive for stock markets. Very few companies are represented in the stock markets due to the predominance of family-controlled businesses that prefer to retain control. With the gradual opening up of various sectors (including banking) to global competition, family-controlled businesses are keener than before to look to capital markets as a source of capital. This provides opportunities for investment bankers and fund managers alike. However, these opportunities should be understood within the context of certain limitations.

The GCC stock markets continue to be volatile, speculative and lack depth and breadth. The industry also faces a serious talent shortage. Lack of an organized database on Gulf companies as well as independent research has rendered these markets speculative. Historical information on companies is still cumbersome to procure with various stock exchange websites enjoying different degrees of advancement. Coverage of GCC companies on international databases like Bloomberg, Reuters, and Thomson DataStream is recent and is not yet fully comprehensive. Due to lack of transparency, it is difficult to produce credible and objective research on Gulf-based companies. Hence, the markets continue to be under-researched and hard to research. Many GCC stock markets still lack a formal authority like Capital Market Authority (CMA) or Capital Market Law (CML) to regulate and control capital markets. Absence of such a structure hinders the progress of the capital market, including arrival of quality foreign investors. Also, regulations surrounding important issues like foreign investment, corporate governance, and insider trading are still evolving and lack the punch when benchmarked with other developed or emerging markets.

Conclusion

The GCC financial sector, especially the banking sector, has shown resilience in the current crisis. However, future progress will require a series of regulatory and structural reforms that can produce sustainable growth rather than volatile growth. The growth of the non-hydrocarbon sector[18] will be a key element of this sustainability goal. The banking sector, after witnessing hectic credit growth, is now in the process of de-leveraging and re-capitalization. With little leeway in terms of monetary policy, fiscal stimulus and counter-cyclical spending will be crucial for the recovery. Regulatory reforms in the area of capital markets will spur development in the asset management industry that witnessed a sharp fall during the global economic crisis. The high net worth nature of the market demands product sophistication along with superior risk management propositions. As the economy expands in size, foreign investment interest is bound to develop rapidly in what is being seen as one of the most prosperous regions in the world.

18. Nearly 95 percent of the labor force is employed in this sector as per an IIF report.

References

Abdullah Al-Hassan, M. K. 2010. *The GCC Banking Sector: Topography and Analysis*. International Monetary Fund.

Abed, G. T. Impact of the Crisis on the Mena Region and the Road to Recovery. *Arab Banker* , no. 10: 29-32.

Ahmed, M. 2010. *GCC: Crisis Highlights Policy Challenges*. Carnegie Endowment for International Peace , March.

AT Kearney. 2010. *GCC Banks: On the Road to Maturity*.

Booz & Co. 2009. *One Year On: the GCC Region's Post-economic Crisis Prospects*. Booz & Co.

Institute of International Finance. 2009. *GCC Regional Overview*. IIF.

International Monetary Fund. 2010. *World Economic Outlook Update*. IMF.

Kamco. 2010. *GCC Banking Sector*. Kamco.

Khamis, A. S. 2010. *Gulf Countries Limit Fallout from Crisis*. IMF.

Layla, M. R. 2010. *GCC Equity Funds*. Kuwait Financial Center "Markaz."

McKinsey & Co. 2010. *Asset Management Survey 2009*.

Mukkamala, M. R. 2009. *Shelter In a Storm*. Kuwait Financial Center "Markaz."

Raghu, L. A.-A. 2010. *GCC Banks: Done with Provisions?* Kuwait Financial Center "Markaz."

Raghu, M. 2006. *GCC Leverage Risk*. Kuwait Financial Center "Markaz."

Ramadoss, V. 2009. *Supply Adjustments in GCC Real Estate - An Update*. Kuwait Financial Center "Markaz."

2

Do GCC Stock Markets Support Their Domestic Economies? An Analytical Overview*

Randa Alami

Introduction

Most Middle East and North African (MENA) financial systems, including the GCC countries, have financial intermediation levels that are below their potential and needs. Similarly, these systems are still largely bank-based, with MENA continuing to raise external finance mostly in the form of loans rather than equity or bonds. Yet, their stock markets, some of which were only created in 2000, are acquiring an increasingly significant role. While they lag behind Turkey and India in terms of maturity and sophistication,[1] these markets have grown spectacularly in terms of aspects like capitalization. Their embryonic nature is also signaled by the fact that they are still considered "frontier" markets: they are yet to earn an emerging market status,[2] and are yet to offer easily accessible or easily disposable

* I am grateful to the workshop participants, Professor Wassim Shahin (Lebanese American University) in particular, for their comments. Any remaining errors are mine.

1. Most regional markets do not have live trading or instant clearing, have yet to allow short selling, and do not offer derivatives or complex financial products.
2. Frontier markets tend to be more thinly traded than emerging markets, have lower market capitalization ratios, restrictions on foreign ownership, and/or low investable capital ratios. Definitions vary, but for example, companies included in the S&P index for emerging markets have a minimum average investable market capitalization of $100 million, with at least $25 million actively traded for one year prior to their inclusion.

world-class assets. The markets are also experiencing rapid regulatory changes, including allowing foreign ownership. Up to the recent global meltdown, their growth had been phenomenal, despite major corrections. The current recession delivered blows not just because of global linkages, but also because of systemic flaws in the economies. Indeed, the buildup to the regional crisis, it will be argued, bears similarities to the sub-prime crisis, if only in terms of the bursting of the real estate bubble in Dubai.

This chapter seeks to investigate the evolving role of the GCC capital markets in supporting their domestic economies. In particular, it will try and gauge the role of equity markets in providing an additional avenue for mobilizing savings and a source of corporate finance. It will do so by investigating their characteristics and status, highlighting the type of firms they represent and their articulation in the real economy. By the same token, the analysis will identify their structural limitations and their medium-term outlook, and will argue that heightened expectations of sustained growth are misguided, misleading, and unhelpful.

The paper begins in Part 1 by looking briefly at the academic literature examining regional markets, in the context of the more general debate about financing and development. This section points to the fact that unless they mature and operate in a well-regulated context, financial markets may not necessarily contribute to growth. Moving on to stylized facts about these markets, Part 2 emphasizes their smallness by placing them within the GCC financial structures. Part 3 then delineates their main features, including a look at participants, ownership structures and sectoral composition. Their smallness, thinness, and illiquidity will become apparent, and the dominance of wealthy families and of government ownership will be revealed. This is followed in Part 4 by a consideration of regulatory aspects, including developments with regard to corporate governance. This sets the scene in Part 5 for an examination of the markets' limited but noted role in raising capital and investments. Beyond data limitation, it will argue that the recent economic shocks were too great for what are still new and embryonic forums of financing. Part 6 concludes by highlighting the implications of the current crisis, namely a protracted growth process, and urgently calls for the consolidation, coordination and even integration of GCC stock markets.

1. Stock Markets and Development in MENA

For all their importance, the academic concern about the role of stock markets in economic growth constitutes but one element of a much wider and multi-faceted debate on finance and development. The key strands of literature have been aptly summarized, among others, by Capasso (2006).[3] In terms of the purpose of this chapter and/or what can be expected of the burgeoning regional markets, the following lessons can be highlighted. Firstly, as financial and economic systems grow, more complex financial intermediation appears, within which stock markets emerge. Secondly, the experience of countries in reliance on various sources of finance is diverse. By the same token, the direction of causality between growth and stock market development is unclear, despite the observed positive correlation between advanced economies and advanced stock markets. In particular, it is unclear how to make markets play desired roles of mobilizing savings, allocating funds efficiently, etc. Thirdly, stock markets can also harm growth: a substantive body of literature also points out that stock markets may cause instability to financial systems as a whole. Specifically, high volatility of stock prices can impact negatively on investment and growth, be it through discouraging the supply of funds from risk-averse individuals, by incorrectly indicating returns on investments, etc. Harmful effects may also emerge in the absence of proper sequencing of financial reforms, and in poorly regulated markets, whose vulnerability may be worsened by their openness.

Beyond that, the current global financial crisis has generated calls, including within international financial institutions, for fundamental revisions of the international financial architecture and of regulatory standards and provisions. Neither the sophistication nor the openness of emerging markets helped them to endure less severe losses, and the shocks sustained went beyond the contagion effects of previous crises. This is why it is not surprising to observe the reaction of Chinese regulators, who moved against complex derivatives and products, having had to foot a massive bill for losses made by large corporations.[4]

In a nutshell, there are no a priori expectations for stock markets to function well, and the harm they can deliver during crises can wipe out the gains made beforehand, pointing to a complex reality and a complex interaction between them and the economy. Within this background, the modest findings of the literature concerned with the MENA region are not surprising. Indeed, a common theme in this literature is that there is little evidence that the financial sectors or stock markets have led or spurred regional economic growth. A key

3. S. Capasso, "Stock Market Development and Economic Growth," WIDER Research Paper 2006/102 (Helsinki: WIDER, 2006).

4. See the *Financial Times,* "China Derivative Rule Changes Hit Banks," November 24, 2009.

reason mentioned is that MENA markets need improvements in their legal and institutional development for them to play a role in financial development or economic growth.

In that spirit, Ben Naceur et al (2007) argue that it is an open question whether stock market liberalization in MENA contributed to investment or economic development.[5] Investment and higher economic growth can increase in response to stock market liberalization, but these effects tend to happen following institutional reform, a conclusion echoed by Beji (2007).[6] In their 2005 paper, Ben Naceur and S. Ghazouani find that the key determinants of stock markets development in the region are: the savings rate (ratio of gross fixed capital to gross disposable income), the ratio of credit to private sector, stock market liquidity; and an indicator of macroeconomic stability.[7] In the case of GCC, we learn from Billmeier and Massa (2007) that their market capitalization is also driven by oil prices.[8]

Thus, there seem to be two key messages. Firstly, it is the real economy which drives stock market development, and the latter can only be as sophisticated as the former. Secondly, it seems MENA and GCC markets have not reached the threshold beyond which they contribute to or support growth. The idea of threshold is also present in Adjasi and Biekpe (2006), who find that stock markets in Africa have a significant role for development and growth, but only in a handful of upper middle income countries with fairly advanced stock markets. Their paper also finds that investment was the most significant determinant of market development indicators. The implication for our purposes is that sustained investment growth across GCC economies should lead to substantive growth for their financial markets. Has this been the case in practice?

Unfortunately, empirical evidence of their role in regional corporate finance is only considered by a handful of studies. Foremost among these are the works by Omran and Bolbol (2003, 2005), who provide a rare study of Arab firms' use

5. S. Ben Naceur, S. Ghazouani, and M. Omran, "Does Stock Market Liberalization Spur Economic and Financial Development in the Mena Region?" (October 2007), http://ssrn.com/abstract=1018742

6. S. Beji, "Financial Openness and Financial Development in the South Mediterranean Sea Countries," 14th ERF Conference, (Cairo: ERF, 2007).

7. S. Ben Naceur and S. Ghazouani, "Stock Markets, Banks, and Economic Growth: Empirical Evidence from the MENA Region," February 2005, http://ssrn.com/abstract=856386.

8. A. Billmeier and I. Massa, "What Drives Stock Market Development in the Middle East and Central Asia--Institutions, Remittances, or Natural Resources?" IMF Working Papers 07/157, (Washington, D.C.: IMF, July 2007).

of stock markets for investment.[9] They suggest that sales and debt growth are significant determinants of choosing equity finance, in contrast to the pecking order theory of finance which predicts that in developing countries, internal cash is preferred source of finance for investment. In Arab economies, managers are often the owners, and equity is not used significantly to finance investments in order not to dilute control. But once listed, the firms tend to have a low retention of cash, partly because investors like receiving periodic income, and partly because firms like to send a positive signal to the market of a strong position to raise debt, suggesting complementarities between the equity and debt as sources of capital. Omet (2009), who considered the stock markets of Bahrain, Qatar, Saudi Arabia, Palestine, Tunisia, and Jordan, also finds that listed firms have low leverage and even lower long-term leverage ratios.[10] Thus despite the emergence of equity markets, retained earnings are still the dominant component of corporate capital structures.

Surprisingly, the larger body of literature (at least 14)[11] is concerned with the efficiency and integration of MENA and/or GCC markets, as if they were fully fledged, mature or well articulated with their economy. A key common concern of this literature is whether these markets are a good option in the portfolio of international investors, even though most markets were closed to foreigners up to 2005. Unsurprisingly, these studies find MENA markets inefficient, and not entirely correlated among each other or with other markets. Nonetheless, a few of these studies shed light on their behavior, the most pertinent for this chapter being two papers.[12] These emphasize their nascent and volatile nature, with much room for speculative and herd behavior, and investors characterized by "irrational exuberance."

9. A. Bolbol and M. Omran, "Investment and the Stock Market: Evidence from Arab firm-level panel Data," *Emerging Markets Review*, 6 (2005): 85-106; M. Omran and A. Bolbol, "Foreign Direct Investment, Financial Development, and Economic Growth: Evidence from the Arab Countries," *Review of Middle East Economics and Finance* 1, no. 3 (2003): 231–249.

10. G. Omet, "Corporate Financing in the MENA Region: Do Country or Firm Specific Factors Explain the Capital Structure?" Paper for the 10th Mediterranean Research Meeting (Florence: European University Institute, 2009).

11. See Abraham (2001); Assaf (2003); Hassan (2003); Haque et al (2004); Neaime (2005); Marashdeh (2005); Squalli (2005); Saadi-Sedik, T., and M. Petri,(2006); al Khazali et al (2006); Hammoudeh and Choi (2006); Elango and Hussein (2007); Khallouli (2008); Hammoudeh et al (2008); Onour (2009); Shreshta and Marashdeh (2010).

12. See M. Haddad and H. Hakim, "Irrational Exuberance on the Saudi Stock Exchange," ERF Conference Paper, (Cairo: ERF, November 2008) and A. Al-Hassan, F. Delgado, and M. Omran, "IPO Behaviour in GCC Countries: Goody-Two Shoes or Bad-to-the-Bone?" IMF Working Paper 07/149 (Washington, D.C.: IMF, July 2007).

2. Main Characteristics of GCC Financial Structures

The general characteristics of Arab capital markets, including those in the GCC, are conveniently described by Abed and Soueid (2005) as follows:[13]

- Financial systems in MENA tend to be more bank-based than any other region.
- The region has one of the least developed markets for fixed income assets.
- Corporate non-governmental bond markets are embryonic.
- Banking systems suffer from: state dominance, concentration, inefficient intermediation, and non-performing loans.

The region also captured a marginal part of international capital flows. Consequently, external financing acquired by the GCC, was modest in relative terms, and was mostly composed of loan syndication, as is clearly shown in Table 1. Foreign bank loans still constitute the largest component of financing packages for projects, indicating continuing need for local financial systems to deepen and widen financial intermediation.

Table 1: External Financing by Type (US$ million)

	2004	2005	2006	2007	2008	1rst Q, 09	2nd Q, 09
Bonds	3,781	11,519	18,154	12,115	4,213	-	8,604
Equity	284	396	1,632	4,773	3,002	-	952
Loans	8,774	29,843	48,122	50,307	38,448	4,239	3,168
TOTAL	12,839	41,759	67,908	67,194	45,662	4,239	12,723

Source: *Global Financial Stability Report* 2009

Table 2 confirms that MENA (including GCC) has the largest share of bank to total financial assets among developing regions. Yet, the table also shows that stock markets have clearly started to make a dent, however small, in regional financial structures. Indeed, data show that stock markets' share of MENA's total financial assets rose from 8 percent to 32 percent between 2002 and 2008, having reached a high of 32 percent in 2006. The progress made by bonds is also remarkable, but at 6 percent of regional financial assets, their share remains too small compared to other regions or to their potential.

The general features of the GCC bonds markets are still as described by

13. G. Abed and M. Soueid, "Capital Markets in the Middle East and North Africa," Presentation, EIB-FEMIP Expert Committee Meeting, Luxembourg, March 2005.

Woertz (2008).[14] Firstly, their actual share vs. their potential share in relation to GDP is low, at 3 percent of GDP, vs. 112 percent in USA and 10 percent in China. Secondly, the bond market is still largely the realm of government securities, and within the thin market of private sector corporate bonds, banks dominate. That is because in the GCC, as in the rest of MENA, the growth of the bond market is hampered by a lack of benchmarks, of yield curves, and sometimes of liquidity. Sustained efforts by the authorities have led to an improvement in the range of maturities offered. The regional market lacks the local currency instruments issued by regional governmental or quasi-governmental bodies that have mushroomed in other developing regions such as Latin America.

Table 2: Capital Markets Structures, 2002-2008

Selected Indicators on the Size of the Capital Markets, 2008

	Stock Market Capitalization	Stock Market	Debt Securities		Bank Assets
			Public	Private	
World	33,513.1	16%	15%	24%	45%
Emerging markets	8,558.9	25%	14%	9%	52%
Asia	5,326.7	24%	13%	10%	54%
Middle East	689.6	32%	2%	4%	63%
Africa	444.5	34%	6%	6%	54%
Selected Indicators on the Size of the Capital Markets, 2002					
World	28,875.1	19%	15%	13%	53%
Emerging markets	1,947.3	14%	11%	6%	70%
Asia	1,310.4	13%	7%	15%	66%
Middle East	63.8	8%	1%	1%	90%
Africa	84.3	13%	7%	2%	79%

Source: *Global Financial Stability Report*, 2009, 2008 & 2004.

A distinguishing feature of GCC bond markets since 2005 has been the phenomenal rise of the *sukuk* (or sharia-compliant bond). According to Wilson (2009), regional *sukuks* amounted to $14.9 billion in 2007 vs. MENA bond issuance of $20.6 billion, giving them a particularly dominant role in the GCC bond market.[15] Up to 2008, the largest category of corporate issuers was UAE banks, whereas Saudi

14. Eckart Woertz, *The GCC Bond Market* (Dubai: Gulf Research Center, April 2008).
15. R. Wilson, *The Development of Islamic Finance in the GCC*, Research Paper, Kuwait Program on Development, Governance and Globalisation in the Gulf States (London: London School of Economics, March 2009).

Arabia was the largest issuer of sovereign debt. As such, there were 48 sovereign issues in a total of 76 for that year (sukuk.net, January 15, 2009). In line with across the board financial contractions, the GCC *sukuk* market contracted in 2008. It hardly began to recover in 2009, when it was devastated by the Dubai problems, with the Dubai World and Nakheel *sukuk* renegotiation causing an earthquake to this category of bonds.

The years 2009-2010 saw attempts to revive the markets by DIFC through its own issuance, followed by mostly local corporations. But the DIFC, Saidi (2010) and other observers share the common view that the bond market, including *sukuks*, needs even more efforts to revive it than equity markets.[16] Efforts are required not only to remove structural limitations such as the lack of benchmarking, but also the lack of expertise of regional financial institutions in leading the underwriting of international bonds or complex project financing. This segment of the capital markets showed promising signs at the beginning of the 2000s when it started to support infrastructural projects. Yet today, it is still unable to support long-term investment in sectors such as energy. Hence, as noted by Sachs et al. (2009)

- "According to data from Dealogic, only seven GCC project financings (out of more than 200) have involved bond issues over the last 14 years, and only one, the Alba aluminum smelter expansion in Bahrain, was outside of Qatar."
- "The regional capital markets currently do not offer tenors long enough to support a power project financing. For that, sponsors would need to look to the international bond market."[17]

Indeed, it will be sometime before GCC markets mature enough to meet long-term financing requirements.

3. Stock Markets

1.1 Main Features

Table 3 presents data for the market capitalization, turnover ratio and number of firms listed on GCC markets between 1995 and 2010.[18] The table leaves no doubt

16. N. Saidi, "The Future of Capital Markets in the Middle East," DIFC Knowledge Series 7 – MENASA Capital Markets (Dubai: DIFC Authority, January 2010).
17. J. Sachs, et al. "Financing GCC Power Projects Post Credit Crunch," *Natural Gas and Electricity 26*, no.1 (August 2009).
18. 2010 data are for the first three months only: these are the only data given by the Arab Monetary Fund, the main source for the previous years.

that although the markets did not maintain the peaks reached in 2005 and 2007, they are not doing too badly compared to their starting point. Inevitably, the current crisis resulted in major trimming in their capitalizations. Except Dubai, all recovered to 2006 level, but only Doha is near the 2007 peak. The combined capitalization for all GCC markets in 2009 equaled that of Hong Kong ($677 billion vs. $690 billion, respectively). Similarly, Saudi Arabia's Tadawul (the largest of the GCC markets) capitalization for 2009 stood between that of Mexico and Russia. Note at one point in 2005, the UAE capitalization in percent of GDP was around 200 percent, about double that of the UK or the US,[19] so a downfall is hardly surprising.

Table 3 also leaves no doubt about the smallness of these markets. Not only is the number of listed firms small, but only half or less of firms listed are traded: 445 in a total of 712. Similarly, market turnover is low throughout the GCC except in Saudi Arabia,[20] this being made worse by the recession. As will be detailed later, the chief reason for the small turnover is the thinness and illiquidity of the markets. Only minority shares of traded firms tend to change hands, because only 5 percent-30 percent of the capital of firms is typically freely floating. To be sure, a key reason why GCC markets are not categorized as emerging markets is because of the narrowness of the investable capital. Furthermore, despite improvement, there is little secondary market trading. The recession and the Dubai meltdown have further undermined that thin trading activity, leading to calls by observers and participants for a consolidation between the markets. The recent market losses have damaged investor confidence, an effect that is likely to last in the medium term, and that is compounded by recession in the real economy. Figure 1, which depicts market capitalizations in 2007 and 2009, clearly captures the losses due to the global and regional meltdown relative to the economy. Figure 2 tracks down market capitalization in absolute terms since the early years.

Table 3: A. Market Capitalization (US$ current, million)

	1995	2000	2001	2002	2003	2004	2005	2006	2007	2008	2009	2010
Bahrain	4,707	6,624	6,601	7,716	9,702	13,513	17,364	21,122	26,796	19,955	16,141	16,677
Doha	-	-	-	10,567	26,702	40,435	87,143	60,905	95,518	76,657	87,932	104,133
Kuwait	14,400	19,848	26,662	35,099	59,528	73,581	123,893	105,950	193,513	113,527	104,226	116,975

19. International Monetary Fund, *Global Financial Stability Reports* (Washington, D. C., 2008), 22.

20. Saudi Arabia has a fairly good turnover ratio compared with emerging and Middle Eastern markets, but activity is often concentrated on speculative plays and large companies.

Muscat	1,971	3,518	2,634	5,268	7,246	9,318	12,062	13,037	22,767	15,643	18,509	19,321
Saudi	40,904	67,166	73,201	74,851	157,306	306,256	646,121	326,852	522,721	246,810	318,785	344,055
Abu Dhabi	-	-	20,376	30,363	55,490	132,413	80,745	71,689	112,160	61,888	72,968	72,591
Dubai	-	-	-	9,470	14,284	35,091	111,993	86,895	138,698	65,218	58,830	54,490
Total	61,982	97,156	129,474	173,334	330,258	610,607	1,079,321	686,450	1,112,173	599,697	677,391	728,244

Source: World Bank (2008); 2007-2010: AMF (Yearly Peformance and Monthly Performance of Arab Capital Markets); 2010 covers January to March.

B. Turnover ratio

	1995	2000	2001	2002	2003	2004	2005	2006	2007	2008	2009	2010
Bahrain	2.3%	3.7%	3.8%	2.7%	2.7%	3.4%	4.1%	6.6%	3.0%	9.5%	2.8%	0.4%
Doha				8.4%	12.1%	15.7%	32.4%	33.8%	25.9%	53.8%	27.6%	2.6%
Kuwait	44.4%	21.2%	43.9%	63.0%	91.9%	70.4%	78.5%	56.3%	62.4%	102.2%	71.2%	9.3%
Muscat	10.7%	15.7%	15.9%	11.0%	18.4%	21.3%	27.5%	17.0%	20.7%	51.4%	29.1%	3.8%
Saudi	15.1%	25.8%	30.4%	41.4%	101.1%	154.4%	170.8%	429.2%	120.2%	195.7%	101.1%	10.2%
Abu Dhabi	-	-	1.8%	3.3%	8.0%	21.5%	23.8%	59.7%	38.2%	99.0%	25.6%	2.4%
Dubai				7.3%	7.2%	39.1%	98.5%	109.0%	64.8%	107.1%	79.3%	7.1%
AVERAGE	18.1%	16.6%	19.2%	19.6%	34.5%	46.6%	62.2%	101.7%	47.9%	88.4%	48.1%	5.1%

Note: The turnover ratio is calculated as value traded as a percentage of market Capitalization.

C. Number of firms listed

	1995	2000	2001	2002	2003	2004	2005	2006	2007	2008	2009	Traded/ Listed*
Bahrain	36	41	42	40	44	45	47	50	51	51	49	10 in 50
Doha	-	-	-	25	28	30	32	36	40	43	44	39 in 43
Kuwait	51	86	88	95	108	125	156	180	196	204	205	135 in 224
Muscat	82	131	96	140	141	123	125	121	125	122	120	67 in 122
Saudi	69	75	76	68	70	73	77	86	111	126	135	138 in 139
Abu Dhabi	-	-	24	30	35	59	60	60	64	65	67	29 in 67
Dubai	-	-	-	12	13	18	30	46	55	65	67	27 in 67
Total	238	333	326	398	426	455	497	533	587	611	620	445 in 712

Source: World Bank (2008); Arab Monetary Fund: Quarterly Bulletin (2008, 2009); Annual Reports for 2009; * www.zawya.com, June 2010

Another feature of GCC markets is that they are volatile, which is partly due to their thinness and to their concentration: at any point, there is a limited

Figure 1: GCC: Market Capitalization in Percent of GDP (2007 and 2009)

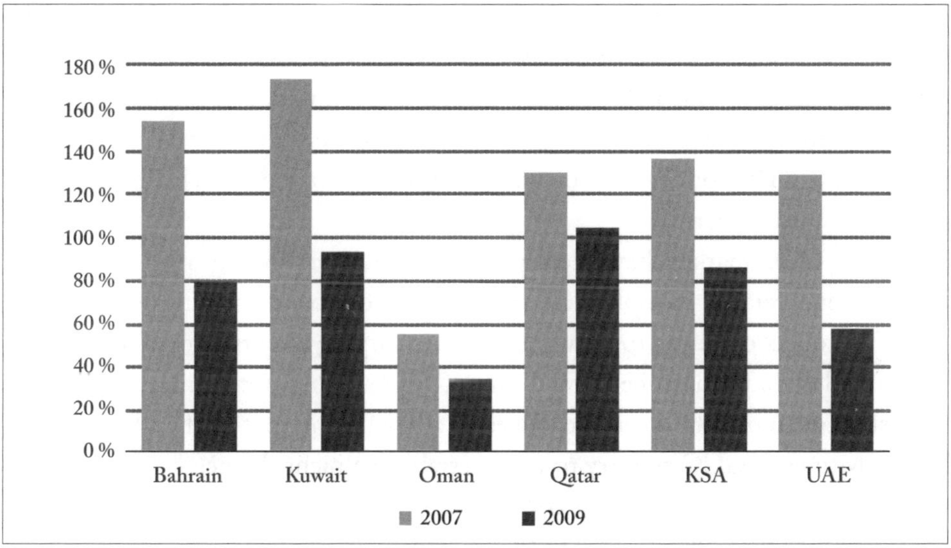

Figure 2: GCC: Market Capitalization 2002 - 2009 (US$ million)

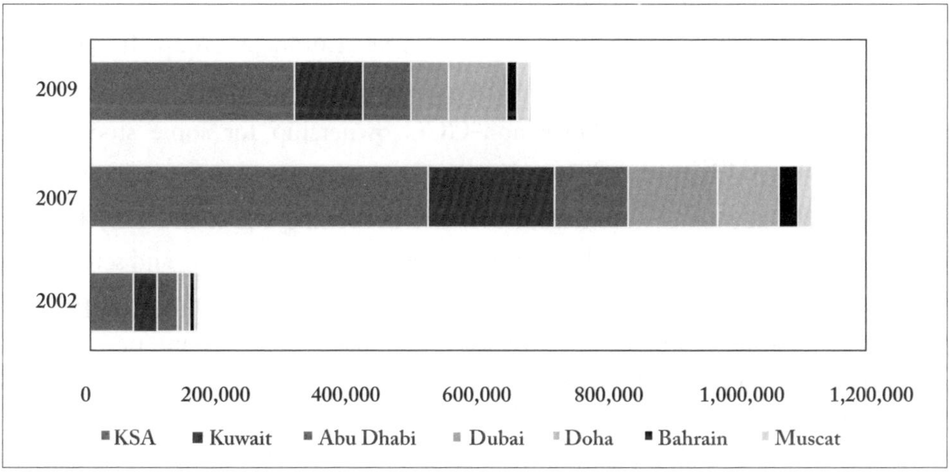

number of shares available. But markets are also volatile because they routinely display herd behavior and asset bubbles, particularly where individual investors are significant. Oversubscriptions (100 times or more) to new IPOs have been a key reflection of such behavior. A major reason for this phenomenon at least up to 2006 was the deliberate under-pricing of shares by governments when floating privatized companies: governments relied on a low offering price as a way of distributing assets widely. The other reason is the lack of experience and unrealistic expectations of individual investors, documented by al-Hassan et al. (2007).[21] Consequently, most IPOs acquired were a loss compared to listing price, especially in the UAE, where investors borrowed at expensive rates to acquire shares. Hence, nowadays, "Muscat SM is the only regional bourse that has an average IPO price in the positive territory compared to its listing day price during the past 5 years."[22]

Thus, GCC markets have seen spectacular but short-lived growth, as well as a marked improvement in sophistication. In a bid to expand the range of investors, the GCC countries moved to allow foreigners to varying extents since 2005, whereas Oman and Bahrain have been forerunners. More significantly, since 2008, there were strategic moves by most exchanges to ally with international exchanges, and luckily, with each GCC country trying to establish a niche. Hence:

- Dubai established DIFX to complement domestic market (the DFM), and NASDAQ now owns a third of that market.
- Abu Dhabi hopes to become the regional center for listing traded funds, and has plans for financial derivatives. In April 2010, it launched the first ETF in the region, with a weak uptake to date.
- Doha sold a 20 percent stake to the NYSE Euronext group. It has now abandoned plans for energy derivatives.
- The Saudi market now allows non-GCC ownership for some stocks, and launched an ETF in June 2010

The main advantages of these moves are deepening the markets by linking with foreign investors, and building on technical expertise in trading and settlement systems. The timing is rather unfortunate: the current crisis meant local exposures to international losses impacted on markets and also wiped out any new foreign investor interest in the medium term.

Such doldrums have underlined the need for coordination and consolidation across the region as a vital measure for revival. Hence, market leaders have started considering mergers in the case of Abu Dhabi and Dubai, with the GCC secretariat

21. A. Al-Hassan, et al. "IPO Behavior in GCC Countries: Goody Two-Shoes or Bad-to-the-Bone?" IMF Working Paper 07/149 (Washington, D.C.: IMF, July2007).

22. P. Gandier, "Global and Regional IPO Impact of Financial Crisis," DIFC Economics Workshop 8: IPOs, M&A & Alternative Investment Markets in the MENA Region, Ernst & Young Presentation (Dubai: February 2010).

establishing a committee to study the possibility for the region.[23] There have also been calls to address practical issues that stand in the way of simple functions such as cross listing in the region. In this context, the head of the union of Arab stock exchanges pointed out that obstacles to increased Arab and foreign investment are obstacles to the growth of GCC markets themselves, the most significant challenges including:[24]

- The failure of companies to seize the opportunity for joint listing on Arab stock markets
- The localization of the issuance of IPOs by new companies and the inability of financial firms to mediate between an investor in a country and an issuing company in another country
- A lack of institutions that serve as a saving or deposit center for securities at the Arab level
- A lack of technical and institutional communication capability among stock saving and deposit institutions in each of the Arab countries

1.1 Sectoral Composition

Table 4 shows the most salient feature of the sectoral composition of GCC and indeed of MENA markets, namely the dominance of banks/financial sector. Banks and/or financial institutions also account for 51 percent of Standard & Poor's Index for MENA, compared to 36 percent in Africa and 16 percent in Latin America. In the GCC, they typically account for a third or more of market capitalization. Except in Dubai, they have the largest market share and often the largest trading value too. The second most important feature of sectoral composition is that it has also been intimately linked to the pattern of economic liberalization and privatization, except perhaps in Kuwait. This was most visible in telecoms and chemicals. Hence, the sale of petrochemical SOEs was a significant addition to the Saudi, Kuwaiti, and Qatari listings.

As such, privatization has been a key source of growth and diversification in regional market capitalization. It is likely to continue to be the case given the lined up sales. Governments have followed what is effectively a policy of being incubators of private sector industries, creating them only to divest them to the private sector. This pattern is necessitated by the fact that governments are at the receiving end of oil wealth, whereas the private sector is very narrow and weak.

23. See *Arabian Business*, March 31, 2010 and *The National*, May 18, 2010.

24. SCA press release, November 22, 2009.

Table 4: Sectoral Composition of GCC Markets

BAHRAIN -Trading value	**2008**	**No of firms**			
Commercial Banks	33.7%	7			
Investment	44.9%	13			
Insurance	2.7%	6			
Industrial	0.2%	2			
Services	18.5%	14			
KUWAIT - Trading value	2008	No of firms			
Banks	33.5	9			
Investments	10.8	47			
Insurance	1.2	7			
Real estate & construction	6.6	39			
Industries & food	11	34			
Services	27	58			
Non Kuwaiti	9.9	14			
OMAN - capitalization	**2008**	**No of firms**			
Banking & Investment	46.9%	30			
Services & insurance	34.8%	38			
Industry	18.1%	52			
Funds	0.13%	2			
QATAR - Trading value	**2008**	**2009**			
Banking & Financial institutions	44.8%	36.3%			
Insurance	2.5%	1.5%			
Industry	15.2%	19.8%			
Services	37.5%	42.4%			
Saudi Arabia - capitalization	**2009**	**No of firms**			
Banks	27.7	11			
Investment	5.6	18			
Insurance	2.0	26			
Real Estate	4.0	7			
Industry	45.3	38			
Services	15.5	35			
ABU DHABI- capitalization	**2009**	**No of firms**	**DUBAI**	**2009**	**No of firms**
Banking and finance	17.4	17	Banks	27.7	12
Insurance	7.7	14	Investments/Finance	19	14
Real Estate	32.6	3	Insurance	4.4	13
Industries	17.7	7	Real Estate & construction	19.5	11
Services	24.6	24	Industries	12.3	5
			Services	16.8	14

Note: Firms have been regrouped to ease comparison. In Tadawul: Industry covers petrochemicals, Cement, Agriculture, Utilities. Services covers Retail, telecoms, transport, media, hotels.

Sources: Bahrain, *Annual Report 2008*; Qatar: *Annual Reports 2008, 2009*; Oman: *Annual Report 2008*; Kuwait:4th *Quarterly Report 2009*, KMEFIC; Dubai: 3rd *Quarterly Bulletin 2009*; Abu Dhabi: *Annual Report 2008*; Tadawul: *Annual Statistical Report 2009*.

Whereas previously, privatization would be restricted to private placements, stock markets offered an additional avenue for the sale of SOEs. The main advantage is that they offered governments the possibility of accessing a potentially wider public, thereby constituting an avenue for diversifying the economy and distributing oil wealth.

Nonetheless, recent years have seen an expansion in the category of listed firms and sectors. Three of these are worth highlighting, namely

- Investment funds (which, as is argued later, contributed to the downfall of Kuwait)
- Large developers and real estate companies, which are also actively traded
- New or growth sectors: media; petroleum sector; utilities; and insurance

Interestingly, there are only a handful of listings relating to oil and gas. This, of course, may well be due to the national ownership of these resources and of the main industrial structures. So the few private listed companies relate to either the few private engineering and servicing companies such as Dana Gas or to downstream retail operations such as Maha Petroleum Products (Oman).

1.1 Types of Firms

In terms of firm size, GCC markets are the realm of large corporations. Indeed, the average size of listed firms is very large compared to listing requirements. According to the website of the markets, minimum capital required varies from under $200,000 in Bahrain to $146 million in Qatar, though no data were available for Kuwait. Except in Oman, average size of listed firms is at least 10 times larger; in Saudi Arabia and Qatar the two are not comparable, due to the weight of giant corporations. As such, GCC markets are highly concentrated, as is clearly illustrated in Table 5. Indeed, the top five to 10 companies typically account for 40 percent-50 percent of market capitalization and even larger share of trading activity (e.g., in Oman, trading is dominated by five stocks, accounting for 20 percent of trading volume between July 2008 to July 2009).

Furthermore, given the small total number of firms, listed companies constitute a minor section of the region's large corporations. Equity markets thus leave out most of the large family-owned businesses and most SMEs, the latter being the case in developed as well as emerging countries. As for family businesses, there have been lots of expectations that stock markets will see the floating of large family businesses. In practice, there has only been a trickle of cases, and often these have involved floating one part of the family holdings.[25] Hence family firms can only be expected to be a minor source of growth for stock markets. According to Ernst and Young, the "strategic rationale for IPOs in the region has not changed – succession planning, institutionalization, monetization, financing, branding etc."[26] One reason is that listing the firms involves both a process of formalizing existing corporate structures and what can be onerous information collection and disclosure requirements.

Table 5: Top Five Firms in GCC Markets (2008/2009)

BAHRAIN	Market share	Government Share	Shareholder
BATELCO	13.9	57.2	Mumtalakat, Pension Fund Commission Bahrain, Social Insurance Organization Bahrain
Allied Union Bank	12.9	39.93	Pension Fund Commission Bahrain, Social Security Kuwait
Arab Banking Corporation	8.2	86.78	Kuwait Investment Authority, Central Bank of Libya, Abu Dhabi Investment Authority
BARKA	8.2		
National Bank of Bahrain	7.5	55.24	Mumtalakat, Pension Fund Commission Bahrain
Total Capitalization	50.7		
Top 5 by value traded	Allied Bank, BBK, Gulf Finance House, Batelco, Salam Bank		
ABU DHABI			
Emirates Telecoms	23.5	60	
National Bank of Abu Dhabi	6.9	70	Abu Dhabi Investment Authority
Qatar Telecommunications	6.8	10	Abu Dhabi Investment Authority
First Gulf Bank	5.0	5.6	Royal family

25. See Ithmar Capital and Dow Jones, "The Impact of Private Equity on GCC Family Businesses," Dubai, 2007, http://www.ithmar.com/pdf/thought_leadership_reports.pdf and K. Remo-Listana, K. "Family-owned Companies See Future in IPO," *Emirates Business* 24/7, April 7, 2008, http://www.zawya.com/story.cfm/sidZAWYA20080407032817.

26. P. Gandier, "Global and Regional IPO Impact of Financial Crisis."

Arkan	4.2	51	General Holding Comp
Total Capitalization	46.4		
Top 5 by value traded	53.5	Aldar, Arkan, Sorouh, Aabar, Methaq Investment	
DUBAI			
Mashreq Bank	16.7		
National Industries	11.3		
Agility	8.0		
National Bank of Dubai	6.7	55.6	
EMAAR	5.9	31.2	
Total Capitalization	48.5		
KUWAIT			
Mobile Telecoms (Zain)	25.3	24	Kuwait Investment Authority
National Bank of Kuwait	12.6		
Kuwait Finance House	9.0		
Commercial Bank of Kuwait	3.8		
National Industries Group	3.0		
Share of Dow Jones Kuwait Index	53.7		
OMAN			
Oman Telecoms	18.3	70	
Bank Muscat	16.7	30.6	17% by Royal Court, the rest govt depts/pension funds
Bank Dhofar	10.2		
National Bank of Oman	6.5		
Raysut Cement	5.6		
Total Capitalization	57.3		

SAUDI ARABIA			
SABIC	20.7	70	
Rajhi Bank	8.9		
Saudi Telecoms	7.4	70	Another 10% by Saudi Pension Fund & Bahraini Social Security
Samba	3.4		
Saudi Electricity Company	3.9	70	
Total Capitalization	44.3		
QATAR			
Ezdan Real Estate	25.3		
Industries Qatar	15.4	70	Qatar Petroleum, another 11% Qatari institutions
Qatar Islamic Bank	4.1		
Q-Telecoms	5.9	55	Qatar Investment Authority; another 9.8% Qatar Retirement Fund
Qatar National Bank	12.2	50	Qatar Investment Authority
Total Capitalization	62.9		
Sources: Bahrain: Annual Trading Report 2009; Kuwait: Dow Jones Fact Sheet 2010; Qatar: 1st Quarter Bulletin 2010; Annual Reports for others; Shareholder information mostly 2008 data from http://www.noozz.com/company/			

1.2 Ownership and Participants

Another distinguishing feature of GCC markets is the concentration of ownership, which is not uncommon in developing countries. Specifically, three types of shareholders dominate:

a) the government;

b) the wealthiest and/or ruling families; and

c) institutional investors.

Table 6: Top Five Firms in GCC Markets (2008/2009)

	Listed Govt Firms	In Top Ten	Market value of board seats by top 10 families
Bahrain	5	3	25.6
Kuwait	3		33.2
Oman	4	1	41.4
Qatar	4	3	57.6
UAE	16	5	19.7 and 36.1 (Dubai)
Saudi	11	3	37.7

http://www.noozz.com/company;
Hawkamah, Power Matters, May 2008, 29-41

A close examination of major shareholders of top listed companies shows that governments own or control typically three of the top 10 companies throughout GCC markets, as is apparent in Table 6. Their presence is further corroborated by the following facts:

- Roughly one-third of the Saudi market's capitalization is owned by the government (including public pension funds), and another third is in strategic holdings by founding families.[27]
- Dubai's domestic DFM market is 80 percent owned by Bourse Dubai, which is itself controlled by the government or government-related holdings.
- Similarly, the Qatar Investment Authority (QIA) owns 70-75 percent of the shares in Qatar Exchange via Qatar Holding. NYSE owns the rest as of August 2009.

So despite the firm commitment to privatization, governments are not withdrawing from the economy: rather they are becoming business partners eager to operate as efficiently as private corporations. The behavioral implications of this form of government capitalism are unclear: is it going to hamper the markets'

27. World Bank, Report on the Observance of Standards and Codes (ROSC) – Corporate Governance Country Assessment Saudi Arabia (Washington, D.C.: February 2009).

ability to become an important component in the region's financial structures? Or will government presence in equity markets simply parallel their reassuring role in bonds markets? The oversubscriptions for IPOs suggest that this may be the case, i.e. that governments may well be crowding in private investors.

The other key category of shareholders in the region is the wealthiest families, which often overlap with the ruling families. While a single such family owns 4 percent or less of stock markets by capitalization, when the shares of the top 10 families are added up, they own between 25 percent in Bahrain and 58 percent in Qatar of the markets.[28] In that sense, capital markets in the GCC are more a millionaires' club rather than a platform for broad-based capitalism.

Bearing in mind the concentrated ownership and the small share of capital available to be traded, it is not surprising that trading is dominated by individuals. Hence retail investors complement strategic holdings by governments and founding families. Their importance varies from a high of over 82 percent in Saudi Arabia to 50 percent-67 percent in Kuwait and UAE, and 41 percent in Qatar. However, their impact on trading and volatility has been disproportionately negative. Aside from "irrational exuberance," inflated expectations, inexperience, etc., retail investors were also described as taking a "relaxed view of management practices, safe in the knowledge that they can sell their shares at any time and for a profit."[29] Regional markets are trying to counter this through ongoing educational efforts and stricter monitoring.

As for foreign participation, this only began a few years ago by allowing GCC nationals, the exercise being extended more recently to other nationals. This move has finally allowed the region to tap portfolio investments. By 2009, the regional picture stood as follows:

- In Bahrain, foreigners, mainly GCC citizens, accounted for just over half of market capitalization, reflecting the importance of investment companies in the market.
- In UAE and Oman, foreigners accounted for 37 percent of traded value and 24 percent of ownership, respectively, in 2009.
- In Kuwait, Qatar, and Saudi Arabia, foreigners account for 5 percent or less of trading activity.

28. Hawkamah, *Power Matters* (Dubai: May 2008), http://www.hawkamah.org/ publications/cg_ reports/ files/Powermatters.pdf

29. Samba Bank, *The Saudi Stock Market: Structural Issues, Recent Performance and Outlook*, Economics Dept Report Series (Riyadh: December 2009).

- Except in Dubai, GCC and other Arabs form the dominant nationality of foreign participants.

Although foreign participation receded in the face of the global and regional meltdowns, it is unlikely to disappear for several reasons. Firstly, in most markets, it remains below the new legislated limits. Secondly, it has only started being allowed in the most lucrative markets, particularly in Saudi Arabia. Ditto for the new form of investment, namely ETFs. If the Omani example is anything to go by – where foreigners' share rose from 18 percent to 24 percent between 2004 and 2009 –, this participation is likely to rise, although this will be a slow and protracted process in the current adverse market sentiment.

Finally, though no consistent data set is available, it is clear that institutional investors are also present. Although many are government entities, this category also includes banks, mutual funds, and pension funds. In Oman, banks dedicated 22 percent of their portfolio investments to the Muscat Stock Market: that was reduced by 61 percent following the crisis.[30] Mutual funds are particularly important in Saudi Arabia, where most banks have established these funds to participate in local equity. According to Tadawul's website, there are at least 61 funds involved in local equity markets. However, according to SAMA's annual report, around two third of total investments by these funds are aimed at the local market.[31] But since they account for only a few percentage points of market capitalization, these investors can be expected to grow in importance.

Most significantly, Private Equity (PE) funds and SWFs have also gained importance. PE funds have mushroomed in the region and in GCC, both in number and volumes. Their activity and numbers are still below their potential: PE in MENA remains at only at 0.3 percent of GDP vs. 1.7 percent in UK. Moreover:

- A majority of PE funds are in the investing phase, and concentrate on M&A or control buyouts.
- Over $19 billion has been raised since 2000, $11 billion was available for investments. At 2007 peak, there were an estimated 108 funds with $16 billion under management[32]

30. International Monetary Fund, *Impact of the Global Financial Crisis on the Gulf Cooperation Council Countries and Challenges Ahead.*
31. SAMA, Annual Report, (Riyadh: 2010), http://sama.gov.sa/sites/SAMAEN/ReportsStatistics/ReportsStatisticsLib /5600_R_Annual_En_45_2009_08_31.pdf, (in Arabic, accessed July 2010
32. *Financial Times*, "Private Equity Has To Face Some Tough Realities," October 15, 2008.

- There are too few venture capital or seed funds.

As for SWFs, these had been present through PE funds: indeed, their main mandate has been to concentrate on investing offshore rather than domestically. The current crisis has led to strategic moves by SWFs to have permanent activity or stakes in the region's markets, particularly in Kuwait, Oman, and Qatar. In Qatar, the QIA acquired substantive stakes in banks as a way of injecting capital, thereby helping to preserve market capitalization.

4. Regulatory Aspects and Corporate Governance

The evolution of the regulatory environments in GCC markets is detailed in the Appendix which also shows that their development is very much a work in progress. Except Kuwait, most countries now have formally independent regulatory and supervisory authorities overseeing markets and market players. Thatcher (2009) reviews the main influences and trends underpinning this evolution.[33] He concludes that both international and domestic factors, including the spread of the British single Financial Services Authorities (FSA) model, led to a regional frenzy of legislation, regulation, and international alliances. In a competitive and globalized world, the region could only follow global trends of adopting corporate governance principles.

Gaping holes remain in practice: firms tend not to have the required transparent and accountable structures. Much work also remains to be done in terms of core standards of operation, disciplinary regulations and firmer sanctions, and small investor protection. Crucially, listed government entities of SOEs must abide by the same corporate code of conduct, auditing requirements, and company laws that apply to private firms, over and above any need to be removed from political interference. Listed family businesses face other pressures: they have to adapt and comply with continuing disclosure requirements and increase the transparency of their actions so as to continuously involve shareholders. Compliance with data and documentation for this purpose has costly operational implications for companies otherwise used to informal ways of doing business and monitoring costs. Transparency implies a shift in local company culture towards complex corporate organizational structures, which may not be suitable for all types of enterprises or sectors.

33. M. Thatcher, "Governing Markets in Gulf States," Working Paper, Kuwait Program on Development, Governance and Globalization in the Gulf States, London School of Economics, March 2009.

Still, progress has been made since the market correction of 2006 in terms, for example, of better regulations against insider trading, separating brokers and clients' money, more transparent trading, and firmer disciplinary actions. Indeed, until 2007, the Emirates' SCA did not have the authority to fine or suspend brokers. Unsurprisingly, the spate of scandals and prosecutions in Dubai in 2008 showed that corruption – mainly insider dealing and creative accounting – was still rampant. Further, a 2008 Hawkamah study confirmed outstanding weaknesses that underlined the immature nature of firms:[34]

- 52 percent of GCC companies did not publish an annual report in English
- More than a third of firms in Dubai and Bahrain trade less than $3000 a day
- 59 percent of companies do not trade every day

The current crisis has similarly accelerated the adoption and implementation of corporate governance codes throughout the GCC markets. But while financial disclosures are now a fairly widespread practice, there are still issues of non-financial disclosure (particularly regarding ownership), board memberships, auditing etc. Uneven progress is also noted in terms of supervisory powers and disciplinary actions. The most visible flagging of the latter has occurred in Tadawul, which launched hundreds of investigations and delivered dozens of fines, which are proudly advertised on its website. The least disciplined or regulated appears to be the Kuwait Stock Exchange, where the only known instance of punishment was overruled by court.

5. Role in Corporate Finance, Investment, and the Crisis

So far, evidence shows that regional markets have been a vehicle for divestiture and partnership between the government and the private sector. But what about their role in mobilizing investments? To recall, the regional literature did not look at such issues at the macro level. Further, while up to 2008, gross domestic investment was helping to fuel GDP growth, figures for 2009 suggest investment growth was grinding down to 0.8 percent.[35] In other words, the period during which investments, the economy, and capital markets, grew simultaneously is very short, restricting room for econometric investigation.

34. Hawakamah, *Power Matters.*

35. World Bank, MENA Economic Development and Prospects, (Washington D.C.: 2008); World Bank, *World Bank Middle East And North Africa Region – A Regional Economic Update: Recovering from the Crisis* (Washington, D.C., April 2010), http://siteresources.worldbank.org/ INTMENA / Resources/MENARecoveringFromCrisispub5-12-10webFINAL.pdf

Nonetheless, there is some evidence at the firm or micro level that is worth revisiting. Firstly, as previously mentioned, three studies suggest that raising equity is not a key strategy for listed firms, mainly because of issues of control, so that both listed and non-listed firms continue to rely primarily on retained earnings and on bank lending. Furthermore, while the listing requirements are fairly modest, in practice, it is well-established large corporations, typically financial firms, which access the markets, floating part of their capital. This practice of minority listings demonstrates that listed firms do use stock markets to raise capital, but prefer to retain control and ownership. Indeed, as is shown below, a good – albeit small – proportion of listed firms raise capital annually through secondary offerings. But not diluting ownership limits the resort to equity financing. A more precise understanding of these patterns across markets or over time is blocked by the dearth of comprehensive studies or surveys of financing strategies at firm level in the GCC.

Looking at capital raised would be one way of gauging the importance of stock markets in mobilizing finance for investment. Apart from problems of data availability and consistency, IPO activity in GCC markets in particular has been plagued by the aforementioned problems of "irrational exuberance," herd behavior, and incredible oversubscriptions.[36] Still, some information about corporate actions to raise capital has been compiled from annual reports of Oman and Qatar and the Saudi regulatory authority, and is presented in Table 7. The table shows that there is an active but small market for IPOs, with capital doubling from $6 billion to $12 billion between 2005 and 2007. Since then, it receded in line with the credit crunch, except in Saudi Arabia. There, IPOs raised $4.8 billion and $9.8 billion in 2007 and 2008, respectively. As such, IPOs were more than half of the value of capital raised in the region, the second most popular avenue being Rights Issues. In fact, the annual reports of stock markets show that most markets have been witnessing a small but increasing number of corporate actions to raise, not just distribute dividends. Thus Table 7 shows new listings have contributed regularly to increased market capitalization, ranging from 4 percent in Oman to 8 percent in Qatar. Despite the absence of a consolidated data set, it can still be said that GCC markets are providing a small – at times minute – proportion of fresh capital and of domestic investments.

36. See Al Hassan et al, "IPO Behaviour in GCC Countries."

Table 7: New Capital Raised on GCC Capital Markets

Regional IPO activitiy	2005	2006	2007	2008	2009
GCC raised ($billion)	6	7.5	12		
MENA raised ($billion)	8.1	7.9	13.5	12.3	2
Number	26	30	53	41	12
Saudi Arabia	**Up to 2005**	**2006**	**2007**	**2008**	**2009**
IPO	6	10	26	13	
Rights Issue	10	3	4	7	
Private Placement	1	-	1	2	
Exempt Offer	10	23	29	19	
Acquisition by Issuing Shares	-	3	1	1	
Oman	**2004**		**2007**		**2009**
Bonus shares	21		27		23
Capital Increase					6
Rights Issues	9		12		9
Bonds	4		2		3
Private Placement	4		8		
New listings	7		20		14
New Issues/Market Capitalization	8.6%		4.5%		
Qatar	**2005**	**2006**	**2007**	**2008**	**2009**
New Issues	11	7	5	11	
New Issues/Market Capitalization	4.6%	4.6%	3.1%	7.0%	

Source: Gulf Capital (2008); Gandier (2010); al-Rumayyan (2009); Annual Reports of Doha and Oman.

On the macro level, a cursory look at the brief regional economic boom in 2004-2008 may initially suggest that markets were both supporting and gaining strength from real economic growth. However, while the 2006 correction revealed that local liquidity was in dire need of investment vehicles, thereafter the situation overran into over-investment in overvalued equity, with corporations unable to sustain continuously high earnings. An asset bubble was being created and was also fuelled by a lending frenzy. Indeed, that episode witnessed a practice that became a key systemic risk in the current downturn: namely use of private credit to buy equity, as investors scrambled to share in the stellar growth. According to the IMF, in the UAE, the ratio of off-balance sheet items to deposits increased from 50 percent in 2000 to 70 percent in 2008,[37] with Dubai piling up $50-$100 billion in foreign debt in an even shorter period. Throughout the region, average real credit growth stood at 23 percent a year between 2003 and 2008. And while proportions vary, in Kuwait at least 12 percent of this lending went to purchasing equity.[38]

A second systemic shock came from the bursting of the real estate bubble in Dubai in particular, but also in places like Qatar. The bursting of that bubble resulted in direct damage to the concerned markets, by wiping out both market value and investors' confidence. Both the lending frenzy and the real estate shock in turn undermined banking and financial sector performance. Given their weight in stock markets, it was inevitable that the latter sustained real and lasting damage. Needless to say, the intimate relationship between state/government entities, core sectors and financial groups make for complex and deep ripple effects. The current problems have also led to an increased cost of borrowing and contributed to reduced access to international finance. That is because the trust in the reliability and guarantees underpinning GREs has been severely dented, the situation being made worse by poor communication and transparency at the peak of the Dubai crisis in December 2009.

The years 2009-2010 also delivered two other shocks with similarly damaging implications for regional financial structures: the collapse of al-Saad and Gossaibi groups in Saudi Arabia and the troubles of Kuwaiti investment firms. Over and above the bill to be footed by the respective governments, the first case, like the Madoff scandal, shows that no one should be too big to be regulated or audited. The problems of Kuwaiti investment firms have more serious repercussions. Beyond the defaults by two giants on the Kuwait markets (Gulf Investment House and al-Dar), they exposed systemic flaws, namely large exposures with a toxic mismatch between short-term loans and illiquid assets.[39] Thankfully, the authorities are very

37. A. Chailloux and D. Hakura,"Systemic Liquidity Management in the U.A.E.: Issues and Options," IMF Working Paper WP/09/261. Washington DC: IMF, December 2009, 20.

38. IMF, *Impact of the Global Financial Crisis on the Gulf Cooperation Council Countries and Challenges Ahead*, Middle East and Central Asia Dept, Departmental paper 1, (Washington, D.C., 2010).

39. R. Wigglesworth, "Kuwaiti Investment Model Feels Strain," *Financial Times*, February 21, 2010.

clear about passing on the message: the underlying models of over-leveraging, rapid haphazard expansion, and heightened expectations and promises of rapid gains are no longer acceptable. Apart from cleaning balance sheets, new monitoring criteria and procedures are to be applied.[40] As in Dubai, the cleaning up will deprive the financial system and banks of liquidity, reducing the availability of funds for lending to other sectors. This is hardly surprising given that the firms' off and on balance sheets equalled Kuwaiti GDP, and the loans secured accounted for at least 11 percent of total lending.[41]

The systemic nature of the crises and the level of losses sustained will certainly slow future progress. They will also have eliminated the majority of retail participants, who had come to expect continuously higher earnings, higher than those from the main alternative, namely bank deposits. The crises also mean that the ability of local markets to provide a significant source of fresh corporate finance will remain at the burgeoning stage for a longer period.

These crises highlight the fact that the real economy and real growth lead stock markets, not the other way round. Unlike some aspects of the East Asian crisis of the late 1990s, speculative attacks and the collapse of stock markets did not cause the economic damage here. Unlike the recent problems of Brazil, regional vulnerability was not due to massive international capital outflows, nor because of the central banks' attempts to react to the international crisis. Rather, the flawed way of financing some of the region's speculative activity and the poor regulatory oversight of sectoral developments (for example, overlooking the practice of "flipping" property even before completion) led to corporate collapses, which in turn undermined market capitalization and market activity. Thus, while the international crisis could have cost temporary losses, these developments imply more serious impairment: it will be sometime before regional markets take off again.

Conclusions and Future Direction

Since being set up, GCC capital markets have clearly grown substantially, improving in depth, diversity and maturity. Between 2004 and 2009, their growth coincided with buoyant economic activity and investment. In this period, they also became a noticeable but very small forum for raising corporate capital. Once foreign

40. "CBK Governor: Economic Crisis Unveiled Shortcomings in Local Investment Firms," www.zawya.com, June 9, 2010.

41. International Monetary Fund, *Impact of the Global Financial Crisis on the Gulf Cooperation Council Countries and Challenges Ahead.*

ownership was allowed, these markets were also able to attract a small number and proportion of international and regional investors.

Clearly, major weaknesses remain. Firstly, due to their immature and volatile nature, the performance of the capital markets has been erratic. They have a number of outstanding regulatory and governance issues, which is why they are yet to match the sophistication, maturity, and depth of capital markets in emerging economies. Secondly, their articulation with the domestic economy remains limited, although they now display more diverse sectoral composition. Further, these markets represent a small section of very large corporations, serving the government and wealthier income quintiles. They are irrelevant for most family-owned businesses and SMEs. They do not yet represent the pooling of the resources of small investors nor have they become a visible platform for the average firm to increased access to credit.

As such, GCC markets are not like others: effectively, by being used as a vehicle for privatization, they have been an incubator for the private sector, as well as a way for traditional family business tycoons to formalize their corporate structures. Their nascent nature, small size, and the weaknesses in regulation have meant that participants include speculators. Bubbles, toxic portfolios, and systemic flaws in the real economy dealt severe blows, worse than any transmission effects from the global meltdown.

The current episode, which wiped out much of the gains since 2005, stresses the point that capital markets ultimately follow the real economy and reflect its sophistication. Consequently, these markets are yet to become a financial pillar for those economies. Not only are equity markets still small, but there is also an urgent need to revive and deepen the once promising bonds market, particularly the corporate end. Hence, in the medium term, capital markets must expect a protracted growth process that will restrict them to a minor role in domestic financing structures, certainly when compared with the importance and sophistication of the banking sector.

The growth in equity markets will continue to be supported by privatization sales, this being subject to the limited absorptive capacity of the private sector. The recession has done much to wipe out investors' interest, resulting in postponed sales. Markets will also grow in line with the expected growth of the embryonic PE sector as well as the continued trickle of large family businesses into the formal corporate world. However, any progress depends on sustaining the current corrective measures in improving regulation and protection mechanisms.

Before the crisis, GCC markets had timidly opened the door to GCC and other nationals. There were also a few calls in MENA and in Africa to overcome the smallness of size by considering the integration of markets. Today's doldrums, abysmally low turnover ratios, and dearth of trading means that this work has to continue: the smallness of individual markets has become a suffocating feature whose logical limit has been reached. By the same token, serious steps towards regional cooperation and integration must be taken as a matter of necessity. In other words, after the stellar growth in the take-off phase, it is time for modesty and hard work on the details.

Appendix

Abu Dhabi Stock Market (ADX)

Regulatory Authority

Emirates Securities and Commodities Authority (SCA), headed by representatives of ministries

Major Regulations

2000 Federal Law No.4 establishing the ESCA
Local Law No. (3) of 2000, the provisions of which vest the Market with a legal entity of autonomous status, independent finance and management

2005 Resolution No.93 regulating Islamic bonds

2007 Regulation of online and margin trading

2009 Tightening Disclosure and Transaction Regulation; Law approving Exchange Traded Funds (ETF)

2010 (April) New UAE Corporate Governance code for publicly listed companies to come into force

2010 ETF launched

Dubai Stock/Financial Market (DSM/DFM)

Regulatory Authority

Emirates Securities and Commodities Authority (SCA), headed by representatives of ministries

Major Regulations

2000 Federal Law No.4 establishing the ESCA

2004 Establishment of the Dubai International Financial Center, regulated by the Dubai Financial Security Authority (DFSA), which also regulates the Dubai International Financial Exchange. DIFC is a financial free zone, with full set of laws (insolvency, trust, personal property).

2005 Resolution No.93 regulating Islamic bonds

2005 (December) DFM set up as a Public Joint Stock Company in the UAE with paid up capital of Dh8 billion, with shares offered for public subscription. Trading in those shares began in 2007.

2007 Plan announced for new corporate governance rules, particularly regarding trading by board members. New accounting and reporting systems also to be adopted.
Borse Dubai was created to own both DIFX and DSM.

2008 New organizational structure, which adds the general assembly as the higher authority, and a Department of Market Authority as well as a Sharia Board

Bahrain Stock Exchange (BSE)

Regulatory Authority

Bahrain Monetary Authority, now called the Central Bank of Bahrain. It acts as the single regulator for the whole financial sector.

Major Regulations

1987 Decree Law No 4 creating the BSE

1999 Amiri Decree No 10 allowed GCC and foreign investment

2000 Disclosure requirements include major shareholders

2002 Capital Markets Supervision Directorate established with responsibility for primary and secondary markets (including listing) and overall intermediation.

2006 Central Bank of Bahrain and Financial Institutions Law (coordination appears effective; a comprehensive and transparent regulatory regime)
BSE is an independent institution but Governor of the Central Bank chairs its board.

2007 New classification of investment funds and committee to accelerate dispute resolution between financial institutions. Rules to reduce insider trading

Operational Aspects

A 10% limit on daily price movements

Doha Stock Market (DSM) (now Qatar Exchange)

Regulatory Authority

Qatar Financial Markets Authority (QFMA), separate from trading or the executive function

Major Regulations

1995 Decree Law No.14 leading to the creation of DSM

2005 Law 33 establishes the Qatari Financial Centre (QFC), including an independent regulatory authority. Law No.13 of 2005 amended to allow foreign investment.

2007 Law 14 amends Law 33, establishing Qatar Financial Markets Authority (QFMA) and Doha Securities Market Company (DSMC). QFMA takes the role of a single regulatory and supervision authority. DSMC takes an executive role in the field of securities trading with regard to execution and clearing and settlement of transactions.

2008 Continuing the work on the QFC Regulatory Authority, which is also to supervise the QFC and the banking system. The authority is to continue to improve listing requirements and disclosure standards and is to regulate new areas such as insurance.

2009 Adoption of Corporate Governance Code
DSM becomes Qatar Exchange, co-owned by Qatar Holding (80%) and NYSE Euronext (20%)

Operational Aspects

A 10% limit on daily price movements

Kuwait Stock Exchange (KSE)

Regulatory Authority

The stock exchange itself and a Market Committee, which includes government representatives

Major Regulations

2007 Rules on disclosure tightened. But capital market supervisor has no judiciary power to enforce ruling: KSE banned Al-Kharafi group from trading but administrative court overturned it
Law at the Council of Ministers to set up a Capital Markets Authorities

Muscat Stock Market (MSM)

Regulatory Authority Capital Market Authority, a government authority

Major Regulations

1988 Royal Decree Law (53/88) establishing the MSM

1998 Royal Decree (80/98) assigned regulatary role to Capital Market Authority

2007 Changes to listing requirements and operating rules, including direct fines for non-disclosure; new corporate governance department within the market.
2008 Clearing is now done by the Muscat Depositary and Securities Registration Company
Cross listing agreement between Oman and Qatar
2010 Creation/Adoption of Omani Corporate Governance Code; changes to the market's organizational structure

Operational Aspects

A 10% limit on daily price movements

Saudi Stock Exchange (Tadawul)

Regulatory Authority As of 2003, Capital Market Authority is the primary regulatory body. It is a government body with appointed board and reports to the prime minister.

Major Regulations

2003 Royal Decree (No.M20) created capital markets law and subsequently the Authority. The law defined the roles and regulations of the CMA and Tadawul.
2006 The CMA passes Corporate Governance Regulations for listed companies following the crash.
2007 Tadawul, which was a department of the CMA, becomes a joint stock company, a move towards separating legal, organizational and regulatory responsibilities. New trading system allows tracking trades. Insider trading: forbidding board members of traded companies from trading around times of disclosures. Many cases (82) investigated and prosecuted.
(December) Tadawul open to GCC nationals. Non Arabs participate through few mutual funds.
2008 (August) Foreigners allowed to participate through swap arrangements
2010 (Spring) ETF launched

Operational & Other Aspects

- A 10% limit on daily price movements
- Clearing time is T+0: Tadawul is the only GCC market to have live trading.

References

Abed, G. and M.Soueid. 2005. Capital markets in the Middle East and North Africa. Presentation, EIB-FEMIP Expert Committee Meeting, Luxembourg, March.

Al-Hassan, A., F. Delgado, and M. Omran. 2007. IPO behaviour in GCC countries: Goody-two shoes or bad-to-the-bone? IMF Working Paper 07/149 (Washington DC: IMF, July).

Al-Rumayyan, Y. 2010. Saudi Arabia: Open for cross-border trading? Presentation, Eleventh Annual Depositary Receipt Issuers' Conference (Egypt: April 2009). http://www.dricworld.com/events/37/3/. Accessed May 2010.

Arabian Business.com. Abu Dhabi and Dubai stock markets in merger talks. http://www.arabianbusiness.com/584939?tmpl. Accessed May 2010.

Arab Monetary Fund. "Yearly Performance" and "Monthly Performance" of Arab Capital Markets. http://www.amf.org.ae/performance

Balli, F., J. Rosmy and M. Osman. International income smoothing and foreign asset holdings. MPRA Paper 10159. Munich: University Library of Munich, 2008.

Beji, S. 2007. Financial openness and financial development in the South Mediterranean Sea countries. 14th ERF Conference. Cairo: ERF.

Ben Naceur, S. and S. Ghazouani. 2005. Stock markets, banks, and economic growth: Empirical evidence from the MENA Region. February. http://ssrn.com/abstract=856386

Ben Naceur, S., S. Ghazouani, and M.,Omran. The determinants of stock market development in the MENA region. August. http://ssrn.com/abstract=856385

Ben Naceur, S., S. Ghazouani, and M. Omran. 2007. Does stock market liberalization spur economic and financial development in the Mena region?" October. http://ssrn.com/abstract=1018742

Ben Naceur, S., N. Boubakri, and Ghazouani. 2008. Privatization and financial market development: A comparison between MENA countries and other regions. ERF Working Paper 390. Cairo: ERF, April.

Billmeier, A., and I. Massa. What drives stock market development in the Middle East and Central Asia -- institutions, remittances, or natural resources? IMF Working Papers 07/157. Washington DC: IMF, July 2007.

Bolbol, A., and M. Omran. 2005. Investment and the stock market: evidence from Arab firm-level panel data. *Emerging Markets Review* 6: 85-106.

Capasso, S. 2006. Stock market development and economic growth. WIDER Research Paper 2006/102. Helsinki: WIDER.

Chailloux, A., and D. Hakura. 2009. Systemic liquidity management in the U.A.E.: Issues and Options. IMF Working Paper WP/09/261. Washington DC: IMF, December.

International Monetary Fund (IMF). 2010. Impact of the Global Financial Crisis on the Gulf Cooperation Council Countries and Challenges Ahead. Middle East and Central Asia Dept, Departmental paper 1. Washington, D.C.

2004, 2008, 2009. Global Financial Stability Reports. Washington, D.C.

Financial Times.

2008. Private equity has to face some tough realities (by R.Wigglesworth), November 15.

2009. China derivative rule changes hit banks. November 24.

2010. Debt threat to Kuwait investment houses (by R.Wigglesworth). February 21.

2010. Kuwaiti investment model feels strain (by R.Wigglesworth). February 21.

2010. Kuwait remains in money market pain (by R.Wigglesworth). March 24.

Gandier, P. 2010. Global and regional IPO impact of financial crisis. DIFC Economics Workshop 8: IPOs, M&A & Alternative Investment Markets in the MENA Region. Ernest & Young Presentation. Dubai: February.

Gulf Capital. 2008. IPO market during 2007. Dubai. www.gulfcapital.com/uploads/research/2008/ IPOs%202007.ppt. Accessed June 2010.

Haddad, M., and H. Hakim. 2008. Irrational exuberance on the Saudi stock exchange. ERF Conference Paper, Cairo: ERF, November.

Hawkamah. 2008. Power Matters. Dubai: May. http://www.hawkamah.org/publications/cg_reports/ files/Powermatters.pdf

Ithmar Capital and Dow Jones. 2007. The impact of private equity on GCC family Businesses. Dubai. http://www.ithmar.com/pdf/thought_leadership_reports.pdf

Khalid, M. 2008. The future of the GCC's emerging capital markets. *Khaleej Times*, February 13.

Madison, K., K. Miller, and C. Martin. 2008. Time to call the Sheriff? - Financial regulation in the Gulf. The Arab Financial Forum, February.

Omran, M., and A. Bolbol. 2003. Foreign direct investment, financial development, and economic growth: evidence from the Arab countries. *Review of Middle East Economics and Finance* 1, no. 3, (December): 231–249.

Omet, G. Corporate financing in the MENA region: do country or firm specific factors explain the capital structure? Paper for the 10th Mediterranean Research Meeting. Florence: European University Institute, 2009.

Remo-Listana, K. 2008. Family-owned companies see future in IPO. *Emirates Business 24/7*, April 7, http://www.zawya.com/story.cfm/sidZAWYA20080407032817.

Sachs, J. et al. 2009. Financing GCC power projects post credit crunch. *Natural Gas and Electricity* 26, no.1, August.

Saidi, N. 2010. The future of capital markets in the Middle East. DIFC Knowledge Series 7 – MENASA Capital Markets. Dubai: DIFC Authority, January.

SAMA. 2010. Annual Report. Riyadh. http://sama.gov.sa/sites/SAMAEN/ ReportsStatistics/ ReportsStatisticsLib/5600 R Annual_En_45_2009_08_ 31.pdf (in Arabic, accessed July 2010).

Samba Bank. 2009. The Saudi stock market: Structural issues, recent performance and outlook. Economics Dept Report Series. Riyadh: December.

Securities & Commodities Authorities. 2009. Al-Turaifi outlines role of UASE in boosting Pan-Arab investment. Press Release November 22, Abu Dhabi Stock Exchange, http://www.sca.ae/English/news/Pages/2009-11-22.aspx. Accessed June 2010.

Sukuk.net. 2010. Significant slowdown in GCC bond market. http://www.sukuk.me/news/print.php?newid=282944. Accessed January 2010.

Thatcher, M. 2009. Governing markets in Gulf States. Working paper, Kuwait Program on Development, Governance and Globalisation in the Gulf States. London: London School of Economics, March.

The National. 2001. ADX chief back tie-up with Dubai bourse. http://www.thenational.ae/apps/pbcs.dll/article?AID=/20100518BUSINESS/705189895/1005/foreign. Accessed May 2010.

World Bank, MENA Economic Development and Prospects, Washington, D.C.: 2008.

World Bank. 2009. Report on the Observance of standards and codes (ROSC)-Corporate governance country assessment Saudi Arabia. Washington, D. C., February.

World Bank. 2010. World Bank Middle East and North Africa region-A regional economic update: Recovering from the crisis. Washington, D.C., April. http://siteresources. worldbank.org / INTMENA / Resources / MEN A Recovering From Crisispub5-12-10webFINAL.pdf

Wilson, R. 2009. The development of Islamic finance in the GCC. Research paper, Kuwait Program on Development, Governance and Globalisation in the Gulf States (London: London School of Economics). http://www.lse.ac.uk/collections/LSEKP/islamicfinance.htm

Woertz, Eckart. 2008. The GCC bond market. Dubai: Gulf Research Center, April.

"CBK governor: economic crisis unveiled shortcomings in local investment firms", www.zawya.com, June 9, 2010

Also:

Most publications of GCC stock markets in Arabic and English (annual reports, trading bulletins, shareholders, rules & regulations, corporate actions, and news)

Abu Dhabi Stock Exchange	www.adx.ae
Bahrain Stock Market	http://www.bahrainstock.com/bahrainstock/index.asp
Doha Securities Market	http://www.dsm.com.qa/dsmsite/
Dubai Financial Market	http://www2.dfm.co.ae/
Muscat Stock Market	http://www.msm.gov.om/
Saudi Stock Exchange	http://www.tadawul.com.sa/wps/portal/HomeAr

3

GCC Bond Markets

Michael P. Grifferty

Introduction

It has become axiomatic to state that the bond markets of the Arabian Gulf have traditionally underperformed equity and especially bank lending for attention as a source of finance. That having been said, progress in developing the fixed income market has been rapid and the potential for further growth is enormous. Longstanding issues in the Arabian Gulf region with allocation of resources, financial market depth and stability as well as corporate and government transparency all came into sharp relief during the global credit crisis. A deeper bond market would have helped to absorb its impact and speed the region's exit from crisis.

Mature and liquid debt markets improve resource allocation by channeling national and regional savings into domestic investments and can diversify the choices available to both institutional and individual investors. Diversification of financing and investment options contributes to the stability of financial markets as well as to corporate and government transparency. This, in a nutshell, is the rationale for being concerned over the development of bond markets in the Arabian Gulf region. It can be expected that, with official and private sector consensus and commitment, bonds will become a key lever of economic growth and financial stability. In this paper, most references to "the bond market" will include the markets for both conventional bonds and *sukuk* or sharia-compliant securities. While the structures of conventional bonds and *sukuk* may differ significantly, their roles in the macro-economy are virtually identical. Lastly, an attempt to describe the bond market in any brevity risks generalizations that will be tested by the considerable diversity of the Gulf economies and markets.

1. The Relative Underdevelopment (or Rapid Development?) of Bond Markets in the Gulf

Depending on which aspects are stressed, the Gulf fixed income market can be correctly described as either extremely nascent, or alternately, as experiencing unprecedented growth. As a share of regional GDP, bonds are underrepresented at only 13 percent, versus 42 percent across emerging markets and 159 percent globally. And while growing, capital markets debt in the MENA region still represents a disproportionately small share of the overall capital structure.

Table 1: Indicators on Size of Capital Markets

	Stock Market Capitalization	Debt Securities	Bank Assets
World	20.3%	39.6%	40.0%
Emerging Markets	29.6%	22.8%	47.6%
Asia	28.1%	20.4%	51.5%
MENA	31.5%	11.1%	57.4%

Source: IMF Global Financial Report, October 2010

1.1 The Rapid Development…

From 2004 until the onset of the credit crisis in 2008, new issue volume increased steadily as government-related entities sought to finance ambitious national development plans and enjoyed easy access to credit markets. The credit crisis, as manifested in various ways in the Gulf put an end to much of the "name lending" that had characterized bank finance, but also marked the end of easy access to capital markets by Gulf issuers. But by the second quarter of 2009, highly rated sovereigns and closely related entities reopened the door to international markets for issuers from the region. Despite the global crisis and Dubai's own credit crisis, 2009 became a record year for issuance by Middle Eastern borrowers. By comparison, bond and *sukuk* activity was constrained in the first part of 2010 compared with the second half of 2009. For that we can point to the uncertainty created by the Dubai World restructuring, various high profile defaults across the region, as well as the local economic downturn and related pessimism. Demand for *sukuk* was tempered by its own set of problems, both real and perceived.

As the market came to grips with the extent of Dubai World's repayment troubles and a restructuring plan took shape, issuance regained momentum in the second quarter. A flurry of large issues in the fourth quarter saw that 2010 almost matched 2009's record volume.

Figure 1: Middle Eastern DCM Annual Issuance

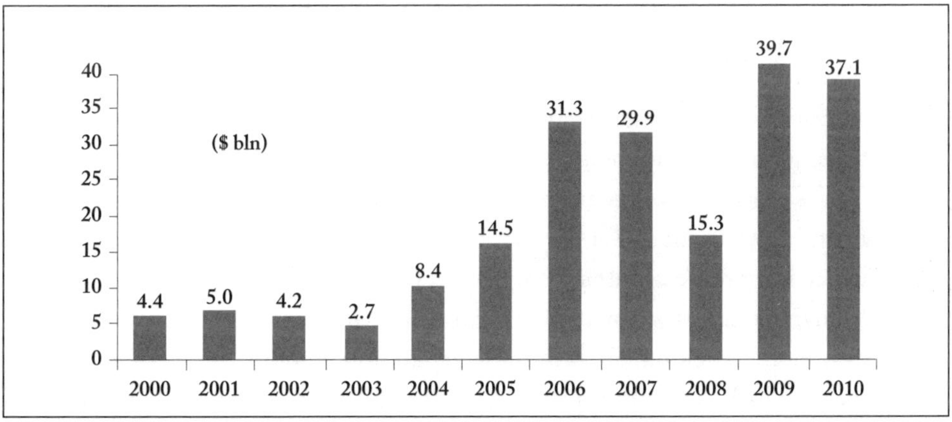

Source: Thomson Reuters

A significant number of Gulf issuers have issued large liquid benchmark bonds and have become well known to discerning international investors. Moreover, a number of these issuers have improved their disclosure in response to demands from international investors, as a perquisite to regaining market access. There is reason to believe that the region will supply considerable new issuance again in 2011.

1.2 The Relative Underdevelopment…

On the other hand, domestic bond markets, the ones that supply the greatest element of economic stability, remain stunted. Some of the Gulf Cooperation Council (GCC) states have histories of issuing either conventional or sharia-compliant instruments on a regular basis. However, as their fiscal stances improved during the period of increasing hydrocarbon prices from 2004, most of those governments drew down their outstanding debt and ceased raising new funds, leaving these markets starved of supply.

A Thumbnail Survey of GCC Government Debt Issuance and Markets

The Central Bank of Bahrain carries out issuance on behalf of the government of conventional short-term treasury bills by auction as well as 91-day *Sukuk* Al-Salam and 182-day Ijara *Sukuk*. The government from time to time issues medium-term domestic Government Development Bonds. The government of Bahrain has also issued benchmark size conventional bonds and *sukuk* in international markets.

The Kingdom of Saudi Arabia used to issue conventional debt across the yield curve in its domestic market, but in line with a policy to reduce its debt to GDP ratio, the Kingdom retired much of its stock of development bonds but continues to issue treasury bills. Saudi Arabia has been encouraging its companies to issue bonds, preferably as *sukuk* in its domestic market for listing and trading on the Saudi bourse, the Tadawul.

The Central Bank of Kuwait issues its own three and six month securities fairly regularly, as well as T-bills and notes on behalf of the government with maturities from three months to two years, mainly for liquidity management.

Oman has a history of auctioning medium and long-term local currency "Government Development Bonds." Outstanding amounts fell and auctions became rare as hydrocarbon prices rose after 2004. Issuance resumed from 2010, but not on a regular basis.

The Qatar government periodically sold domestic securities to its banks up to 2005, and then halted the practice. In 2010 and 2011, Qatar conducted two large placements of conventional and sharia-compliant medium terms bonds with its banks. Interest and profit rates were defined by the issuer. It is not clear whether this will become a regular practice.

The UAE federal government has not previously been authorized to borrow. Issuance was confined to individual emirates like Dubai or Abu Dhabi. However, UAE is in the process of setting up a debt management office and a law on public debt has been adopted by the Federal National Council, and is awaiting the Presidential signature. It has been suggested that the UAE could issue dirham instruments beginning late in 2011 or early 2012.

Since the global financial crisis there has been a growing recognition that developed domestic markets could have helped the region absorb the shocks of squeezed bank liquidity and limited access to international capital markets. Consequently, the voices calling for development of these markets have multiplied with the economic leadership in virtually every Gulf state calling for deepening of bond markets. These calls have translated into some actions at the national level. What has been absent from these discussions is recognition that the respective sizes of the national markets are, for the most part, not sufficient to support a diverse, liquid market.[1] Moreover, there has been no coordination among the states in terms of issuance policy or approach to market infrastructure. Likewise, the GCC has not provided direction that would allow harmonized market policies or structures. This points to an elemental irony: a region that is a large net capital exporter, financing its development through international capital markets and international investors. For the time being, the international capital markets are where the vast majority of capital will be raised.

2. Key Issues for Developing Regional Bond Markets

2.1 A Strong Base Is Needed to Support the Market

Issuance from the region has been nothing if not volatile - first surging to unprecedented levels in 2008 and then braking sharply, only to resume rapid growth. Even in periods where markets have been open there has been a tendency toward opportunistic issuance with issues coming to market in quick succession to take advantage of perceived windows of opportunity. Some of that has to do with preference for known, sovereign-linked issuers and vanilla products in turbulent times. There are also the well-known debates and public comments about sharia compliance as well as recent issues of priority in case of insolvency. But the basic underlying reality is that local capital is not organized in a way that could provide an effective investor base sufficient to accommodate regional aspirations.

Distribution of Bonds Issued from the Region

If we consider that the majority of GCC bonds are issued in USD in international markets, then it comes as no surprise that the majority of buyers and holders are outside of the region. But choice of market reflects issuers' recognition that adequate demand does not exist in the region. Analysis is difficult since detailed breakdowns of distribution by investor category tend to be closely held. Moreover, it has been suggested that regional issuers sometimes specifically favor international investors in the allotment process, at the expense of regional ones, for the purpose

1. The Saudi market is the only possible exception as it has a greater investor depth and corporate breadth for issuance, though with characteristics of a captive market.

of establishing their credits and gaining a following in the larger international investment community. It has even been suggested that bonds repatriate to the region after the original distribution, but at a premium. Within the region, the largest set of buyers is commercial bank treasuries. This is not a particularly helpful situation as the purchases are mainly funded by banks' deposits with a far shorter profile, thereby contributing to the maturity mismatch between banks' assets and liabilities. In the case of *sukuks* coming out of the region, they have tended to go into the hands of banks, including Islamic banks within and outside the region, foreign institutions seeking regional exposure, high net worth retail and family offices. In some cases, transactions are tailored practically for non-institutional buyers who have no expectation to trade and or particular need for liquidity.

2.2 What is Missing from the Demand Side?

If the GCC region is to begin to fund more of its own development via the debt markets, then it will need to take steps to mitigate the shallowness of its institutional or professional investor base.

The Gulf States have in differing degrees acted as guarantors of their citizens' social security through a wide variety of channels. An implication of this paternalism has been that private savings could remain on the back burner. At another level, the various sovereign wealth funds (SWFs) existing across the Gulf are in a sense the ultimate guarantors for the states that they can provide for the future welfare of the citizenry. SWFs, for their part, have mainly been outwardly focused in their investment guidelines and so do not, in the first place, serve to build the local markets or to fund domestic development. While this remains the general rule, the world of Gulf SWFs has diversified to include some relatively smaller ones that are open to domestic investment; besides, there are some signs that larger outwardly focused ones may find space for supporting local investment. But the SWFs cannot, and probably should not, be expected to be a principal means of channeling local wealth into regional investment.

Likewise, in spite of the wealth resident in the region, the Gulf has not developed its potential as a center for asset management, in spite of the fact that at least three jurisdictions, Dubai, Bahrain and Qatar, are vying for the role of regional asset management hub. The relative paucity of mutual funds in the region derives in part from the relatively small size of capital markets generally, from lack of sophisticated investment management tools that limit hedging, and preferences of the local investor base. The last is explained by a regional fascination with measurable gains in the short term that characterizes retail investors including to an extent, high net worth investors (HNWIs). Further, many HNWIs use professional asset management to access international markets but are comfortable dealing directly with the domestic bourses. The number of locally managed funds offering fixed income products has increased over the past two years, but their growth has not been proportionate to the increase issuance of bonds from the region.

The fundamental challenge for mutual fund development, as for other aspects of the capital market, is the lack of an incentive structure to foster or mandate development of a deep domestic/regional institutional investor base. A full range of investors would figure more prominently private pension funds and insurance companies.

3. Pensions in the GCC

Pension systems in the GCC tend to be state operated defined, benefit schemes operating on a pay-as-you-go basis (PAYG). Some have been unfunded and it is feared that those that are funded may be significantly under-funded in the face of early allowable retirement ages, rich benefits and a declining ratio of contributing workers to beneficiaries. According to a 2009 study by Booz & Co, systems are currently sustainable with a ratio of 25 workers to one beneficiary – but that ratio will drop to three to one in some countries by 2050.[2] Further, current pension schemes contribute little to financing of long-term private sector investment or to development of the domestic financial systems. Social security retirement funds exist throughout the region, mainly for state employees, but are generally not subject to best practice management, including for investment guidelines.GCC workers are not encouraged to save for their retirements and there is no equivalent of the voluntary retirement mechanisms that exist in more mature economies. Further, there is little evidence that GCC residents are looking after their financial futures in a systematic manner. A recent commercial survey found that three quarters of respondents declared their savings not as much as they had planned and that the same percentage does not save regularly.[3] Likewise, financial literacy is generally accepted to be fairly low.

In developed markets much of the demand for private mutual funds is driven by personal contributions to programs to fund retirement or education. A concerted

2. Richard Shediac and Samer Bohsali, "The Case for GCC Pension Reform," *From Sinking to Sustainable* (Booz & Co, 2009).
3. "National Bonds GCC Savings Index," survey commissioned by National Bonds Corporation, PJSC and conducted by YouGov Siraj, 2010.

effort to raise the level of the capital markets would involve gradual reform of the social safety net for citizens to involve them more in their own future planning. There is considerable international experience to draw upon should the Gulf choose to do so. The World Bank promotes a three-tiered format for pension reform that starts with publicly-run schemes supplemented by additional layers that tend to deepen private savings. The primary tier is a government-sponsored, mandatory pension fund; the second tier would be mandatory as well, but administered by employers, providing defined benefits. The third tier would be an optional defined contribution framework that is directed by the employee. When governments introduce nonpublic pension tiers, they typically do so with the goal of shifting responsibility to the worker and private fund managers, and lessening their own roles. Pension system reform would require a great deal of care and public preparation but could also prove quite popular as it would empower individuals with their own financial futures. In any case, such changes would be phased in over a period of years, giving people who are still in the workforce time to adjust their thinking and modify their financial behavior.

Another powerful driver could be incentivizing the millions of expatriate workers in the region to save a portion of their earnings in the country where earned. This would serve the purpose of providing long-term savings to be tapped for development. This could be accomplished in large part through adjustment of end-of-service practices and mandating that employers make available savings options, even for modest earners. These contributions would accumulate rapidly into significant size and could serve as the basis for a much strengthened mutual fund industry. Care would have to be taken to ensure that asset accumulation does not lead to asset bubbles. In fact, there is a rich spectrum of possibilities if pension reform is to be considered. Singapore's compulsory Central Provident Fund provides a multi-purpose savings vehicle. Chile provides a template for a pension system based on private providers and choice for savers. There is opportunity for GCC countries to make reforms to their pension systems now in a way that would strengthen existing systems and contribute to the development of regional debt capital markets.

4. Insurance in the GCC

Another potential pillar of GCC bond markets, the insurance sector, is growing rapidly. Premiums in the GCC were estimated by one source to have grown 28 percent from 2008 to 2009.[4] However, this growth starts from a very low base and

4. Value Partners, "GCC Insurance Premiums Rocket by 28% in 2009," Press Release, March 15, 2010.

so the insurance sector remains relatively underdeveloped. Non-life premiums as a percent of GDP among the GCC states were .87 percent while life premiums were only .23 percent. Overall industry assets as a share of GDP were 4.4 percent, well below an OECD rate of 45 percent and below the share of most emerging markets, including East Asia and Pacific which were at 14 percent.[5] A market study found that only 15 percent of total premiums were accounted for by life coverage, compared with 60 percent in Europe.[6] With the bulk of policies in the GCC being non-life, the typical investment horizon of an insurance company investment will be correspondingly shorter than global averages. It should be added that there is considerable variance within the GCC states with overall penetration highest in Bahrain and very low in Qatar and Saudi Arabia, where life coverage is negligible. While it has been said life insurance has not been in demand for cultural reasons, the overall insurance sector is also constrained by lack of compulsory insurance in some areas, weak regulatory and supervisory regimes, and lack of professional skills, i.e. lack of a supportive framework. Moreover, regional insurers have shown a propensity to invest disproportionately in volatile property and stock markets, adding an additional risk element that has been cited in evaluations of their financial strengths. A number of GCC countries are making unprecedented efforts to improve their environments for insurance including by establishing dedicated oversight bodies and upgrading regulation. But there is considerable distance to make up before insurers become important regular participants in the debt capital market.

Countries with successful markets tend to possess regulatory frameworks for pensions and insurance that include prudential investment guidelines to ensure safety first of all, and secondarily, liquidity of investments. Portfolios, whether publicly or privately run, would have to meet prudential regulations that would likely include minimum portfolio allocations for highly rated or risk free assets, including bonds and *sukuk*. Improving the basis for institutional investors in the region for both conventional and sharia-compliant requires a comprehensive look at private savings and a commitment to promoting them. Both pension reform and insurance deepening will take a number of years if not decades to be fully instituted, but that period can be minimized if they are actively taken on as priorities.

---

5. Rodney Lester, *The Insurance Sector in the Middle East and North Africa: Challenges and Development Agenda*, The World Bank, November 2010.
6. Value Partners, "GCC Insurance Premiums Rocket by 28% in 2009."

5. Other Pressing Issues for GCC Bonds

5.1 Secondary Market Liquidity

A liquid market can be defined as one where participants can execute large transactions without substantially impacting prices. Bond market liquidity encourages efficient market pricing and efficient decisions on borrowing and investing. The vast majority of trading of bonds issued from the Gulf region takes place on over-the-counter markets, even where bonds or *sukuk* are listed in London or Luxembourg or on local bourses. Trading desks of a modest number of large regional and international banks are responsible for the bulk of trading, much of which is routed through inter-dealer brokers (IDBs) located in the region or in London who act as intermediaries between the dealers. IDBs serve the market by promoting price discovery while maintaining anonymity among the dealers who may prefer not to indicate their intentions to other dealers.

Within the Gulf region, there is reasonable liquidity for large issuances (sovereigns and quasi-sovereigns) among the banks that maintain significant trading operations. Data from a quarterly survey published by the Emerging Market Traders Association (EMTA) indicate that the most traded instruments from the region are conventional bonds issued by Qatar, Abu Dhabi and Bahrain governments (for example, Qatar 4 percent due 2015, Bahrain 5.5 percent due 2020 and Abu Dhabi 5.5 percent due 2014).[7] While this set of benchmark sized sovereign bonds and a number of benchmark corporate issues enjoy good liquidity, much of what has been issued from the region is traded little and real time price data is hard to obtain.

Likewise, trading volume data is sketchy as compared with other regions. The same survey of emerging market traders reports on volumes by country and instrument. Middle East bonds account for almost 8 percent of global emerging market trading. But if the amounts for Turkey and Israel are stripped out, the figure drops to 3.5 percent. Bonds issued from GCC states account for less than 1 percent of global emerging market turnover.[8] Even if the survey understates somewhat the Middle East figures due to underreporting, the implication is still that Middle East bonds trade less as a share of outstanding issues than bonds from other regions.

7. Trade Association for the Emerging Markets, Second Quarter 2010 Debt Trading Volume Survey, August 12, 2010; Standard and Poor's, "S&P Launches New Credit Rating Scale for GCC," Press Release, February 23, 2010.

8. Ibid.

Figure 2: Emerging Markets Trading Volumes Q2 2010

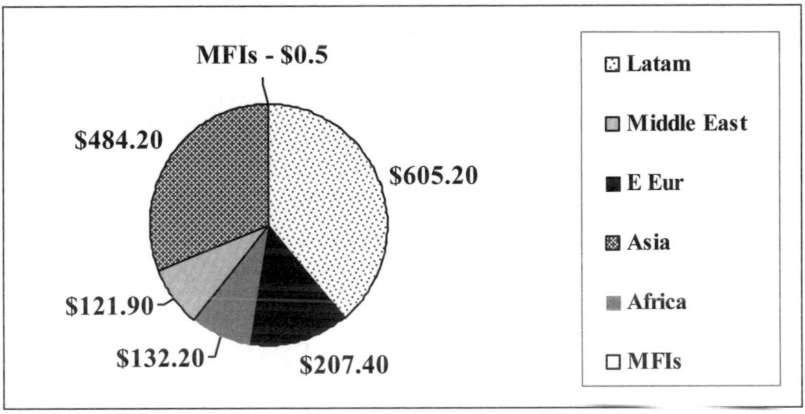

Figure 3: EM Trading Volume GCC Focus Q2 2010

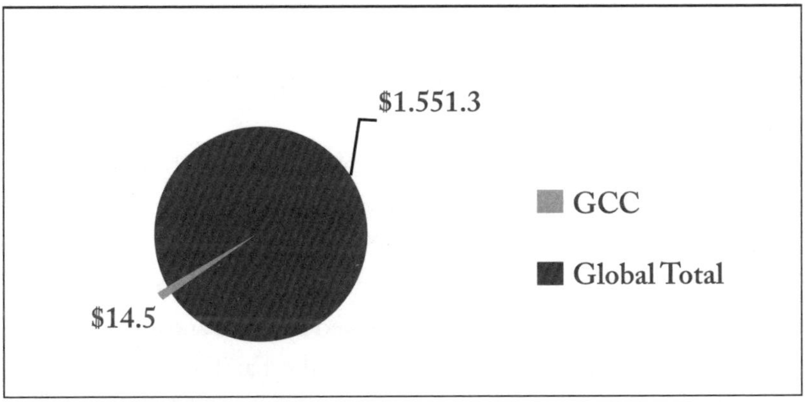

Source: Emerging Markets Traders Association

5.2 Towards Greater Liquidity

If the key to developing a vibrant debt market is in achieving secondary market liquidity, then the Gulf region can take advantage of experiences elsewhere. Most who have been involved in efforts globally would observe that achievement of secondary market liquidity is considerably more challenging than primary placement of debt instruments with investors and requires cooperation among stakeholders on a sustained basis. They would also contend that an environment created to facilitate trading of shares will not likely serve trading of bonds without considerable adaption to recognize the special characteristics of fixed income. For example, costs associated with fixed income trades must be particularly low and central banks should have an ability to conduct open market operations only with designated counterparties. Several regional bourses have opened bond trading platforms and others are developing strategies to do so. But it remains to be seen whether these platforms will offer liquidity enhancing features. Ultimately, whether trading remains over-the-counter or migrates to one or more platforms that have been proposed will ultimately be decided by traders on the basis of efficiency, flexibility and cost. World experience, including the relevant example of East Asia, suggests that it would be practical to focus initially on trading conventions and practices that support firm two-way market making within the over the counter market.

Likewise, other factors indirectly but significantly affect liquidity and should be addressed.

- Sufficient market supply is a necessary but not sufficient perquisite for liquidity. The instruments need to be designed simply and issued to an investor base that is incented to trade.
- Accurate and reliable benchmark yield curves enable market participants to attach prices to different credits and maturities. In this respect, there is no substitute for the sovereign as it is the only entity that is suited to maintain a permanent presence in the market.
- Good faith, predictability and regular information flow from borrowers, both corporate and official, enables better trading decisions.
- Transparency in pricing in secondary market adds to liquidity. But ill-designed efforts to maximize transparency can detract from liquidity.
- Fixed income instruments need to be served by a safe and efficient framework for trading and settlement. In this regard, the bar for reducing transaction costs has to be set higher than for share trading since debt will not be traded unless costs are very low. The systems also have to recognize central banks' requirements for flexibility and counterparty risk.
- The regulatory environment should provide for needed capabilities to accompany bond liquidity such as futures and swaps markets, repo markets and securities lending to facilitate investors constructing their investment portfolios and risk management strategies.

Most of the issues that relate to liquidity in conventional instruments are equally relevant for sharia-compliant instruments such as *sukuk*. Most of the issues that relate to liquidity in conventional instruments are equally relevant for sharia-compliant instruments such as *sukuk*. However, *sukuk* face some special challenges to achieving liquidity due to differing opinions about the suitability of trading sharia-compliant instruments, the preference of many investors to buy and hold, and the generally shorter tenors of *sukuk* in the market.

5.3 Corporate Transparency: Disclosure, Investor Relations and Ratings

Gulf corporates have long been criticized for lack of transparency and shortcomings in corporate governance. Here too, bond markets have begun playing a special role. Whereas only several years ago bankers despaired that issuers had little or no concern for their debt investors once a deal was completed, there is now a much keener sensitivity among corporates and indeed among governments about the secondary market performance of their debt. Moreover, the financial crisis that affected the region's access to international markets has had the very positive effect of raising the level of both primary and ongoing disclosure. However, there still remains considerable distance to make up.

Investor relations offices have been mainly oriented to satisfying the needs of equity investors but there is growing attention to debt. A survey conducted in 2010 by the Gulf Bond and Sukuk Association (GBSA) revealed that a majority of bond investors have become more demanding over the past two years and that an overwhelming majority feel that good investor relations (IR) can lead to more aggressive pricing of new issues. A majority of investors in regional bonds still consider the information provided by issuers to be insufficient. Most had met issuers on roadshows, but many were not satisfied with the quality and quantity of information provided. A corresponding survey of issuers revealed a growing appreciation for debt IR, with the vast majority sharing the opinion that equity and bond investors have different information needs and that fixed income investors require more information in times of stress. A majority of issuers indicated that their IR staff deal with fixed income, but few have dedicated staff. Most issuers do not benchmark their IR activity to industry guidelines or to comparable companies. GBSA is developing a set of best practice guidelines for debt IR.

Likewise, the number of credit ratings published in the region has increased substantially over the past five years, albeit from a low base. Moody's corporate ratings within the GCC have increased from just two in 2006 to 26 in 2011. At least as interesting is increasing diversity in the spectrum of ratings outstanding which suggests growing differentiation among investors for particular credits, as well as a willingness of corporates to see value in maintaining ratings, even if in the lower investment grade and non-investment grade categories.

Standard and Poor's launched in 2010 a local ratings scale in expectation of a pick-up in local currency debt issues and with the intention to give a clearer picture of the rating spectrum for investors in regional debt issues.

Figure 4: Moody's Corporate Ratings GCC

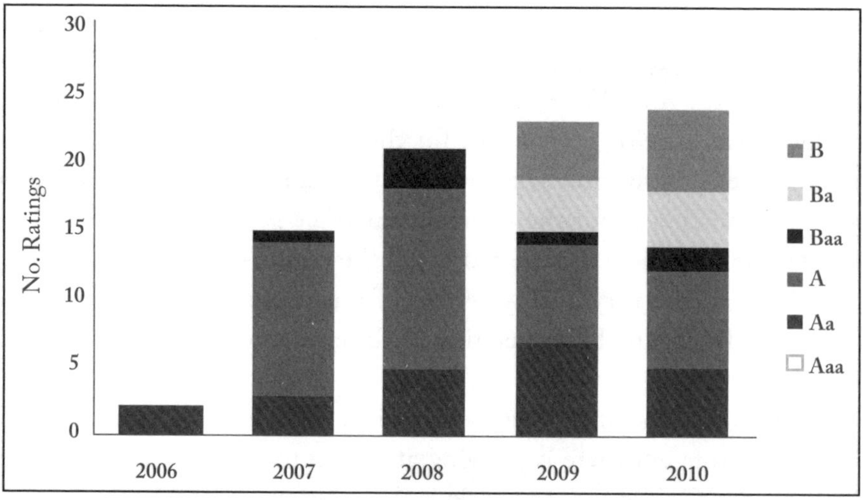

Source: Moody's Investors Service

5.4 Growth Outlook for Gulf Bond and Sukuk Issuance

Since the global credit crisis, emerging market debt issuance has increased to record leve ls driven by sustained low dollar interest rates and the faster recovery of developing economies. That trend should be sustained for as long as US rates remain low, which seems likely to last into 2011, given the absence of

Figure 5: Middle Eastern DCM Quarterly Volume ($ bln)

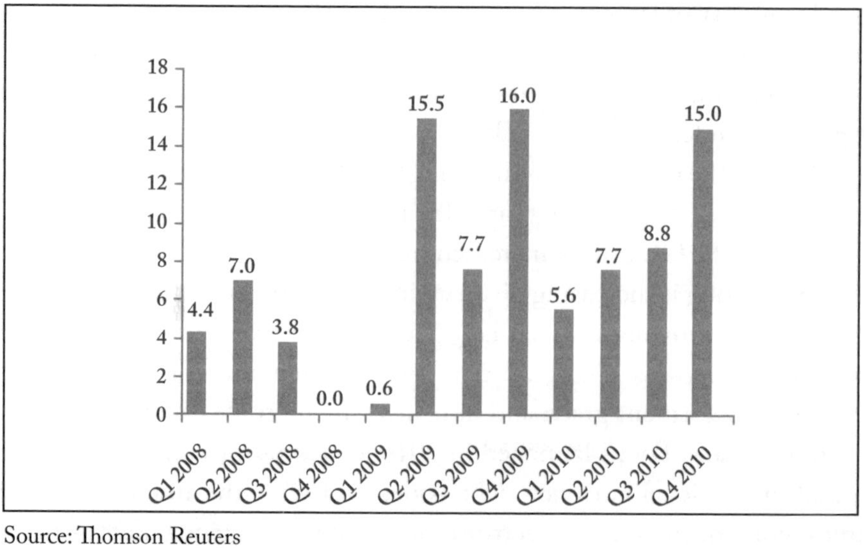

Source: Thomson Reuters

evident inflationary pressures in the US. In line with the global trend, 2010 was a significant year for bond sales for the MENA region with an unprecedented variety of issuers ranging from sovereigns to government-related entities, through to straight corporates and some high yield propositions. The global investor base is trending positive on the region and is paying attention to the volume and frequency of new issuance, suggesting a critical mass has developed.

The questions remain: Will the volume be sustained over time and what factors will drive new issuance? Refinancing will be a key driver. Moody's Investors Service has estimated that rated and unrated GCC corporates combined have $212 billion outstanding of which 28 percent (for the unrated companies) is of short-term nature.[9] We can expect that some of these companies will be looking to lengthen their maturity profiles to address risk and also to lock in low dollar interest rates.

Figure 6: Short-term Debt Exposure

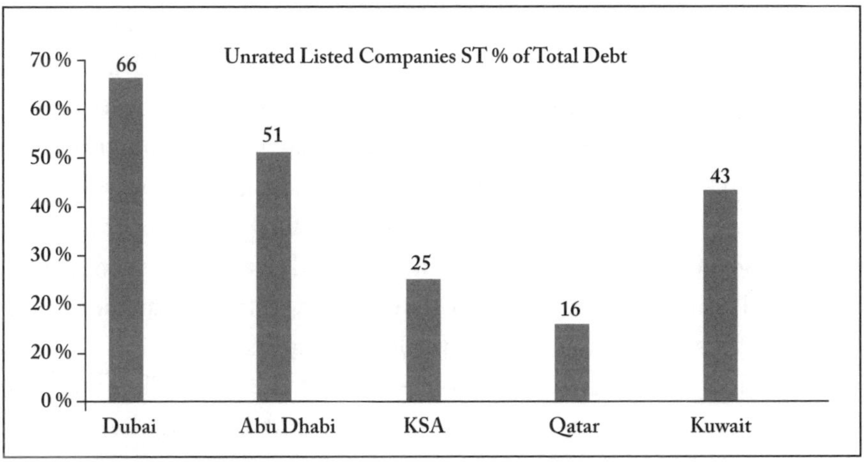

Source: Moody's Investors Service

What is more, corporate indebtedness is skewed towards bank debt, with many listed companies having no capital markets debt outstanding. The Moody's study suggests the short term debt is concentrated in sectors such as telecom, investment holding, real estate and construction.

To some extent, bond issuance may be more out of necessity, than love for

9. Moody's Investors Service, "Refinancing Corporate Debt in the Arabian Gulf," Special Comment, September 14, 2010.

Figure 7: Bank Debt Exposure Unrated V. Rated Companies

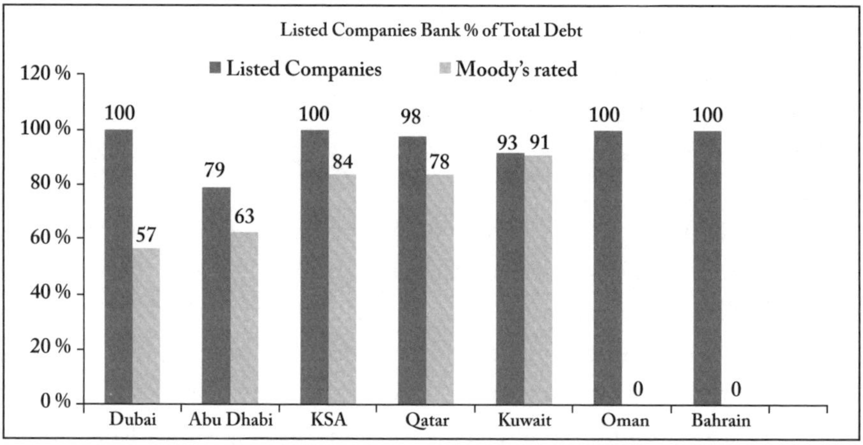

Source: Moody's Investors Service

the rigors and transparency of debt capital markets. Banks, generally speaking, remain risk averse, not ready to revert to their previous role as lender of first resort. While deposits have started to recover and grow in some institutions, liquidity remains at a premium in some banks, especially in UAE. But even where liquidity does not pose a principal constraint, lending to the private sector has grown at a lower pace. Credit to some sectors is particularly constrained, such as real estate, where banks are more closely monitoring their overall exposure as well against some companies which bump against single borrower limits. Banks are also more conscious of the maturity mismatch between assets and liabilities. This mismatch incidentally may drive additional issuance from the banks themselves as they issue bonds for longer tenors.

Conclusions that can be drawn are 1) that there are likely to be new corporate entrants to the public debt markets, and 2) with the refinancing numbers involved, even a modest number of new entrants to the bond market from this pool can impact volume significantly.

Issuance may also be supported by the willingness of states that can afford to continue to pursue strongly counter-cyclical fiscal policies, namely in Saudi Arabia, Kuwait and Abu Dhabi. The region's needs and ambitions for infrastructure are well known and various estimates have been put forward for the next decade, usually over a trillion dollars. So capital spending, particularly on public and quasi-public infrastructure will provide support over the medium to long term, be it for development of entire districts and cities, conventional and alternative power to address chronic supply bottlenecks, water supply, roadways, oil and gas, smelters, air and seaports and public transport projects such as GCC railway network, or domestic rail schemes. Social infrastructure such as for health and education requires massive investment as well, though it does not attract as much attention. How it will be that many of these large projects will be financed remains an unknown. The extent to which governments resist the tendency to spend current or reserve funds on these projects will have a lot to do with the growth of debt capital markets.

5.5 Headwinds to Growth of New Issuance

In the near term, investors will continue to reward strong sovereign and sovereign-related credits and these will always be the first back into the market as conditions ease. This brings up the whole debate about the value and role of government guarantees. The sovereign guarantee model allowed much capital to be raised and development to take place before it began to be tested. But the model also detracted from the defining beauty of the capital market – its efficiency in allocating capital. Rather than looking for the best business models and penalizing the worst projects, capital was, and to an extent continues to be attracted to those projects most likely to be supported in case of trouble.

It is fair to ask whether the experience has fostered a reliance on guarantees, explicit or implied; and if so, has this condition hobbled development of the market? On a positive note, more explicit language is being applied in prospectuses to describe the relation of issuers to governments. And investors, taking their cue from the ratings agencies, have to a much greater extent sorted out who is under the sovereign umbrella and who is not. But it remains far too early to judge that the grey areas have all been cleared.

The sovereign led return to the market is welcome and the region needs more issuance. But throughout the various pauses in issuance some have worried that a rush to issue would not be particularly constructive. The financial press has echoed these concerns, putting into relief a major irony of the region; that is, excessive reliance by companies and projects on foreign capital in a region that is itself a leading capital exporter. A concern is how sharply risk appetite among international investors will drop off after the sovereigns and the quasi-sovereigns.

Holding back project finance as a source of issuance in the Gulf is the absence of comprehensive frameworks for public-private partnerships, as is moving forward in Egypt, for example. In the near to medium term, family companies will continue to avoid the capital markets and seek other means of financing for the usual reasons of maintaining confidentiality and flexibility, even at cost. As non-rated and largely non-listed entities, they do not need to respond to shareholder demands to maximize return on equity. For non-investment grade or lower tier investment grade, the cost of funding in the international markets can be high. For the combination of country and sector risk and relative illiquidity investors may require high single or even double digit yields, and there are few projects that can sustain that kind of funding cost.

5.6 Mobilizing Domestic Government Debt Markets

The single most important action that can underpin a regional debt capital market would be action by the states to develop government yield curves in their own currencies, thereby providing critical mass for development of an indigenous market.

In many cases, the central banks well appreciate the need for a robust yield curve. But as monetary authorities, they are unlikely to be able to support issuance of securities beyond a year without the fiscal authority taking responsibility as obligor. Specifically, it is the ministries of finance, as developers and executors of the state budget, that are in a position to act as borrowers and thereby as market catalyst. However, in conditions of fiscal surplus, as in a number of Gulf States, it can be difficult to establish consensus on a strategy for the bond market that includes incurring debt. Reference can be made to the experiences of countries with sustained surpluses such as Norway, Singapore and Australia that have kept a critical mass of government debt as a public good.[10] It is the actions of the fiscal authorities that will have most to do with whether a bond market takes hold or does not, including a corporate bond market. In fact, sovereign debt management and bond market development are highly inter-dependent. If this approach is to succeed, the fiscal authorities have to commit to developing internal capacity in the form of a debt management office that may start simply but should eventually carry out the role of front, middle and back office.

Practically, the ministries should commit to maintaining borrowing practices that support market development in the long term. This commitment will likely entail short-term costs that the issuer has to be prepared to explain. As a benchmark issuer, the government can standardize its structures and

10. "Impact of the Global Financial Crisis on the Gulf Cooperation Council Countries and Challenges Ahead," International Monetary Fund, Middle East and Central Asia Department, 2010.

commit to regular issuance practices. Government bonds often require a special mechanism for primary issuance and, therefore, need a clearly defined legal framework that defines the borrowing authority and lists a sufficiently broad range of purposes. These could include the ability to borrow to finance public sector investment in addition to financing deficits, as well as for refinancing, cash management and for market development. The relationship between the government as an issuer and the fiscal agent should be clearly defined as should all contractual relationships including between government and underwriters, regardless of distribution method. There is every reason to believe that this well established path to market development can succeed within the GCC region.

6. A Medium-term Outlook for Gulf Bond Markets: Consensus and Commitment Needed

Decisions by Oman and UAE to withdraw from the common currency project took the wind out of the sails of an already slow voyage toward financial market integration. Practical planning for monetary union was well behind where it needed to be with the bond markets a striking example. But the process of harmonizing markets is a worthwhile goal unto itself that will pay dividends with or without currency union, if companies and projects can lower their costs of capital by accessing a wider pool of investors familiar with the region.

The case for deepening the GCC bond markets has never been more urgent or better understood. But national initiatives risk cancelling out growth of a regional debt capital market if they produce a zero sum game based on competing financial centers. In order to prevent this happening, there needs to be a Gulf-wide vision developed that is bought into by the industry, the governments and the GCC itself. Proactive efforts on the part of the government authorities, regulatory bodies and market participants are essential for creating an environment conducive to the development of the bond market. If the regional markets are to realize their potential, a vision has to be developed and shepherded with official leadership in active partnership with the industry. Industry associations are a critical means to mobilize and channel the input of the market players in a productive manner by helping develop relevant regulation, advising government agencies as issuers, providing input to regulators on market trends and developments, documenting market practices and conventions, and promoting professional standards.

What is dawning in the region is the realization that bond markets are not simply for opportunistic use in a pro-cyclical manner, but are at least as well suited to act as a strategic counter-cyclical shock absorber. Bond markets are contributing to the region's development and the past years have seen tremendous growth. For the next steps, there needs to be consensus on a regional vision and an organized official commitment, starting at the level of GCC and involving the states, central banks, and national regulators with help from the industry.

4

Prospects of the Banking and Finance Sector and the Development of Financial Centers

Eckart Woertz

Introduction

Rapid economic growth in the GCC countries has led to large and varying financing needs, which, in turn, meet a relatively underdeveloped financial sector with only nascent regulatory institutions. The financial sector is characterized by a lack of bond and derivative markets, difficult access to credit for small and medium enterprises (SMEs), dominance of international banks in the project finance market, and heavily concentrated equity markets in terms of sectors and ownership.

Bahrain, Dubai, Qatar, and Saudi Arabia (with the King Abdullah Financial District) have all started to establish international financial centers which try to remedy some of these shortcomings and try to connect their respective countries more with international capital markets. The goal is to attract foreign capital, know-how, and business and at the same time open up new channels for local funds to invest abroad. This is in line with a development strategy that has been recommended by Frederic Mishkin for emerging markets, but its shortcomings have been revealed in the current global financial crisis.[1] While following a similar development approach, the different financial centers vary considerably with regard

1. Frederic S. Mishkin, *The Next Great Globalization. How Disadvantaged Nations Can Harness their Financial Systems to Get Rich* (Princeton, N.J.: Princeton University Press, 2006).

to their legal frameworks, degree of realization, and the niche markets they intend to occupy.

This chapter analyzes the different segments of the GCC financial markets and assesses the future development prospects of the four international financial city projects in the region, their complementarities and possible areas of competition. It also critically examines how such centers could contribute to the development of domestic capital markets which, in turn, vitally influence the policy options for GCC monetary authorities as they face a global financial crisis and plan for a GCC monetary union.

1. The Structure of GCC Financial Markets

It is important to take stock of some major characteristics and challenges of GCC financial markets to understand the environment in which the financial center projects in the GCC operate. As evident from other chapters in this book, the GCC capital markets are characterized by a striking under-representation of bond markets as a means of finance. An increase of their relative importance in the overall capital structure of the GCC is certainly warranted, and governments in Qatar and Abu Dhabi have already formulated their intention to develop them further, for example by increasing the issuance of government bonds in order to provide a benchmark yield curve for the corporate bond sector. An improved bond market could lead to better capital access, efficiency gains, and improved price discovery and risk assessment. Derivatives have fallen from grace in the wake of the global financial crisis; still the nearly complete lack of derivative markets in the GCC could be a disadvantage and needs to be carefully assessed. As banks in the MENA region show a strong bias towards large companies and access to bank credit for small and medium enterprises (SMEs) is more difficult than in other world regions according to the World Bank, the over-reliance on bank finance is a particular handicap for this important segment of the economy.

The limited number of listings and lack of free float of existing listings are a problem in the young GCC stock markets. They are dominated by a few big companies, which have the state as a majority shareholder, while most of the larger private enterprises are family-owned and not listed. The same is true for the biggest state companies, namely the oil sector. Thus the largest 20 or so companies in each of the GCC countries are not listed at all (e.g., Saudi Aramco and other national oil companies, Dubai Holding, Alba, Dubal, Airlines, ADIA, KIA and other investment bodies).[2] On the other hand, among the listed companies, the largest 10 companies in each country make up between 50 percent and 80 percent of market capitalization. The GCC stock market bubble of 2005-06 would probably not have reached such lofty proportions if too much money had not chased so few stocks. It has thus been argued that increased privatization on the one hand and going public of private family enterprises on the other would lead to broader markets and higher free floats, which would be beneficial for the further development of GCC stock markets.

While the biggest companies in the GCC are state-owned, the huge realm of small and medium enterprises (SME) is dominated by family-owned private sector companies. Some of these companies have reached the size of big conglomerates. The Olayan, Al-Futtaim, Kanoo and Zamil group of companies are cases in point. Family members hold key executive positions in these firms, and the family mostly holds full ownership. Family enterprises elsewhere in the world have gone public, and often the respective families do not retain a majority stake anymore. Examples are Wal Mart (38 percent family ownership), Ford (40 percent) or BMW (47 percent).[3] Usually, family members do not have an exclusive grip on executive positions anymore in such enterprises, nor do they rank prominently on the boards of these companies. They mostly confine themselves to a controlling role in the background; in some cases, like the German Haniel Group, this is even stated policy. In the GCC, such a trend has not been observed so far. Shuaa Capital is one of the few examples of a family enterprise subsidiary in the UAE (Al Ghurair) that has gone public, and there are a couple of other examples in Saudi Arabia (e.g., Al Rajhi Bank, Al Abdullatif Industrial Investments) and Kuwait (e.g., Sultan), but generally that has remained the exception.[4]

The advantage of trust within established family relationships is valued higher than the advantages of increased corporatization and going public, namely enhancement of the available talent pool and accountability and easier access to

2. OECD, "Ownership Structures in MENA Countries: Listed Companies, State-Owned, Family Enterprises and Some Policy Implications," Working Paper 2005, available at http://www.oecd.org/dataoecd/26/2/35402110.pdf

3. Others would be Fiat (30 percent), Peugeot (42 percent) and Carrefour. For a detailed list of the 250 biggest family enterprises in the world, see http://www.familybusinessmagazine.com/topglobal.html

4. United Nations Economic and Social Commission for Western Asia (ESCWA), "Responding to Globalization. Stock Market Networking for Regional Integration in the ESCWA Region," (New York: 2003), 39, available at http://www.escwa.org.lb/information/publications/edit/upload/grid-03-37.pdf

financing from the capital markets. Instead financing via retained earnings, and sometimes banks, still remains the rule, and GCC family enterprises are reluctant to give up unlimited control and succumb to the increased accountability standards that come with a public listing, like quarterly reports and the appointment of independent directors to the supervisory board. On the other hand, GCC family enterprises mostly follow broad business interests in conglomerate-like structures; the specialization on core competencies, which is usually more appealing to stock market investors, is not very common so far. The initiative of the Dubai International Financial Exchange (DIFX, now NASDAQ Dubai) to reduce the minimum free float for its IPOs to 25 percent from the current 55 percent at the bourses in Dubai and Abu Dhabi was launched with an eye towards such family enterprises, which are hesitant to give up their majority stakes. But so far there have been no corresponding listings, and it remains to be seen whether the initiative will prove successful.

One reason for the relative reluctance of private companies to enter the stock market may be attributable to their relative distance from the capital markets in general. Astonishingly, access to loans from banks is difficult for many companies, despite the huge credit growth that has taken place in the region, which apparently has been mainly directed toward a selected minority of large companies and consumer financing. The World Bank has deplored the disconnect between the financial sectors and the real private economy in Middle Eastern countries.[5] While on the macro level a reasonably high degree of financial intermediation of about 60 percent of GDP can be observed,[6] it is only few large companies that profit from it, while the majority seems to rely on retained earnings: About 75 percent of company financing in MENA countries stems from this source and only 12 percent from the banking sector, while the corresponding figure for high income countries stands above 20 percent. In Saudi Arabia, for example, less than 40 percent of companies reportedly have an overdraft facility with a bank and only slightly more than 20 percent have a loan from a bank.[7] More access to the capital markets could certainly facilitate the expansion and modernization drive of many companies in light of increased opening up and competition in the wake of the WTO process. But before

5. World Bank, "Middle East and North Africa. Economic Developments and Prospects 2006: Financial Markets in a New Age of Oil," available at http://siteresources.worldbank.org/INTMENA/Resources/MENA-EDP2006.pdf, 50.

6. This is the average of Middle Income Countries and slightly below the 84 percent average of High Income Countries. Ibid.

7. Ibid.

thinking about family enterprises going public or issuing bonds, the natural first step would be to improve the cooperation with the financial sector on the very basic level of loan facilities.

2. Islamic Banking as a Niche Sector

An important niche segment in the GCC is Islamic banking, which has been growing 15 percent on average in recent years. These growth rates are considerably higher than those for the conventional banking market, although it has to be taken into consideration that it is a young market that has started from a low statistical base and growth rates will trend lower going ahead. The GCC region is a center of the global Islamic banking market followed by Asia and Europe. Therefore, it is in a good position to capitalize on this competitive advantage and use it for expansion not only in the Gulf but also abroad. As rival financial centers like London are also eyeing the Islamic banking market as an important growth segment, the region needs to live up to this competition. The most important segments of the Islamic banking market have been consumer financing, car and mortgage financing, and Islamic credit cards. In the fields of debt securities, Islamic bonds (*sukuks*) have enjoyed increasing popularity and actually formed a majority of bond issuance in 2007-08.

Some have argued that Islamic banks have been less exposed to the global financial crisis. This is true in the sense that Islamic banks are not allowed to invest in derivatives and have thus avoided exposure to complex securities that were often at the heart of the crisis. However, they invested heavily in the local real estate market, which also showed a characteristic boom-bust scenario. As an overwhelming majority of business of Islamic banks is in some sort of "disguised" fixed income, there are many inter-linkages with the conventional banking system. *Murabaha* contracts, for example, are largely used by treasury departments of Islamic banks and use the trade of commodity baskets and deferred payments to generate a cash flow that constitutes "fixed income" all but in name. Yields of such *murabaha* contracts closely track the LIBOR, and counterparts are often international conventional banks. There is, therefore, clear exposure to developments in the conventional banking system. As the global economy soured, Islamic banks were equally exposed to the increased occurrence of credit events. Issuance of *sukuks* declined more than conventional issuance and came to a virtual standstill in early 2009, as there were increasing doubts about their legal structure. Even though issuance recovered afterwards, there seems to have been a shift of the investor base from international investors to more domestic players. The Accounting and Auditing Organization of Islamic Financial Institutions (AAOIFI) in Bahrain damaged market sentiment for *sukuks* in 2008 when it argued that they were not sharia-compliant as they did not constitute real risk sharing on the part of the investor but rather were some form of disguised fixed income. And while the financial crisis unfolded, it was unclear whether *sukuk* holders really have recourse to the underlying basket of physical securities, i.e., whether they are "asset-backed" or whether they are only "asset-based", i.e., that they have been only identified in the sales contract to serve cash flow payments in order to satisfy the legal requirements of sharia law, but are not subject to some form of privileged recourse by creditors in case of a credit event.

These concerns about the legal viability of *sukuks* were amplified by the eruption of the Dubai debt crisis when Dubai World and its subsidiary Nakheel asked for a debt standstill at the end of November 2009. The Nakheel *sukuk* that was maturing on December 14, 2009 was governed by English law, but it was ambiguous whether this would be applicable in the UAE; it was also unclear to what extent investors would have recourse to underlying assets, how they would be ranked in payment priorities in case of a default, and whether recourse to government-owned assets would be legal in the UAE at all. These ambiguities greatly affected market sentiment for *sukuks* and went beyond a mere reputation loss for Dubai and its ambitions to become a financial hub. Other *sukuks* had already defaulted earlier in 2009, including a $100 million issue by Kuwaiti Investment Dar and a $650 million issue by a Bahraini subsidiary of Saudi-based Saad group.

Islamic banks in the Gulf can be divided into independent Islamic banks (e.g. Dubai Islamic, Al Rajhi) and Islamic banking subsidiaries of conventional banking parent companies (e.g. Emirates Islamic, HSBC Amanah). The Islamic banking market has witnessed strong growth rates of 15 percent on average in recent years. As Islamic banking assets are still less than 1 percent of the total assets of the top 1,000 banks in the world, these growth rates are coming from a low statistical base. In the Gulf its relative importance is much higher with Islamic banking mustering 22 percent of total bank assets, while in 2003 this ratio stood at only 10 percent, according to S&P. Although some Gulf Islamic banks like Al Rajhi, Kuwait Finance House or Dubai Islamic Bank have begun to expand internationally to countries such as Malaysia and Pakistan, the Islamic banking market is still relatively segmented along regional and national lines. The Gulf is a leading Islamic banking market worldwide with 49 percent of all Islamic banking establishments, followed by Asia (20 percent) and Europe (14 percent). In terms of value, the GCC countries manage 43 percent ($353 billion) of global sharia-compliant assets, with the world total being $822 billion.[8]

Table1: Global Share of Islamic Finance Establishments

	Share	Notes
Gulf Countries	49%	The leading countries are UAE, Bahrain, Saudi Arabia and Iran
Rest of Middle East	7%	
Asia	20%	Mainly Malaysia as key player
Europe	14%	UK is the key player, boosted by FSA regulatory initiatives
USA & Canada	5%	
Others	5%	Africa, Australia and South America have only a marginal market share
Total	100%	

Source: Shariah Fortune Report available at: http://www.pr.com/press-release/149391

The Asian market is dominated by Malaysia, while the European market musters the largest asset base per customer of the three. In terms of potential, Muslims represent about 20 percent of the world population but only 4 percent of world GDP. There is large room for growth as, in terms of purchasing power, Muslims of the MENA region command approximately the same purchasing power as the smaller number of Muslims in Europe and the larger number of Muslims in South Asia (see Table 2). It is conceivable that Islamic banking will become a more unified market on a global scale. Given the strong market share of the Gulf, its banks would be well positioned to capitalize on such a trend and expand abroad. Domestic Islamic banks from the region have not yet tried to establish a global brand like HSBC Amanah. Because of a lacking institutional investor base, most Islamic bond (*sukuk*) issues of the Gulf are paradoxically bought by investors in OECD countries and do not remain in the region. Hedge funds specialized in distressed capital have also been attracted to *sukuks* of Nakheel and a Saad group subsidiary after steep price declines because of a looming default.

8. "Islamic Banks Assets up 29 Percent," *Arab News*, November 9, 2009, available at http://www.arabnews.com/?page=6&section=0&article=128271&d=9&m=11&y=2009 .

However, in the longer run, these events might be damaging for *sukuk* sentiment among the larger public of international investors.

Table 2: Muslim Population Worldwide and GDP Weight

Region	Population (mn)	%of total	GDP ($bn) represented by Muslim population*
North America	7	0.6	86
MENA	461	37	667
Malaysia, Singapore, Indonesia	212	17	134
Bangladesh, Pakistan, India	506	41	538
Europe	51	4	634
Total	1237	Approximately 20 % of world population	Approximately 4% of world GDP

*Assuming share in GDP same as population share

Source: Royal Institute of International Affairs, "The Gulf as a Global Financial Centre. Growing Opportunities and International Influence," Chatham House Report, London 2008.

3. Regulatory Issues

Rising oil prices and massively increased bank lending led to super-abundant liquidity in the GCC countries and an unprecedented stock market rally in 2004 and 2005. However, the resulting overvaluations could not be maintained and, at the beginning of 2006, the stock markets collapsed. Small investors, who often had speculated on margin at the height of the market, were hurt in particular. Though lack of corporate governance did not directly cause the GCC stock market corrections in 2006, better regulations and more transparency are badly needed. Clear and reliable reporting and investor relations, enforcement of margin requirements, and prevention of insider trading are cases in point. The improvement of corporate governance in the Arab financial markets is the mission of Hawkamah, a non-profit institute located in the Dubai International Financial Centre (DIFC).[9] It has initiated a host of activities since 2006 and

9. See www.hawkamah.org.

increased awareness of the problem considerably. It also published the first Corporate Governance Survey of the GCC in cooperation with the Equity Advisory Group of the Institute of International Finance (IIF), similar to a series of reports done by the IIF in other emerging markets like Brazil, South Africa and Turkey earlier. The IIF, an association of worldwide banks, focuses on five broad areas in its reports:

- Minority shareholder rights
- Structure and responsibilities of the Board of Directors
- Accounting and auditing
- Transparency of ownership and control
- Regulatory environment

The GCC region still shows ample potential for improvement in these areas. Even the better positioned countries like Kuwait and Oman show a compliance rate of only 70 percent with IIF standards, while UAE and Qatar at the lower end only attain 40 and 35 percent, respectively. The dominance of state ownership in most of the big companies is usually not helpful for the rights of minority shareholders. There is a lack of independent directors on the board of directors-in the case of government companies, it is mainly government representatives, and in family enterprises, it is the family and close friends. In both cases, there is insufficient disclosure of potentially conflicting interests. Insider trading and decision making detrimental to minority shareholders are a frequent occurrence. As books are often kept for the taxman who is enforcing accounting principles, and as the GCC states rarely tax enterprises, the standards of accounting and auditing are equally underdeveloped in the GCC countries with their young stock markets. Finally, with the exception of Oman, regulatory authorities in the GCC often lack sufficient power to ensure actual enforcement of rules and regulations. Many of the GCC regulatory authorities also still lack full independence from third parties like the state or the respective stock markets.

Table 3: Regulatory Structure in GCC Countries

Country	Regulatory Structure
Bahrain	The Central Bank of Bahrain regulates the Bahrain Stock Exchange. No formal Capital Market Authority (CMA) yet.

Kuwait	Kuwait Stock Exchange (KSE) is an independent financial institution. The Market Committee within the KSE regulates the exchange. Kuwait does not have an independent regulator thus far, but wants to establish one according to the Capital Market Law, which was passed in February 2010.
Oman	In 1998, Oman became the first GCC country to establish a separate regulatory body - the Capital Market Authority (CMA). The CMA regulates the Muscat Stock Market.
Qatar	Doha Securities Market (DSM) has been regulated by the Qatar Financial Markets Authority (QFMA) since 2005. QFMA is an independent regulatory agency. No formal Capital Market Authority (CMA) yet.
Saudi Arabia	Tadawul, Saudi Arabia's stock market, was established in 2001 and is an independent organization. In 2003, the government created the Capital Markets Authority (CMA), which regulates the Tadawul. CMA is a government organization, but has financial, legal, and administrative independence.
UAE	The Emirates Securities & Commodities Authority (ESCA) was established in 2001 to regulate the Abu Dhabi Securities Market (ADSM) and the Dubai Financial Market (DFM). ESCA is a government organization, but has financial, legal, and administrative independence. ADSM is a legal entity of autonomous status with financial and managerial independence. DFM is a public institution having its own independent corporate body.

Source: Hawkamah, The Institute for Corporate Governance/ Institute of International Finance (IIF), Comparative Survey of Corporate Governance in the Gulf Corporation Council – An Investor Perspective, Task Force Report, September 2006, p. 5 and press reports

Notable progress has been made though. Many GCC countries have drafted corporate governance codes or have included such requirements in capital market and commercial company legislation. Enforcement of rules and ad-hoc regulations has also seen some improvement. In the UAE, for example, regulators suspended IPOs of companies that had just been founded and that did not have a history of at least two years of successful operations. Thus, a potential flooding of the market with shell companies, as witnessed in the Kuwaiti Souk Al Manakh in 1982, has been avoided.

The GCC stock market crash of 2006 and the current impact of the global financial crisis have drawn attention to areas where regulation and reform is necessary ranging from corporate governance to credit bureaus and monetary policy. The worry of monetary authorities in the GCC about high inflation rates gave way to an accommodative stance in the second half of 2008 as the global credit crunch raised the potential threat of a deflationary contraction.

4. Impact of Global Financial Crisis

The direct impact of the global financial crisis in the GCC countries was limited. Altogether the hitherto announced subprime exposure of GCC banks of about $3 billion has been small compared to that of Europe and the US. Part of this may be attributable to a lack of transparency with more exposure likely to surface over time. But the main reason is that GCC banks have been relatively conservative compared to their American and European peers. In many cases, the investment criteria of banks did not allow the purchase of non-investment grade bonds or complicated structured products, and an occasional lack of sophistication may have proven to be beneficial for some banks, now that such products are literally discredited. The losses of SWFs are something different and were substantial. It has been estimated that some of them lost 30-40 percent of their assets over 2008. However, this money has been offshore and was only meant to be repatriated at a later stage, possibly in an after-oil age and for future generations. Its loss has certainly been painful and has reduced the options of the local governments but it does not have a direct connection to the local economy at this stage.

The most visible effects of the global financial crisis thus far have therefore not been caused by direct exposure to troubled subprime assets but in indirect form, as the GCC countries and their burgeoning project finance markets have been affected by the rising costs of borrowing and declining availability of large credit facilities. While GCC central banks were preoccupied with runaway credit growth and inflation during the first half of 2008, they started to react to the liquidity crunch in late 2008 by monetary easing and other stabilizing efforts such as guarantees on bank deposits. However, they have acted unilaterally thus far and have not found a common policy like the European Union. If interbanking rates start to differ considerably due to different policies and their differing reception in each country, the more successful one country is in bringing down rates, the more likely it will attract borrowers from neighboring countries. Authorities will need to address this, otherwise they may be tempted to impose some kind of capital controls to make sure that the accommodative measures they are undertaking will benefit their own economies and not evaporate via open capital markets.

Figure 1. GCC Corporate Bonds:
Spread above LIBOR, HSBC/ DIFX GCBI Index

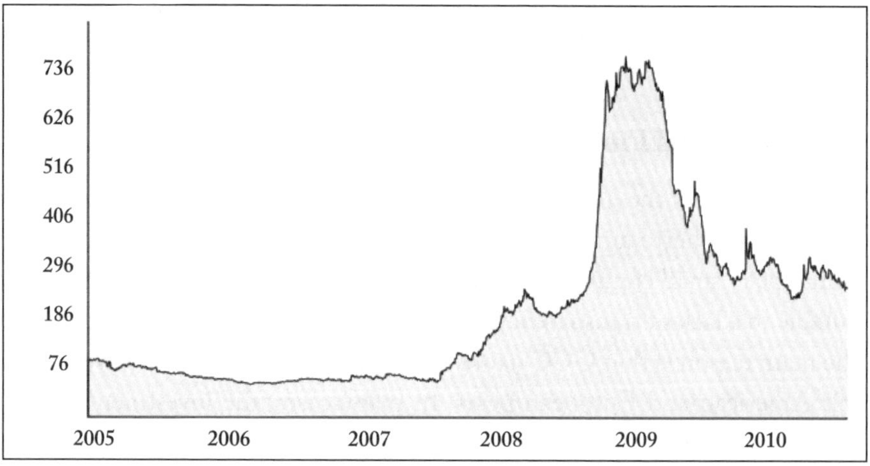

Source: HSBC/ DIFX, available at: http://www.hsbcdifxindices.com/

After the spike in spreads in Q4 2008 and Q1 2009, there has been significant improvement since March 2009 alongside a global recovery of financial markets. Refinancing costs have eased, although they still stayed significantly above their level in 2006/2007. Following the Dubai debt crisis at the end of 2009, however, renewed worries resurfaced. The economic structures of the oil-rich GCC countries are significantly different from the one in Dubai. Still, there was some contagion effect, with spreads rising in neighboring countries and in Abu Dhabi, which has a relatively high financial exposure to the problems of Dubai.

5. Structure of the Banking Sector and Possible Future Developments

The banking universe of the GCC countries is diverse. The domestic retail markets are mostly served by national banks that often have the state as a major shareholder and are still considerably shielded from regional and international competition (e.g., Emirates Bank/National Bank of Dubai, National Bank of Abu Dhabi, and National Commercial Bank). One challenge for these banks will be to define areas of specialization and venture into new fields like project finance and private banking as the environment they are operating in becomes more competitive.

International banks are more present in the corporate and project finance market, and only in some cases do they have a large branch network like HSBC or Citibank in the UAE. Other banks focus more on local investment and corporate banking services as well as private banking for high net worth individuals (e.g.,

CSFB, Merrill Lynch), while still others restrict themselves to representative offices, trade finance and occasional participation in syndicated loans.

There is an apparent lack of an institutional investor base in the country as the market for mutual funds and life insurance products is underdeveloped. There are some locally-based private equity funds (e.g., Al Abraj, Injazat, International Financial Advisors, Investcorp), and some banks are offering mutual fund products that invest in the local market (e.g., Mashreqbank, NCB), but overall the market is in a very nascent stage and could profit from an increased offering of pension schemes. Government pension funds as far they exist (e.g. in Saudi Arabia) are usually not very active, long term investors, but can occasionally play an important role as provider of liquidity for markets if ordered by the government. There are sales teams of foreign funds (mutual, closed end, private equity, hedge, e.g. Mellon, Forsyth, Templeton, Man), but these funds mostly invest in international markets and not in those of the region. Finally, the large SWFs of the region like the investment authorities of Abu Dhabi, Qatar or Kuwait (ADIA, QIA, KIA), also manage large offshore assets that do not directly affect the local capital markets and their development.

Given the burgeoning economic development in the region and its increased needs for focused financial services, the following fields may witness the most development:

- Growing investment banking and corporate banking services for domestic companies and venturing of national banks into the project finance market, which is thus far dominated by international banks
- Increased M & A of GCC companies and increased FDI of foreign companies in the GCC
- Development of capital markets, notably bond and derivative markets; this includes a nascent fund industry ranging from mutual funds to pension schemes and private equity funds. Tackling of associated regulatory issues
- Increased role of insurance companies. So far there is a predominance of non-life insurance, a reliance on international reinsurance companies, and low ratios of insurance to GDP. Growth for sharia-compliant takaful insurance could be particularly brisk.
- Development of private banking services for a growing number of high net worth individuals, who have become more sophisticated investors
- Advanced asset management solutions for sovereign wealth funds, which manage the increasing oil wealth. Trend towards strategic equity stakes that can

help diversification of the local economy instead of mere portfolio investments

- White labeling of products (e.g. funds, structured products) and know-how acquisition by national banks
- Back office and custodian solutions for GCC capital markets, which have growing intersections with international markets. While a tendency towards unification has not been seen yet, it would be highly desirable and could lead to cross-country trading platforms
- Growing role of Islamic banking, although growth rates are likely to level out as we approach a higher statistical base. There is potential for local banks acquiring international status via this niche market (e.g., cooperation with Asia including Malaysia). Specific requirements in regulation (Basle II), customer care and risk management solutions, as well as controversial discussions about sharia compliance of various products have to be taken into consideration.
- Growing credit for SMEs and microcredit. The disconnect between SMEs and the banking system in the GCC has to be tackled; there have also been some initiatives for microcredit in the GCC (Al Jameel Group, PlaNet Finance, IFC).

6. GCC Financial Centers

The GCC countries saw a flurry of newly-designed International Financial Centers that aim to attract foreign banks and investors and try to connect the financial sector of these countries more closely with the international banking scene. While there is similarity of motivation among them, there are considerable differences in the various approaches and stages of implementation. The question has also been raised whether there is the risk of oversupply and whether there is enough business for all the newly-launched projects. In September 2004, the Dubai International Financial Centre (DIFC) started operations and the Qatar Financial Centre (QFC) opened for business in May 2005. Saudi Arabia announced the King Abdullah Financial District project in Riyadh in 2006 and construction started in 2007. The Bahrain Financial Harbour (BFH) project was completed in 2009, but Bahrain has been a regional financial hub since the seventies and already offered a sophisticated financial infrastructure before.[10]

The Global Financial Centres Index by the City of London ranks Dubai

10. City of London, *The Competitiveness of the Gulf as a Global Financial Center*, Study by ICMA Centre of University of Reading, May 2008.

highest in the region (rank 21), followed by Qatar (rank 43), Bahrain (rank 45) and Riyadh (rank 68).[11] Kuwait and Oman do not figure in the global overview that also serves to gauge competition to London's most important business, the financial industry. The Index takes five major categories into consideration: People, Business Environment, Market Access, Infrastructure and General Competitiveness. In recent years, Bahrain has fallen behind relatively in the rankings and has been surpassed by Qatar. Dubai is now less frequently named as an upcoming financial center as the global financial crisis and the Dubai real estate bust have left an impact. On the contrary, the discussions about a possible opening of the Saudi stock market to foreigners may have prompted an inclusion of Riyadh in the ranking for the first time in 2009.

6.1 Bahrain Financial Harbour

With the outbreak of civil war in Lebanon in 1975, financial business suffered greatly in the Levantine country, which used to be the Middle East banking hub until then. Bahrain at that time took on the mantle of regional financial center and chose a conscious strategy to offer a new home to Middle East banking business. This was not only helped by the push factor of Lebanese civil war but also by the pull factor of rapidly rising oil revenues, which moved the center of economic gravity of the Middle East to the Gulf. While it has played host to offshore banks since 1978, Bahrain also has a core strength in Islamic banking. Apart from hosting many Islamic banks and regular *sukuk* issuance by the Bahrain government, the country also hosts the Accounting and Auditing Organization of Islamic Financial Institutions (AAOIFI) and teaching bodies such as the Bahrain Institute of Banking and Finance.[12] But its position has been eroding with the establishment of the DIFC and the QFC. With the ascendance to the WTO of Saudi Arabia and Kuwait and the requirement to comply with its rules, many foreign banks and insurance firms have also received licenses to operate in Saudi Arabia and Kuwait, taking away business from Bahrain. Despite the debt crisis of Dubai and its concomitant reputation loss, there is debate whether Bahrain will be able to regain lost market share from it

Still, Bahrain had a head start and a well-developed regulatory framework administered by the Bahrain Monetary Agency (BMA), the Kingdom's central bank,

11. City of London, *The Global Financial Centres Index 6*, September 2009, available at http://217.154.230.218/NR/rdonlyres/4A05FE0F-4CD1-46EB-ADB5-84672ACC05FE/0/GFCI6.pdf.
12. http://www.bibf.com.bh/content/index.htm.

which maintains stringent controls over the financial industry. The BMA also has a well-developed process for establishing special purpose vehicles (SPVs) to issue *sukuks*, or Islamic bonds. In 2007-08, the central bank quelled speculation on an appreciation of the local currency early and thus avoided the ensuing withdrawal of hot money that has caused considerable problems in Saudi Arabia and the UAE. Large sub-prime losses at Arab Banking Corporation and Gulf International Bank in 2008, however, have dented the otherwise positive reputation of the Bahraini regulators.

The Bahrain Financial Harbour (BFH) is a waterfront commercial development project. It aims to strengthen Bahrain's position as a financial hub for the Middle East, with particular expertise in Islamic banking, insurance and asset management. By attracting regional and international foreign investments, it is hoped that BFH can recapture some of the ground that Bahrain has lost to competitors in the region like Dubai and Qatar.[13] BFH also hosts the Bahrain Financial Exchange (BFX), launched in 2010. It is the first multi-asset exchange in the MENA, which will allow for trading of *sukuks*, derivatives and structured products alongside conventional fixed income and equities.[14] Bahrain has fared relatively well during the current global financial crisis and has faced less fallout than competitors such as Dubai or Saudi Arabia. Bahrain also offers the opportunity to set up businesses without local partners. In the wake of Dubai's debt crisis and its concomitant reputation loss, Bahrain has embarked on a marketing drive to lure business back from Gulf competitors. However, political turmoil at the beginning of 2011 has thwarted such aspirations.[15]

6.2 Dubai International Financial Centre (DIFC)

Dubai International Financial Centre (DIFC) is an offshore financial market place, which has its own exterritorial jurisdiction, trades in US dollar only, has tax exemption for 50 years, and guarantees unlimited repatriation of profits. Since opening in September 2004, the DIFC has aimed to bridge the time gap between the financial centers of Hong Kong and London. September 2005 saw the opening of the Dubai International Financial Exchange (DIFX) which has since been rebranded NASDAQ Dubai after an intense bidding for Scandinavian bourse OMX

13. Digby Lidstone, "Manama Builds on Market Strength," *MEED*, October 22, 2009, available at http://www.meed.com/sectors/economy/government/manama-builds-on-market strength/3001423.article

14. Ibid.

15. Matthew Martin, "Bahrain Seeks to Regain its Financial Crown," *MEED*, February 8, 2009, available at http://www.meed.com/sectors/finance/bahrain-seeks-to-regain-its-financial-crown/1985500.article\

led to cross holdings between the two partners, Bourse Dubai and Nasdaq.[16] The Dubai Financial Services Authority (DFSA) has synthesized the financial services regulations of UK, US, and Canada jurisdictions to produce laws that incorporate international best practices. DIFC, along with international organizations and government ministries, has also been instrumental in backing Hawkamah, the first institute for corporate governance in the region.

DIFC has undoubtedly succeeded in attracting major names of the international finance business. It has created a vibrant financial community that is also attracted by the urban lifestyle advantages that Dubai has to offer in comparison to other Gulf countries. However, it has to be noted that often it was only the sales people who moved in and larger contingents of traders and asset managers are still missing. Thus, Dubai has not yet succeeded in becoming a major trading hub of currencies, equities and bonds between the time zones of Asia and Europe. Also DIFX/NASDAQ Dubai has not attracted any meaningful quantities of trading in its fourth year of existence. Its only real primary listing is Dubai Ports World, but otherwise it mainly houses secondary listings of foreign equities and certificates. Such secondary listings have failed to attract meaningful liquidity at developed market places such as NYSE. For this reason, many German companies, for example, have regretted their move to make a secondary listing at the New York Stock Exchange (NYSE), because it led to increased reporting requirements but has not provided any benefits – a US fund manager still prefers to buy German stocks in Germany as liquidity and prices are usually better. If an established market place like NYSE has failed to provide a liquid market for secondary listing, it is very unclear how DIFX/NASDAQ Dubai was supposed to succeed with such a strategy. Unless it was able to develop into the preferred market place of UAE, and possibly Gulf securities, it was unlikely to awake from its doldrums. But trading of such domestic securities has remained firmly in the hands of onshore exchanges like the Dubai Financial Market (DFM) or the Abu Dhabi Securities Markets (ADSM), which

16. Nasdaq and Borse Dubai were initially fighting for the control of OMX. The Qatar Investment Authority entered the fray later and started buying OMX shares as well. Instead of starting a bidding war, Borse Dubai and Nasdaq finally reached a complex deal. Borse Dubai went on with its public offer for OMX shares and once it owned at least 67 percent of the OMX shares, it was agreed to transfer it all to Nasdaq. In return, Borse Dubai received an equivalent share of NASDAQ's equity base, which took a minority holding of 33 percent in Dubai International Financial Exchange (DIFX). Borse Dubai has thus about 20 percent of the share capital of Nasdaq, but only 5 percent of its voting rights. The rest of the shares that it might acquire in the deal will be placed in a trust fund. As part of the deal, Borse Dubai has also acquired Nasdaq's stake in the London Stock Exchange, of which it currently controls about 21 percent.

are currently engaged in talks for a possible merger. Not surprisingly, NASDAQ_Dubai has finally decided to integrate its trading operations with DFM and Shebab Gargash, a director of the Dubai Chamber of Commerce and Industry and CEO of Daman Investments, deemed it "a failed experiment."[17]

DIFC has also announced its intention to become one of the world's leading fund centers following the enactment of a collective investment law. A company official said that this covered all funds including mutual funds, property funds, Islamic funds, hedge funds, funds of funds, and private equity funds. Furthermore, DIFC aims to become a major trading hub for Islamic securities, most notably *sukuks*, and it has managed to attract a large number of listings of *sukuks* at DIFX/NASDAQ_Dubai. As bonds are usually traded over the phone, a listing on an exchange does not mean necessarily traded volume; still, the initiative is a clear competition to Bahrain and its vested interest in the Islamic banking sector.

However, a severe blow to DIFC's ambitious plans was dealt with the debt crisis of Dubai World and Nakheel that erupted with a debt standstill request on November 25, 2009. Until then, the market had assumed an implicit government guarantee for such government-owned companies, to which DIFC belongs as well. As this government guarantee did not materialize, and Abu Dhabi has shown up for the rescue only selectively, financing costs for Dubai entities have increased considerably. The lack of transparency and the unprofessional conduct surrounding the Dubai World debt crisis has also shattered trust in the regulatory and management capacities in the emirate. These shortcomings were particularly striking in the case of the default of the Nakheel *sukuk* in December 2009. It revealed severe ambiguities in the legal framework of the sharia-compliant security, i.e. in the Islamic finance sector where DIFC wanted to grow in particular. The *sukuk* is governed by English law, but it was unclear whether such law would be applicable under UAE law and whether there would be any legal recourse to underlying assets or other assets of the holding company, Dubai World.[18] DIFC, like many other companies, was rocked by a corporate scandal when its former governor Omar bin Sulaiman was arrested under embezzlement charges and only released after repaying $14 million in allegedly unauthorized bonuses. With its new governor Ahmed al-Tayer, DIFC has tried to focus on its core business, refrain from foreign investment adventures, and review its high office rents in order to retain customers.[19]

---

17. Andrew White, "Nasdaq Dubai a 'Failed Experiment' – Gargash," *Arabian Business*, September 26, 2010.

18. Eckart Woertz, *Implications of Dubai's Debt Troubles*, GRC Report, December 2009.

19. "FT interview: Ahmed al-Tayer," *Financial Times*, June 24, 2010.

Competitors in the region like Bahrain or Qatar will undoubtedly try to take advantage of Dubai's setbacks in order to lure market share away from it. In order to reestablish confidence, the DIFC bankruptcy law will henceforth be applicable to possible bankruptcy cases of Dubai World, according to ruler's decree no. 57. As the onshore jurisdiction of Dubai does not have a real bankruptcy law except for stipulating jail for defaulting debtors, the internationally recognized jurisdiction of DIFC is also sought in other cases, among them a pending lawsuit against real estate developer Damac.

6.3 Qatar Financial Centre

Unlike the DIFC, the Qatar Financial Centre (QFC) is an onshore market place that only guarantees tax exemption for a period of three years, after which listed companies are required to pay the predominant tax rate of 10 percent. Since making the strategic choice to allow foreign investment in oil and gas and spending large sums on infrastructure and hydrocarbon projects, Qatar has seen a lot of international financial companies setting up shop in Doha. Qatar has the world's third-largest gas reserves, and it is estimated that its gas will last for many decades at planned levels. Hence, Qatar set up QFC with a long-term view towards appealing to project financiers and addressing the economic boom in the country. Rather than being international as its name suggests, QFC is more geared towards the domestic market and its finance needs. It has not attracted the same amount of bankers as DIFC, and many offices only consist of a representative and a secretary. The aim is to gain a foothold in the burgeoning domestic market rather than set up an office for regional expansion. The Qatar Investment Authority (QIA) tried to compete with Borse Dubai in the acquisition of OMX and LSE. In the process, it accumulated nearly 10 percent interest in OMX, which it sold at the beginning of 2008 after losing out to Dubai. It has also purchased a large share of LSE of which it still owns 15 percent. However, in 2008, Qatar made a far-reaching technology and management partnership agreement with NYSE, which took a 25 percent stake in the Doha securities market for $250 million. At this stage it is unclear how ownership of LSE could lead to a more international profile for QFC and what the strategic rationale behind it is.

QFC opened for business in May 2005, and includes the Qatar Financial Centre Authority, the fully-independent Qatar Financial Centre Regulatory Authority (QFCRA), and an arbitration body, which will adjudicate appeals. Qatar also has set up the International Mercantile Exchange (IMEX), which is supposed to be an energy trading platform, but has not attracted any meaningful business thus far, and the plan to offer energy derivatives has fizzled out. It is QFC-regulated and was originally scheduled to move to a newly-built Energy City. The QFC has also been deliberating recognizing the Doha Securities Market (DSM) as one of its approved bourses; the QFCRA has indicated that it would first look at the DSM's global compliance issues. An attempt to apply the advanced regulatory framework of QFC to the overall Qatari market in 2007 has failed, and the Doha securities market continues to be regulated by the Qatar Financial Markets Authority (QFMA), which was also founded in 2005. Therefore, the intended role of QFCRA to function as a pacemaker of domestic financial market reform has not materialized thus far. However, in 2010, Qatari authorities reiterated their intention to unify the three regulators under one umbrella shortly. QFC's regulator, the stock market, and the central bank's supervision of the local banking industry would then be merged. QFC has also launched an overhaul of its business model in 2010, downsized its staff, and wants to focus on asset management, captive insurance and re-insurance going ahead. [20]

6.4 King Abdullah Financial District, Riyadh

Work on the King Abdullah Financial District (KAFD) started in 2007 and the first phase of the $60 billion project is scheduled to be completed in 2011. The Public Pension Agency (PPA) is its landowner and its master developer. With a planned site of 1.6 million meters and a gross floor area of 3.5 million meters, it would dwarf London's Canary Wharf, which is built over an area of 345,000 meters.[21] The KAFD will replace the business district in Olaya and will be the headquarters of the Capital Market Authority (CMA) and the Stock Exchange (Tadawul), with the latter to be renamed the Saudi Arabian Financial Exchange. It will also house the commodity market headquarters and banks like Samba, Alinma Bank or Al-Rajhi Bank and the Public Investment Fund (PIF).[22]

On the anvil is also a financial academy for 5,000 students, which will provide capacity-building skills. The project, aims to 'consolidate Saudi Arabia's position as the

---

20. Simeon Kerr, "Qatar Changes Tack to Boost Financial Centre," *Financial Times*, February 1, 2010, available at http://www.ft.com/cms/s/0/bcd59adc-0f74-11df-a450-00144feabdc0.html?nclick_check=1 .

21. Mohamed Ramady, "King Abdullah Financial District - a New Value Proposition in the Middle East," in *Investing in the GCC Markets: Regional Opportunities and Challenges,* ed. CPI Financial Books, 2010.

22. Colin Foreman, "Samba Launches Tender for Deal to Build Headquarters," *MEED*, November 2, 2009, available at: http://www.meed.com/sectors/construction/real-estate/samba-launches-tender-for-deal-to-build-headquarters/3001816.article

world's oil capital and capture the position of Middle Eastern financial capital.' Like the King Abdullah Economic City north of Jeddah, it is a greenfield development with large ambitions and, like Bahrain and QFC, it is an onshore entity that does not have the international and exterritorial design of DIFC. KAFD also will not offer tax-free incentives for companies to set up shop. However, this has not deterred international players, such as Deutsche Bank, Morgan Stanley and Goldman Sachs, from registering.[23] As KAFD is more geared towards the domestic Saudi market, the potential of improved access to the largest GCC financial market is incentive enough. The pending mortgage law and the Saudi government's announcement that it would consider the introduction of a government-owned mortgage guarantee institution similar to Fannie Mae could give a massive impetus to the development of Saudi financial markets, as home ownership is still under-developed. Equally, it is hoped that the Saudi stock market will be opened to foreign institutional investors in the future. The Saudi authorities hope that KAFD will create about 43,000 new jobs for its growing youth population. While it is conceivable that it could develop into an important access point for the largest Gulf financial market, it is not completed yet and there are many question marks. Access of foreigners to the Saudi stock market is still limited. For non-GCC and non-resident aliens it is only possible via mutual funds and proxy products of banks. Furthermore, the restrictive social environment and visa practices, gender segregated workplaces, and limited lifestyle quality impose difficulties in attracting international banking talent, most notably female ones.

7. Commodity Trading: Dubai Mercantile Exchange (DME) and Dubai Multi Commodities Centre (DMCC)

While the idea to establish an international financial center for mainstream banking products in the Gulf may sound audacious, trading in commodities has more obvious advantages in the region. The Gulf (including Iraq and Iran) produces about 40 percent of world oil supplies, and Dubai houses a vibrant gold trade, where about 15 percent of worldwide physical gold is traded on good days. While a lot of it is re-exported to neighboring India, a sizable portion also stays in the Gulf region itself.

Dubai Mercantile Exchange (DME) is a joint venture between Tatweer, a member of Dubai Holding, the New York Mercantile Exchange Inc. (NYMEX),

23. "KSA's King Abdullah Financial District," MEED, July 2009, available at: http://www.zawya.com/story.cfm/sidZAWYA20070703102850/KSA's%20King%20Abdullah%20Financial%20District%20%20%20%20

and the Oman Investment Fund (OIF). It was founded in 2007. Its motivation is to establish a benchmark for Gulf sour crude variants that are considerably different from the dominating WTI and Brent contracts against which the region's oil is still priced. The DME offers the possibility of physical settlement; its futures are not mere paper contracts. The DME is setting the monthly Official Selling Prices (OSP) for Oman's crude exports since its launch, and the Dubai Petroleum Authority has announced recently that it will base the pricing of its benchmark crude (Dubai Fateh) on differentials of the DME Oman OSP.[24] DME has not yet been able to attract the bigger players of the region like Saudi Aramco and Abu Dhabi National Oil Company (ADNOC).[25] It has also struggled to attract more traders from Asia where about two-thirds of the Gulf's oil exports head to. DME also needs more financial companies to get involved besides strategic investors who trade on it like Goldman Sachs, Morgan Stanley, Shell and Vitol. Should DME succeed in attracting large Gulf oil companies like Aramco to use DME contracts as a base for pricing, this would increase the importance of the exchange dramatically.[26]

For the time being, though, liquidity on DME has remained low for the mentioned reasons. But it has improved – physical deliveries of DME contract hit 10 million barrels in October 2009, which marks a 60 per cent increase in physically delivered volumes from its launch in August 2007.[27] DME has also tried to increase its attractiveness to Asian traders by launching new products besides its existing DME Oman Futures flagship products, such as a DME Brent-Oman Swap or options on Oman sour crude.

Dubai Multi Commodities Centre (DMCC) is the first free trade zone for commodities in the Middle East. It was founded in 2002 and houses the Dubai Gold and Commodities Exchange (DGCX). It aims at providing trading platforms for a wide variety of commodities ranging from gold, silver and currency derivatives to gemstones, diamonds and steel. It has developed the Dubai good delivery

---

24. "Dubai to Set Crude Oil Selling Price Based on DME Oman Contract," *AME*, June 23, 2009, available at http://www.ameinfo.com/201439.html

25. Shashank Shekhar, "DME Needs a Big Player to Raise Liquidity Level," *Emirates Business*, June 28, 2009, available at: http://www.business24-7.ae/Articles/2009/6/Pages/27062009/06282009_956d5404e4db46afbfbdafde28cc128b.aspx

26. "Interview-DME Seeks More Oil Producers to Beef up Liquidity," Reuters, November 3, 2009, available at http://www.futurespros.com/news/commodities---futures-news/interview-dme-seeks-more-oil- producers-to-beef-up-liquidity-97457

27. Babu Das Augustine, "Dubai Mercantile Exchange Has Got Fundamentals Right, says Sharaf," *Gulf News*, November 30, 2009, available at http://gulfnews.com/business/oil-gas/dubai-mercantile-exchange-has-got-fundamentals-right-says-sharaf-1.541995

standard for physical trading in smaller gold bars and an electronic infrastructure for securities and trade finance instruments like the Dubai Gold Receipt and the Dubai Commodity Receipt.

The DMCC also houses the Dubai Tea Trading Centre, the Dubai Diamond Exchange, and the Dubai Gems Club, where physical trade in the respective items is already up and running. Furthermore, DMCC has launched the initiative for the Dubai Cotton Center, which aims at becoming a trading and storage hub for cotton from Uzbekistan.[28] While DMCC has achieved good trading volumes in precious metals, gemstones and diamonds, the launch of a fuel oil futures contract, which was a joint venture with the Multi-Commodities Exchange of India (MCX) and Financial Technologies (India) Limited (FTIL), was not successful. The contract has been discontinued for lack of liquidity, as investors were not familiar with derivatives in this item and the area also lacked spot barges.[29] It remains to be seen whether planned futures contracts on steel, plastics and gasoline will be more successful.[30] Contrary to base metals such as copper, steel is hardly traded in the form of futures; only Shanghai offers such a contract thus far. Together with LNG Impel, DMCC is also planning to set up a LNG storage hub to provide more flexible services which will offer customers the ability to trade, store and plan supplies of LNG.

Conclusion

The Gulf region has the potential to develop into an important niche player in the international financial system. Awash in petrodollars, its sovereign wealth funds look for foreign investment opportunities, while domestic companies are modernizing themselves and increasingly engaging in mergers and acquisitions. Multi-billion projects in the Gulf are in need of project finance, while the banking retail market is in many fields, such as mortgage financing or insurance, still undeveloped. In commodity trading, the region has obvious advantages in energy-related items and precious metals, and some of the Dubai-related initiatives have good chances to grab more international market shares going forward – the trading in Omani sour crude and gold especially could prove to be successful. The region is also in an advantageous position to profit from an expansion of Islamic banking, although the

28. See DMCC website, http://www.dmcc.ae/media-files/2009/11/02/20091102_DMCC-Cotton-Bro-Oct-2009-1.pdf

29. See DMCC website, http://www.dmcc.ae/en/dmcc-news/dmcc-news/energy-related-commodities-news/30-january-2008-lng-is-set-to-become-a-globally-traded-commodity.html/

30. See DMCC website, http://www.dmcc.ae/en/base-metals-steel/steel/introduction-base-metal.html

recent Dubai debt crisis and contradictory statements of sharia scholars about the legal viability of *sukuk* contracts have marred sentiment.

With an aggressive marketing campaign and its lifestyle advantages, Dubai has managed to push itself into the pole position in rankings of the region and is widely seen as the most promising financial center of the region. However, other financial centers must not be forgotten and Dubai's ambitions have been compromised in the wake of its debt crisis. Bahrain as the oldest banking center in the region will try to use this to its advantage and regain market share, especially in Islamic banking where it has long experience and a regulatory framework. However, political turmoil at the beginning of 2011 has thwarted such aspirations. QFC largely focuses on its domestic energy sector and its project finance needs. It has not developed a more international profile yet, despite high profile deals like the acquisition of a share of London Stock Exchange (LSE) and NYSE's partnership with the Doha Stock Market (DSM). Financial liberalization in Saudi Arabia and Kuwait could also pose serious competition to the banking centers on the Gulf coast with a more international outlook. It remains to be seen whether Saudi Arabia can overcome problems of cultural perception abroad and the resulting difficulties in attracting international talent. But the ambitious King Abdullah Financial District in Riyadh clearly aims to play a major role as financial hub of the largest GCC economy in the future.

Advertisements of Gulf financial centers often involve a "mixture of slick marketing and public relations, financial acumen and a lot of real estate projects thrown together."[31] The former head of the Dubai Financial Services Authority Habib Al-Mulla has conceded that the DIFC is "more of a shopping centre and (...) a real estate project" and that DIFC has somehow "lost its vision."[32] In a region whose GDP equals that of the Netherlands, hardly every city can become an "international financial center," and the dynamic of domestic GCC capital markets often relies on exchanges and institutions outside the financial center projects. Thus, a word of caution is in order, and it remains to be seen which niches the respective projects can occupy, possibly after a period of consolidation.

---

31. Mohamed Ramady, "King Abdullah Financial District - a New Value Proposition in the Middle East," 91.

32. "DIFC Vision 'Has Been Lost' Says Ex-DFSA Boss," *Arabian Business Magazine*, July 18, 2010, available at http://www.arabianbusiness.com/592894-difc-vision-has-been-lost-says-ex-dfsa-boss.

5

The Determinants of Capital Structure Choice: Case of GCC Listed Companies

Lamia A. Obay

Introduction

"There is no universal theory of capital structure, and no reason to expect one. There are useful conditional theories, however. . . . Each factor could be dominant for some firms or in some circumstances, yet unimportant elsewhere." (Myers, 2003, p. 216)

Whether financing decisions affect the value of the firm has long been discussed. How managers make financing decisions is still very much a 'puzzle.' The aim of this paper is to explore the determinants of the financing decisions within GCC listed firms. There are several features that characterize the GCC financial system. Firstly, the system is bank dominated. Secondly, stock markets have been operating for less than two decades. Thirdly, businesses are mostly family-owned with ownership highly concentrated in the hands of a few family members. Besides, the combined number of firms listed on GCC markets is less than 1,000 which represents a very small percentage of businesses operating in the area. Except for Saudi Arabia, the market for initial public offerings dried out after the flurry of 2005. Private credit from banks averaged 30 percent to 60 percent of total GDP during 2000-2008 (Figure 1), an indication of low financial deepening of the GCC financial system.

Capital markets also failed to capture a sizable proportion of financing needs of GCC businesses. Market capitalization to GDP shot up from a low 34 percent in 2000 to above 180 percent, then fell to less than 60 percent in

2008 (Figure 2). Figure 3 clearly shows that stock markets did not play a role in raising funds until the year 2004. Stock issues practically dried out after the advent of the global financial crisis. The bond market (Figure 4), still very much underdeveloped, is dominated by sovereign issues with governments capturing more than 70 percent of the total volume of bond issues. The *sukuk* (sharia-

Figure 1: Sources of Funds - Private Credit as a Percentage of GDP

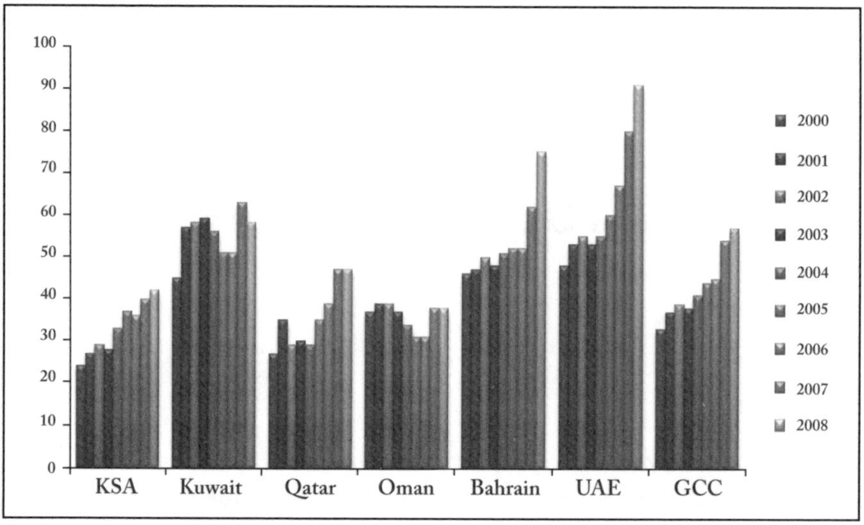

Source: GCC Countries' Central Banks

Figure 2: Market Capitalization as a Percentage of GDP

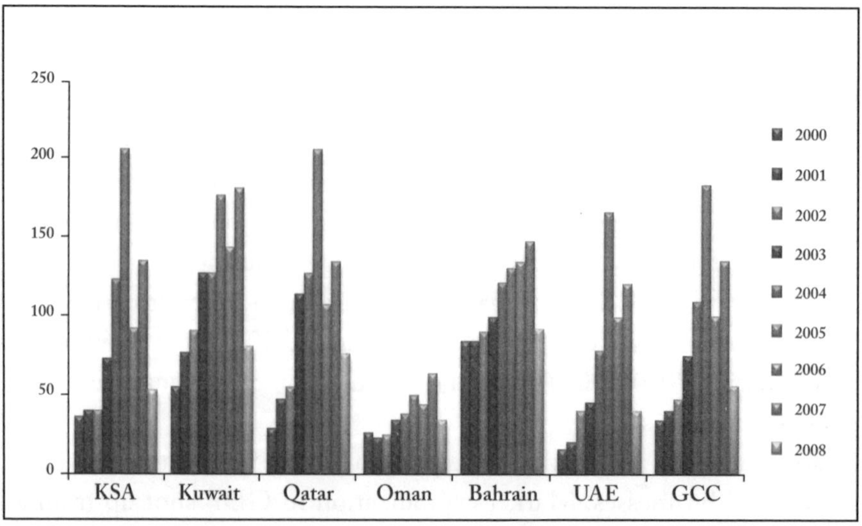

Source: GCC Countries' Central Banks

compliant bonds) market was hit hard with the default of Dubai World and its subsidiary Nakheel.

The paper is structured as follows: Section 1 reviews the literature of capital structure. Section 2 defines the variables that affect the capital structure's choice of firms and develops the hypotheses. The sample and estimation methods

Figure 3: Source of Funds: Use of Stock Market by GCC Firms

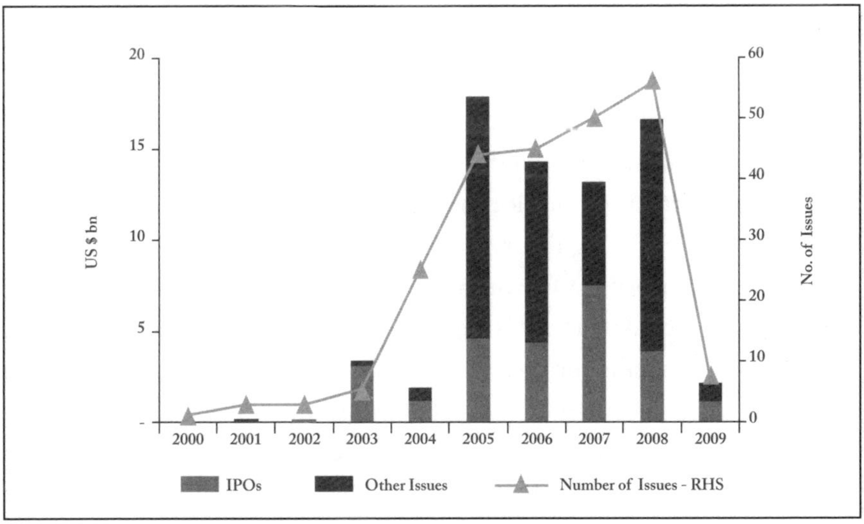

Source: Zawya.com and author's compilation.

Figure 4: Use of the Bond Market by GCC Countries

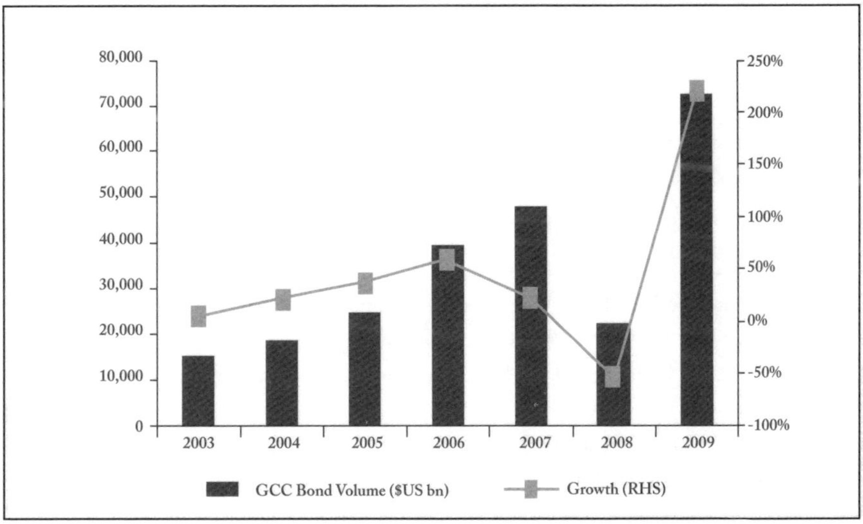

Source: Markaz.com. Includes sovereign, corporate, conventional and Islamic bonds

are discussed in section 3. The analysis and empirical results are presented in section 4.

1. Literature Review

The seminal work of Modigliani and Miller forms the basis for modern thinking on capital structure.[1] They state that the firm's value is unaffected by its capital structure decision as long as the firm is operating in a well-functioning capital market with no transaction costs and symmetric access to credit market allowing rational investors to 'undo' the firm's capital structure by holding negative or positive debt. Several empirical studies were conducted based on the debate around the irrelevance of these assumptions and three main theories emerged in an attempt to explain the capital structure 'puzzle': the trade off theory, the pecking order theory, and the equity market timing theory.

The trade-off theory (TOT), originally introduced by Kraus and Litzenberger (1973), states that capital structure is a balancing act between the cost of bankruptcy and the tax saving benefits (or the tax shield in the case of GCC countries, given the absence of taxation) of debt.[2] This proposition was fiercely criticized by Myers (1984) on the basis that tax-benefits are real and large, whereas costs of bankruptcy are remote and small, a view that was also upheld by Warner (1977).[3] In addition, the adoption of the TOT would mean a much higher level of debt than what is actually observed. Despite such criticisms, the TOT, mainly through its dynamic version, has found wide acceptance among researchers. Dynamic trade-off models such as in Fischer et al. (1989) suggest firms have an optimal leverage range within which their leverage ratios are allowed to vary. Hovakimian et al. (2001) find that more profitable firms are more likely to issue debt over equity.[4] They note that this is consistent with firms trading off the risks of bankruptcy with the tax benefits of debt.

Several authors challenge the M&M proposition. Jensen and Meckling (1976), Jensen (1986); Hart and Moore (1994), in their challenge of the M&M

1. F. Modigliani and M.H. Miller. "The Cost of Capital, Corporate Finance and the Theory of Investment," *American Economic Review* 48 (1958): 261-296.
2. A. Kraus and R. H. Litzenberger, "A State Preference Model of Optimal Financial Leverage," *Journal of Finance* 28 (1973): 911-922.
3. S.C. Myers, "The Capital Structure Puzzle," *Journal of Finance* 39 (1984): 575–592; J.B. Warner, "Bankruptcy Costs: Some Evidence," *Journal of Finance* 32 (1977): 337-348.
4. A. Hovakimian, T.C. Opler and S. Titman, "The Debt-Equity Choice," *Journal of Financial and Quantitative Analysis* 36 (2001): 1–24.

proposition, recognize the need to account for agency costs when investigating determinants of firms' capital structure.[5] Debt disciplines managers and mitigates agency problems of free cash flow since debt must be repaid to avoid bankruptcy. Equity-holders of a levered firm, for example, can potentially extract value from debt-holders by increasing investment risk after debt is in place: the "asset substitution" problem. Such behavior creates agency costs which the choice of capital structure must recognize and control. Friend and Lang (1988) argue that empirical results indicate that agency problems are an important determinant of capital structure.[6]

The Pecking Order Theory (Myers and Majluf, 1984 and Myers, 1984) advances that businesses adhere to a hierarchy of financing sources and prefer internal financing whenever available and debt is preferred to equity in the case of external financing.[7] The rationale behind such hierarchy arises from managers' unwillingness to dilute existing shareholders claims (Autore and Kovacs, 2004).[8] Frank and Goyal (2004) argue that high growth firms (with large financing needs) will end up with high debt ratios because of managers' reluctance to issue equity.[9] Baker and Wurgler (2002) further argue that firms with high market-to-book ratios that reflect growth or investment opportunities may exhaust their internal sources of funds to finance an investment.[10] This model implies the existence of information asymmetry between corporate managers and the market, since little information is disclosed in the process. It also implies the absence of a targeted optimal capital structure, or debt to equity ratio.

---

5. M. Jensen and W. Meckling "Theory of the Firm: Managerial Behavior, Agency Costs and Capital Structure," *Journal of Financial Economics* 3 (1976): 305–360; M.C. Jensen, "Agency Costs of Free Cash Flow, Corporate Finance, and Takeovers," *American Economic Review* 76 (1986): 323–329; O. Hart and J. Moore, "A Theory of Debt-based on the Inalienability of Human Capital," *Quarterly Journal of Economics* 109 (1994): 841–879.
6. I. Friend and L. Lang, "An Empirical Test of the Impact of Managerial Self-interest on Corporate Capital Structure," *Journal of Finance* 43 (1988): 271-281.
7. S. Myers and N. Majluf, "Corporate Financing and Investment Decisions when Firms Have Information that Investors Do Not Have," *Journal of Financial Economics* 13 (1984): 187-221; Myers, "The Capital Structure Puzzle."
8. D.Autore and T. Kovacs, "The Pecking Order Theory and Time Varying Adverse Selection Costs," Working paper, Virginia Technical University, 2004.
9. M. Z. Frank and V.K. Goyal, "The Effect of Market Conditions on Capital Structure Adjustment," *Finance Research Letters* 1 (2004): 47-55.
10. M. Baker and J. Wurgler, "Market Timing and Capital Structure," *Journal of Finance* 57 (2002): 1-31.

More recently, Baker and Wurgler (2002) have suggested that the current capital structure is the cumulative outcome of past attempts to time the equity market.[11] Market timing implies that firms would issue new shares when they perceive they are overvalued and would repurchase their own shares when these are perceived to be undervalued. Empirical support for such theory has been rather limited. Bie and Haan (2004) in their study of Dutch firms did not find "strong and persistent effect of market timing on capital structure."[12] Similar conclusions are reached by Mahajan and Tartaroglu (2007) in their study of firms within major industrialized (G-7) countries.[13] They find the impact of equity market timing attempts on leverage to be short lived, which is inconsistent with the prediction of the equity market timing hypothesis and more in line with dynamic trade-off model.

Studies on emerging markets such as Booth et al. (2001) and Wiwattanakantang (1999) only appeared in recent years.[14] Booth et al. (2001) look at determinants of capital structure in 10 developing countries, including Jordan, and conclude that the capital structure decision is affected by the same observed variables in developed countries, albeit country specific differences persist. Later studies (Al Najjar and Taylor 2008, and Tien 2007) demonstrate that Jordanian firms follow the same determinants of capital structure as occur in developed markets, namely: profitability, firm size, growth rate, market-to-book ratio, asset structure and liquidity.[15]

2. Data and Methodology

Data Sample

The sample of this study includes non-financial firms listed in three GCC countries, namely the United Arab Emirates (UAE), Bahrain, Qatar, and Saudi Arabia. Firms'

11. Ibid.

12. T. Bie and L. Hann, "Does Market Timing Drive Capital Structures? A Panel Data Study for Dutch Firms," Working paper no. 14, The Nederlandsche Bank NV, 2004.

13. A. Mahajan and S. Tartaroglu. "Equity Market Timing and Capital Structure: International Evidence," *Journal of Banking & Finance* 32 (2008): 754-766.

14. L. Booth, V. Aivazian, A. Demirguc-Kunt and V. Maksimovic, "Capital Structures in Developing Countries," *Journal of Finance* 56 (2001): 87-130; Y. Wiwattanakantang, "An Empirical Study on the Determinants of the Capital Structure of Thai Firms," *Pacific-Basin Finance Journal* 7 (1999): 371-403.

15. B. Al-Najjar and P. Taylor, "The Relationship between Capital Structure and Ownership Structure: New Evidence from Jordanian Panel Data," *Managerial Finance* 34 (2008): 919-933.

accounting and market data for 10 years (2000-2009) have been hand collected from the firms' websites and from Abu Dhabi Securities Exchange (ADX), Dubai Financial Market (DFM), Doha Securities Market (DSM) of Qatar, Bahrain Stock Exchange (BSE), and the Saudi financial market, Tadawul. Both ADX and DFM belong to the UAE. Overall, our sample includes 150 companies with 16 firms listed on BSE, 24 on DSM, 25 between DFM and ADX, and 85 on Tadwaul.

Dependent Variables; Capital Structure

Our model is tested using four measures of capital structure: total debt to total assets (BTDTA), long-term debt to total assets (BLDTA), short-term debt to total assets (BSDTA), and total debt to total equity (BDE). Our choice of leverage ratios is guided by earlier empirical studies.

Performance Measurement (Independent Variables)

Due to the limitations of the data available, five factors are set as performance measurement: Profitability, growth opportunities, size, asset structure, and risk. The ratios used for these factors are derived mainly from the empirical studies.

Profitability

There is no agreement in the literature about the relationship between leverage and profitability. The trade-off model suggests that the higher the profitability of a given firm the greater is the leverage deployed (Brealey et al., 2007).[16] According to Jensen and Meckling (1976), the agency-based models show the same type of relationship.[17] As a firm's profit increases, more leverage should be deployed so that management discretion is hindered. Nearly all empirical studies results used in this research are not consistent with the trade-off model. However, they are consistent with the pecking order theory. The pecking order theory suggests that as profitability grows, leverage decreases due to the fact that firms will first raise money from internal funds and then will resort to debt financing and finally equity (Brealey et al., 2007).[18] In the case of developing economies, however, some empirical studies (Delcoure, 2007; and Chen, 2003) suggest a modified pecking

---

16. R.A. Brealey, S.C. Myers and A.J. Marcus, *Fundamentals of Corporate Finance* (New York: McGraw Hill/Irwin, 2007).
17. M. Jensen and W. Meckling. "Theory of the Firm: Managerial Behavior, Agency Costs and Capital Structure," *Journal of Financial Economics* 3 (1976): 305–360.
18. Brearley et al., *Fundamentals of Corporate Finance*

theory is followed – retained earnings, equity, and lastly, debt.[19] The profitability measure that is used for the purpose of this research is net operating income over total assets.

Growth Opportunities

According to Myers (2003), and Jensen and Meckling (1976) the higher the growth opportunities, the lower debt is used.[20] With the opportunity to grow, managers are enticed to use more debt in a way that may expropriate wealth from debt holders to stock holders, that is undertake riskier projects so as to generate higher returns for stockholders at the expense of bondholders. Bondholders, when suspecting such behavior, may either ask for higher risk premium, or add more protective covenants to deter such behavior. They may even chose to stop funding altogether. These actions restrict managers' ability to issue debt and accordingly lead to lower debt ratios. Market-to-book ratio of total assets is used to measure growth opportunities. Studies done by Wiwattankantang (1999) and Delcoure (2007) support this view.[21] Market to book value ratio is used to measure growth opportunities.

Size

The relationship between leverage and size is not clear yet. Most of the empirical studies used for the purpose of this paper show that size is positively correlated to leverage. This can be attributed to the fact that firms that are large in size are well diversified and thus exhibit lower bankruptcy risk (Brealey et al., 2007). Size is measured as the natural logarithm of total asset.

Tangibility

The existence of debt requires firms to have assets as collateral to secure the debts. Whether a firm has collateral depends on its asset structure. The more tangible assets a firm has, the more the debt is secured and thus is deployed. Tangibility is measured as net fixed assets over total assets.

---

19. N. Delcoure, "The Determinants of Capital Structure in Transitional Economies," *International Review of Economics & Finance* 16 (2007): 400; J. Chen, "Determinants of Capital Structure of Chinese-listed Companies," Journal of Business Research 57 (2003): 1341-51.
20. S.C. Myers, "Financing of Corporations," in *Handbook of the Economics of Finance: Corporate Finance* edited by G. Constantinides, M. Harris and R. Stulz (North Holland: Elsevier, 2003); Jensen and Meckling, "Theory of the Firm."
21. Y. Wiwattanakantang, "An Empirical Study on the Determinants of the Capital Structure of Thai Firms." ; Delcoure, "The Determinants of Capital Structure in Transitional Economies."

Risk

As the trade-off theory suggests, the higher risk a firm entails the lower leverage is used for the reason that loss would be amplified (Brealey et. al.2007). Empirical studies support this theory. Risk is measured by the ratio of the standard deviation of net operating income to total assets.

3. The Model

We model leverage based on the set of the above-mentioned firm-specific factors and control for market conditions by adding real GDP growth rate, inflation, and growth rate of money supply (M2).

(1) $Yit = \alpha + \sum \beta KXK,it + \eta t + \varepsilon it$

where Yit is a measure of leverage of firm i at time t, X is the vector of explanatory variables. These are measures of profitability, growth opportunity, risk, tangibility, and size. ηt represents time specific macroeconomic effects, in our case, GDP growth, money supply growth and inflation.

Because of the high correlation between GDP, inflation, and M2, the assumption of independence of the explanatory variables is not met. This may cause the regression coefficients to be overestimated, underestimated, or with the wrong algebraic sign. Accordingly, the instrumental variable technique is used, where inflation and GDP are used as explanatory variable for M2. The model specification becomes:

(2) $Yit = \alpha 0 + \Sigma \beta KXK,it + m2t + \varepsilon it$

(3) $m2t = \alpha 1 + \lambda 1gdpit \ \lambda 21inflationit + \omega it$

To estimate equations 2 and 3, the data for all four countries is pooled and three country dummy variables are used representing Saudi Arabia, Qatar, and UAE. The dummy variable for a given country takes a value of 1 if the firm operates in that particular country and 0 otherwise. A significant coefficient of a country dummy would suggest that there are country-specific determinants of leverage.

Differences in results between OLS and 2SLS are reported in Table 5a (see Appendix to this chapter).

4. Findings

Descriptive statistics about the DVs and the IVs are presented in Table 2 and Table 3, respectively (see Appendix to this chapter). Correlation matrix is presented in Table 4. Table 3 shows that leverage is predominantly in the form of short term-debt, as the ratio of bsdta is consistently higher than that of bldta. This is mainly due to the fact that banks impose tenure on several types of business loans, giving no choice to firms but to borrow short term even when financing long-term capital budgeting needs. It also shows that firms in the UAE use more leverage than their GCC counterparts, followed by Qatar. Bahraini firms are the least leveraged. They are also the least likely to use long-term debt. Eight out of the 17 Bahraini firms in the sample have not contracted any long-term debt in the 10 years under study. In the case of Saudi Arabia, 39 out of the 85 firms in the sample have made either no use or occasional use of long-term debt. This may be due to religious reasons, as firms will avoid interest bearing financing and may opt to use different forms of sharia-compliant modes of financing. Given these constraints, it can be assumed that firms are using internal funds for financing, in line with the 'modified' pecking order theory. Table 3 also reveals that the average debt to equity ratio, bde, is negative in the case of Qatari firms, leading to major departure from normality (large skewness and kurtosis). This rather unusual observation for listed firms was due to one firm, a gas company, having a negative equity in 2008 due to large hedging reserves against its interest rate exposure.

Like Rajan and Zingales (1995),[22] and Booth et al. (2001),[23] I find that leverage in GCC countries is influenced by size (lassets), profitability (profit) and collateral (fata). Like Antoniou (2007),[24] I also find a positive country effect, mostly in the case of Qatar and the UAE. However, I also find differences; I find that growth opportunities (mbr) have no significant effect on leverage. An inverse relationship is reported in the case of US and other developed countries (Rajan and Zingales, 1995).[25]

The results in Tables 5 b-e and summarized in Table 6, reveal a strong positive relationship between assets and leverage. The variable 'lassets' is consistently significant at the 1 percent level irrespective of the leverage measure used. Its effect on leverage varies, however. Its effect is higher when using debt to equity ratio, as opposed to debt (total, long-term, or short-term) to total asset ratios. Similar

---

22. R. G. Rajan and L. Zingales. "What Do We Know About Capital Structure? Some Evidence from International Data," *Journal of Finance* 50 (1995): 1421-60.

23. Booth et al., "Capital Structures in Developing Countries."

24. A. Antoniou, Y. Guney, and K. Paudyal, "The Determinants of Capital Structure: Capital Market oriented versus Bank oriented Institutions," *Journal of Financial and Quantitative Analysis* 43 (2008): 59-92.

25. R. G. Rajan and L. Zingales, "What Do We Know About Capital Structure? Some Evidence from International Data."

findings are reported by Al-Ajmi et al. (2009) in the case of Saudi firms,[26] and Barakat (2008) in the case of MENA firms.[27]

The results also indicate a significant inverse relation between profit and leverage, except when short-term leverage is used. This inverse relation is consistent with the pecking order hypothesis that internal funding is preferred to the more expensive external sources. Higher profitability reduces the need for external financing, as reported by Antoniou (2007) and Flannery and Rangan (2006).[28]

The variable ndts is a positive and significant determinant of capital structure, except when long-term leverage is used. Since the GCC countries have no taxes, this implies that ndts can be construed as a proxy for collateral (Barakat 2008).[29]

Interestingly enough, risk is barely significant, and has, for the most part, a positive relation to leverage. The lack of significance may indicate poor credit analysis by credit providers, mostly banks. It may also be due to the predominantly short-term tenure of firm loans, requiring less credit analysis from banks.

Conclusion

Financial systems are bank-dominated in the GCC countries. Firms' access to bank credit is still limited when measured against GCC countries' GDP. The bond market is still underdeveloped and is dominated by sovereign entities. Stock markets lost their appeal after the downturn they witnessed in recent years. This greatly constrains the GCC firms' ability to raise funds.

GCC firms' financing is mostly short term and is determined by size and profitability for the most part. Around 25 percent of firms in the sample have no long-term debt. This assumes a 'modified' pecking order in the case of GCC firms, that is, firms will use internal funds, short-term debt, the equity market, and whenever possible, the bond market.

---

26. J. Al-Ajmi, H. Abo Hussain, and N. Al-Saleh, N. "Decisions on Capital Structure in a Zakat Environment with Prohibition of Riba: The Case of Saudi Arabia," *The Journal of Risk Finance* 10 (2009): 460+.
27. M. Barakat, "Determinants of Corporate Borrowing in the Arab World," OSU Ph.D. dissertation, 2003.
28. M. J. Flannery and K.P. Rangan. "Partial Adjustment toward Target Capital Structures," *Journal of Financial Economics* 79 (2006): 469-506.
29. M. Barakat, "A Test of the Agency Conflict and Control Effect on Capital Structure: the Case of Middle Eastern Arab Countries," *Journal of Academy of Business and Economics* (February 2008), available at http://www.accessmylibrary.com/article-1G1-192587633/test-agency-conflict-and.html (accessed July 24, 2010).

An area of future research could be to introduce industry classifications into the analysis. Industry classification is not standardized across GCC countries. Ship building, for instance, and airline companies are both classified as 'transportation' with Zawya classification. Industry effect will be tested once classification is finalized. Differences are likely to exist between different sectors, mainly the real estate and construction sectors.

Appendix

Table 1: Variables, Definitions

Variable	Definition	Expected Sign	Selected Studies on Capital Structure
Capital Structure Measures - The dependent variables			
BTDTA	Book value of total debt to total assets		
BLTTA	Book value of long-term debt to total assets		
BSTTA	Book value of short-term debt to total assets		
BDE	Book value of total debt to total assets		
M2	The residuals from regressing M2 growth on GDP and INFLATION in the two-stage least square.	+	
Capital Structure Determinants -Firm specific variables			
LASSETS	Natural logarithm of assets	+	Frank and Goyal (2009), Antoniou et al. (2008), Flannery and Rangan (2006), Hovakimian et al. (2004)

NDTS	Non-debt tax shield = (Depreciation + amortization)/total assets	+/-	(+) Antoniou et al. (2008), Titman and Wessels (1988) (-) Hovakimian et al. (2004)
FATA	A measure of tangibility. Fixed Asset Ratio = Net fixed assets / Total Assets	+/-	(+) Frank and Goyal (2009), Flannery and Rangan (2006) (-) Hovakimian et al. (2004)
RISK	Standard deviation of Operating Profits/total assets	-	
MBR	Measure of Growth Opportunity. MBR= (Total assets - Book value of Shareholders Equity + Market capitalization)/Total Assets	+/-	(+)Frank and Goyal. (2009), MacKay and Philips (2005) (-) Antoniou et al. (2008), Flannery and Rangan (2006), Hovakimian et al. (2004)
PROFIT	Profit=Net Operating Income/Total assets	-	Frank and Goyal (2009), Antoniou et al. (2008), Flannery and Rangan (2006)
L1(DV)	Lagged leverage (ex. L1BTDTA = Book value of Total debt to total assets, lagged one year)	+	Antoniou et al. (2008), Frank and Goyal (2004), Ozkan (2001)
Control variables			
GDP	Growth rate of real GDP	+	
INFLATION	Price change, %	?/+	(+) Frank and Goyal (2009)
COUNTRY DUMMIES	Dummy variables that take the value of 1 if listed on the stock market of a particular country, 0 otherwise. Used to test for Country effect.		

Table 2: Descriptive Statistics - Independent Variables, by Country

This table reports descriptive statistics of the variables used in our main regressions. Table 1 provides the definitions and data sources for these variables. The sample period is 2000 to 2009.

Country		lassets	ndts	fata	risk	mbr	profit	gdp	inflation	m2
Bahrain	mean	11.35	1.57	26.11	7.00	142.90	5.12	6.31	2.55	16.01
	sd	1.15	1.94	21.84	11.65	73.94	11.52	1.66	0.74	11.56
	skewness	0.87	1.17	1.04	4.88	1.62	-1.95	-0.98	-1.05	0.92
	kurtosis	3.76	3.38	3.08	33.63	6.33	10.60	2.99	5.98	2.80
KSA	mean	12.60	3.76	43.84	4.75	253.28	7.49	11.95	3.26	16.12
	sd	1.63	3.48	23.60	5.34	188.10	8.75	4.18	3.23	5.51
	skewness	0.89	4.44	-0.16	4.06	3.19	0.45	-0.31	1.00	-0.09
	kurtosis	4.16	35.07	2.07	26.44	17.60	3.44	1.90	2.85	1.44
Qatar	mean	13.13	1.96	31.55	7.34	274.74	5.13	12.39	7.74	26.69
	sd	1.68	1.80	25.19	11.18	277.28	9.13	3.84	6.91	10.20
	skewness	-0.18	0.83	0.72	2.99	3.71	0.22	-0.34	-0.75	0.39
	kurtosis	2.45	2.68	2.48	12.75	20.03	6.34	1.84	2.23	1.53
UAE	mean	12.44	2.92	30.95	6.28	184.01	6.40	6.80	6.71	23.25
	sd	1.94	2.81	21.43	6.22	161.41	6.62	3.69	3.81	10.29
	skewness	0.25	2.02	0.47	2.45	2.55	0.80	-0.71	0.01	0.57
	kurtosis	2.59	9.54	2.44	10.94	9.67	6.35	2.78	1.57	2.17
Overall	mean	12.51	3.11	37.83	5.64	232.10	6.69	10.47	4.43	18.88
	sd	1.71	3.14	24.29	7.55	194.52	8.87	4.56	4.35	9.12
	skewness	0.58	4.03	0.19	4.71	3.64	-0.18	-0.11	0.65	0.93
	kurtosis	3.35	34.29	1.97	36.91	22.92	6.98	2.20	2.77	3.58

Table 3: Descriptive Statistics - Dependent Variables, by Country

This table reports descriptive statistics of the variables used in our main regressions. Table 1 provides the definitions and data sources for these variables. The sample period is 2000 to 2009.

btdta is book value of total debt to total assets. bldta is long-term debt to total asset. bsdta is book value of short term debt to total assets, bde is book value of total debt to total equity. mtdta is market value of total debt to total assets. mldta is long-term debt to total asset. msdta is market value of short term debt to total assets, mde is market value of total debt to total equity.

country	Stats	btdta	bldta	bsdta	bde
Bahrain	mean	17.03	1.30	13.90	27.62
	sd	16.07	3.22	13.38	39.54
	skewness	1.33	3.59	1.55	3.19
	kurtosis	3.95	18.06	5.10	16.99
KSA	mean	33.17	8.59	19.37	69.30
	sd	19.82	12.28	14.62	73.34
	skewness	0.41	1.86	1.17	2.28
	kurtosis	2.17	6.22	3.82	10.63
Qatar	mean	34.29	15.86	15.93	-3145.74
	sd	22.77	19.48	13.25	39232.65
	skewness	0.78	1.63	1.16	-12.00
	kurtosis	2.88	5.58	3.58	145.00
UAE	mean	37.23	10.66	23.16	90.53
	sd	21.68	14.97	14.58	109.17
	skewness	0.23	1.50	0.75	3.11
	kurtosis	2.12	4.17	3.58	16.38
Total	mean	32.24	9.18	18.94	-390.92
	sd	20.96	13.93	14.52	14828.15
	skewness	0.52	2.08	1.10	-32.03
	kurtosis	2.38	7.77	3.76	1026.92

Table 4: Correlation Coefficients

This table provides correlation coefficients of the variables used in our main regressions. Table1 provides the definitions and data sources for these variables. The sample period is 2000 to 2009.

	btdta	bldta	bsdta	bde	ndts	fata	risk	mbr	profit	m2	gdp	inf
btdta	1.00											
bldta	0.66	1.00										
bsdta	0.69	-0.04	1.00									
bde	-0.10	-0.20	0.04	1.00								
ndts	0.12	-0.09	0.20	0.03	1.00							
fata	0.16	0.32	-0.11	-0.06	0.38	1.00						
risk	-0.04	-0.10	0.05	0.02	0.01	-0.08	1.00					
mbr	-0.05	-0.08	0.00	0.02	0.14	0.08	0.40	1.00				
profit	0.04	-0.10	0.15	0.02	0.18	0.11	0.12	0.22	1.00			
m2	0.01	0.06	-0.01	0.00	-0.13	-0.15	-0.06	-0.06	-0.03	1.00		
gdp	0.03	0.02	0.00	-0.04	0.06	0.08	-0.08	0.05	0.10	0.31	1.00	
Infl.	0.13	0.15	0.05	-0.08	-0.10	-0.08	-0.13	-0.14	-0.03	0.49	0.25	1.00

Tables 5a: Determinants of Capital Structure Using Book Value of Long-term Debt/Total Assets as a DV

This table presents regression estimates of capital structure on firm variables and macro control variables. The regression variables are described in Table 1. The sample period is 2000 to 2009. These models are estimated using OLS and 2SLS. The associated t-statistics are reported in parentheses. *, **, and *** denote significance at the 10%, 5%, and 1% levels, respectively.

	OLS		2SLS	
bldta	Coef.		Coef.	
_cons	-38.0414	***	-38.339	***
	(-12.8800)		(-12.050)	
lassets	3.3487	***	3.371	***
	(14.5500)		(14.720)	
ndts	-0.5944	***	-0.595	***
	(-4.7800)		(-4.790)	
fata	0.2093	***	0.209	***
	(13.1000)		(13.020)	
risk	-0.0900		-0.096	*
	(-1.6200)		(-1.720)	
mbr	0.0010		0.001	
	(0.4300)		(0.410)	
profit	-0.3070	***	-0.309	***
	(-7.0700)		(-7.130)	
m2	-0.0540		-0.063	
	(-1.0700)		(-0.730)	
inflation	0.0822			
	(0.8200)			
gdp	-0.0738			
	(-0.7000)			
S.Arabia	1.4854		1.096	
	(1.0700)		(0.890)	
Qatar	7.9263	***	7.971	***
	(4.8700)		(4.550)	
UAE	6.0380	***	6.384	***
	(4.1800)		(4.240)	
R2	0.3780		0.3774	
No.of Obs	984		984	

Tables 5b: Determinants of Capital Structure Using Book Value of Total Debt/Total Assets as a DV

This table presents regression estimates of capital structure on firm variables and macro control variables. The regression variables are described in Table 1. The sample period is 2000 to 2009. These models are estimated using 2SLS. The associated t-statistics are reported in parentheses. *, **, and *** denote significance at the 10%, 5%, and 1% levels, respectively.

btdta	Coef.		Coef.		Coef.		Coef.	
_cons	-34.8274	***	-40.4629	***	-36.5670	***	-37.7446	***
	(-7.24)		(-7.5600)		(-7.6700)		(-6.8900)	
lassets	5.0720	***	5.1186	***	4.5612	***	4.7159	***
	(13.54)		(13.2200)		(11.7600)		(11.9800)	
ndts	0.9517	***	1.0079	***	0.8140	***	0.8212	***
	(4.51)		(4.6700)		(3.8500)		(3.8400)	
fata	0.0714	***	0.0787	***	0.0783	***	0.0716	***
	(2.65)		(2.7800)		(2.8900)		(2.5900)	
risk	-0.0151		0.0212		0.0185		0.0373	
	(-0.17)		(0.2200)		(0.2100)		(0.3900)	
mbr	-0.0022		-0.0018		-0.0044		-0.0042	
	(-0.63)		-(0.4800)		(-1.2200)		(-1.1000)	
profit	-0.2239	***	-0.2395	***	-0.1915	***	-0.2094	***
	(-3.04)		(-3.1900)		(-2.6200)		(-2.8100)	
m2			0.2360	*			-0.0306	
			(1.7900)				(-0.2100)	
S.Arabia					8.2217	***	8.2758	***
					(3.9000)		(3.9100)	
Qatar					9.1767	***	9.3043	***
					(3.6400)		(3.0900)	
UAE					14.1600	***	14.1493	***
					(6.0400)		(5.4700)	
R2	18.75%		18.33%		21.65%		22.16%	
No. of Obs.	1008		984		1008		984	

Tables 5c: Determinants of Capital Structure Using Book Value of Long-term Debt/Total Assets as a DV

This table presents regression estimates of capital structure on firm variables and macro control variables. The regression variables are described in Table 1. The sample period is 2000 to 2009. These models are estimated using 2SLS. The associated t-statistics are reported in parentheses. *, **, and *** denote significance at the 10%, 5%, and 1% levels, respectively.

bldta	Coef.		Coef.		Coef.		Coef.	
_cons	-38.42	***	37.98	***	-42.47	***	-38.40	***
	(-13.44)		(-13.54)		(-13.60)		(-12.07)	
lassets	3.56	***	3.25	***	3.60	***	3.37	***
	(15.98)		(14.24)		(15.95)		(14.74)	
ndts	-0.61	***	-0.58	***	-0.60	***	-0.60	***
	(-4.85)		(-4.64)		(-4.73)		(-4.79)	
fata	0.19	***	0.21	***	0.20	***	0.21	***
	(12.00)		(13.11)		(12.28)		(13.02)	
risk	-0.07		-0.10	*	-0.06		-0.10	*
	(-1.27)		(-1.81)		(-1.00)		(-1.74)	
mbr	0.002		0.001		0.002		0.001	
	(0.75)		(0.48)		(0.89)		(0.48)	
profit	-0.35	***	-0.31	***	-0.35	***	-0.31	***
	(-7.95)		(-7.25)		(-7.97)		(-7.16)	
m2					0.16	**	-0.06	
					(2.02)		(-0.73)	
S.Arabia			1.19				1.08	
			(0.96				(0.88)	
Qatar			7.43	***			7.94	***
			(5.01)				(4.54)	
UAE			6.23	***			6.37	***
			(4.52)				(4.24)	
R2	32.58%		36.20%		34.20%		37.75%	
No. of Obs.	1008		984		1008		984	

Tables 5d: Determinants of Capital Structure Using Book Value of Short-term Debt/Total Assets as a DV

This table presents regression estimates of capital structure on firm variables and macro control variables. The regression variables are described in Table 1. The sample period is 2000 to 2009. These models are estimated using 2SLS. The associated t-statistics are reported in parentheses. *, **, and *** denote significance at the 10%, 5%, and 1% levels, respectively.

bsdta	Coef.		Coef.		Coef.		Coef.	
_cons	9.0589	***	7.0519	*	7.3618	**	6.5905	*
	(2.5800)		(1.8100)		(2.1100)		(1.6400)	
lassets	0.8091	***	0.7913	***	0.6280	**	0.6502	**
	(2.9600)		(2.8100)		(2.2100)		(2.2500)	
ndts	1.2771	***	1.3302	***	1.1658	***	1.1977	***
	(8.3100)		(8.4800)		(7.5200)		(7.6300)	
fata	-0.1280	***	-0.1297	***	-0.1289	***	-0.1360	***
	(-6.5100)		(-6.3000)		(-6.5000)		(-6.7000)	
risk	0.0716		0.1012		0.1042		0.1295	*
	(1.1000)		(1.4600)		(1.5800)		(1.8400)	
mbr	-0.0042	*	-0.0043		-0.0050	*	-0.0051	*
	(-1.6400)		(-1.6000)		(-1.8800)		(-1.8300)	
profit	0.1796	***	0.1692	***	0.1829	***	0.1680	***
	(3.3400)		(3.1000)		(3.4100)		(3.0700)	
m2			0.1107				0.0355	
			(1.1500)				(0.3300)	
S.Arabia					4.7672	***	4.9303	***
					(3.0800		(3.1700)	
Qatar					2.1545		1.8217	
					(1.1700		(0.8200)	
UAE					7.5077	***	7.3232	***
					(4.3700		(3.8600)	
R2	10.42%		10.09%		12.46%		12.70%	
No. of Obs.	1008		984		1008		984	

Tables 5e : Determinants of Capital Structure Using Book Value of Total Debt to Total Equity Ratio as a DV

This table presents regression estimates of capital structure on firm variables and macro control variables. The regression variables are described in Table 1. The sample period is 2000 to 2009. These models are estimated using 2SLS. The associated t-statistics are reported in parentheses. *, **, and *** denote significance at the 10%, 5%, and 1% levels, respectively.

bde	Coef.		Coef.		Coef.		Coef.	
_cons	-196.74	***	-212.23	***	-199.32	***	-198.95	***
	(-9.11)		(-8.81)		(-9.24)		(-7.99)	
lassets	21.71	***	22.00	***	20.26	***	20.84	***
	(12.91)		(12.62)		(11.55)		(11.63)	
ndts	1.63	*	1.81	*	1.52		1.55	
	(1.72)		(1.86)		(1.59)		(1.60)	
fata	0.17		0.19		0.24	*	0.22	*
	(1.42)		(1.52)		(1.94)		(1.73)	
risk	-0.21		-0.14		-0.26		-0.26	
	(-0.53)		(-0.33)		(-0.65)		(-0.60)	
mbr	-0.01		-0.01		-0.01		-0.01	
	(-0.66)		(-0.57)		(-0.79)		(-0.76)	
profit	-1.68	***	-1.73	***	-1.54	***	-1.58	***
	(-5.07)		(-5.11)		(-4.66)		(-4.65)	
m2			0.56				-0.39	
			(0.94)				(-0.58)	
S.Arabia					13.20		13.24	
					(1.38)		(1.37)	
Qatar					30.33	***	33.77	**
					(2.66)		(2.46)	
UAE					40.31	***	42.48	***
					(3.80)		(3.61)	
R2	15.82%		15.82%		17.52%		18.12%	
No. of Obs.	1008		984		1008		984	

Table 6: Summary of Findings across Different Model Specifications

This table presents summary results of regression estimates using different definitions of capital structure. The regression variables are described in Table 1. The sample period is 2000 to 2009. These models are estimated using 2SLS. The associated t-statistics are reported in parentheses. *, **, and *** denote significance at the 10%, 5%, and 1% levels, respectively.

		Expected Sign	btdta	bldta	bsdta	bde
cst	Significance level		1%	1%	1%	1%
	Sign		(-)	(-)	(+)	(-)
lassets	Significance level		1%	1%	1%	1%
	Sign	+	(+)	(+)	(+)	(+)
ndts	Significance level		1%	1%	1%	10%1
	Sign	+/-	(+)	(-)	(+)	(+)
fata	Significance level		1%	1%	1%	10%2
	Sign	+/-	(+)	(+)	(+)	(+)
risk	Significance level		.	10%2	10%3	.
	Sign	-	(+)	(-)	(+)	(+)
mbr	Significance level		.	.	10%4	.
	Sign	+/-	(-)	(+)	(-)	(-)
profit	Significance level		1%	1%	1%	1%
	Sign	-	(-)	(-)	(+)	(-)

m2	Significance level		10%1	5%1	.	.
	Sign	+	(+)	(+)/(-)5	(+)	(+)/(-)5
S.Arabia	Significance level		1%	.	1%	.
	Sign		(+)	(+)	(+)	(+)
Qatar	Significance level		1%	1%	.	1%
	Sign		(+)	(+)	(+)	(+)
UAE	Significance level		1%	1%	1%	1%
	Sign		(+)	(+)	(+)	(+)

Notes:

1. Significant in the absence of country dummies.
2. Significant in the presence of country dummies only.
3. Significant only when country dummies are present, and m2 is not included in the model
4. Significant only when country dummies are present.
5. Negative when country dummies are introduced.

References

Al-Ajmi, J., H. Abo Hussain, and N. Al-Saleh. 2009. Decisions on capital structure in a Zakat environment with prohibition of Riba: The case of Saudi Arabia. *The Journal of Risk Finance* 10, 460+.

Al-Najjar, B. and P. Taylor. 2008. The relationship between capital structure and ownership structure: New evidence from Jordanian panel data. *Managerial Finance* 34, 919-933.

Antoniou, A., Y. Guney and K. Paudyal. 2008. The determinants of capital structure: capital market oriented versus bank oriented institutions. *Journal of Financial and Quantitative Analysis* 43, 59-92.

Autore, D. and T. Kovacs. 2004., The pecking order theory and time varying adverse selection costs. Working paper, Virginia Technical University.

Baker, M. and J. Wurgler. 2002. Market timing and capital structure. *Journal of Finance* 57, 1-31.

Barakat, M. 2008. A test of the agency conflict and control effect on capital structure: the case of Middle Eastern Arab countries. *Journal of Academy of Business and Economics* (February), available at http://www.accessmylibrary.com/article-1G1-192587633/test-agency-conflict-and.html (accessed July 24, 2010).

Barakat, M. 2003. Determinants of corporate borrowing in the Arab world. OSU Ph.D. dissertation.

Bie, T. and L. Hann. 2004. Does market timing drive capital structures? A panel data study for Dutch firms. Working paper no. 14. The Nederlandsche Bank NV.

Booth, L., V. Aivazian, A. Demirguc-Kunt, and V. Maksimovic. 2001. Capital structures in developing countries. *Journal of Finance* 56, 87-130.

Brealey R.A., S.C. Myers and A.J. Marcus. 2007. *Fundamentals of corporate finance.* New York:McGraw Hill.

Chen, J. 2003. Determinants of capital structure of Chinese-listed companies. *Journal of Business Research* 57, 1341-51.

Delcoure, N. 2007. The determinants of capital structure in transitional economies. *International Review of Economics & Finance* 16, 400.

Fischer, E., R. Heinkel, and J. Zechner. 1989. Dynamic capital structure choice: theory and tests. *Journal of Finance* 44, 19–40.

Flannery, M.J. and K.P. Rangan. 2006. Partial adjustment toward target capital structures. *Journal of Financial Economics* 79, 469-506.

Frank, M.Z. and V.K. Goyal. 2003. Testing the pecking order theory of capital structure. *Journal of Financial Economics* 67, 217–248.

Frank, M.Z. and V.K. Goyal. 2004. The effect of market conditions on capital structure adjustment. *Finance Research Letters* 1, 47-55.

Frank, M.Z. and V.K. Goyal. 2009. Capital structure decisions: which factors are reliably important? *Financial Management* 38, 1-37.

Friend, I. and L. Lang. 1988. An empirical test of the impact of managerial self-interest on corporate capital structure. *Journal of Finance* 43, 271-281.

Hart, O. and J. Moore. 1994. A theory of debt based on the inalienability of human capital. *Quarterly Journal of Economics* 109, 841–879.

Hovakimian, A., G. Hovakimian, and H. Tehranian. 2004. Determinants of target capital structure: the case of dual debt and equity issues. *Journal of Financial Economics* 71, 517-540.

Hovakimian, A., T.C. Opler and S. Titman. 2001. The debt-equity choice. *Journal of Financial and Quantitative Analysis* 36, 1–24.

Jensen, M.C. 1986. Agency costs of free cash flow, corporate finance, and takeovers. *American Economic Review* 76, 323–329.

Jensen, M. and W. Meckling. 1976. Theory of the firm: Managerial behavior, agency costs and capital structure. *Journal of Financial Economics* 3, 305–360.

Kraus, A. and R. H. Litzenberger. 1973. A state preference model of optimal financial leverage. *Journal of Finance* 28, 911-922.

MacKay, P. and G. M. Phillips. 2005. How does industry affect firm financial structure? *Review of Financial Studies* 18, 1433-1466.

Mahajan, A. and S. Tartaroglu. 2008. Equity market timing and capital structure: international evidence. *Journal of Banking & Finance* 32, 754-766.

Modigliani, F. and M.H. Miller. 1958. The cost of capital, corporate finance and the theory of investment. *American Economic Review* 48, 261-296.

Myers, S.C. 1984. The capital structure puzzle. *Journal of Finance* 39, 575–592.

Myers, S.C. 2003. Financing of corporations. In *Handbook of the Economics of Finance: Corporate Finance* edited by G. Constantinides, M. Harris and R. Stulz, R. North Holland: Elsevier.

Myers, S. and N. Majluf. 1984. Corporate financing and investment decisions when firms have information that investors do not have. *Journal of Financial Economics* 13, 187-221.

Ozkan, A. 2001. Determinants of capital structure and adjustment to long run target: evidence from UK company panel data. *Journal of Business Finance and Accounting* 28, 175-198.

Rajan, R.G. and L. Zingales. 1995. What Do We Know About Capital Structure? Some Evidence from International Data. *Journal of Finance*, 1995, 50 (5): 1421-60.

Tian, G.G. 2007. Capital structure and corporate performance: evidence from Jordan. *Australasian Accounting Business & Finance Journal.* FindArticles.com. May 9, 2010. http://findarticles.com/p/articles/mi_qa5450/is_200712/ai_n24392959/

Warner, J. B. 1977. Bankruptcy costs: some evidence. *Journal of Finance* 32, 337-348.

Wiwattanakantang, Y. 1999. An empirical study on the determinants of the capital structure of Thai Firms. *Pacific-Basin Finance Journal* 7, 371-403.

6

Repercussions of Dubai's Debt Crisis

Eckart Woertz

Introduction

For long, Dubai has been regarded as a specific development model, an alternative to the dominating oil-based rentier states in the region. Traditionally more trade-minded than neighboring emirates like Abu Dhabi, it embarked on a course of economic diversification early on, even before the exploitation of oil, which started in the 1960s. In the 1950s, the Dubai Creek was dredged to accommodate seagoing traffic more easily; at the end of the 1970s, the Jebel Ali Port was built; and in 1983 and 1985, Dubai Dry Docks and Emirates Airline were founded. All these projects mixed entrepreneurial spirit and openness towards trade with a sizable debt component. In the case of the Dubai Creek project, credit was extended by the ruler of Kuwait; in recent times, international capital markets have played an ever growing role. Encouraged by the early successes, Shaikh Mohammed bin Rashid Al-Maktoum, UAE Vice-President and Prime Minister and Ruler of Dubai, who is the mastermind behind the contemporary vision of Dubai as a trade and service hub, pulled out all stops at the end of the 1990s. The growth in projects and debt was unprecedented, especially after real estate investments in specified zones were legalized for foreigners in 2002. Real estate and construction have formed a mainstay of the economy with a share of about 25 percent.[1] If multiplier effects are considered, their importance is even higher: they required ancillary services like

1. See Figure 4 in Appendix to this chapter.

marketing, and the sizable workforce in these two sectors has been an important demand factor in the city's retail sector.

The Dubai debt crisis exposed the perils of reliance on debt-financed and often speculative real estate investments. At the same time, many of Dubai's outward-looking sectors like aviation, logistics or aluminum have been affected by a business slump in the wake of the global financial crisis. The debt standstill request for the government-owned companies Dubai World and Nakheel in November 2009 marked a watershed event in the economic development of Dubai. Before this, markets had assumed an implicit government guarantee for such companies; now that such a guarantee has not materialized, and Abu Dhabi has shown up to the rescue only selectively, refinancing on international markets has become more expensive and difficult for Dubai entities. Matching increased costs of capital with growing economic activity is a challenge in the prevailing global environment. Therefore, reliance on Abu Dhabi in the ongoing restructuring process will increase and come with trade-offs. A possible outcome will be greater centralization of the UAE and a recalibration of Dubai's development strategy. While the real estate sector is still troubled and has failed to deliver on its lofty promises, Dubai has reached critical mass as a regional trading hub and can build on this strength.

This chapter first examines the debt structure of Dubai and analyzes how Dubai's refinancing conditions have changed. Then it assesses the effect on different Dubai companies and which sectors have been most affected by the crisis. Islamic banking is given special consideration as Dubai had been one of the largest issuers of dollar-denominated Islamic bonds (*sukuk*) before the crisis. Problems of the legal framework, most notably the bankruptcy law, are outlined subsequently. The chapter also discusses the crisis management of the Dubai government and whether Abu Dhabi's increased role will likely lead to increased centralization of the UAE. Finally, the troubled Dubai model is juxtaposed with prevailing theories about the rentier state.

1. Dubai's Debt Structure

Transparency is missing when it comes to Dubai's debt situation. Official data about the consolidated gross debt of the government and the companies it owns is not published. One has to rely on estimates of debt in the form of bonds and syndicated loans for which information is available in the public domain. In November 2009, Moody's gauged this debt load to be between $80 billion and $100 billion, with a preference of erring at the upper end of that range at $100 billion.[2] The IMF put this number slightly higher in February 2010 at $109 billion.[3] This number, however, does not include other forms of debt for which no public data exists such as syndicated loans with incomplete documentation, bilateral loans from local and international banks, accounts payables and suppliers' credit or derivatives, credit commitments and other liabilities.[4] If estimates on these are included, the number grows further and could be as high as $130 billion-$170 billion, the investment bank EFG Hermes opined in its UAE 2010 Yearbook.[5] These numbers have been disputed, especially the estimate of up to $24 billion possible exposure of Emirates Bank NBD to Dubai Inc. entities, which appears hardly reconcilable with publicly available data about the bank's overall outstanding loans and liabilities.[6] The wide range of the estimates reveals considerable uncertainty, especially with regard to bilateral loans of local banks. In February 2010, Moody's estimated the overall exposure of local UAE banks to Dubai World alone at $15 billion.[7] In April, it reduced its estimate to around $10 billion and regarded the exposure as "manageable."[8] Given Dubai's GDP of $82 billion, debt load estimates represent between 100 and nearly 200 percent of GDP, depending on the estimate, which is in any case substantial. If the lower end of $80 billion is taken, it represents nine times the Dubai government's 2008 revenues and has the potential to severely stress fiscal abilities.[9]

The restructuring of Dubai World will apply only to a fraction of this debt and only to the holding company and two of its real estate subsidiaries, Nakheel and Limitless. Dubai Ports World (DPW) and Jebel Ali Free Zone (JAFZ) have been exempted from the restructuring. Both these entities have viable business models with ongoing cash flows and have benefited from the recovery in international freight rates since March 2009. They are seen relatively favorably by analysts; not everything in Dubai is as apocalyptic as a cursory glance at newspaper headlines

2. Moody's, "Dubai Inc. Credit Environment. Update & Outlook," Special Comment, November 2009.
3. IMF, *United Arab Emirates: 2009 Article IV Consultation – Staff Report*, IMF Country Report No. 10/42, Washington D. C., February 2010.
4. Ibid.
5. *Daily Star*, January 21, 2010. Publicly known debt of syndicated loans and bonds was estimated to be at $96.6 billion in this report.
6. Sher View Blogspot, "Is Dubai Inc's Debt Really $170 Billion?" January 19, 2010, available at http://aqsher.blogspot.com/2010/01/is-dubai-incs-debt-really-170-billion.html .
7. Moody's, Weekly Credit Outlook, February 22, 2010.
8. "Dubai World Plan Not to Affect Banks," *Khaleej Times*, April 10, 2010.
9. Moody's, "Dubai Inc."

sometimes seems to suggest. JAFZ has actually paid a coupon in time only a few days after the standstill request of its parent company. That the DW subsidiaries Istithmar World and Infinity World have been exempted from the restructuring as well has come as a surprise to many as these companies have engaged in leveraged and ill-fated foreign investments that can be hardly regarded as the core business of DW (e.g. MGM Mirage Casino Las Vegas or Barney's New York). In the meantime, however, they and other Dubai Inc. entities have started to divest some of their overseas assets in order to improve their liquidity position. Istithmar has sold its share in Indian budget airline Spicejet and is trying to find a buyer for its holding in Inchcape Shipping Services, a London-based marine services group, while Dubai Holding is looking to sell its 40 percent share in Malaysia's Bank Islam. [10]

Dubai World's liabilities amount to a widely quoted $59 billion. However, this figure refers to liabilities, not debt instruments alone but also unpaid contractor bills or land grants, according to Deutsche Bank.[11] The amount of debt proper has been estimated to be $22 billion-$24 billion, and on the eve of further announcements, Barclay's assumed that $18 billion of this amount would be part of the restructuring process. After a nerve-wracking weekend without detailed information, Dubai World finally specified that a higher amount of $26 billion of debt will be restructured.

Immediately after the standstill request, Barclay's identified ca. $16 billion of debt at the three entities that are up for restructuring: $8.5 billion at Nakheel (including local currency debt), $5.5 billion at Dubai World holding company, and $1.2 billion at Limitless. This left ca. $10 billion of debt for which no public information exists and which most likely consists of private bilateral loans at Dubai World or Limitless, as Barclay's assumes that Nakheel has not borrowed much additional funds since its last balance sheet date before the standstill request (December 31, 2008).[12]

With regard to the overall debt load of Dubai, two factors are worrisome: First, the maturity profile of outstanding debts is very short term. From 2010 to 2012, $50 billion of debts are due, $12-$13 billion in 2010 and a staggering $25 billion in 2011 alone. Dubai will need to refinance this debt at significantly higher costs, as markets have dropped their assumption of an implicit government

10. *Gulf Times*, February 7, 2010; *Financial Times*, February 9, 2010.

11. Wayne Arnold, "Exploding Dubai's Debt Myth," *The National*, December 2010, available athttp://www.thenational.ae/apps/pbcs.dll/article?AID=/20091130/BUSINESS/711309922&SearchID=73386884052317 .

12. Barclay's Capital, "Dubai's Debt – Whose Problem is It?" *Emerging Market Research*, November 30, 2009.

guarantee. Secondly, there is a substantial amount of bad debt, which is not backed anymore by viable assets or business models. As per Moody's estimates, this bad debt may amount to $25 billion.[13] Eventually someone will need to take this loss in a bailout or a restructuring. The bargaining on who that will be has arguably begun with Dubai World's standstill request. According to Dubai World's debt restructuring proposal that was revealed in March 2010, it will not be the Nakheel bondholders, as its two outstanding *sukuk* bonds are scheduled to be paid in full and in time. Banks will be less well off. They will receive tradable securities with maturities of five and eight years for their outstanding principal, with sub-commercial levels of interest payments that are still under negotiation. Suppliers will need to take haircuts as well. They will receive a cash payment of Dh500 ($135), which would satisfy a lot of the smaller contractors. The larger companies will only receive 40 percent of their receivables and will get paid the remaining 60 percent in the form of a "tradable security" with a maturity of five years, whose specifications are still under negotiation as well. Dubai and Abu Dhabi will foot part of the bill. The Dubai World owner, Dubai government, will inject $9.5 billion into the company; $5.7 billion have been earmarked from the earlier $10 billion bailout bond of Abu Dhabi and another $3.8 billion will come out of the pockets of the Dubai government itself.[14]

Overall, the proposal has been received positively by stock markets, and large banks like HSBC have taken the lead in endorsing it. In May 2010, a deal was cut with a core group of seven leading creditor banks which held 60 per cent of the $14.4 billion debt of the Dubai World holding company. Finally, on September 10, a formal agreement with 99 percent of the creditors was reached thus avoiding costly lawsuits and arbitration procedures. Only one US fund continued to oppose the agreement which commits to restructuring a total of $24.9 billion, including $10 billion that are owed to the government of the UAE. Property developer Nakheel would negotiate its $10.5 billion of bank loans and unpaid bills separately and would be split from the conglomerate as part of the restructuring proposal. Dubai Holding, a large conglomerate owned by the Dubai ruler personally, is also at the beginning of negotiating a restructuring of its debt. Its non-financial arm asked for a deferring of loan payments for a second time in September 2010.[15]

13. Moody's, "Dubai Inc."

14. Andrew England, Simeon Kerr, Robin Wigglesworth, "Dubai World in Line for $9.5bn Injection," and "Bondholders Have Most Reason to be Happy," *Financial Times*, March 25, 2010.

15. Robin Wigglesworth, James Drummond, "Dubai World Agrees Terms with Creditors," *Financial Times*, September 10, 2010.

2. Changing Conditions for Refinancing

Dubai has always been proud to be a state that is run like a corporation. Given the lack of a tax base and the small share (11 percent) of government spending in the overall Dubai GDP, one could in fact argue that the state is its corporations and is as much in trouble as them if they are in dire straits. The market discounted this; with the breakout of the global financial crisis, its assumption of an implicit government guarantee relied increasingly on Abu Dhabi's willingness to help Dubai out if need be. This view seemed to be vindicated by Abu Dhabi's actions. At the beginning of 2009, it helped to refinance struggling Borse Dubai and via the Central Bank it provided liquidity support of Dh120bn ($32bn) to the UAE's banks. Most notably, it purchased a $10 billion bond issued by Dubai under a $20 billion bond program in March 2009. The unsecured five-year bond formally had no strings attached and its very preferential rate of 4 percent would not have been achievable for Dubai on the free market at that time.

Dubai executives encouraged the market's view of an implicit government guarantee by self-confident statements, and the market continued to treat companies owned by the government (e.g. Dubai World) or the ruling family (e.g. Dubai Holding) as "quasi-sovereign" proxies for the credit quality of the Dubai government, which itself has issued only a few debts of $3.7 billion in dollar and local currency and does not have a credit rating.

The first signs of retreat appeared in October 2009, when the Dubai government was able to tap international debt markets for the first time in a year after the eruption of the global financial crisis. It raised $2 billion in an Islamic bond issue. In the bond prospectus it distanced itself from its corporations by denying an explicit government guarantee in order to look more attractive for investors in its new bond. This prompted Moody's to downgrade five of the six Dubai government-related companies it is currently rating, even before the recent standstill request.[16]

As the implicit government guarantee has disappeared, markets now need to value Dubai's government-owned companies on a stand-alone basis. However, this task is extremely difficult, if not impossible, given the lack of transparency and data. Before the standstill request, Moody's gave Dubai companies investment grade rating only because of the implicit government guarantee, which in turn was tied to Abu Dhabi's support waiting in the background. With the exception of DPW, it regarded all of them (DEWA, DIFC Inv., Dubai Holding, JAFZ, Emaar) as

16. Moody's, "Dubai Inc."

speculative grade on a stand-alone basis and in fact has further downgraded them after the debt standstill request.

Standard & Poor's (S&P) has also cut credit ratings of National Bank of Dubai, Dubai Islamic Bank, Mashreqbank and Emirates Bank International after the standstill to account for their Dubai World debt exposure. Without implicit government guarantee, companies like DP World, DIFC Investments, JAFZ, Dubai Multi Commodities Center Authority, Dubai Holding Commercial Operations Group and Emaar Properties PJSC were downgraded to junk status. In a remarkable move, S&P withdrew its rating of Dubai Holding in January 2010, citing insufficient and untimely provision of information as reason. Dubai Holding reacted one day later by dropping S&P as its rating agency, arguing that it has shown "lack of understanding of the holding firm's business, its operations and relationship with the Government of Dubai."[17]

Reassessment of credit risk has also extended to Abu Dhabi related entities that do not have explicit government guarantees. Moody's downgraded the ratings of seven government-owned companies in Abu Dhabi in March 2010, such as Mubadala Development Company, International Petroleum Investment Company (IPIC), Tourism Development & Investment Company (TDIC), Abu Dhabi National Energy Company (TAQA), Emirates Telecommunications Company (Etisalat), Dolphin Energy (Dolphin), and Aldar Properties (Aldar).[18] Subsequently, the announcement of the DW debt restructuring plan – most notably the proposal to repay the two outstanding Nakheel bonds in full and restrict haircuts to loans – had a positive impact on markets. This led again to reassessments, this time to the upward side. S&P put the credit ratings status of five Dubai government-linked firms under review with a possible upgrade in the future.[19]

The changed refinancing conditions can be gauged from Figure 1. The costs of credit started to skyrocket at the end of 2008 as a result of the global liquidity crunch. After reaching a plateau, they eased as expansive monetary policies by central banks around the world eased pressure. At the end of 2009, there was a

17. "S&P Deals Blow to Dubai Hldg Unit, Pulls Rating," Reuters, January 25, 2010; Issac John, "Dubai Holding Drops S&P as its Rating Agency," *Khaleej Times*, January 26, 2010.

18. Andrew White, "Moody's Downgrades Seven UAE Companies," *Arabian Business*, March 4, 2010, available at http://www.arabianbusiness.com/58 2988-moodys-downgrades-seven-uae-companies .

19. Shaheen Pasha, "S&P's to Review Status of Five Dubai Govt Firms," *Arabian Business*, March 25, 2010, available at: http://www.arabianbusiness.com/584596-saampp-to-review-status-of-five-dubai-govt-firms .

renewed spike due to the eruption of the Dubai debt crisis. Initial confusion over lack of government support eased somewhat when Abu Dhabi decided to provide funds for the repayment of the Nakheel *sukuk* that was due on December 14, 2009. Still, Abu Dhabi support is clearly selective and it is not willing to foot the whole bill. Thus, considerable uncertainty prevailed until the announcement of an official proposal for debt restructuring by Dubai World at the end of March 2010 and the formal restructuring agreement in September. While relative credit costs are lower than during the height of the global financial crisis, they continue to be much higher than during the preceding five years and the sale of large bond issues is more difficult.

Figure 1: UAE Sukuk US Dollar Bond Index (AESI): Spread over LIBOR

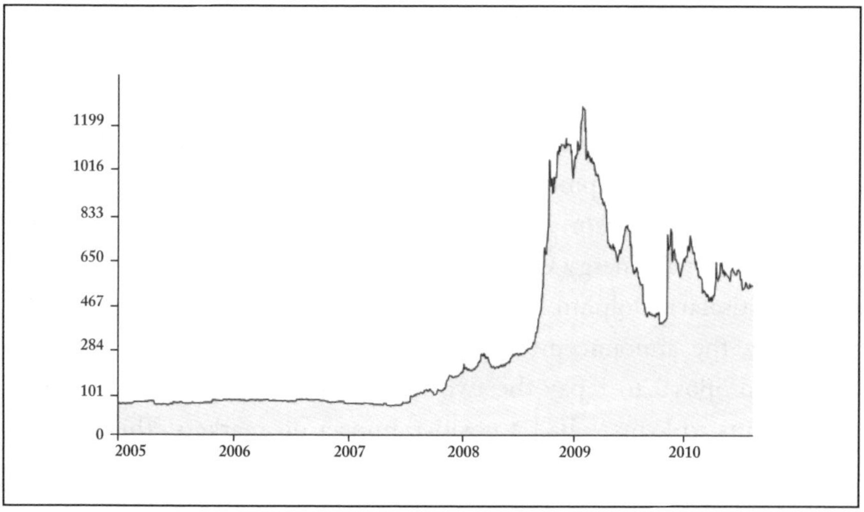

Source: HSBC, NASDAQ Dubai

3. Effect on Dubai Companies and Their Credit Risk

Apart from the problems at Dubai World, markets wonder whether credit risk may materialize at other Dubai companies. Real estate companies have been at the heart of Dubai World's debt problems and have the most pressing need for restructuring. A merger between Emaar and the real estate companies of Dubai Holding (Tatweer, Sama, Dubai Properties Group) was planned beginning the summer of 2009 but was abandoned by Emaar in December of the same year. Markets were concerned about the lower level of transparency at Dubai Holding subsidiaries and feared that the merger might have exposed Emaar to additional default risk while the land bank assets of Dubai Holdings have declined in value in the wake of the real estate slump in the emirate.[20]

A merger of the two real estate financers Tamweel and Amlak under the umbrella of the Abu Dhabi-based Real Estate Bank and the Emirates Industrial Bank (EIB) has been pending since late 2008 and shares of the companies were suspended from trading. However, on September 26, 2010, Dubai Islamic Bank announced an increase in its share in Tamweel from 20 percent to 57.33 percent, and many observers felt that this renewed assertiveness of Dubai might mark an end to the prolonged merger talks, although the fate of Amlak continued to be murky.[21] While Dubai Holdings also has a pronounced exposure to the Dubai real estate market, the maturity profile of its debt spreads out until 2017 and is a less pressing issue compared to the decidedly short-term payment schedule of Dubai companies on average. Still, its credit default swaps rose the most (146 percent) of all Dubai entities in the immediate wake of Dubai World's standstill announcement, and it must be regarded as the most vulnerable, also because of leveraged foreign investments by its subsidiary Dubai International Capital.

Pressure on the Dubai real estate market will continue, especially in less attractive areas and for unfinished projects. Modest price recoveries in the third quarter of 2009 were not fundamentally underpinned but rather a technical reaction to massive losses of about 50 percent since the price peak in the summer of 2008.[22] An already underdeveloped mortgage market collapsed by 73 percent in 2009, according to the Dubai Land Department (DLD) and cannot stimulate demand at the moment.[23] In commercial real estate in particular, a high level of inventories weighs on the market, while a simple counting of lights in apartment buildings at night reveals low occupancy rates. Foreign investment demand was crucial for the erstwhile real estate boom, but it has faded away because of the global financial crisis. With the lost trust in the wake of the Dubai World debt affair, it will be even more difficult to attract. UBS estimates that it will be difficult to raise the additional finance of $11 billion for an estimated 40,000 unfinished flats as half of the investors will likely default by the end of 2010. As trust in developers has fallen and prices in the secondary market are below initial purchasing prices, there is an incentive for investors to walk away from ongoing projects, even if this means

20. "Emaar Ends Dubai Holding Merger Talks, Debt Fears Weigh," Reuters, December 9, 2009.

21. "DIB Takes Reins at Tamweel," *The National*, September 26, 2010.

22. See for example Global Investment House, *GCC Real Estate Sector Quarterly*, March 2010.

23. Shane McGinley, "Dubai Mortgage Market down 73% in 2009," *Arabian Business*, January 11, 2010, available at: http://www.arabianbusiness.com/578467-dubai-mortgage-market-down-73-in-2009 .

forfeiting earlier down payments. Overall, UBS expects real estate prices to decline a further 30 percent in 2010.[24]

At the beginning of 2009, research by investment banks estimated that there would be a significant population decline in Dubai. These estimates varied from 8 percent of UBS to 17 percent of EFG Hermes. Shuaa Capital estimated that population declined by 9 percent to 1.54 million until the beginning of 2010.[25] However, official figures by the federal Ministry of Economy have maintained a population increase in 2009 of 7.5 percent to 1.8 million people, mainly due to migration.[26] Although traffic congestion has eased visibly, Dubai is certainly not a ghost town as some media reports wanted to make believe, and the mass exodus of expatriates that some had expected did not materialize. Still, it is difficult to see where the alleged newcomers have supposedly found work, given the obvious decrease in construction activity and the layoffs of white collar expatriates in the real estate, finance and media industries. Interestingly, collected waste officially decreased from 6.2 million to 4.9 million tons between the first and the last quarter of 2009 and puts the alleged population increase into question.[27] Statistics in the UAE are not very reliable or detailed. To add to the confusion, different official institutions use different numbers. The "official" population figures of the UN, the UAE Federal National Council (FNC), the UAE Ministry of Economy (MoE) and the UAE Ministry of Labor all differ considerably.[28] It remains to be seen whether the release of the 2010 census data will bring more clarity. Given the varying estimates and figures, suffice to say that population figures can be politically sensitive and that the officially stated increase in Dubai's population in 2009 was not enough to ward off a significant deterioration of its real estate market.

Compared to the ailing real estate sector, companies with ongoing cash flows and established business models are more resilient. In international comparison, DPW, the world's fourth largest port operator, has fared sufficiently

24. Sarmad Khan, "Dubai World Plan 'Not a Quick Property Fix'," *The National*, March 31, 2010, available at: http://www.thenational.ae/apps/pbcs.dll/article?AID=/20100331/BUSINESS/703319940/1042 .

25. Shuaa Capital, *UAE Vision* 2010, January 12, 2010, 19.

26. UAEinteract, "10,000 New Residents Arrive in Dubai Per Month," available at: http://www.uaeinteract.com/docs/10,000_new_residents_arrive_in_Dubai_per_month/40354.htm .

27. Damian Reilly, "Dubai Numbers Make Great Reading," *Arabian Business*, March 18, 2010.

28. Study by Madar Research, see "Glaring Inaccuracies in GCC Population Figures Result in Skewed Development Outlook for Gulf Countries," AMEinfo, January 4, 2010, available at: http://www.ameinfo.com/news/Company_News/M/Madar_Research_Group .

well. It may face only a slightly negative revenue growth and its maturity profile stretches out as far as 2037. The preliminary economic recovery since March 2009 has helped a lot of Dubai companies with an internationally diversified risk exposure: JAFZ, DPW and Emirates Airline benefitted from recovering trade and freight rates, while Dubai Aluminum (DUBAL), which contributes around 7 percent to Dubai GDP, was helped by improving aluminum prices after the steep correction in commodity prices in the second half of 2008. Many of the more viable companies are organized under the umbrella of the Investment Corporation of Dubai (ICD), which is increasingly emerging as Dubai's "good bank" of assets.

Established free zones such as Media City and Internet City, which are run by Dubai Holding-owned Tecom, have a relatively stable base of long-term tenants. In comparison, newer economic cities such as Silicon Oasis or the Dubai Biotechnology and Research Park (DuBiotech), will be less resilient as they are in an earlier stage of development and have less obvious competitive advantages, particularly with regard to available qualified human resources.

DIFC might also be in a less advantageous position. The financial sector has been particularly hit by the global crisis, and Dubai's image as a financial hub has been severely tarnished by the Dubai World debt saga. Regional competitors like Bahrain and Qatar may be able to use this to their advantage. Abu Dhabi has financial ambitions of its own with a planned financial city on Sowwah island, and it aspired to host the Central Bank of the planned GCC currency union before withdrawing from the project when the seat went to Riyadh. Remarkably, the exchanges in Abu Dhabi and Dubai are currently in merger talks to create a larger and more liquid trading platform.[29] With Saudi Arabia's accession to the WTO, the GCC's largest economy is also in a better position to realize ambitions in the financial field, which it has formulated with the King Abdullah Financial District project in Riyadh. Currently, DIFC is revisiting its business plan and considering lowering its rents which are up to three times higher than comparable onshore office space in Dubai.

The Dubai Electricity and Water Authority (DEWA) is the only government-owned company whose debt has an explicit government guarantee. As a utility provider, it has a more stable business model by nature and might actually profit from the economic downturn. It has been under immense

29. Simeon Kerr, Andrew England, "Abu Dhabi and Dubai Exchanges in Merger Talks," *Financial Times*, March 30, 2010.

pressure to increase power generation and water desalination capacity in order to keep pace with the city's rapid growth, and such capacity expansion is now cheaper to buy. DEWA was even able to refinance $2.2 billion at the height of the global financial crisis in April 2009. Only days after the standstill request, DEWA appointed Citigroup and Standard Chartered Bank on November 30, 2009 to arrange a bond issue of up to $2 billion in the first quarter of 2010. In April 2010, DEWA then went on a roadshow and sold a $1 billion bond, which was 11 times oversubscribed, thus showing a positive market view of an explicit Dubai government guarantee. Thus an important litmus test was passed, as it was the first time that a Dubai entity tested the market after Dubai World's standstill request and the failure of the implicit guarantee assumption.[30] In September 2010, a $1.25 billion *sukuk* of the Dubai government was four times oversubscribed and Emaar was mulling the issuance of a $375 million convertible. Thus, some conditional risk appetite seemed to have returned to the market place, also because of a renewed strong interest in emerging markets on a global level.

The effect on banks in the UAE is difficult to gauge, as most of their exposure is likely to be in bilateral loans that are not in the public domain. National Bank of Abu Dhabi (NBAD) is the only UAE bank that has made an official announcement about its aggregate exposure to Dubai World. It has put it at $345 million, which would be rather modest and double its non-performing loan ratio only to 2 percent in case of default. Standard Chartered points out that "in the absence of detailed disclosure from the banks, the large exposure limit set by the Central Bank of the UAE (25% of the bank's capital to commercial public sector entities)" can be taken as "a better indication of what the 'worst case' maximum exposure to Dubai World and Nakheel could be for each bank." As there is no aggregation of exposure to different legal entities, banks could treat Dubai World and Nakheel as two different entities, which could theoretically increase aggregate exposure to 50 percent in the worst case scenario. Based on this methodology, and by comparing the capital of UAE banks with their total outstanding loan volume, Standard Chartered arrives at a maximum exposure of $13.4 billion of UAE banks in a worst case scenario, which would increase their NPL ratio to 10-16 percent (with the exception of NBAD which has declared its exposure, and in its case this ratio would be 2 percent).

30. Robin Wigglesworth, "Dubai World Gives Debt Markets a Boost," *Financial Times*, April 7, 2010, available at http://www.ft.com/cms/s/0/b62074ae-425b-11df-8c60-00144feabdc0.html .

Table 1: Standard Chartered's Worst Case Scenario

	Estimated worst case exposure ($ bn)	Worst case NPL ratio in %	NPL ratio June 09 in %
Emirates NBD	4.4	9.7	1.5
NBAD	0.3*	2.0	1.1
ADCB	2.7	12.8	4.2
First Gulf Bank	3.0	13.4	1.1
UNB	1.4	11.6	1.3
Mashreqbank	1.6	15.7	2.2

*has been officially declared
NPL= Non Performing Loan
Source: Standard Chartered, "Dubai World – Impact on the UAE Banks," Credit Research, December 1, 2009.

Citing unnamed banking sources, an AFP story on November 29, 2009 put the exposure of Abu Dhabi and Dubai banks to Dubai World at between 30 and 40 percent of banks' capital, with Abu Dhabi Commercial Bank (ADCB) having exposure between $2.18 billion and $2.45 billion and First Gulf Bank of $1.36 billion. In the case of ADCB, this would be pretty close to Standard Chartered's worst case scenario given in Table 1.

While this certainly would affect the profit quality at banks and might even make their bondholders nervous, it has to be stressed that there is a three-year guarantee by the UAE government on bank deposits since October 2008. The guarantee was implemented in the wake of the global financial crisis and extends to all national and international banks with "significant operations," excluding regional and Iranian banks. The UAE Central Bank also made additional liquidity facilities available to UAE banks to underscore this guarantee and quell any speculation about possible bank runs.

4. Risk of Regional and International Contagion

Markets initially feared substantial risk of contagion on a regional and even international level. Credit default swaps of other GCC countries rose as well, albeit to a lesser extent than the ones of Dubai (see Table 2), and international equity markets tumbled as they feared that Dubai could spark a crisis of emerging market debt in general.

Table 2: Market Reaction to DW Standstill Request: Spreads of Credit Default Swaps (CDS)

	5y CDS Nov. 23	5y CDS Nov. 27	Relative change in %
Dubai Holding	670	1650	146
Emirates Bank	345	800	132
Dubai	317	630	99
DP World	355	700	97
NBAD	135	250	85
Abu Dhabi	100	175	75
Mubadala	133	225	69
ADCB	210	305	45
Bahrain	175	225	29
Qatar	94	120	28
Russia	191	215	13
Hungary	217	242	12
BarCap USD GCC bonds index	237	302	27
BarCap USD EM Sovereign Index	315	323	3

Source: Barclay's Capital, "Dubai's Debt – Whose Problem is It?" Emerging Market Research, November 30, 2009

Such fears say more about the still fragile nature of global financial markets than about the contagion potential of Dubai, which is limited. Neighboring countries with significant oil revenues and foreign reserves have a very different economic structure from Dubai. Saudi Arabia actually has one of the lowest levels of government debt in the world with a share of only 13.4 percent of GDP, as Calyon/ Bank Saudi Fransi points out.[31] This is a number other countries can only dream of; the US is at 50 percent and rising and India is at 81 percent, not to mention countries like Italy or Japan. The real estate bubble of Dubai has also been unique

31. Calyon/Banque Saudi Fransi, Dubai: *After the Plunge*, Emerging Market Focus, November 27, 2009.

in the region – many neighbors started to copy it, but in hindsight they were lucky to be late. There is certainly exposure by GCC investors to Dubai investments, but a full fledged contagion of the Dubai debt crisis is unlikely, also because oil prices have held out pretty well around $75 per barrel.

After the initial shock, markets started to increasingly differentiate between Dubai and, to a lesser extent, Abu Dhabi on the one hand and the rest of the GCC on the other. By the beginning of January, credit default swaps (CDS) spreads of GCC sovereign issuers had returned to their pre-crisis level of November 23 while CDS spreads for Dubai but also for Abu Dhabi remained on elevated levels even though they had fallen from their highs in November/December 2009.[32] GCC issuers other than Dubai like Bahrain's government, Saudi Arabian developer Dar Al Arkan, National Bank of Abu Dhabi, and Banque Saudi Fransi have also been able to tap international capital markets since the announcement of Dubai World's standstill request.

The lack of potential contagion applies all the more to international markets. Dubai is not comparable to China, Brazil or the US real estate market. It has also not functioned as counterparty for deals in trillions of dollars of OTC derivatives like Lehman Brothers or AIG. To put it into perspective, one can take a look at the magnitude of GDP figures: world GDP is at $61 trillion, while the GCC GDP is only $1.1 trillion, and that of the UAE is $228 billion of which $82 billion accrues to Dubai. International banks have lent substantial sums in the UAE, but compared to their overall loan volume the exposure should be manageable, as JP Morgan points out. The largest exposure is with HSBC, Standard Chartered, Barclay's, and RBS/ABN Amro (see Table 3).

Table 3: Foreign Banks: Exposure to UAE in 2008

	Outstanding Loans in $ bn	Loans to UAE as % of Total Group Loans
HSBC	17.03	1.8%
Standard Chartered	7.77	4.4%
Barclays Bank	3.58	0.4%
RBS/ ABN Amro	2.24	0.4%
BNP Paribas	1.69	0.2%

Source: JP Morgan, "UAE-Exposure at Risk Analysis," Europe Equity Research, November 27, 2009

32. IMF, "Impact of the Global Financial Crisis on the Gulf Cooperation Council Countries and Challenges Ahead," Middle East and Central Asia Department, Washington, D. C., 2010.

5. Dubai's Reaction to the Debt Crisis

In February 2009, Dubai received a first $10 billion help from Abu Dhabi and in July 2009, it established the Dubai Financial Support Fund (DFSF) to centralize decision-making and coordinate capital allocation to struggling government-related entities in a more efficient way. The DFSF reports to Dubai's Supreme Fiscal Committee (SFC), but nothing is known about its allocation strategy and priorities beyond a general reference to projects with strategic significance within Dubai. A cursory look at statements of Dubai officials in the run-up to the crisis suggests that they were in a state of denial. In October 2008, at the Cityscape real estate fair, Nakheel announced the building of a 1000-meter tower and Shaikh Mohammed maintained that the unfolding global financial crisis would constitute an opportunity for Dubai as it could attract money from frustrated investors who were losing money elsewhere. Only weeks before the Dubai World standstill request in November 2009, he told a conference audience that people who questioned Dubai's ability to pay and Abu Dhabi's willingness to step in should "shut up."

When disaster struck, the handling of the standstill request did not inspire the confidence of markets. It revealed lack of professionalism on the part of the Dubai government and Dubai Inc. companies. The announcement was scant in detail and was made before major holidays in the Muslim World (Eid) and the US (Thanksgiving). Only two hours before, two government-related Abu Dhabi banks had released $5 billion for the Dubai Economic Support fund, which had been awaited as part of a second $10 billion tranche of the bailout program. Investors who banked on this statement and added to their positions in the Nakheel bond were naturally not amused to see more than 30 percent of their investment evaporate only two hours later. The exemption of DPW and JAFZ from the restructuring process was only announced later and, in the meanwhile, investors were left with the rumor mill and statements by non-DW executives who revealed no further details. Instead they preferred to shoot the messenger by blaming the press and analysts. From a city that has self-confidently declared its intention to become a regional if not international financial center by aspiring to best practices, markets had expected otherwise. It was announced in December 2009 that Abu Dhabi would give a further $10 billion, but officials had to backpedal a month later as they clarified that this would include the $5 billion support that was announced on the same day as the debt standstill request. Thus, a $10 billion announcement in fact only represented $5 billion in fresh money.

With time passing, transparency has somewhat improved. The announcement of Dubai World's debt restructuring proposal in March 2010 was handled much more professionally. Still the question has been asked, whether human resources at many Dubai Inc. entities were experienced enough to handle a crisis of such magnitude and whether the leadership was ready to heed the advice of the public relations companies it had hired to explain its investment strategy.[33]

Overall, a picture emerges where the leadership's vision of rapid urban development was stimulated by low interest rates on international capital markets and ample oil revenues in the wider Gulf region. Once the strategy of "build and they will come" yielded impressive initial results, there was a tendency for lieutenants at the various Dubai Inc. entities to outcompete each other in ever larger project launches in order to vie for the favor of the leadership. Irrational exuberance was encouraged by poor oversight and already daring investment approaches were reinforced by an approving long leash from above. Shaikh Mohammed himself had declared that the only speed he knows is "full throttle" and maintained that the substantial building activity in Dubai would only constitute 10 percent of his "vision." When Emaar chairman Mohammad Alabbar approached him with a proposal for a 90-storey building, the Dubai ruler replied, "why waste your time on 90 stories?" and the highest building of the world, the Burj Khalifa (formerly known as Burj Dubai) was built. In an interview with *Business Week*, Alabbar said that Shaikh Mohammed "takes the fear of failure away from you because he is with you."[34]

Such unlimited confidence and mutually reinforcing euphoria has faded with the advent of the crisis. Alabbar and several other lieutenants, like Dubai Holding chairman Mohammed Gergawi or DW chairman Sultan bin Sulayem, have been demoted; they had to leave the board of Investment Corporation Dubai (ICD) and now only hold positions as leaders of their respective companies. Sulayem had also to give up chairmanship of the Dubai World subsidiary, Nakheel. Oversight has been increased and the head of the ruler's court Al Shaybani is widely acknowledged as Shaikh Mohammed's new strong man and closest aide. The influence of the meritocratic, slick and Western-educated executives like Alabbar and Gergawi who do not hail from well-established families has been fading, while members of conservative business families like Al Lootah and Al Tayer have been brought on board. Ahmed Humaid Al-Tayer has become the new governor of the DIFC and Ali Rashid Ahmed Lootah has replaced Sulayem as new chairman of Nakheel.

There has also been a string of investigations and indictments. Former vice-

33. Andrew England, "Dubai Faces Self-made Public Image 'Disaster'," *Financial Times*, December 12, 2009, available at: http://www.ft.com/cms/s/0/2c21584c-e67e-11de-98b1-00144feab49a.html .

34. "The Master Builder of the Middle East," *Business Week*, July 2, 2007, available at: http://www.businessweek.com/magazine/content/07_27/b4041056.htm .

chairman of Istithmar World Adel Shirawi, former Deyaar chairman and former UAE minister of finance Mohammed bin Kharbash, and Omar bin Sulaiman, the former governor of DIFC have been linked to corruption cases, just to mention a few (see Table 4 in appendix). It would be misleading, however, to reduce the Dubai debt crisis to moral failures of individuals. Crises of this magnitude are not brought about by individual failures but by the volatility of capitalist development and contagious exuberance that is eerily reminiscent of earlier boom-bust scenarios going back to the Dutch Tulip mania in the 17th century.[35]

6. Abu Dhabi's Role and the Growing Centralization of the UAE

As Dubai's access to international capital markets has diminished, it will need to rely increasingly on Abu Dhabi besides making the necessary restructuring moves. Despite its support on numerous occasions at the beginning of 2009, Abu Dhabi only reluctantly provided funds for repayment of the $4.1 billion Nakheel *sukuk* on December 14, 2009 after violent market reactions threatened to hurt the reputation of the wider UAE and Abu Dhabi as well.[36] An unnamed senior Abu Dhabi official told Reuters that Abu Dhabi would support Dubai on "a case by case basis" and that it will "pick and choose" which companies it will support.[37]

On November 25, Dubai did not receive the full second $10 billion tranche of a $20 billion bond program as originally expected but only $5 billion, and it was announced that the proceeds of the bond were not supposed to be used for the bailout of Dubai World and Nakheel but for other liquidity needs of the emirate that are administered by DFSF. Abu Dhabi's support for Dubai in the current financial crisis is selective and not unconditional. Abu Dhabi shows that it is ready to practice tough love and force a restructuring of Dubai business entities that are currently not viable or might not fit into its own and the UAE's overall development plans. While it remains committed to a selective bailout, it seems unwilling to foot the bill all by

35. For a classic on early financial crashes in history, see Charles Mackay, *Extraordinary Popular Delusions and the Madness of Crowds* (Boston: 1956, original 1841).

36. Speculation about the backroom politics between November 25 and December 14 are widespread and range from Abu Dhabi letting Dubai hang out to dry to get a meaningful participation in the restructuring process to Dubai trying to pressurize Abu Dhabi to release more support, which it finally got. Another interpretation makes a link to the UAE's 123 nuclear agreement with the US that was awaiting approval of Congress at that time. A prolonged negative press about business practices and politics in the UAE could have hurt prospects of the agreement that Abu Dhabi regards as vital for power provision in the UAE.

37. Reuters, November 29, 2009.

itself. It is ready to accept a considerable reputation risk for Dubai and the UAE as a whole by letting Dubai walk the thin line of debt restructuring and default and making international investors bear part of the burden. Speculation about trade-offs is increasingly shifting from rumored secret buyout arrangements that are impossible to verify to a power shift to Abu Dhabi within the federal structure of the UAE.

Payoffs for Abu Dhabi's bailout might rather be on a political level. Abu Dhabi could demand a strengthening of federal authority, while Dubai would need to relinquish certain sovereign rights, such as control of customs, which so far remains on the level of individual emirates. Hints at increased centralization are already discernible, with Abu Dhabi and federal institutions playing a more visible role in national development policy and Shaikh Mohammed of Dubai increasingly appearing in his role as Vice President and Prime Minister of the UAE rather than as Ruler of Dubai. Shaikh Mohammed launched a dedicated website at the beginning of 2009 that highlights his prominent role in federal politics.

It is important to keep in mind that the various emirates of the UAE, especially Dubai and Ras Al Khaimah, had shown a strong sense of independence during the genesis of the federation. In the 1970s, the UAE still resembled a confederation than a federation in many ways, and consensus about further unification steps had to be delicately balanced. Individual emirates were reluctant to cede authority and revenues to a central government that still had to assert itself amidst tribal allegiances and unresolved border issues.[38]

In 1979, a proposal by Abu Dhabi to strengthen federal ministries and reduce the autonomy of individual emirates faced stiff resistance from Dubai and Ras Al Khaimah, which preferred the rather loose confederation that had prevailed until then. The compromise that ensued led to a greater integration of Dubai into federal politics. Besides being Vice-President of the UAE, the ruler of Dubai would henceforth also be its Prime Minister presiding over the Council of Ministers – a compromise that has proven to be successful and has lasted to this day. Still, Dubai continued to maintain a local military force that was only integrated into the federal Union Defense Force (UDF) in 1996.

While the UAE has shown a tendency towards more unity, lack of centralization has remained an issue even in foreign affairs. During the Iran-Iraq war of the 1980s, Abu Dhabi, Ras Al Khaimah, Ajman and Fujairah supported Iraq, while Dubai, Sharjah and Umm Al Quwain leaned more towards Iran, their most important

38. For more details, see Christopher M. Davidson, *Dubai. The Vulnerability of Success*, (New York: Columbia University Press 2008) and Christopher M. Davidson, *The United Arab Emirates: A Study in Survival* (Boulder: Lynne Rienner, 2005).

trading partner and home country of a large merchant expatriate community in these emirates. Operation Desert Storm for the liberation of Kuwait and the US invasion of Afghanistan equally led to considerable disagreement between different emirates. Until 9/11, the UAE was one of the three states recognizing the Taliban regime besides Pakistan and Saudi Arabia. The Abu Dhabi-led anti-Iranian group among the emirates had favored a "Sunni axis" that also included Taliban-led Afghanistan in order to counter perceived "Shi'a expansionism."

Centralized control of customs authority in exchange for financial help would give Abu Dhabi a firmer grip on implementation of sanctions policies against Iran, which the US has repeatedly demanded in the past. Such a move would also be in line with its own tough stance with regard to the regional ambitions of Iran. The UAE has been firm in its opposition of the Iranian occupation of three UAE islands in the Gulf and has put it repeatedly on the agenda of the Arab League and other international organizations.

Control by the individual emirates is also evident in other areas such as the police force, parts of the judiciary, education, transport, utility companies, compilation of statistics and stock markets. The country's Central Bank was only founded in 1980 and its role in the overall banking framework is relatively underdeveloped when compared to other countries in the region.

The UAE needs increasing unification of policies and standards for its ambitious development drive. It also needs substantially improved statistics which so far are often not available in a timely, complete and consistent fashion. Like elsewhere, there will need to be more regulation of capital markets, while a unification of the stock markets in Dubai and Abu Dhabi could strengthen the position of the UAE as a niche player in international capital markets. In this context, it needs to be remembered that Abu Dhabi played a major role in the refinancing of Borse Dubai in February 2009 and merger talks have been undertaken between the exchanges in Abu Dhabi and Dubai. A looming electricity shortage will require the development of Abu Dhabi's sour gas reserves and new power generation capacities, possibly fueled by nuclear and renewable energy. Urban development is increasingly intertwined with people living in one emirate and working in the other, and coordinated planning will be required especially in the field of transport networks and railroads. More unification and centralized control of the judiciary could contribute to furthering the rule of law and improve the international image of the UAE as an investment destination, which has been bruised recently by lack of corporate governance and investor protection. Finally, education plays a pivotal role in Emiratization efforts which aim at increased integration of young nationals in the workforce.

7. The Nakheel *Sukuk* and Implications for Islamic Banking

Dubai has played a major role in the nascent global *sukuk* market, and its treatment of payment procedures carries important implications for this segment of the Islamic banking market. The GCC countries constitute about 40 percent of the global *sukuk* market; in terms of dollar-denominated *sukuks*, its importance is even bigger as Malaysian *sukuks* are mainly issued in local currency, the ringitt.[39] The UAE has issued a majority of GCC *sukuks* in the boom years of 2006 and 2007 as Figure 2 shows. Most of this issuance came from Dubai and was often related to real estate and banks. As dynamics in these sectors slowed, the share of the UAE in GCC *sukuk* issuance declined from 63.3 percent in 2008 to 41.9 percent in 2009. Remarkably, this share shot up to 91.2 percent in the fourth quarter of 2009 and was attributable to a larger bond issue by the Dubai government in November shortly before the eruption of the Dubai debt crisis. Overall, the share of governments in GCC *sukuk* issuance increased from 65 percent in 2008 to 91 percent in 2009.

Figure 2: GCC Issuance of Islamic Bonds (*Sukuks*)

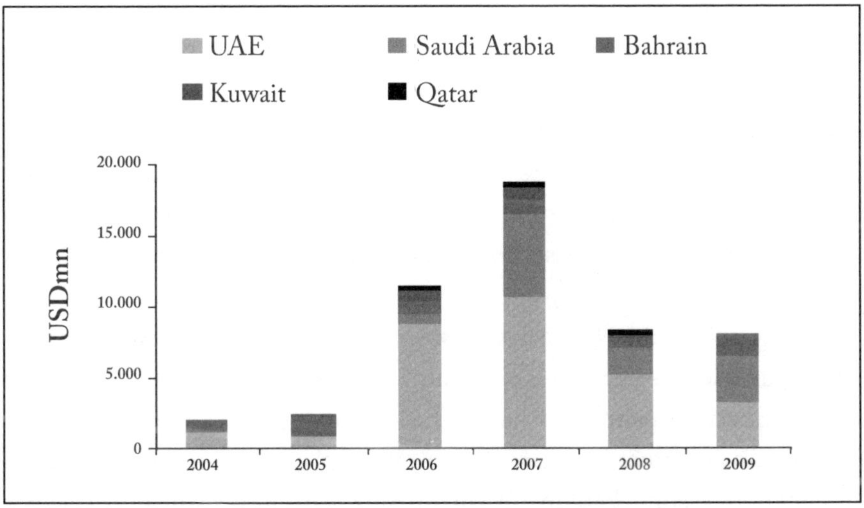

Source: NCB Capital, GCC Debt Market Tracker, January 2010

Ahead of the due date of the Nakheel *sukuk* on December 14, 2009 rating agencies assumed that a postponement of bilateral loans behind the scenes might happen, but made it repeatedly clear that repayment of publicly traded debt instruments would be regarded as a litmus test and involuntary rescheduling as a

39. NCB Capital, *GCC Debt Market Tracker*, January 2010.

default, which would seriously harm credit sentiment for Dubai. For a voluntary restructuring, 75 percent of the bondholders would need to approve changes to the terms of the *sukuk* at an extraordinary general meeting.

A group of international investors led by the US hedge fund QVT Financial LP hired Ashurst, a London law firm, to advise them on their options, according to a report by the London-based newspaper *The Times*.[40] The group accounted for more than 25 percent of Nakheel's bonds by value and would thus have had a veto power at a possible general meeting of bondholders. According to *The Times*, the group examined two possible approaches in case of a default. One would have sought to seize Nakheel's real-estate assets in Dubai, the other would have focused on Dubai World's parent-company guarantee on the debt, which could have opened the way for a claim against more valuable assets abroad, such as P&O Ferries Ltd. or the Queen Elizabeth 2 cruise liner. As the underlying assets of the Nakheel *sukuk* were undeveloped plots of the Dubai Waterfront project, which is currently on hold, their current market value has likely been low.

There is no legal precedent for recourse to assets in case of a *sukuk* default thus far. *Sukuk*s are "asset based" rather than "asset backed." They were designed to satisfy legalistic requirements of sharia law in order to circumvent the ban on interest, not to establish a waterproofed recourse to underlying assets like an Asset Backed Security (ABS) in conventional financial markets. The Declaration of Trust in the Nakheel *sukuk* contract was governed by English law, and considerable ambiguity existed whether all its stipulations would be applicable under UAE law or whether assets of government-related entities could be seized under UAE law at all.

As repayment of the Nakheel *sukuk* was ensured by support of Abu Dhabi in the eleventh hour, a legal solution for a default scenario did not have to be found. Still, markets have become painfully aware of the legal ambiguities of *sukuk* securities. As Dubai, Bahrain and other Gulf countries aspire to play a leading role in the growing global market of Islamic banking, it will be important to convincingly clarify such legal ambiguities and improve regulation.

Doubts about the viability of *sukuk* contracts were raised by a verdict of the Bahrain-based Accounting and Auditing Organization for Islamic Financial Institutions (AAOIFI) in 2008 when it declared a majority of them as non-sharia compliant for lack of real risk sharing on the part of the investor. The Nakheel *sukuk* would have been the third one to default after Kuwait Investment Dar's $100

40. Helen Power, "Dubai World's Creditors May Claim its Trophy Assets," *The Times*, December 2, 2009.

million *sukuk* in May 2009 and the one of Bahrain-reigstered Saad Group subsidiary for over $650 million in June 2009. Currently there is a curious law case pending in London, where the defaulting Kuwaiti Investment Dar has raised arguments that are similar to the verdict of AAOIFI. Investment Dar appeals to pay the stipulated "profit rate" on its outstanding *sukuk*, maintaining that its structure has not been sharia-compliant and would hence fall outside the company's remit.[41] This outlines the worst nightmare of *sukuk* creditors as it could give debtors a legal tool to renege on initially agreed contract specifications.

While a bond default can happen, it would be important to establish convincing legal clarity of *sukuk* structures in such a situation, otherwise their future issuance and tradability might be seriously affected. A second Nakheel *sukuk* has been repaid in 2010 and another one that is still outstanding in 2011 is scheduled for full repayment according to Dubai's proposal of a debt restructuring. Thus, the Nakheel *sukuk* saga will not lead to a legal precedence. However, Dubai has started to acknowledge shortcomings in its murky legal framework, most notably the bankruptcy law, which is non-existent as far as Dubai's onshore jurisdiction goes: there is no well-established process on how to arbitrate bankruptcy cases, defaulting debtors simply go to jail. For this reason Ruler's decree 57 stipulates that a modified version of the bankruptcy law of the offshore DIFC will be applicable for legal cases pertaining to Dubai World although the company is registered onshore. The Tribunal applying the law would be located in DIFC, but different from the DIFC court proper.[42] Contrary to Dubai's onshore jurisdiction, DIFC follows mainly English common law, has English as working language and not Arabic, and allows foreign lawyers to represent their clients. In a first case, a foreign investor is suing Dubai developer Damac over contractual breaches at DIFC. So far Damac has appealed DIFC's jurisdiction, although it is registered there.[43] Going ahead it will be interesting to see whether DIFC jurisdiction could play a pilot role for reform of the UAE's onshore jurisdiction. This could happen in the form of increasing its reach as in the case of Dubai World or by offering onshore parties possibilities of "opting into" its jurisdiction and take advantage of its internationally accepted standards.[44]

---

41. Robin Wigglesworth, "Court Concession Raises Islamic Finance Risk," *Financial Times,* March 25, 2010.
42. Latham & Watkins, "New Dubai Decree Relating to any Future Restructuring of Dubai World and its Subsidiaries," *Client Alert*, no. 972, January 8, 2010.
43. Angela Giuffrida, "'VIP Investor' Sues Damac," *The National,* January 17, 2010.
44. Paul Stothard, "Comment: UAE Needs More Law Reform," *Financial Times,* March 10, 2010.

Conclusion: Rentier State, Dubai Model and Globalization

Dubai's debt predicament requires decisive restructuring, especially in the ailing real estate sector. Compared to other countries in the Middle East, Dubai has a competitive advantage in terms of infrastructure, lifestyle and business facilitation. It also has a successful role to play as a regional trading hub, provided it can rid itself of past exuberance. Markets can stomach frankness if it is administered with a clear strategic vision and decisive action, but they are very sensitive to prolonged periods of uncertainty. With declining oil revenues in Dubai and the impact of the financial crisis, funding of UAE's development efforts will depend more on Abu Dhabi than in the past. The ambitious development goals of the UAE and its wish to play a more visible role in international affairs will also require a more centralized approach to planning and institution building. Rather than aiming at rumored equity buy-outs, Abu Dhabi will possibly try to forge a consensus for more concentration of responsibilities on the federal level in exchange for its ongoing financial help to Dubai and other emirates.

Dubai has been long hailed as a model of economic diversification. Oil nowadays constitutes less than 5 percent of its GDP; as oil production has declined from a peak of 400,000 barrels per day at the beginning of the 1990s to well below 100,000 bpd, economic diversification has indeed been a necessity. In reality, however, Dubai has retained a considerable indirect dependency. A large chunk of its investments have been driven by capital inflows from surrounding oil exporters. As Dubai functions as a window to the world to Iran and is its most important trading partner, Iranian inflows have been of particular importance. They have been estimated at around $13 billion per annum during the boom years, and Iranians purchased about 15 percent of Dubai's real estate. Other sizable inflows came from the Gulf countries, South Asia, Russia and Great Britain. Thus, to a degree, the real estate hype like oil was reliance on external rents due to location.[45] As the boom was indirectly fueled by oil income in the region, Dubai also did not escape a Dutch disease-like focus on non-tradables: while nominal currency appreciation was not possible due to a dollar peg, inflation led to an appreciation of the real effective exchange rate and a concomitant loss of competitiveness in tradables.

Having said that, Dubai, like the rest of the Gulf, is beyond the classic rentier

45. For an outline of the classic rentier state theory, see Giacomo Luciani, "Allocation vs. Production States. A Theoretical Framework," in *The Rentier State*, eds. Hazem Beblawi, Giacomo Luciani (London, New York: Croom Helm, 1987).

state paradigm, with some role for the private sector, pockets of efficient government industries and nascent constitutional reform.[46] Internationally competitive industries like Emirates Airline or Dubal have been created, and it remains to be seen whether changes in governance can lead to the kind of "embedded autonomy" (Evans) that has characterized developing states in South-East Asia.[47] However, global capitalism is in crisis, the Washington consensus has been discredited, while efforts to resuscitate Keynesianism seem to be blithely unaware of fiscal constraints and threats of currency devaluation. Whether globalization-based growth will resume is therefore an open question and the abilities of a small city state in the Gulf to influence its fate are limited.

46. For the relationship between public and private sector see Giacomo Luciani, "From Private Sector to National Bourgeoisie: Saudi Arabian Business," in *Saudi Arabia in the Balance. Political Economy, Society, Foreign Affairs*, eds. Paul Aarts and Gerd Nonneman (New York: University Press, 2005), 144-181 and Steffen Hertog, *Princes, Brokers, and Bureaucrats. Oil and the State in Saudi Arabia* (Cornell University Press, 2010). For constitutional reform, see Michael Herb, *All in the Family. Absolutism, Revolution and Democracy in the Middle Eastern Monarchies* (Albany: State University of New York Press, 1999); Anoushivaran Ehteshami, "Reform from Above. The Politics of Participation in Oil Monarchies," *International Affairs* 79 (2003): 1); Joshua Teitelbaum (ed.), *Political Liberalization in the Persian Gulf* (New York: Columbia University Press, 2009).

47. See the excellent discussion in the introduction of Tim Niblock (with Monica Malick), The *Political Economy of Saudi Arabia* (London, New York: Routledge, 2007). Remarkably, Saudi Arabia has not cut back the reform efforts that it has started in the 1990s despite high oil prices.

Appendix

Figure 3: Structure of Dubai Inc.

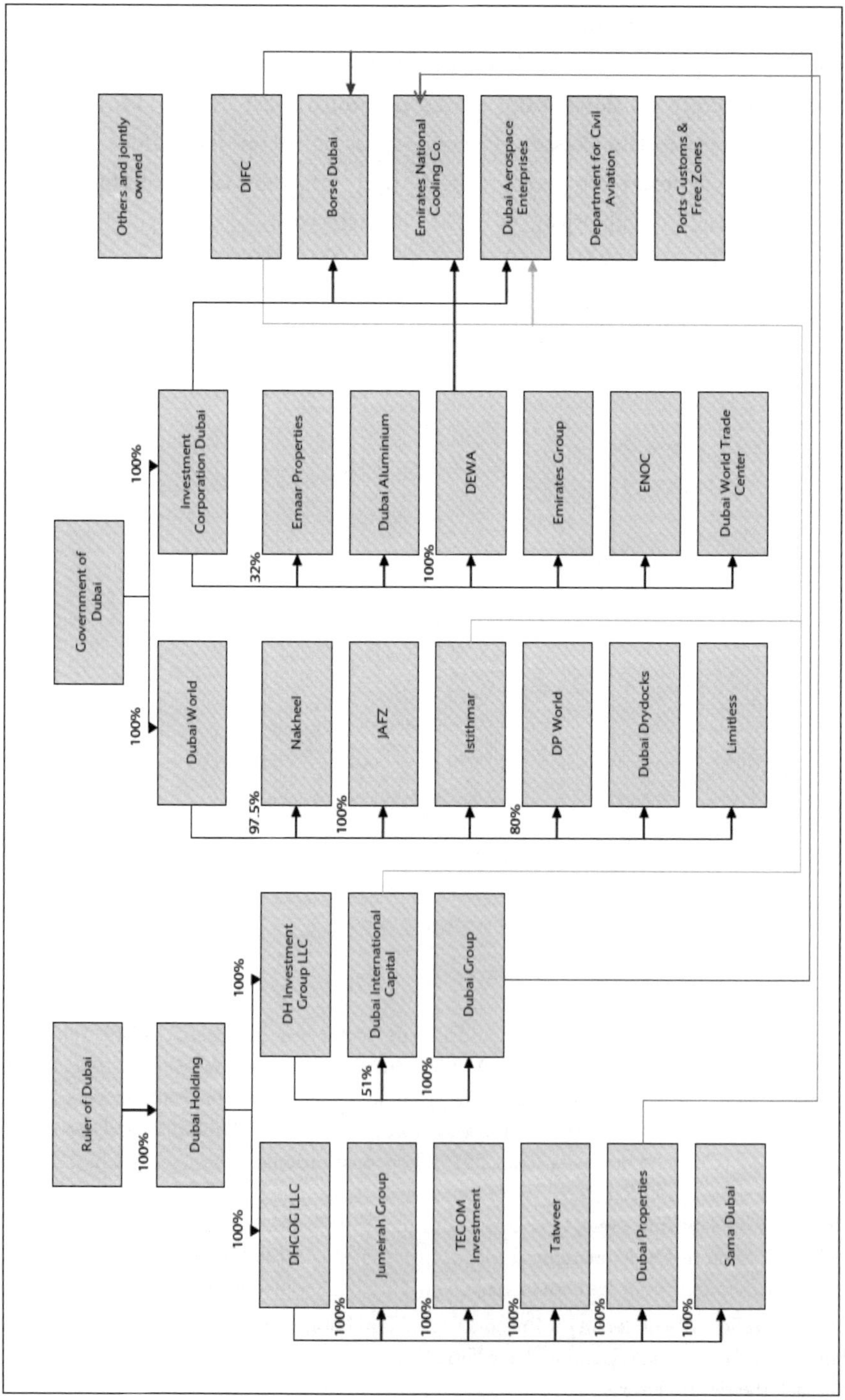

Source: Barclay's Capital

Figure 4: Dubai GDP by Economic Activity (Basic Current Prices),2008

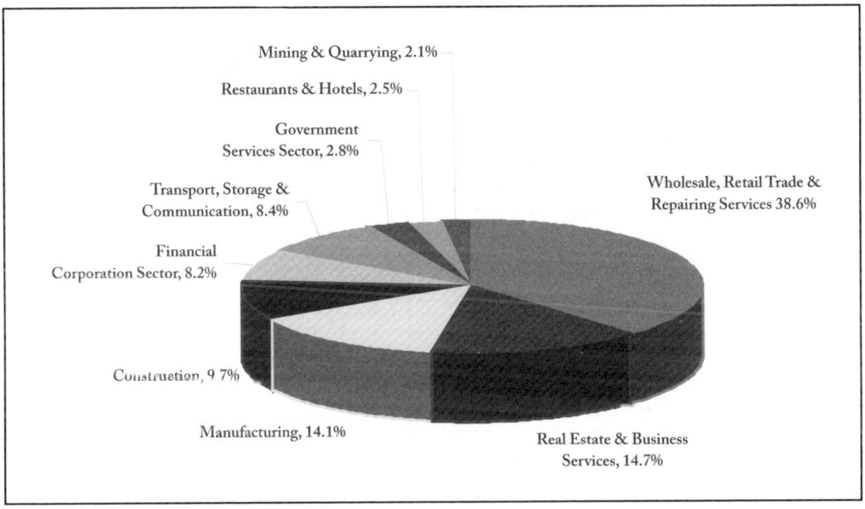

Source: Dubai Statistics Center, 2010

Table 4: High Profile Corruption Cases in Dubai

Name of Individual	Affiliation	Case Details & Status
Omar bin Sulaiman	Former Governor, Dubai International Financial Centre	Accused of abusing his authority for profiting from public funds. Illegally diverted funds amounting to $13.6 million to his own account as "performance bonuses. Public Prosecution ordered his detention pending further investigation and soon to be referred to courts
Saad Abdulrazak	Former chief executive of Dubai Islamic Bank	Sentenced to three years in prison and fined $31 million for accepting a bribe and unlawful commissions.
Zack Shahin	Former CEO, Deyaar Development	An American of Lebanese origin, he is accused of embezzlement of more than Dh98 million ($27 million) and is the longest-serving top executive in police custody
Mohammad bin Kharbash	Former chairman of Deyaar and Dubai Islamic Bank and former UAE Minister of Finance	Charged with helping and abetting Zack Shahin, embezzlement, and "damaging state interest."
Adel Shirawi	Former vice chairman of Istithmar World and former head of Tamweel	Charged with embezzlement and mistrust.

Michael Bryan Smith	Former personnel manager for Limitless	Embezzlement of $150 million, to be extradited from Thailand
Kabir Mulchandani	Chairman, Dynasty Zarooni	Allegedly defrauded investors of more than $100 million. The Dubai prosecutor's office issued an arrest warrant in March 2010
Tawhid, Tawfiq, and Tamjid Abdullah	Founders of Damas International	Were fined $3.72 million by Dubai's Financial Services Authority (DFSA) over a series of 'unauthorized transactions.'
A list of more than 60 people mainly from government-linked companies are under investigation.	Tamweel, Nakheel, Istithmar World, Dubai Islamic Bank and Sama Dubai	Under investigation. Several senior executives have been detained.
An Emirati and an Egyptian national guilty of bribery	Nakheel	The UAE Supreme Court upheld the convictions of the two employees
Two Australians charged with bribery in a separate case	Nakheel	Under trial
Seven people, including two Pakistanis, charged of receiving a total of $1.7 million in alleged bribes to facilitate the financing of deals	Dubai Islamic Bank	Under trial
A senior executive and an engineer of Lebanese nationality were charged with bribery and financial irregularities, amounting to nearly Dh49 million.	Mizin	Under trial
Five senior executives are facing charges of bribery involving more than Dh46 million.	Tamweel and Bonyan Holding	Under trial

Sources: Local Newspapers and Official News Agency WAM

7

The Impact of Monetary Policy and Financial Sector Development on Economic Growth in GCC Countries

Elias El-Achkar and Wassim Shahin

Introduction

The framework of monetary policy in each of the GCC countries has been clearly formulated to preserve the exchange rate peg to the US dollar except in Kuwait (since 2007) which pegs to an undeclared weighted basket of currencies. The peg to the dollar provides an anchor for monetary policy; the role of such policy is circumscribed by the exchange rate regime with GCC interest rates tracking the dollar rates. In addition, the GCC countries have been benefiting from an increase in their levels of financial development especially in the areas of financial deepening in bank intermediation to the private sector and bank liquid liabilities. The purpose of our paper is two-fold. We first examine the impact of the current framework of monetary policy in the GCC countries, in terms of pegging exchange rates, on economic growth. The aim is to address the significance of this relationship using our own measure of the exchange rate variable as an additional argument in recommending a monetary policy framework for the future Gulf Monetary Union. Second, given the current exchange rate arrangement, we examine the impact of financial sector development on economic growth using some suggested indicators of financial sector development in the literature.

The paper relies on empirical methodology reflected in panel data estimation for the six GCC countries from 1975 to 2008. The findings show that exchange rate arrangements are an important determinant of economic growth. The significant relationship between exchange rates and economic growth does not coincide with some of the results reached in the literature showing a weak or non-existent relationship. However, the results are in line with the studies that have shown a significant relationship in the sense that different exchange rate arrangements may impact economic growth. The result in our paper clarifies the impact of the monetary policy framework adopted by the GCC countries on economic growth. It also allows us to examine the appropriateness of this framework and to consider monetary policy options for the GCC monetary union given that the exchange rate arrangement seems to impact growth. The results we reach on the importance of financial sector development for economic growth in the GCC countries are mixed as reflected in the significance of some indicators of financial development and the insignificance of others.

The paper is organized as follows. Section 1 discusses the actual conduct of monetary policy in the six GCC countries. Section 2 reviews the findings of the empirical studies conducted on the relationship between the nature of the exchange rate regime and economic growth and also analyzes the literature addressing the relationship between financial sector development and economic growth. Section 3 develops the testing methodology and highlights the empirical results reached. Section 4 relies on the findings in section 3 and on the existing monetary policy framework to analyze future prospects for monetary policy after the achievement of the Gulf Monetary Union. Section 5 contains some concluding remarks on policy implications.

1. Monetary Policy in GCC Countries: Past and Current Arrangements

This part presents the past and current monetary policies adopted in the GCC countries as reflected in their exchange rate arrangements. GCC currencies have been de facto pegged to either one currency, the US dollar, or a basket of currencies for decades, inconsistent most of the time with the de jure, or the officially declared exchange rate arrangement or policy to the IMF, except for Kuwait and Oman. Table 1 illustrates this inconsistency as it shows that from 1980 until 2001, Saudi Arabia, UAE, Qatar, and Bahrain currencies were formally pegged (de jure) to a basket of currencies, the SDR (IMF's Special Drawing Rights), but effectively (de facto) they were fixed to the US dollar. Kuwait and Oman currencies were both officially and actually pegged to an undisclosed basket of currencies and the US dollar, respectively. Based on a joint decision taken during a summit meeting at the end of 2001, all GCC members officially pegged their currencies to the US

Table 1: Exchange Rate Arrangements of GCC Countries

	Officially announced (de jure)	Actual arrangement (de facto)
Bahrain	1980-2001: domestic currency pegged to SDR. 2002-currently: domestic currency pegged to USD.	Classified by the IMF under Other Conventional Fixed Peg Arrangements where the country pegs its currency at a fixed rate to a major currency or a basket of currencies and where the exchange rate fluctuates within a narrow margin of at most +/- 1 percent around a central rate. The peg is against a single currency.
Kuwait	1975-2002: domestic currency pegged to a currency composite other than the SDR. 2003-mid 2007: domestic currency pegged to USD. Mid 2007- currently: domestic currency pegged to a currency composite other than the SDR.	Classified by the IMF under Other Conventional Fixed Peg Arrangements. The peg has been against a composite until 2001 but changed later to against a single currency and then again, starting mid 2007, to against a basket.
Oman	1970s-currently: domestic currency pegged to USD.	Classified by the IMF under Other Conventional Fixed Peg Arrangements. The peg is against a single currency.
Qatar	1975-mid2001: domestic currency pegged to SDR. Mid 2001-currently: domestic currency pegged to USD.	Classified by the IMF under Other Conventional Fixed Peg Arrangements. The peg is against a single currency.
Saudi Arabia	1970s-mid 1986: domestic currency pegged to SDR. Mid 1986-currently: domestic currency pegged to USD.	Classified by the IMF under Other Conventional Fixed Peg Arrangements. The peg is against a single currency.
UAE	1970s-2001: domestic currency pegged to SDR. 2002-currently: domestic currency pegged to USD.	Classified by the IMF under Other Conventional Fixed Peg Arrangements. The peg is against a single currency.

Source: International Monetary Fund, International Financial Statistics

dollar by the end of 2002 as a big step towards the monetary union. But in May 2007, Kuwait announced its intention to shift from the dollar peg to an undisclosed currency basket peg again, without dishonoring its commitment to the monetary integration and the common currency. The de facto classification of exchange rate regimes in Bahrain, Oman, Qatar, Saudi Arabia, and UAE has been therefore conventional fixed peg arrangements against a single currency. The Kuwaiti de facto regime shifted between conventional fixed peg arrangement against a composite and conventional fixed peg arrangement against a single currency.

As for exchange rate behavior, the period average exchange rate per US dollar has been fixed since 1981 in Bahrain, Qatar and UAE at 0.3760, 3.6400, and 3.6725, respectively, following a currency appreciation of 3 percent in 1980. The exchange rate against the US dollar was maintained in Oman at 0.35 from 1975 till 1985 and then at 0.3845 from 1986 till present, whereas it has been stable at 3.7500 in Saudi Arabia since 1987. Before that date, the Saudi Riyal fluctuated within a range of +/- 4 percent. The largest currency appreciation of the Kuwaiti Dinar against the US dollar was around 5.9 percent in 2007, when Kuwait abandoned the dollar peg, and the largest depreciation was close to 5 percent in 1989. These facts explain the very low exchange rate volatility or strong currency stability in the GCC countries for the period 1975-2008. It is worth mentioning that, on average, large oil export revenues and current account surpluses have helped the GCC countries to accumulate, over the years, considerable foreign exchange reserves necessary to reinforce the peg credibility, limit currency fluctuations, and discourage speculation on the currency.

Thus, in order to achieve the previously discussed exchange rate arrangements especially with the beginning of 2001, the GCC countries pursue the following monetary policy especially with regard to interest rates by having these rates adjust in line with interest rates in the USA to preserve the currency peg (see various GCC Central Bank Reports). Taking them one country at a time, the peg to the dollar of the Bahrain Dinar provides an anchor for monetary policy which contributes to controlling inflation and protecting the external value of the domestic currency. This arrangement implies that policy interest rates are closely aligned to US interest rates. In Oman, the monetary policy framework is conditioned by the fixed exchange rate whose main objective is to defend the peg to the US dollar. Therefore, as the US federal funds rate declined from 5.25 percent in August 2007 to 2 percent in April 2008, Oman eased its monetary policy stance reflected in its lowering of its policy rates and inter-bank money market rates. The weighted average interest rate on the Central Bank of Oman CDs declined from 3.63 percent in December 2006 to 1.975

percent in December 2007 and the overnight domestic inter-bank lending rate fell from 3.39 percent to 1.47 percent in the same period. In Qatar, the Qatar Central Bank (QCB) states that the objective of monetary policy is to keep the Qatari Riyal (QR) stable against the US dollar with aspects other than the exchange rate such as cyclical developments being of no high priority in relation to monetary policy. Thus, the QCB monetary policy is implemented to manage the short-term interbank interest rates by keeping QCB overnight interest rates closely related to the federal funds rate to preserve the fixed parity between the domestic currency and the US dollar. In Saudi Arabia, the objective of monetary policy is to maintain the peg of the Saudi Riyal to the US dollar. Thus, the role of monetary policy is circumscribed by the exchange rate policy with Riyal interest rates following US dollar rates. In the UAE, monetary policy is tied to exchange rate policy by pegging the Dirham to the US dollar. As a result, domestic interest rates are aligned to those of the dollar reducing, if not eliminating, their effectiveness as monetary policy instruments. The interest rate on CDs Repo fell from 4.5 percent in December 2007 to reach 1 percent in January 2009 in line with US rates. Starting 2007, the Central Bank of Kuwait dropped the policy of pegging against the US dollar and began fixing domestic currency to an undeclared special weighted basket of currencies of a set of countries with major financial relations with Kuwait. It is believed by the Kuwait monetary authority that this system provides more relative flexibility in defining and implementing monetary policy. As a result, Kuwait's interest rates ceased solely following movements in the federal funds rate and started adjusting to other international interest rates as well.

2. Literature Review on Exchange Rate Arrangements, Financial Sector Development and Growth

The empirical literature on the impact of various exchange rate arrangements and regimes on economic performance is large. Alternatively, there also exists a vast literature on the relationship between the level of financial development and economic growth. This section offers a literature review on both of these issues by addressing the results of some of the studies especially the ones that have incorporated the MENA countries, including the GCC member states.

2.1 Exchange Rate Arrangements and Growth

The literature addressing the relationship between exchange rate regimes and economic growth is very vast. We will confine the analysis to seven of these studies that are the most relevant for our paper and the most reflective of the existing literature. The present paper relies on the empirical methodology developed in the existing studies with an application on the GCC countries. One of the earliest studies on the subject by Ghosh, Gulde, Ostry and Wolf (1997)[1] uses data covering nine regime types over the period 1960-1990 to examine for 136 countries the relationship between the type of the exchange rate arrangement, economic growth and inflation. The authors note that whereas there exists a strong negative link between the flexibility of the regime and the volatility of output and employment, there is only a weak link between the exchange rate arrangement and output growth. However, they report that under pegged regimes, investment ratios are higher and trade growth lower than under flexible ones. Domac and Shabsigh (1999) examined the impact of real exchange rate misalignment on economic growth in four MENA countries, namely, Egypt, Jordan, Morocco and Tunisia in the 1970s and 1980s.[2] During these years, the countries adopted exchange rate arrangements motivated by the need to protect the external balance from external shocks and domestic expansionary policy. The results reached confirmed the adverse effects of this misalignment on growth using all measures of misalignment adopted in endogenous growth models. Levy-Yeyati and Sturzenegger (2001) examine the impact of exchange rate regimes on output growth along with inflation, real interest rates, and nominal money growth.[3] The sample used covers 1,925 annual observations for 154 countries over the period 1973-1999. The authors found that for industrial countries, there exists no significant link between exchange rate regimes and economic performance. For non-industrial economies, both short and long pegs (pegs that have been in place for at least five consecutive years) are significantly and negatively related to per capita output growth. For both groups of countries, hard pegs display significantly smaller growth rates than floating arrangements. Nabli and Veganzones-Varoudakis (2002) addressed the impact of overvaluation in the 1970s and 1980s in 10 selected MENA countries on economic activity as measured by the competitiveness of manufactured exports.[4] The findings show that

1. Atish Ghosh, Anne-Marie Gulde, Jonathan Ostry, and Holger Wolf, "Does the Nominal Exchange Rate Regime Matter?" *NBER Working Paper Series* 5874, 1997.

2. Ilker Domac and Ghiath Shabsigh, "Real Exchange Rate Behavior and Economic Growth: Evidence from Egypt, Jordan, Morocco, and Tunisia," *IMF Working Paper* WP/99/40. Washington, International Monetary Fund, 1999.

3. Eduardo Levy-Yehati and Federico Sturzenegger, "Exchange Rate Regimes and Economic Performance," *IMF Staff Papers* 47 (2001): 62-98.

4. Mustapha Nabli and Marie-Ange Veganzones-Varoudakis. "Exchange Rate Regime and

overvaluation affected manufactured exports negatively. In addition, when some countries reduced overvaluation in the 1990s, their manufactured exports increased due to the significant decline in exchange rate misalignment. Bailliu, Lafrance and Perrault (2003) estimate the impact of exchange rate arrangements on growth using a panel data set of 60 countries between 1973 and 1998.[5] The results suggest that pegged, intermediate (crawling pegs or target zones) and flexible exchange rate regimes have a positive impact on economic growth when there is a monetary policy anchor. However, the opposite holds true in the absence of an anchor as intermediate and flexible exchange rate regimes become detrimental for growth. In this sense, the findings imply that the presence of a monetary policy anchor rather than the type of exchange rate regime is what matters for economic growth. The study by Husain, Mody and Rogoff (2005)[6] differs from previous ones in that it draws on new data and advances in exchange rate regimes' classification developed in Reinhart and Rogoff (2004).[7] This study relies on the new classification to also examine exchange rate regime durability and performance in developing and industrial economies. The findings imply that for highly developing economies with little access to international capital markets, pegged exchange rate regimes deliver relatively low inflation and high exchange rate durability without sacrifices in economic growth. As countries become more financially developed, they gain from moving to more flexible exchange rate regimes achieving higher growth without higher inflation. However, for emerging markets, exchange rate arrangements do not seem to have a systematic effect on output growth. Finally, Aghion, Bacchetta, Ranciere and Rogoff (2006) using a data set of 83 countries between 1960-2000 reached empirical results that real exchange rate volatility can impact long-term productivity growth with the effect largely depending on the level of financial development.[8] This volatility reduces growth in countries with low levels of financial development whereas for financially developed countries, there seems to be no significant effects.

Competitiveness of Manufactured Exports: The Case of MENA Countries," *MENA Working Paper No 207*. Washington: World Bank, 2002.

5. Jeannine Bailliu, Robert Lafrance, and Jean-Francois Perrault, "Does Exchange Rate Policy Matter for Growth," *International Finance* 63, no.3 (2003): 381-414.
6. Aasim Husain, Ashoka Mody and Kenneth Rogoff. "Exchange Rate Regime Durability and Performance in Developing versus Advanced Economies." *Journal of Monetary Economics* 52, no. 1, (2005): 35-64.
7. Carmen Reinhart and Kenneth Rogoff. "The Modern History of Exchange Rate Arrangements: A Reinterpretation." *The Quarterly Journal of Economics* CXIX, no. 1, (February 2004): 1-48.
8. Phillipe Aghion, Philippe Bacchetta, Romain Ranciere, and Kenneth Rogoff, "Exchange Rate Volatility and Productivity Growth: The Role of Financial Development." *NBER Working Paper* 12117, 2006.

The findings of the previously mentioned studies can be generalized as follows. For cases of pegged exchange rates, there seems to be either a weak or no significant relationship between the exchange rate arrangement and growth or in few cases a negative relationship. In addition, cases of exchange rate overvaluation or misalignment seem to be detrimental for growth. Cases of more flexible arrangements also show a weak relationship between various exchange rate regimes and growth. However, in some studies, flexible regimes seem to be more conducive for growth than fixed ones. The GCC countries were included in some of these studies that have mostly used a large sample of countries in a panel data framework. Thus, the specificities of some of the GCC countries, such as the large share of oil in exports and relatively low elasticities of demand for this product, may not be accurately captured in the studies.

2.2 Financial Sector Development and Growth

The recent literature addressing the relationship between financial sector development and economic growth centered first around determining measures of financial sector development to examine their significance on growth. These measures relate to the development of financial intermediaries as well as development of financial markets. Important measures of financial intermediaries' development relate to the ratios of private domestic credit to GDP, domestic credit to total credit, broad money to GDP, and liquid liabilities of banks to GDP. Measures of financial market development include stock market capitalization as a share of GDP, stock market capitalization, and private and public bond capitalization as a share of GDP. The rationale for a positive relationship between financial development and economic growth is based on the idea that financial development improves the efficiency of capital allocation conducive for growth. According to Khan and Senhadji (2000), three ongoing debates govern this relationship, namely, the measure of financial depth, the direction of causality between financial depth and growth, and whether a banking-based financial system is superior to a market-based one.[9]

One of the earliest studies examining this relationship is King and Levine (1993) in which 80 cross country evidence for the period 1960-1989 are used to examine whether the financial system can promote economic growth.[10] The results

9. Mohsin Khan and Abdelhak Senhadji. "Financial Development and Economic Growth: An Overview," IMF Working Paper, WP/00/209. Washington: International Monetary Fund, 2000.

10. Robert King and Ross Levine, "Finance and Growth: Schumpeter Might be Right," *The Quarterly Journal of Economics* 108, no. 3 (1993): 717-737.

reached show that the four financial sector development indicators used – such as the size of the formal financial intermediary sector to GDP, the importance of banks relative to the central bank, the percentage of credit allocated to private firms and the ratio of credit issued to private firms to GDP – are all significant in impacting the growth indicators such as real per capita GDP growth, the rate of physical capital accumulation, the ratio of domestic investment to GDP and a residual measure of the improvements in the efficiency of physical capital allocation. In a more recent study, Khan and Senhadji (2000) use four measures of both financial intermediaries and financial market development to examine their impact on growth.[11] Interestingly, the first three measures are cumulative in the sense that the first one being a subset of the second one relates to domestic credit to the private sector as a share of GDP, the second one includes in addition to the first measure the stock market capitalization as a share of GDP, whereas the third measure includes the second measure plus the private and public bond market capitalization as a share of GDP. The fourth measure includes only stock market capitalization. Thus, the third measure becomes the most exhaustive measure for financial depth and is only available for highly financially developed economies. The coefficients of all four indicators of financial depth are of the positive sign and highly significant in impacting growth. These results are in line with previous empirical evidence. Thus, to sum-up, there exists strong evidence on a general positive relationship between financial sector development and economic growth even though different indicators of financial depth may not be equally significant with some being insignificant in some countries and some studies as will be shown in the next section.

3. Testing Methodology and Empirical Results

The testing methodology is based on the previously discussed models in the second section that have addressed the impact of exchange rate regimes and financial development on economic performance. The resulting empirical specification is represented by:

RGDPit = a0 + a1GCEit + a2GFCFit + a3EGSit + a4IGS + a5DCRit + a6MQMit + a7EXSDRit + Uit

Where i stands for the ith country and t for the tth time period and where:

RGDP = Growth rate of real GDP

11. Mohsin Khan and and Abdelhak Senhadji, "Financial Development and Economic Growth: An Overview."

GCE= Growth rate of real government consumption expenditure
GFCF= Growth rate of real gross fixed capital formation
EGS= Growth rate of real exports of goods and services
IGS= Growth rate of real imports of goods and services
DCR= Growth rate of real domestic credit to the private sector
MQM = Growth rate of real broad money
EXSDR= Growth rate of the exchange rate
U= error term.

The exchange rate variable (EXSDR) is measured as the value of domestic currency units in terms of the Special Drawing Rights (SDR) such that an increase in this value reflects a depreciation in the domestic currency (and the US dollar) vs the SDR. This measure is included to capture the effects of the GCC adopted exchange rate regime on growth, which is one of the main purposes of the study. We could not include exchange rate dummies to reflect regime differentials as domestic currencies of the GCC countries were all of the pegged type over the period of the study as per the de facto classification in Table 1. Alternatively, we could not report the actual value of the exchange rate as it was largely constant and pegged to the US dollar. Therefore, to examine changes in this variable, we measured it in relationship to the SDR so that any change in the US dollar/SDR value will be reflected in a change of the domestic currency in terms of the SDR mirroring its appreciation or depreciation. Additionally, all variables in the equation are measured in percentage changes in real term during the corresponding year. We tried several specifications such as, for example, expressing each variable as a percent of GDP. However, our results and especially the R 2 kept improving when we moved to the current measure. Our sample consists of annual observations for the six GCC countries over the period 1975-2008. The considered period could provide, therefore, a large or acceptable number of annual observations for a suitable dataset consisting of 34 observations per country and thus a total of 204 observations as a whole. However, lack of some data caused fewer observations which totaled 178. The main sources of our data are the IMF International Financial Statistics CD-ROM and the World Economic Outlook Databases. In very rare cases, and when necessary to fill missing data, we relied on Central Bank Bulletins and reports of countries in question.

The results of our econometric investigation are displayed in Table 2. The aim of the paper, as stated earlier, is twofold. The first is to examine the relationship between exchange rate arrangements and economic growth while the second is to study the impact of financial sector development on economic growth. The findings show that the exchange rate variable is significant and of the negative sign,

Table 2: Macroeconomic Variables Associated with Economic Growth

Dependent Variable is Growth Rate of Real GDP (RGDP)

Growth rate of Real Government Consumption Expenditure (GCE)	0.017 (0.033)
Growth rate of Real Gross Fixed Capital Formation (GFCF)	0.101*** (0.029)
Growth rate of Real Exports of Goods & Services (EGS)	0.202*** (0.028)
Growth rate of Real Imports of Goods & Services (IGS)	-0.051 (0.032)
Growth rate of Real Domestic Credit to the Private Sector (DCR)	0.002 (0.007)
Growth rate of Real Broad Money (MQM)	0.054** (0.022)
Growth rate of the Exchange Rate (EXSDR)	-0.102** (0.049)
Time period	1975-2008
Number of observations	178
Cross sections	6
R-squared, Adjusted R-squared	0.52, 0.49
F-statistic	20.24***
Durbin-Watson stat	2.10

Note: Standard errors are in parentheses. One, two and three asterisks indicate significance levels of 10, 5 and 1 percent, respectively

implying that domestic currency appreciation against the SDR (under a peg to the US dollar) is likely to impact positively economic growth. Therefore, the result reached suggests that the dollar peg exchange rate regime for the GCC can contribute to economic growth under an appreciating dollar against other major currencies. In turn, a weakening of the dollar can slowdown economic growth. This supports the idea that the nature of the exchange rate regime adopted in the GCC countries to achieve macroeconomic discipline or to promote the external sector does have a significant impact on growth. It is to be noted that the paper does not address the issue of successful versus unsuccessful exchange rate pegs and arrangements but their growth implications. The findings on the significance of the exchange rate variable do not coincide with some of the results reached in the literature on the weak or non-existent relationship between exchange rate arrangements and economic growth but are generally in line with the studies that have shown a significant relationship.

Regarding the second aim of the paper, two measures of financial development variables were used: The rate of growth of real domestic credit to the private sector and the rate of growth of real broad money. The first measure was shown to be insignificant. This is in line with studies such as the one by Hakura (2004)[12] where this variable was dropped from the analysis due to its insignificance. It is also in line with some of the mixed results in Aghion, Bachetta, Ranciere, and Rogoff (2006)[13] as well as some other studies where this variable was either shown to be insignificant or with a negative sign implying that it impedes growth such as in Bailliu, Lafrance, and Perrault (2003).[14] However, this result is not in line with the ones reached by King and Levine (1993) and Khan and Senhadji (2000) where this indicator was significant throughout various specifications.[15] In fact, in the last mentioned study, the authors discuss some probable reasons for the insignificance of this indicator such as the inadequacy of the various linear specifications to capture growth dynamics and that the relationship between growth and financial depth may involve a threshold effect where countries need to reach a certain level of depth before there is a significant effect on growth. The second indicator or the rate of growth of real money was shown to be significant in line with many studies in the literature corroborating this result such as King and Levine (1993).[16] Thus, according to this measure, financial development is a significant determinant of GCC's economic growth.

Our results also show that some other explanatory variables are significant and of the expected sign. Gross fixed capital formation is positively correlated with economic growth in line with other studies reflecting this result such as Khan and Senhadji (2000), and Levy-Yeyati and Sturzenegger (2001).[17] Exports seem also to

12. Dalia Hakura, "Growth in the Middle-East and North Africa," *IMF Working Paper* WP/04/56. Washington: International Monetary Fund, 2004.
13. Aghion, Bachetta, Ranciere, and Rogoff, "Exchange Rate Volatility and Productivity Growth."
14. Bailliu, Lafrance, and Perrault, "Does Exchange Rate Policy Matter for Growth."
15. King and Levine, "Finance and Growth: Schumpeter Might be Right"; Khan and Senhadji, "Financial Development and Economic Growth: An Overview."
16. King and Levine, "Finance and Growth: Schumpeter Might be Right."
17. Khan and Senhadji, "Financial Development and Economic Growth: An Overview"; and Levy-

be a major determinant of growth similar to other studies showing the significance of trade openness such as Bailliu, Lafrance, and Perrault (2003).[18] Government consumption expenditure is insignificant in line with studies that have addressed this issue. In several of these studies, such as Levy-Yeyati and Sturzenegger (2001), Bailliu, Lafrance, and Perrault (2003), the impact of this variable on economic growth was shown to be even negative as it is believed that excess government spending impedes growth.[19] In the GCC countries, a key finding in Hakura (2004) is that large governments appear to have stifled private sector growth and impeded the diversification of production.[20] Standard errors reported are corrected for heteroscedasticity and serial correlation and some of the diagnostic tests to assess the goodness of fit of the model are reported at the bottom of the table.

4. Future Prospects for Monetary Policy

The GCC countries have decided to establish a monetary union in the next few years, knowing that currently only four of them are still committed, with Oman in 2008 and the UAE in 2009 making a decision not to join the Union. In designing the monetary and exchange rate policy framework for this union and its common currency, decisions have to be taken on both the strategic and operational levels. One of the key strategic decisions, and perhaps the most prominent, is the choice of the optimal exchange rate regime. Operational related decisions deal with issues such as the future role and functions of the unified central bank and of each GCC country monetary authority, rules on domestic credit growth to the private and public sectors, the extent of harmonization of banking regulation and supervision and payment and settlement systems among member countries, the management of international foreign exchange reserves and other foreign assets. Given that operational-related issues are beyond the scope of this paper, this section discusses the future prospects for monetary policy in the GCC countries as reflected in the choice of the exchange rate regime after achieving the Gulf Monetary Union. The stated exchange rate regime for the monetary union has so far been the use of the US dollar peg as an external anchor for monetary policy. The decision was largely based on the belief that the peg can maintain macroeconomic stability, strengthen

Yeyati and Sturzenegger, "Exchange Rate Regimes and Economic Performance."

18. Bailliu, Lafrance, and Perrault, "Does Exchange Rate Policy Matter for Growth."

19. Levy-Yeyati and Sturzenegger, ""Exchange Rate Regimes and Economic Performance," and Bailliu, Lafrance, and Perrault, "Does Exchange Rate Policy Matter for Growth."

20. Hakura, "Growth in the Middle-East and North Africa."

confidence in the GCC economies, and allow member countries to adopt the single currency at the existing parities. In light of the above mentioned facts, it was natural therefore for GCC to give the dollar peg priority over other alternatives because of the policy familiarity among economic agents and its wide acceptance. Additionally, the pegging to the dollar for the past few decades has proved its credibility and efficiency, firstly, in keeping inflation relatively low on average in the region, except for the period 2004-2008 in certain countries like UAE and Qatar partly due to imported inflation through the dollar peg and a weakening US currency; and secondly, in facilitating and promoting trade and financial transactions with the rest of the world. It is well known that the peg implies for countries adopting such an exchange rate arrangement that they cannot defend in the short run against imported inflation contrary to the long run where higher inflation in trading partners is likely to be offset by the depreciation of their domestic currencies against the US dollar. The dollar peg is also easy to administer and manage for reasons explained later. It is worth noting that the GCC countries have practiced fiscal and labor policies consistent with the exchange rate peg to support domestic and external stability.

Yet one may ask whether, with ongoing and planned structural changes in their economies, the dollar peg will remain the most advantageous system for the GCC countries in the future and the best policy option. The fact that the peg arrangement has served their objectives in the past does not mean that future benefits are assured especially in a world characterized by deepening and broadening world economic and financial integration and rapidly changing operating environments. In an attempt to find answers to this legitimate question, we examine whether the GCC ought to keep the current monetary arrangement when establishing the union or adopt a different one by highlighting the several advantages and disadvantages of each arrangement along with the salient features of the GCC countries, their future path for financial development, and the empirical results attained. We suggest, based on qualitative and empirical analysis, the most suitable regime for the single currency under the existing conditions and what could be an alternative choice in the future if the GCC economies are to become more sectorally diversified and integrated in international trade and finance.

4.1 The Peg to the US Dollar

Recently, there have been valuable and well-founded arguments for the peg to the US dollar as an exchange rate regime for the intended single GCC currency. First, the peg to the US dollar tends to stabilize the value of export revenues or more accurately smoothen potential fluctuations in the financial inflows from external trade and finance resulting from volatility in foreign exchange markets, as most of the GCC exports (oil and gas) and the bulk of their external financial assets are US dollar denominated. In fact, oil and gas production in these economies at present account for around 75 percent of their exports. However, this could become a weaker argument in case the share of GCC non-oil exports in other than the US dollar becomes relatively much larger or external assets turn out to be broadly diversified in the currency of denomination. But this is very unlikely to be the case in the short to medium term.

Second, holding imported inflation constant, the peg to the US dollar can bring price stability to GCC countries as it has proved to be for many years a strong anchor for monetary policy and can prevent domestic inflation from deviating too much from the US rate of inflation for an extended period of time, provided there are no significant divergences between GCC and US business cycles. In general, fixed exchange rates constrain expansionary aggregate demand policies for the fear of jeopardizing the peg and depleting international reserves. But domestic inflation in many GCC countries has deviated very substantially from the US in recent years and the dollar peg has been partly blamed for this though inflation has been low on average in the Gulf region for the rest of the years with considerable differences in inflation among GCC member countries and consequently in their real effective exchange rates. This is because the imported monetary policy from the US due to the peg at that time was not appropriate for local needs. Specifically, lower US interest rates policies were unsuited to the needs of the GCC business cycles where higher interest rates might have dampened the excesses of the ensuing oil boom. In this respect, supportive fiscal policies and policies aiming at enlarging the absorptive capacity of the GCC economies remain a must to ensure price stability.

Third, the fixed exchange rate against the US dollar in GCC countries can ensure international competitiveness under high labor market flexibility in the private sector as it is currently the case in the GCC economies. However, there are doubts in the willingness and ability of GCC countries to maintain such flexibility in the long run, as there are emerging trends indicating that the national labor force in the non-oil private sector is gaining importance and its share of the total work force is expected to increase in the future consequent to the rapidly growing population and the tendency of the government sector not to be playing the role of employer of first and last choice. The flexibility will be undermined also by efforts to nationalize the labor force and complicate the employment of expatriate workers.

To the above arguments, one can add also that a fixed exchange rate encourages capital inflows as it provides a kind of implicit guarantee against the risk of exchange rate changes. As such, a fixed exchange rate regime can encourage large dependence on foreign capital irrespective of the consequences. An external shock such as an increase in foreign interest rates can then result in capital outflows and loss of international reserves. Under a fixed exchange rate regime, borrowers have also much less incentive to hedge their foreign exchange positions though the exchange rate risk can be much easier hedged than under other regimes.

4.2 The Peg to a Basket of Currencies

Pegging to a basket of currencies has its own advantages and disadvantages. On the benefits side, such a peg can in general reduce the adverse effects of nominal exchange rate volatility of major currencies and introduce more stability in external trade and related receipts. However, it is a minor benefit for the GCC countries at present given the characteristics of their economies and exports. The basket peg can also serve as a transitory regime before the implementation of a more flexible exchange rate arrangement as it allows market participants and economic agents to get more acquainted with the foreign exchange rate risk and the way to manage such risk. This implies therefore that market participants have to bear the exchange rate risk and possess the right hedging tools and techniques which may not be affordable or could be costly.

Another shortcoming is that basket pegs are more difficult to manage than a single peg given that different weights are attached to the currencies of the country's trade and financial partners. In addition, basket pegs are more opaque and hard to explain to the general public, which could encourage speculative attacks on the domestic currency under certain circumstances as has happened in many countries with such regimes. To overcome this latter obstacle, it has been suggested to peg to a small and transparent basket easy to interpret and manage, such as one consisting of two currencies, the US dollar and the Euro. Such a basket would allow the GCC countries to embrace most of their transactions in trade and finance with the rest of the world and to manage efficiently the exchange rate risk with only the dollar and Euro hedging instruments. One can add that the build-up of large foreign exchange reserves in GCC countries can in turn play an important role in discouraging speculative attacks on the single currency.

4.3 Managed Floating

The most interesting arguments in favor of alternative exchange rate classifications to the conventional peg to the US dollar relate to the improved ability to contain both domestic and imported inflation. It has been contended specifically that monetary policy independence associated with a more flexible exchange rate regime would allow GCC countries to pursue better their goals of low inflation and output growth. A flexible exchange rate regime would make room for a more independent and efficient monetary policy. Therefore, the exchange rate and not the interest rate can be used to absorb adverse external shocks and stabilize output. However, some have argued that the effectiveness of an independent or more active monetary policy in achieving stability could be undermined by distortions in the monetary transmission mechanism specifically in the effectiveness of the interest rate channel as in the case of GCC countries. This argument may be valid if investment and consumption decisions in these economies are largely insensitive to change in interest rates and highly dependent on government spending. However, as the empirical results show in our work and the literature, the role of government spending seems to stifle and impede growth on average and at best is not a major cause of it, though it could be argued that despite the fact that government spending in the GCC countries is mere redistribution of rents, the recent countercyclical stimulus by them contributed to growth or at least prevented negative growth. Thus, under such conditions of negative government spending contribution to economic growth, monetary policy rather than fiscal policy is likely to play the leading role in absorbing shocks on the domestic economy, necessitating at least a partial independence.

It has been advocated as well that by abandoning the peg to the dollar the GCC countries can avoid imported inflation resulting from a sustained depreciation of the US currency. But it could be argued as well that administrative price controls like the ones in many GCC countries and low pass-through effects tend to limit imported inflation. Hasan and Alogeel (2008) investigated the factors behind inflation in the GCC region and found that demand and money supply shocks affect inflation in the short run but the main driving force for inflation in the long run is the trading partners' inflation followed by the pass-through effect and oil prices.[21]

Furthermore, allowing the exchange rate to float would obviously increase the exchange rate risk and that would probably necessitate hedging, which could be costly and difficult in an environment of underdeveloped capital markets. Despite the fact that this paper does not address such issues, the literature results on the efficiency of financial markets in GCC do not have strong support. Changing the exchange rate policy could also cause difficulties for business planning, accounting, and budgeting in the corporate sector, which has become accustomed to operate

21. Maher Hasan and Heshan Alogeel, "Understanding the Inflationary Process in the GCC Region: The Case of Saudi Arabia and Kuwait," IMF Working Paper 08/193 (Washington: International Monetary Fund, 2008).

under completely different conditions for a long time and where the peg facilitated these issues.

To conclude, many believe that the peg to the US dollar remains the most viable policy option for GCC countries to achieve macroeconomic and external stability under existing conditions reflected in economies largely based on the performance of the hydrocarbon sector, the bulk of exports and foreign assets being denominated in the US dollar, and adequate labor and capital markets mobility, though labor mobility is likely to lessen over the coming period for reasons mentioned before such as the sponsorship system. Over the past decades under similar conditions, the dollar peg has proved its credibility as a nominal anchor for monetary policy for GCC countries and has assured for these economies the desired stability objectives without hindering their international competitiveness or their ability to quickly adjust to shocks. It also facilitated trade, finance and accounting transactions in addition to monetary coordination among GCC member countries, allowing the determination of the entry parities. However, despite the many advantages, the empirical results reached in this study show that there is a significant relationship between the exchange rate variable and economic growth in the sense that a depreciation in the value of the US dollar and thus the domestic currency tends to impede growth. Based on this, the GCC authorities should pay attention in pegging to one single currency irrespective of the path this currency takes. The exchange rate regime of pegging to a basket followed by Kuwait since 2007 may be worth considering and may signal the beginning of a general move towards this policy. In addition, a larger monetary and economic entity reflected in the new union may lead to a shift to a more diversified economic and exports structures away from the heavy dependence on the oil sector, and to more international market integration in trade, services and assets, coupled with changing labor policies and flexibility from growing employment opportunities in the non-oil private sector. Under the new conditions, we believe that exchange rate flexibility is a necessity for the monetary union to ensure external stability and international competitiveness. Over the medium term, the GCC countries can introduce an intermediate regime between the peg to a single or basket of currencies and the float to enable economic agents to acquaint themselves on how to operate under a more flexible regime and manage the exchange rate risk.

Conclusion and Policy Implications

The monetary policy framework in the GCC countries has been based on pegged exchange rate arrangements to achieve macroeconomic discipline and promote external stability. The results reached in this paper show that such arrangements can significantly impact economic growth in the sense that a depreciation in the value of the US dollar and thus GCC currencies influences growth negatively. As a result, by pursuing pegged exchange rate arrangements, these countries may leave themselves open to domestic negative output fluctuations whenever economic conditions in the US, and to a lesser extent worldwide, dictate a depreciation in the value of the US currency. In addition, the results also show that while some measures of financial development are not significant in impacting growth in GCC countries, other measures reflect the significance of financial depth. These results ought to be considered in the formulation of the Gulf Monetary Union in the context of the monetary policy framework and the exchange rate arrangement to be adopted. Monetary Unions should be more protected from the US dollar fluctuations to be able to adjust their common currency in line with the objective of preserving the Union's convergence framework without losing their independent monetary policy. Until now, however, many believe that pegged exchange rate arrangements remain the most viable policy option for the GCC countries to achieve macroeconomic internal and external policy goals. Additionally, pursuing an independently floating exchange rate arrangement at this stage would increase the exchange rate risk necessitating hedging, which could be costly and difficult in an environment of low level of financial development. However, over the medium term, to insulate their economies further against the depreciation of the US dollar and minimize output fluctuations until more financial depth has been achieved, the GCC countries can move towards an intermediate regime starting with pegging to a diversified basket of currencies while adjusting their economies to operate under a more flexible arrangement and manage the exchange rate risk.

Bibliography

Aghion Philippe, Philippe Bacchetta, Romain Ranciere, and Kenneth Rogoff. "Exchange Rate Volatility and Productivity Growth: The Role of Financial Development." In *NBER Working Paper* 12117, 2006.

Bailliu Jeannine, Robert Lafrance, and Jean-Francois Perrault. "Does Exchange Rate Policy Matter for Growth." In *International Finance* 63, no.3 (2003): 381-414.

Central Bank of Bahrain website, www.cbb.gov.bh

Central Bank of Kuwait website, www.cbk.gov.kw

Central Bank of Oman website, www.cbo-oman.org

Central Bank of Qatar website, www.qcb.gov.qa

Central Bank of Saudi Arabia website, www.sama.gov.sa

Central bank of the UAE website, www.centralbank.ae

Domac, Ilker and Ghiath Shabsigh. "Real Exchange Rate Behavior and Economic Growth: Evidence from Egypt, Jordan, Morocco, and Tunisia." *IMF Working Paper* WP/99/40. Washington, International Monetary Fund, 1999.

Ghosh, Atish, Anne-Marie Gulde, Jonathan Ostry, and Holger Wolf. "Does the Nominal Exchange Rate Regime Matter?" *NBER Working Paper Series* 5874, 1997.

Hakura, Dalia. "Growth in the Middle-East and North Africa." *IMF Working Paper* WP/04/56. Washington: International Monetary Fund, 2004.

Hasan, Maher, and Alogeel Heshan. "Understanding the Inflationary Process in the GCC Region: The Case of Saudi Arabia and Kuwait."*IMF Working Paper* 08/193. Washington: International Monetary Fund, 2008.

Husain, Aasim, Ashoka Mody and Kenneth Rogoff. "Exchange Rate Regime Durability and Performance in Developing versus Advanced Economies." *Journal of Monetary Economics* 52, no. 1, (2005): 35-64.

IMF, *Annual Reports*, various issues.

IMF, *International Financial Statistics*, CD-ROM.

IMF *World Economic Outlook*, Database.

Khan, Mohsin and Abdelhak Senhadji. "Financial Development and Economic Growth: An Overview.",IMF Working Paper,WP/00/209. Washington: International Monetary Fund, 2000.

King, Robert and Ross Levine. "Finance and Growth: Schumpeter Might be Right." *The Quarterly Journal of Economics* 108, no. 3 (1993): 717-737.

Levy-Yehati, Eduardo and Federico Sturzenegger. "Exchange Rate Regimes and Economic Performance." *IMF Staff Papers* 47 (2001): 62-98.

Nabli, Mustapha and Marie-Ange Veganzones-Varoudakis. "Exchange Rate Regime and Competitiveness of Manufactured Exports: The Case of MENA Countries." *MENA Working Paper* No 207. Washington: World Bank, 2002.

Reinhart, Carmen and Kenneth Rogoff. "The Modern History of Exchange Rate Arrangements: A Reinterpretation." *The Quarterly Journal of Economics* CXIX, no. 1, (February 2004): 1-48.

8

The Establishment of a Monetary Union among the Member States of the GCC

*Erwin Nierop and Gabriela Lippe-Holst**

Introduction

In 2001, the Heads of State of the Gulf Cooperation Council (GCC) decided that the bloc would embark on the establishment of a Gulf Monetary Union (GMU). The basic assumption was that the GMU would be created in the style of the Economic and Monetary Union (EMU) established by the European Union (EU) towards the end of the last and beginning of this century.

The legal basis for the GCC initiative was laid down in Article 4 of the 2001 Economic Agreement, which states the following:

"For the purpose of achieving a monetary and economic union between Member States, including currency unification, Member States shall undertake, according to a specified timetable, to achieve the requirements of this union. These include the achievement of a high level of harmonization between Member States in all economic policies, especially fiscal and economic policies, banking legislation, setting criteria to approximate rates of economic performance related to fiscal and monetary stability, such as rates of budgetary deficit, indebtedness, and price levels."

By the end of 2009, another legal act relating to GMU entered into force: a Monetary Union Agreement (MUA[1]), inclusive of the Statute of a Gulf Monetary

* Views expressed in this research paper are those of the authors and not necessarily those of their employers or any other party

1. The Monetary Union Agreement among the member states of the Cooperation Council for the

Council (GMC[2]).[3] It is noted that the MUA has not been signed by Oman and the United Arab Emirates. Oman is of the opinion that it has to invest in the development of its infrastructure first and will thus for the time being not meet the convergence criteria for participation in the monetary union. The UAE has reconsidered its participation in GMU after the GCC's decision to locate the headquarters of the GMC in Riyadh, Saudi Arabia, rather than in the UAE capital, Abu Dhabi.[4] The MUA foresees that this set of legal instruments will be completed with the Statute of a Gulf Central Bank (GCB), which will have to be prepared by the GMC.

In March 2010, the GMC was inaugurated. Its main task is to prepare for GMU and it will no doubt wish to look into the EU's experiences in this respect. While the EU may indeed provide for many useful examples, which may save valuable time for the GCC, a word of caution is warranted as well. EMU is embedded in the institutional framework of the EU, which has developed over a period of more than five decades. Arrangements for other monetary unions cannot be simply copied from the EU, but should be tailored to their specific context.

It may be premature to predict an accurate timetable for the achievement of GMU, since the timetable will among other matters depend on the time required for technical preparatory work to lay the operational and regulatory foundations for GMU. Yet, it is obviously important to develop a strategy towards GMU, including a timetable. First, the lack of a strategy may lead to a situation where political momentum is lost. Second, the establishment of a monetary union is a society wide development where all parties involved (public authorities, the private sector, the public at large) will have a role to play and therefore will require a compass to

---

Arab States of the Gulf (GCC), dated December 30, 2008 and ratified on June 7, 2009 by Bahrain, Kuwait, Qatar, and Saudi Arabia. The MUA appears to be a stand-alone agreement, which is not intended to be merged into the overall legal and institutional framework of the GCC.

2. The Statute of the Monetary Council of the member states of the Cooperation Council for the Arab States of the Gulf (GCC), of the same date as the MUA to which it is annexed.
3. The MUA and the GMC Statute remind to the 1992 ("Maastricht") treaty on European economic and monetary union, which included a general part on economic and monetary policy (title VII), a Statute of the European Monetary Institute (EMI), and a Statute of the European System of Central Banks (ESCB) and of the European Central Bank (ECB). In 2009, the provisions relevant to EMU were incorporated in the ("Lisbon") Treaty on European Union and the Treaty on the Functioning of the European Union, while the EMI Statute had already earlier become obsolete as a result of the EMI's dissolution upon the establishment of the ECB.
4. This decision is formalized in Article 4.4 of the MUA as repeated in Article 3.3 of the GMC Statute.

prepare themselves properly and in a timely fashion for the events to come and particularly the introduction of the single currency.[5]

1. General Foundations for Gulf Monetary Union

The establishment of a monetary union is often considered to be a stage in the following process: free trade area – customs union – internal or common market – monetary union and – political union. A monetary union is usually seen as the crown on the internal market with different advantages such as the creation of a single market for goods and services, the elimination of foreign exchange risks, and the integration of financial markets. In the case of the GCC, it is clear that the feeling of a common identity and destiny among the citizens is also an important factor for the initiative to establish a monetary union. That said, in order to optimally reap the benefits of a monetary union and to ensure its smooth functioning, it is also generally considered that a sufficient degree of regional integration is required. For the purpose of this paper, a distinction may be made between: (a) market integration and financial market integration, (b) economic convergence, and (c) legal convergence.

1.1 Market Integration and Financial Market Integration

It goes beyond the scope of this paper to provide an in-depth analysis of the requirements for GMU and the present state of affairs in the area of market integration and financial integration.[6] However, on the basis of the EU's experience,

5. By way of comparison, the timetable for the achievement of EMU was as follows:
   - 13 years (1989 – 2002) from the political agreement to realize EMU to the final completion of the undertaking.
   - 7 years (1992 – 1999) from the signing of the legal framework for EMU to the start of "Stage 3" of EMU with the introduction of the scriptural euro, followed in 2002 by the introduction of the physical banknotes and coins.
   - The above 7 years were fully used by EU member states to reach the necessary degree of economic and legal convergence and by Community bodies (in particular the EMI) as well as the member states to complete preparations necessary for the start of EMU, for which a deadline was set in the Treaty of Maastricht of July 1, 1998.
6. The ECB considers the market for a given set of financial instruments or services to be fully integrated, when all potential participants in such a market (i) are subject to a single set of rules when deciding to buy or sell those financial instruments or services, (ii) have equal access to this set of financial instruments or services, and (iii) are treated equally when they operate in the market. The term "market" is used in a broad sense, covering all possible exchanges of financial instruments or services, be these via an organized market, such as a stock exchange, or via an over-the-counter market created by a financial institution supplying a financial instrument or service.

it is possible to define the following areas for specific attention:

- free movement of goods
- freedom of movement for workers
- right of establishment and freedom to provide services
- free movement of capital
- company law
- financial services (for example, legislation on: banking; securities trading and investment services; payment and securities settlement systems; collateral and enforceability of contracts; insolvencies)
- economic and monetary policy (including the prohibitions on monetary financing and privileged access, the principle of central bank independence)
- statistics, and
- customs union

As far as financial integration is concerned, there are several reasons why this is important for the smooth functioning of GMU. First, financial integration is of key importance for the conduct of the single monetary policy, as it fosters a smooth and balanced transmission of monetary policy throughout the single currency area. Second, financial integration is also relevant for financial stability; on the one hand, it enhances the opportunity for risk diversification and improves access to financial markets; on the other hand, it may increase the scope for spill-over effects and contagion. Moreover, financial integration is linked to the GCB's task of promoting the smooth operation of payment systems, including the safe and efficient functioning of securities clearing and settlement. Finally, it is generally accepted that financial integration contributes to increasing the potential for stronger non-inflationary economic growth.[7]

The ECB has developed quantitative indicators of financial integration in the euro area, which provide the basis for a comprehensive assessment of both the current level of financial integration and its evolution overtime.

7. See in this context, for example, the ECB's report on Financial Integration in Europe dated April 2010. The Eurosystem attaches great importance to furthering progress in European financial integration through different activities such as:

- enhancing knowledge and raising awareness of the state of and need for European financial integration and measuring the progress made (monitoring, speeches, research together with academics and practitioners);
- acting as a catalyst for private sector activities by facilitating collective action and assisting with possible coordination problems (for example, in the area of retail payments);
- providing advice on the legislative and regulatory framework for the European financial system

1.2 Economic Convergence

The general foundations for monetary union include a sufficient degree of convergence of the economies proposing to form the monetary union (to compensate for the loss of national discretion in monetary and exchange rate policy, which is an inescapable feature of monetary union) and sufficient economic and financial integration to enable them to enjoy the benefits of lower transaction costs and exchange rate risk from the start of monetary union. Monetary union itself will promote integration and convergence (as much of the academic literature recognizes), but this will take time. Inherent to monetary union is the conduct of a single monetary and exchange rate policy in the interests of the single currency area as a whole. It cannot be tuned to suit the needs of individual member states. Owing to the impossibility of conducting a national monetary and exchange rate policy by individual member states in monetary union, it is important to start from a position in which such a loss of national discretion in macroeconomic policy can easily be borne and will not (by inflicting strains on the national economies) outweigh the benefits of introducing the single currency in terms of reduced transactions costs and exchange rate risks and the prospect of greater economic integration. Therefore, to function smoothly and to bring about economic benefits for all GCC member states, GMU should start with a high degree of sustainable monetary and economic convergence and compatibility among the member states. These states should have broadly synchronous economic cycles, experience similar external shocks (arising, for example, from fluctuations in world commodity prices), and have comparable inflation and growth rates. Similar income levels may also be important. Their public finances should be under control. Their interest rates should align, and they should have a high degree of stability in nominal bilateral exchange rates.

The GCC has indeed recognized the importance of macro-economic convergence. In 2006, it adopted the following six convergence criteria (which are very similar to the EU's convergence criteria):

- The inflation rate should not exceed by more than 2 percent the weighted average of inflation rates of the six GCC countries
- The average short-term interest rate should not exceed by more than 2 percent

(contributions to public consultations initiated by the European Commission, opinions on draft Community and national legislation in the ECB's field of competence, participation in EU committees); and
- providing central banking services that also foster European financial integration (for example, the TARGET2 payment system, TARGET2 Securities for the settlement of securities transactions, the Correspondent Central Bank Model2).

the average of the lowest three interest rates

- Foreign exchange reserves should cover good imports for at least four months
- Annual fiscal deficit should not exceed 3 percent of GDP
- The public debt ratio should not exceed 60 percent of GDP
- The GCC currencies should maintain a fixed peg to the USD.

Fiscal policy is the most important element of economic policy which, it may be assumed, would remain at least initially within the competence of GCC member states in a monetary union. But sustainable monetary union will require permanent commonly agreed standards for sound fiscal policies. The enforcement of such fiscal rules would require political acceptance.

1.3 Legal Convergence

Currently, a process of harmonization of the legal framework in the areas most affected by the monetary union needs to be put in place. The concept, objectives, instruments and powers of central banks need to be aligned. The concept and legal regime of credit institutions, payment systems, basic securities laws, statistics, etc., need to be similar before single institutions such as the GCB can operate throughout the monetary union jurisdictions. This process has been termed in the EU as "legal convergence" and a distinction is usually made between three areas where adaptation of national legislation is required:

- Central bank independence. If the GCC will follow the ECB's approach towards central bank independence,[8] this would imply that a distinction will be made between:

  (a) institutional independence: the prohibition for the GCC and its member states to issue instructions to the GMC, GCB, and the NCBS[9]

---

8. The notion of central bank independence is in this context restricted to ESCB-related tasks. In the area of independence of prudential supervisors, a distinction may be made between:
   - regulatory independence, associated with a wide autonomy in setting prudential rules and regulations;
   - supervisory independence from political interference and industry intimidation;
   - institutional autonomy associated with the security of tenure of supervisors; and
   - budgetary (financial) independence.

9. For example, Article 38 of statute of the Central Bank Law of Kuwait states the following: "The Governor shall keep the Minister of Finance continuously informed of the monetary and credit policy pursued or intended to be pursued by the Bank. If the Minister has a different view, he may issue general directives to be followed by the Bank and such directives shall become binding on the Bank ..." This Article is clearly in contradiction with the principle of institutional independence

(b) personal independence: security of tenure of members of decision-making bodies of the GMC, GCB, and the NCBs (a minimum term of office and dismissal only on grounds of incapacity or serious misconduct)[10]

(c) functional independence: the GMC and GCB should have adequate powers and tools at their disposal to achieve their statutory objectives, and

(d) financial independence: the GMC and the GCB should avail of adequate financial means to fulfil their tasks.

- Integration of NCBs in a new structure geared towards a single monetary policy to be conducted in a new single currency area.
- Adaptation of legislation other than the statutes of NCBs

The need for adaptation of national legislation is also recognized in Article 17.1 of the MUA, which reads as follows: "The Member States shall take all measures and procedures to ensure the consistency of their national legislation, including the statutes of their national central banks, with this Agreement in order to allow the Central Bank to perform its tasks and conduct its functions." In this context it is interesting to note that Article 7 of the MUA as repeated in Article 5 of the GMC Statute states that "The Monetary Council shall be consulted by the Member States on any proposed legislation relevant to the Monetary Union." This obligation is very useful, since it enables the member states to profit from the GMC's experience in this respect and it will allow the GMC to contribute to the harmonization of legislation in the monetary and financial field. That said, the provision may also merit further clarification. First, "any proposed legislation relevant to Monetary Union," is a broad formulation and, in order to avoid confusion, it may be wise to specify this further.[11] Second, the GCC and GMC

and therefore requires adaptation.

10. For instance, Article 9 of the statute of the Saudi Arabian Monetary Authority reads as follows: "The Minister of Finance nominates the Governor and the members of the Board of SAMA wit the approval of the Council of Ministers and the appointment is valid for five years by way of a Royal Decree. The Governor and the members of the Board can be removed from office through the same procedure and by Royal Decree." This Article does not define and delimit the grounds for dismissal and it would therefore require adaptation.

11. In the case of the EMI, a similar obligation existed under Article 5.3, second paragraph, of the EMI Statute with regard to "any draft legislative provision within its field of competence." This obligation was further elaborated in a Council decision of November 22, 1993 on the consultation of the European Monetary Institute by national authorities on draft legislative provisions (93/717/EC). This Council Decision defined draft legislative provisions as follows: "Any such provisions which, once they become legally binding and of general applicability in the territory of a Member State, lay down rules for an indefinite number of cases and are addressed to an indefinite number

may be well-advised to reflect on the consequences of non-compliance with this obligation.[12] Third, procedural matters, such as the time limits for consultation procedures, may require attention. Fourth, the adoption of legislation relevant to GMU will be a moving target and extend well beyond the scope of the starting date of GMU. As a consequence, it is appropriate to extend the obligation to the GCB (which has not been done yet in the MUA, but could be achieved through the GCB Statute).[13] Last but not least, the GCC may wish to consider the creation of a mechanism of consultation at a Community level in order to avoid that the GMC's, and later the GCB's, expertise can only be mobilized at the stage that GCC resolutions, recommendations, and possibly in the future other measures are implemented in national legislation. In fact, once the GMC or the GCB have advised on draft GCC measures, it may not be necessary anymore to have consultations on national implementing measures.[14]

2. Legal and Institutional Framework for Gulf Monetary Union

2.1 Monetary Union Agreement

A monetary union needs to be prepared for and subsequently operated within the framework of a comprehensive set of pre-established rules (the legal framework) and an adequate institutional structure, including the establishment of regional monetary institutions (the institutional framework) embedded in the existing GCC institutional framework. For this purpose, the MUA lays down the legal and institutional foundations of GMU.

- Article 3 specifies the basic features of the GMU as follows: "The monetary union shall entail:

---

of natural or legal persons, excluding provisions of which the exclusive purpose is the transposition of Community directives into the law of Member States." This Council decision also defined the EMI's field of competence to in particular cover draft legislation in the following areas: (a) currency matters; (b) means of payment; (c) national central banks; (d) the collection, compilation, and distribution of monetary, financial, banking, payment systems and balance of payment statistics; (e) payment and settlement systems; and (f) rules applicable to financial institutions insofar as they materially influence the stability of financial institutions and markets.

12. Under EU law, non-compliance with the obligation to consult led to invalidity of the legislation concerned.

13. In the case of the ECB, this was done in a Council decision of June 29, 1998 on the consultation of the European Central Bank by national authorities regarding draft legislative provisions (98/415/EC).

14. See in the same vein also the second part of the definition of the notion of "draft legislative provisions" in footnote 8 ("excluding ... Member States").

1. the coordination of economic policies of the Member States so as to ensure that they are conducive to monetary and fiscal stability with a view to securing a high degree of sustainable economic convergence throughout the single currency area;
2. preparing the payment systems infrastructure essential for the monetary union;
3. the adoption of banking legislation and common rules in the field of banking supervision to sustain monetary and financial stability;
4. the establishment of the Monetary Council to prepare for the establishment of the Central Bank as an independent institution with main goals that include conducting the monetary and exchange policy for the single currency area;
5. issuing a single currency to substitute the currencies of the Member State."

Furthermore, the MUA contains provisions on: the GMC (which are repeated in its Statute); the single currency; and the GCB (which will no doubt be repeated in its Statute); [...]

2.2 Gulf Monetary Council

The Gulf Monetary Council (GMC) serves two main purposes. First, it serves as the institutional forum for the analytical and technical preparation of the central banking function in the forthcoming GMU, replacing the institutional arrangements which already existed under the auspices of the GCC for cooperation between the NCBs of the GCC member states. As such, it is supposed to: (a) enhance cooperation between NCBs of the GCC member states; (b) foster coordination of national monetary and exchange rate policies and operations; and (c) act as the institutional hub for organizing, coordinating, and monitoring preparations for GMU. Second, it serves as the institutional nucleus from which the new monetary authority (the GCB) will evolve.[15] It thus foreshadows the future monetary authority in charge of the single monetary policy and exchange rate stability.

Objectives and Tasks of the GMC

The GMC's objectives and tasks are detailed in Article 6 of the MUA as repeated in Article 4 of the GMC Statute, which read as follows:

"The core objective of the Monetary Council is to prepare the necessary

15. While it would be possible to establish the GCB well ahead of the start of GMU with the task of leading all necessary preparations, following the EU's experience with the EMI, the GCC member states have decided to set up the GMC as an interim institution and a precursor to the future GCB.

infrastructure for the monetary union; in particular, the establishment of the Central Bank and the development of its operational and analytical functions, along with the following:

1. empower cooperation among the National Central Banks with a view to establishing the conditions necessary for the realization of the monetary union;
2. foster coordination of national monetary and exchange rate policies until the Central Bank is established;
3. monitoring National Central Banks lending to public entities in Member States, and issuing the rules necessary to implement that;
4. decide the regulatory, organizational and logistical framework necessary for the Central Bank to perform its functions in cooperation with the National Central Banks;
5. develop the statistical framework necessary for the single currency area;
6. prepare the banknotes and coins denominated in the future single currency and develop the general framework for issuing and circulating banknotes and coins in the single currency area;
7. ensure the readiness of the payments and settlement systems to operate in the single currency area;
8. monitor the compliance of the Member States to their commitments toward the monetary union and the introduction of the single currency, in particular with respect to economic convergence;
9. decide the timetable for the issuing and introduction of the single currency;
10. make recommendations on the legislations necessary to the establishment of the monetary union, establishment of the Central Bank, and issuing of the single currency."

Reading in sections 4 and 9 that the GMC "decides" the regulatory, organizational, and logistical framework as well as the timetable for the issuing and introduction of the single currency, it is clear that the GMC is a very important institution. This conclusion is also supported by the fact that, in accordance with Article 9 of the MUA, the GMC shall "determine" the name of the single currency, its denominations, its design, its security features, and its exchange rate against foreign currencies. In addition, in accordance with Article 11 of the GMC Statute, the Governing Board of the GMC may, inter alia, adopt "directives" (seemingly an GMC internal instrument to ensure the proper fulfilment of the GMC's mandate) and "mandatory procedures" towards the establishment of the GCB and to ensure compliance by the GCC member states with their commitments, in particular under the MUA. In this context, it is interesting to note that the MUA and the GMC Statute do not provide for mechanisms ensuring accountability of the GMC vis-à-vis other parties.[16] In addition, the MUA and the GMC Statute do not foresee an allocation of competences relating to the establishment of GMU to other parties such as political authorities at a GCC level.[17]

Decision-making Bodies

The GMC has two decision-making bodies: the Governing Board and the Executive Body. In accordance with Articles 9.1 and 12.4 of the GMC Statute, the Governing Board of the GMC is composed of the Governors of the National Central Banks, and the executive president of the GMC may participate in its meetings, but has no voting rights. This is different from the situation in the EMI, where its President chaired the EMI's Council, was responsible for the day-to-day management of the EMI, and was also accountable to political bodies at a Community level for progress made towards EMU. Another interesting difference between the EMI and the GMC is that in the EMI Statute the rule for voting was a simple majority and the exception unanimity, while in the case of the GMC the rule is unanimity and there are no exceptions.

Independence of the GMC

The GMC should enjoy the same degree of autonomy as the future GCB. Thus, when carrying out its tasks in line with its mandate, the GMC should act independently vis-à-vis the member states and organs and institutions of the GCC. Institutional independence and autonomy should also be safeguarded by the right of the GMC to organize its work as it sees fit to fulfil its statutory tasks. In this context, it is noted that the provisions on independence of the GMC and the GCB differ. Article 7 of the GMC Statute reads as follows:

"The Monetary Council, members of its governing board, and its executive body are prohibited from receiving orders or directions, which would influence their performance of duties and tasks as assigned by this Statute, from any of GCC bodies or the Government Entities or anyone else."

Article 15 of the MUA reads as follows:

"The GCC and the Government Entities of the Member States are prohibited from issuing any directions to the Central Bank and the National Central Banks

16. For example, in the context of the EU this would be the European Parliament.

17. For example, in the context of the EU this would be the European Council.

or any of their executive bodies that would influence the performance of their tasks and functions as assigned by this agreement and their respective statutes. The GCC, the Government Entities, and the Public entities of the Member States shall respect those principles and shall not seek to influence the members of the executive bodies and the staff of the Central Bank and the National Central Banks while performing their jobs."

Dissolution of the GMC and Succession by the GCB

The GMC is intended to be an interim body. Its mission will be completed at the latest when GMU starts. This is clearly laid down in Article 4.2 of the MUA, which reads as follows: "The established Monetary Council shall carry out its tasks until the establishment of the Central Bank, which will replace the Monetary Council as the steps towards the establishment of the Central Bank are concluded." The details of the dissolution of the GMC and its succession by the GCB are laid down in Article 18 of the MUA. It is interesting to see that, in accordance with Articles 15 and 18.3 of the GMC Statute, the costs relating to the GMC are supposed to be shared equally between the National Central Banks. In view of the different size of the GCC member states in terms of population and economies, an alternative would have been allocation of shares in the costs in accordance with a capital key (as was the case for the EMI), but the solution chosen for the GMC underscores the political dimension of the project in terms of an expression of solidarity in the process towards a common monetary future for the GCC member states.

2.3 Gulf Central Bank

GMU will require a regional institution responsible for the single monetary and exchange rate policy. Monetary policy is indivisible because, with the free movement of capital and efficient markets, liquidity conditions within a single currency area will tend to equalize at any particular point in time. Furthermore, since the exchange rate is an important variable of monetary and financial conditions, monetary policy and exchange rate policy are closely interrelated. The MUA envisages that the regional institution should take the form of a central bank, established primarily to provide centralized decision-making on monetary and exchange rate policies. Its Community status will ensure that its decisions are guided by the objectives of the single currency area as a whole. As the GCB performs a public function, it needs to be provided with a clear and unambiguous mandate, stating as its primary objective preferably maintaining price stability, which is an objective that leaves relatively little room for interpretation. This is in line with current standards in central banking, not only in Europe but also in other parts of the world.

Objectives and Tasks of the GCB

In article 14 of the MUA, these features are captured as follows:

"The primary objective of the Central Bank shall be to ensure price stability in the single currency area within the framework of the optimal utilization of economic resources to ensure economic stability. Its tasks include the following:

1. Defining and executing the monetary and exchange rate policy of the single currency area and ensuring consistent implementation of the monetary and exchange rate policy of the single currency area through national central banks.
2. Managing the foreign reserves of the single currency area.
3. Issuing banknotes and coins denominated in the single currency.
4. Promoting effective operation of the payment and settlement systems within the single currency area.
5. Performing the operational, statistical, and advisory tasks necessary for the execution of its functions.
6. Laying out general rules for prudential supervisory measures with regard to financial institutions."

Reviewing the above Article on the GCB's objectives and tasks, the following points may be noted:

Secondary Objective of the GCB

The secondary objective of the GCB is the "optimal utilization of economic resources to ensure economic stability. This secondary objective deviates somewhat from the often used reference to "without prejudice to the primary objective of maintaining price stability, support the general economic policies" of a Community or government (as the case may be).

Single Central Bank or System of Central Banks

Theoretically, the GCB could be organized as a single regional central bank to replace the existing NCBs (which could become its local administrative offices) or as the leader and core of a system of central banks, whereby the NCBs would act under its guidance as points of access to the central banking facilities of the single currency area.[18] Whilet the MUA does not explicitly use the word "system", reading through

18. The EU has opted for the system-model, whereby a distinction is made between the ESCB, comprising the ECB and all EU NCBs, and the Eurosystem, composed of the ECB and the NCBs of those EU member states which have adopted the euro as their currency.

these legal texts, it seems clear that the GCC has chosen the system approach. For example:

- Article 6.4 of the MUA refers to the performance of the GCB's functions "in cooperation with" the NCBs.
- In addition, Article 14.1 of the MUA refers to the implementation of the monetary and exchange rate policy of the single currency area "through" NCBs.
- Furthermore, Article 18.1 of the MUA, which states that "The financial institutions in the single currency area shall perform their activities in compliance with the rules and decisions issued by the Central Bank as conveyed to them by the National Central Banks."

In the experience of the ESCB/ECB, a system approach whereby the tasks of the system are executed in a decentralized fashion by the NCBs as the operational arms of the system raises a wide range of issues with regard to the relationship between the center of the system (the GCB) and the NCBs, which have to be addressed in rules of procedure and other legal acts where it is important to define this relationship.[19] The most important aspect in this respect is that a single monetary policy also requires harmonization of monetary policy instruments and procedures.[20]

Central Bank Independence, Transparency, and Accountability

Legal, institutional and functional independence help the GCB to achieve the primary objective of price stability. An independent central bank is not only in a better position to pursue the primary objective of price stability; it is also perceived by the financial markets and the general public to be more credible than a central bank which is dependent on a government. These considerations are especially important for a regional central bank which operates in a monetary union formed by otherwise sovereign states, and which must take decisions and conduct operations with a whole currency area perspective and without national bias. While independence is a prerequisite for the fulfilment of the GCB's objectives and tasks, the importance of transparency and accountability should also be recognized. Transparency enhances the effectiveness of monetary policy and makes it easier to hold an independent

19. In the case of the ESCB/ECB, the principle of decentralization is laid down in Article 12.1, third paragraph, of the ESCB/ECB Statute, which states that the ECB "to the extent deemed possible and appropriate ... shall have recourse to the national central banks to carry out operations which form a part of the tasks of the ESCB."
20. In the Eurosystem, this has been achieved through a Guideline, which allows the Eurosystem NCBs to choose the legal means to execute monetary policy operations, which may either be done under contractual or statutory arrangements, as long as a level playing field across the euro area is maintained.

central bank accountable. The GCB may meet this obligation by, in particular, issuing regular reports, providing an ex-post explanation and justification of its decisions and actions, which will allow the GCC, the Member States, the financial markets, and the general public to assess how far the GCB has achieved its objectives. As mentioned in section 3 above, the independence of the GCB is catered for in Article 15 of the MUA, but the MUA does not contain any provisions on the GCB's transparency and accountability, which may feature in the future Statute of the GCB.

Role of the NCBs

In view of the above choice for a system approach, the NCBs will in particular assist the GCB in the performance of its operational and statistical functions and carry out the tasks delegated to them in conformity with the regulations and decisions of the GCB. In this context, the MUA contains some interesting features.

International Representation of the System of NCBS

First, Article 19 states that "The Central Bank shall represent the single currency area in organizations and for international and financial cooperation whenever such organizations and for a deal with monetary and exchange rate policy matters or other issues which are relevant to the tasks and functions of the Central Bank, including the signing of international bilateral or joint agreements with other countries as well as regional and international organizations." The words "shall represent" give the impression that the GCB will have a stronger position in this field than the ECB at present, where the ECB (i.e. its Governing Council, composed of the Governors of the euro-area and the members of the ECB's Executive Board) decide on the ECB's international representation, as a result of which the ECB has an observer status in the IMF and is thus not in the position to "represent" the euro area.

Role of the GCB and NCBs in Prudential Supervision

Second, as opposed to the situation in the EU where prudential supervision is still rather fragmented and dispersed over a number of different authorities, all GCC NCBs are also banking supervisory authorities. This may make it easier to harmonize banking regulation at a GCC level and expand the role of the system of NCBs beyond monetary and exchange rate policy and financial stability[21] to a higher profile in financial supervision.

21. The ECB defines financial stability as a condition in which the financial system which comprises financial intermediaries, market, and market infrastructures – is capable of withstanding shocks and the unravelling of financial imbalances, thereby mitigating the likelihood of disruptions in

- Article 3.3 states: "The monetary union shall entail the adoption of banking legislation and common rules in the field of banking supervision to sustain monetary and financial stability."

- Furthermore, Article 14.6 adds that the GCB's tasks include "laying out general rules for prudential supervisory measures on financial institutions."

- Article 18.2 concludes that the GCB "shall lay out the principles and conditions for prudential supervision on financial institutions in the Member States, and procedures and measures necessary for financial stability."

These Articles give rise to several questions. First, will the GCC and the GCB have any legislative or regulatory powers in the field of prudential supervision? Referring to the paragraph on legal acts, the expectation is that the GCC and GCB will mainly work with recommendations in this field, which require implementation at a national level. The use of the words "common or general rules" and "principles and conditions" seem to support this expectation. Second, how will the division of competencies be between the GCC and the GCB? The impression exists that the GCB will have a right of initiative to adopt resolutions or recommendations in this field and that the GCC may perhaps play a lesser role in this respect. Third, the scope of the role of NCBs requires further reflection. In view of the expected level of decentralization within the system, the expectation seems warranted that this scope is broad. It will then depend on the implementation of harmonization measures at a national level whether a level playing field may be achieved across the GCC member states or at least the single currency area. Fourth, the GCB's role in the area of financial stability requires further definition.[22] In conclusion, the realization of GMU necessitates a review of the current arrangements for financial stability and prudential supervision. The above MUA Articles may be considered as enabling clauses providing for the possibility of establishing a GCC-wide regime for financial stability and prudential supervision with a shared responsibility. The GCB may set the rules and standards for a uniform and consistent exercise of prudential supervision, while the NCBs are responsible for the prudential supervision of their financial intermediaries.

---

the financial intermediation process that are severe enough to significantly impair the allocation of savings to profitable investment opportunities. See the ECB's half-yearly *Financial Stability Review.*

22. In the EU, the role of the ESCB in the area of financial stability is currently being expanded through the establishment of a European Systemic Risk Board.

GCB Legal Acts

It is difficult to conceive how a single monetary policy may be implemented and executed without the adoption of legal acts and particularly binding legal acts.[23] This gives rise to the question as to which legal instruments may eventually be adopted by the GCB. For the GCC, Articles 8 and 9 of its Charter provide for the possibility to adopt resolutions and recommendations, which are non-binding and require implementation at a national level. For the GMC and the GCB, in the MUA and the GMC Statute, different terms are being used for acts which appear to be intended to have legal effects such as decisions; mandatory procedures; directives, common or general rules, principles and conditions; and recommendations. However, the impression exists that such measures are not defined in their legal nature, still require implementation at a national level, and may perhaps only be enforced vis-a-vis NCBs through financial penalties without recourse to a court or arbitration tribunal (see Article 22 of the MUA) and vis-à-vis member states through peer pressure in an arbitration procedure (see Article 24 of the MUA).

2.4 Other Adaptations of the GCC's Institutional Framework

Pending the adoption of the Statute of the GCB, there are several further aspects which seem to require further reflection and perhaps adaptation of the GCC's current institutional arrangements.

Accountability

First, although the GCB would be performing its functions and tasks independently and in conformity with its Statute, it will not operate in a political vacuum. Thus, without prejudice to its independence, the GCB would need to be integrated into the institutional framework of the GCC. This framework would need to ensure that:

- the GCB can be held properly accountable;
- a forum is established where the GCB can conduct a dialogue with the authorities of the member states (which remain responsible for economic policies other than monetary and exchange rate policy in the single currency area); and

23. By way of comparison, the legal framework for EMU is mostly composed of Community and national legislation. As far as Community legislation is concerned, a distinction may be made between areas where one authority is exclusively competent (for example, the ECB for monetary policy) or where there is a shared competence between different authorities (for example, the ECB and the European Commission and Parliament in the area of payment and settlement systems). As far as the ECB is concerned, in its field of competence it may adopt binding regulations, decisions, guidelines, and instructions and non-binding recommendations and opinions.

- the GCB is recognized as the initiator of and/or adviser on all legislation falling within its areas of competence.

Surveillance and Enforcement of Fiscal Discipline

Second, the institutional framework needs to be adapted to establish procedures and mechanisms to regularly monitor and assess economic convergence and to foster fiscal discipline in the GCC member states.

Judicial Control

Third, in order to ensure that the GCC bodies act within a predefined rule of law regime, their legal acts (imposing obligations on third persons) should be subject to judicial review by an independent body which would make its decisions solely on the basis of the law of the GCC, without considering any underlying national interests. The existence of a mechanism for judicial review creates a counterweight to regulatory and sanctioning powers in the monetary and prudential supervisory field, and ensures uniform implementation of the relevant statutory provisions throughout the single currency area. At present, the MUA only provides for an arbitration clause and this may be felt to be insufficient for the settlement of monetary union related disputes. Therefore, the GCC may wish to consider establishing a Monetary Union Court to adjudicate on such matters.

Status of Oman and the UAE

It is noted that Oman and the UAE are not signatories to the MUA and the Statute of the GMU, obviously since they have opted out of GMU for the reasons mentioned in the introductory chapter. However, this gives rise to at least two issues. First, although both countries may, at least for the time being, wish to stay out of GMU, there will be areas of common interest between the "ins"and "outs", for example in the field of exchange rate policies. These issues, on the one hand, require coordination between the two different groups, but on the other hand, there seems to be no legal obligation under the relevant legal texts to do so. The question arises whether this issue should perhaps in the future be accommodated. Second, the impression exists that this may eventually turn out to be a temporary situation, notwithstanding the fact that there is no indication at present how long this situation may last. Assuming, though, that all parties (the "ins" on the one hand and the "outs" on the other hand) share a common interest to align their efforts towards Gulf economic and monetary union, the question arises how Oman and the UAE will be treated in the future and whether any adaptations of the GCC's institutional framework are warranted in this respect.[24]

3. Preparatory Work for Gulf Monetary Union

3.1 Master Plan

Preparatory work for GMU will be challenging, since it is bound to cover a wide range of interrelated topics involving different groups, and proceed to a timetable taking account of different, often long, lead times on the various projects. Accordingly, it is advisable to start with detailed preparatory work well in advance of GMU and to carry this out in a coordinated and synchronized fashion on the basis of a Master Plan. The purpose of such a Master Plan is to: (a) identify tasks; (b) allocate responsibilities; (c) identify interrelationships between projects (and consequently the need for consultation between the parties involved); (d) guide the organization and monitoring of activities; and (e) determine priorities. Preparatory work has already started under the aegis of the GCC's Committee of Central Bank Governors and is bound to be intensified within the framework of the GMC.

3.2 Committee Structure

In cooperation with the NCBs, the GMC carries out the bulk of the preparatory work. In order to organize cooperation between the GMC and the NCBs, a number of specialized committees composed of GMC/GCB and NCB representatives could be established (representing a development of the past sub-committee structure of the GCC's Committee of Central Bank Governors).[25] These committees could contribute at all stages of projects to establish GMU, namely in the setting of strategic goals, in technical preparations, and in implementation (including testing). Such committees and their main tasks could be as follows.

---

24. By way of comparison, in the EU a distinction is made between those member states which have adopted the euro as their currency (16 at present) and those which have not yet adopt the euro (11 at present). In the latter group, a distinction is made between those member states, which are obliged to adopt the euro once they qualify, and those member states, which have negotiated that they may decide this for themselves (Denmark and the United Kingdom). That said, all NCBs of all member states are represented in the ESCB.

25. The EMI had, and the ECB still has, a similar structure in place. Particularly in a decentralized system of central banks, a committee structure supports the coherence of preparatory work and its implementation; the center of the system benefits from the expertise of the NCBs and, the other way around, the NCBs profit from expertise gathered through the discussions in the committees.

Monetary Policy Committee (MPC)

- coordination of the monetary and exchange rate policies and operations of member states in the period before GMU
- convergence assessments, other monitoring/economic reporting tasks
- preparation of the infrastructure for area-wide projections
- framework for managing a smooth transition to GMU
- preparation of the GCB's monetary policy strategy
- development of monetary policy instruments, procedures, and operations for GMU; and
- development of a conceptual framework for the interrelationships between a single monetary and exchange rate policies and national fiscal policies.

Banknotes and Coins Committee (BCC)

- design (including substrate and security features)
- printing and minting (including quality control)
- preparing and managing the cash changeover
- stablishing requirements and ensuring a smooth and continuous supply of cash; and
- monitoring and analyzing the counterfeit situation

Market Infrastructure Committee (MIC)

- GCB market infrastructure policies and objectives
- payment systems arrangements and instruments
- trading, clearing, and settlement of financial instruments
- collateral policy and settlement
- definition and maintenance of the operation facilities/services of the system of central banks
- means to promote harmonization and integration and thereby competition and efficiency; and
- oversight and regulatory issues

Financial Supervision and Financial Stability Committee (FSC)

- defining the GCB's role and its relationship with financial supervisors/regulators and relevant international/supranational bodies.

Statistics Committee (STC)

- immediate needs to support coordination of monetary and exchange rate policies, monitoring convergence, etc.
- requirements for GMU
- program for developing harmonized data
- organization of statistical work in GMU; and
- IT infrastructure

Accounting Committee (ACC)

- financial resources and accounting standards for the GMC
- central bank accounting, financial statements, statistical reporting in GMU; monitoring developments in International Accounting Standards/International Financial Reporting Standards;
- financial structure of the GCB – capital structure, distribution of seigniorage and other elements of profit/loss; and
- user requirements for IT infrastructure relating to accounting and financial reporting

Information Technology Committee (ITC)

- telecommunications including conferencing facilities
- secure document exchange
- statistical data exchange; and
- facilities for exchange of operational data (if different); databases for common use within the system of central banks (for example, eligible collateral, counterparties, banknotes, statistics); on-line or other facilities to allow speedy access across the system.

Communication Committee (COC)

- informing about preparations for GMU generally
- information campaign to prepare for cash changeover; and
- communication channels for use in GMU (including regular publications)

Legal Committee (LEC)

- recommendations by GMC and GCB for complementary legislation
- complementary legislation for GMU, where there is a competence
- legal instruments for adoption by GCB

- opinions on draft legislation referred to GMC/GCB for consultation
- compliance with GMC/GCB legal acts
- legal and institutional matters affecting the system of central banks; and
- legal support to work of other committees.

Human Resources Committee (HRC)

- organization of training on all matters relating to GMU; and
- recruitment of staff for the system of central banks with the skills and expertise for preparatory work and subsequently for GMU.

Senior Committee (SEC)

Since the number of topics to be decided is very large, it may be advisable to appoint a senior group of NCB officials, perhaps at the level of Vice-Governor and chaired by the GMC's Vice-President to prepare for the Governing Board's deliberations and decisions. This Senior Committee could also pay particular attention to organization and governance issues for the system of central banks, including its relationship with the GCC and other bodies, and to capacity building in the system.

Since the committees will have to deal with many technical and time-consuming topics, it may be useful to consider the establishment of task forces to deal with well-defined topics. Some topics may warrant the creation of special, perhaps multidisciplinary, groups, for example convergence reports and the cash changeover (the replacement of existing national banknotes and coins by the new single currency banknotes and coins).

Obviously, most of the work will have to be completed before the start of GMU. However, this may not always be the case; certain items may be deferred or prepared so as to leave room for later refinement when time permits. It is important to conduct the work of the committees on the basis of well-defined mandates and precise work plans. If time becomes of essence, committees may distinguish between three different types of preparatory work:

- preliminary work (for example, tasks related to the coordination of national monetary and exchange rate policies, convergence reports, and other economic reporting, where relevant to the committees area of expertise);
- minimal essential provisions for the proper start of GMU; and
- later enhancements of such provisions, since developing and implementing such enhancements will take time and it is therefore important to plan them well in advance.

3.3 Changeover to the Single Currency

The changeover from the existing national currencies to the single currency will give rise to many legal, organizational, and communication issues, for example: changeover scenario; name of the single currency and its sub-divisions; conversion rates; legal implications (e.g. continuity of contracts); changeover in the financial sector; cash changeover; and communication strategy. The single currency will serve as a unit of account, medium for transactions, and store of value. The changeover to the single currency will affect all aspects of economic life and involve all sectors of the economy. It will thus be a great challenge for all bodies, and in particular for the GMC and thereafter the GCB, given their responsibility for its successful implementation. To ensure transparency and public acceptance, the changeover will need to be guided by principles of legal certainty, simplicity and user-friendliness, cost-effectiveness, and avoidance of competitive distortions.

4. Operational, Regulatory Framework for Gulf Monetary Union

As mentioned earlier, the establishment of a monetary union requires the adoption of basic legal instruments, but in the legal field more needs to be done. In addition to such basic legal instruments, the legal underpinnings of the operational framework for a monetary union need to be created. For example:

- The introduction of a single currency gives rise to issues such as: continuity of contracts in legacy currencies; rounding rules; and provisions against counterfeiting.
- The choice of a decentralized central bank system will require the operational frameworks of the NCBs to be harmonized in order to ensure that the relevant parties are treated equally (at least in material respects), for example in access to liquidity in the single currency.
- The conduct of a single monetary policy needs to be supported by accurate statistics, and non-compliance by reporting agents with their obligations to deliver the necessary data will have to be sanctioned through uniform rules applicable across the single currency area.
- The smooth operation of an area-wide payment system for the single currency requires harmonized rules on issues such as the finality of payments and the implications of insolvency of a participant in the payment system.

- In order to reap the benefits of a single currency, market conventions may need to be created or amended, which may require the adoption of legislation to make them enforceable, for example in the field of netting.

In the experience of the ECB, the above requires the adoption of a variety of legal acts. The operational regulatory framework for EMU provides a wealth of examples of such legal acts, from which the GCC may profit. However, as mentioned earlier, the EMU's operational regulatory framework is much influenced by the features of the EU, in particular its institutional characteristics, and each new regional monetary union will have to adapt the arrangements to the requirements of its specific situation. The operational regulatory framework for EMU is nevertheless likely to provide many examples which may at least provoke further reflection, and may even, in certain cases, be partially or fully copied thus saving valuable time.[26]

5. Recommendations on the Way Forward

In the final analysis, while the GCC has made considerable progress towards the establishment of GMU, there are obviously many points which require further reflection and work, several of which are listed non-exhaustively below.

- The GMC will have to be made operational, which requires a number of logistical and human resources related actions (preparation of headquarters, establishment of employment conditions, election of Executive President, recruitment of staff, establishment of an organizational structure which is geared towards the fulfilment of the GMC's mandate[27]).
- The Statute of the GCB will have to be completed. While the MUA contains already important provisions on the GCB, a number of issues still require further reflection, such as: governing bodies; operations; financial provisions (capital, transfer of foreign reserves, distribution of monetary income); and, last but not

26. The relevant legal acts may be found at the websites of the ECB (www.ecb.europa.eu) and the European Commission (www.ec.europa.eu).

27. Based on the EMI's experience, perhaps the following structure could be chosen:
   - a General Secretariat in charge of preparatory work for GMU and the preparation of Governing Board meetings;
   - an Economics and Research Department, in particular in order to support preparatory work;
   - an Administration Department responsible for issues such as employment related matters, premises, security; and
   - an IT Department in charge of the information systems requirements of the GMC, but also the preparation of the IT infrastructure necessary for the smooth functioning of GMU.

least, the legal acts which the GCB is empowered to adopt. Since this Statute or at least the underlying principles will serve as a compass for preparatory work to be carried out by the GMC, it appears important that work in this area progresses at an appropriate speed.

- The GMC will have to prepare the operational, regulatory framework for GMU. It is highly advisable to do this on the basis of a Master Plan in a coordinated and synchronized fashion among all actors involved. For all practical purposes, the GMC could take the endeavors of the EU's Committee of Governors and the EMI in this field as a basis for further reflection and action, topped up with the experiences of the EU and the ESCB/ECB with the operation of EMU over the past 10 years.
- Requirements for economic convergence and in particular fiscal discipline will have to be further detailed. While the GCC's economic convergence criteria appear to reflect the state-of-art, recent experiences in the EU have shown that it is important to have a robust framework in place with regard to the surveillance and enforcement of fiscal discipline.
- Pursuance of the goal of integration of (financial) markets as envisaged in the GCC's Charter and Economic Agreement is likely to require considerable additional efforts. It seems advisable to do this on the basis of an action plan, determining objectives and setting timetables to achieve these objectives, which ties into the strategy and timetable for the introduction of the single currency.
- Further reflection seems desirable on legislative powers at a Community level (i.e. GCC and GCB level) to support the smooth functioning of GMU. It is difficult to conceive that the present legal instruments of resolutions and recommendations are sufficient to cater for the requirements of a fully-fledged GMU. The introduction of the single currency will require the adoption of a large number of measures at a GCC level, and this will in turn require careful planning and coordination among all actors involved. The same holds true for the system of arbitration currently foreseen in the MUA. In particular, the adoption of binding legal acts and the imposition of sanctions on credit institutions appear to inevitably require recourse to independent courts.
- The requirement in the MUA that national legislation be made consistent with the requirements for GMU, will lead to the adaptation of the statutes of NCBs as well as abolition or adaptation of old legislation or the adoption of new legislation in a variety of fields. This could be done through umbrella, "catch-

all" legislation or through adoption of legislation on a piece-meal basis or a mix thereof. This requires, also at a national level, the development of an action plan for the introduction of the single currency.

- The name of the single currency will have to be chosen, the conversion rates determined, and the changeover scenario fixed, and all this has to be communicated to the financial markets and public at large well in advance of the start of GMU in order to ensure that all parties can prepare themselves properly and in a timely fashion for the introduction of the single currency.
- Last but not least, the essential preparations for GMU cannot be completed, nor the capacity built to enable the GMC to function, without substantial efforts to recruit, train, and retain suitable staff, and to provide the necessary material resources.

9

Approaches to Islamic Banking in the Gulf

Rodney Wilson

Introduction

Islamic banking is more developed in the Gulf region than anywhere else in the world. Although there is much information and writings on Islamic banking on the Arab side of the Gulf, much less is available on the workings of the Islamic banking system in Iran. The aim here is to examine the very different approaches taken by Iran and its Gulf Arab neighbors to Islamic banking. The political factors that determined these different approaches will be analyzed and their implications explored.

Consideration will also be given to what has been the more successful approach, which inevitably raises the issue of how success is measured in a political economy context. Measuring Islamic bank assets or deposits provides a quantitative indication of relative size, but of greater significance is the dissemination of ideas and the building of international alliances. The outward globalist approach of Islamic bankers in the Gulf Cooperation Council (GCC) countries contrasts with the inward-looking, more nationalistic approach in Iran. In particular, the market-driven, competitive model of Islamic banks in the GCC contrasts with the statist model of Iran where it is the role of government which is crucial. Ultimately the future of Islamic banking in Iran will depend on the resilience of the Islamic Republic, whereas in the GCC arguably it is a bottom up phenomenon with much popular support which governments cannot ignore irrespective of political factors. In other words, in the GCC, Islamic banking is primarily seen as a business, whereas in Iran, politics has determined developments and will continue to do so.

1. Iran's Islamic Banking Law

Legal, regulatory and sharia compliance systems are also very different on the Iranian and GCC sides of the Gulf. Islamic banking in Iran is governed by a law enacted in 1983, but there are no Islamic banking laws in the GCC apart from some limited and belated provisions in the United Arab Emirates (UAE), and in the case of Kuwait, amendments to the banking legislation with new sections introduced to cover Islamic banking. For the other GCC states, it is at the regulatory level that provision is made for the particular requirements of Islamic banks.

Iran's Law on Usury (Interest) Free Banking of 1983 was only enacted four years after the Islamic Republic was declared and over eight years after the establishment of Dubai Islamic Bank, the first sharia compliant financial institution in the region. Article 1 of the law provides for the establishment of a monetary and credit system based on rightness and justice as delineated by Islamic jurisprudence. The implication is that this will be free of *riba*, which the current English translation of the law equates with both usury and interest, although this was ambiguous in earlier translations which only specified usury.

The main support for introducing an Islamic financial system into Iran came from Abdulhassan Banisadr, the first president of the Islamic Republic, who wrote a doctoral thesis on Islamic banking for the Sorbonne in Paris. However, Banisadr's Presidency lasted only just over a year as he fell out with Ayatollah Khomeini, and as a result, he was impeached in June 1981, two years before the Islamic banking law was finally enacted. Despite widespread support in the *majlis* (the Iranian parliament), there was confusion about how an Islamic banking system would actually operate. It was largely through the efforts of Bank Markazi (Iran's Central Bank) that the new law was drafted, but the staffs of the commercial banks were skeptical and unenthusiastic, and although these institutions were state-owned, they enjoyed considerable autonomy. It was only in 1985 that sharia-compliant financing was introduced; most deposits were not Islamized until 1987.

Iran's Islamic banking law provides for deposits on a *qard hassan* basis, the concept being that of an interest free loan by depositors to the bank, the only type of lending permitted under sharia. Those who drafted the law however recognized that depositors expect some return, especially in inflationary conditions. Hence article 6 of the law provides for non-fixed bonuses in cash or in kind. In practice, prizes are given to depositors, with the lucky account holders selected through a lottery.[1] As gambling (*maisir*) is forbidden in Quranic teaching (Sura 2:219), it is unclear how

1. Bank Melli, *Annual Report*, 2007, 11.

awarding such prizes can be viewed as justified, especially as most depositors, as in any lottery, do not receive prizes.

Article 3 of Iran's Islamic Banking Law provides for term investment deposits which the banks can use for *mudaraba* financing and direct investments, the so-called restricted *mudaraba* which the influential Iraqi Shi'a cleric, Muhammad Baqir As Sadr, recommended.[2] With restricted *mudaraba* contracts, the bank acts as an agent and the depositor shares in the profits from the project being financed rather than receiving interest. The contract is regarded as just, as the depositor as financier (*rabb al mal*) is sharing in the risk with the businessmen or entrepreneur (*mudarib*) undertaking the project. In practice, term investment deposits rates in Iran are determined by the Bank Markazi at the macroeconomic level and are unrelated to the performance or profitability at the microeconomic level of particular projects. For 2009, for example, the term deposit rates for one year were 14.5 percent rising to 17.5 percent for five-year deposits,[3] these rates largely reflecting inflationary expectations, a subject on which *fiqh* is silent.

2. Legal and Regulatory Developments in the Arab Countries of the Gulf

Islamic banking development in the Arab countries of the Gulf has been largely ad hoc, with no comprehensive legislation attempting to Islamize financial transactions as in Iran. Within the GCC states Islamic banking is regarded as a matter of customer choice, with conventional banks competing for business in what is usually described as a dual financial system. The resilience of the GCC conventional banks is largely because they offer overdraft facilities, which gives clients more flexibility in the timing of their spending. As overdrafts incur interest charges, they cannot be offered by Islamic banks; instead clients have to enter formal sharia-compliant contracts which specify what is being financed and the timing of repayments. Much of the population in the GCC has a preference for banking services which are consistent with Islamic teaching, but many remain to be convinced that Islamic banking as it is currently practiced provides the best solutions, and therefore they remain content to deal with conventional banks, especially for services not provided by Islamic banks. Indeed many Islamic bank clients also maintain accounts with conventional banks without having pangs of conscience, the aim being to get the best of both worlds.

2. Rodney Wilson, "The Contribution of Muhammad Baqir Al-Sadr to Contemporary Islamic Economic Thought," *Journal of Islamic Studies* 9.1 (1998): 46-59.
3. Central Bank of Islamic Republic of Iran, *Economic Trends* 57.2 (2009/10): 16.

Given these popular attitudes, GCC governments have not felt pressurized to introduce Islamic banking laws; rather they take a pragmatic approach and introduce regulation where it is necessary. Dubai Islamic Bank, the first commercial Islamic financial institution in the world, was established in 1975, but without any specific law governing its activities when it was awarded a license by the Government of Dubai, five years prior to the Union Law Number 10 of 1980 establishing the Central Bank of the UAE. In practice, the Dubai Islamic Bank was barely regulated in its early years of operation, and it was only in 1985 that a Federal Law was enacted covering Islamic banks, financial institutions and investment companies (UAE Federal Law 6).

There are four significant provisions in the Federal Law of 1985, one regarding the rights of Islamic banks, two dealing with consequential exemptions and the final provision dealing with sharia governance. The first significant provision is under Article 3 which states that Islamic banks have the right to form companies, either on their own account or with partners, the latter presumably applying to *mudaraba* and *musharaka* partnership contracts, although these are not specifically mentioned.

Two exemptions are referred to under Article 4 of the Federal Law. The first is the exemption given to Islamic banks from Article 90 Clause (a) of the earlier Union Law of 1980 which stipulates that banks should not trade in goods. As the *murabaha* contracts offered by the Dubai Islamic Bank involved the bank acquiring commodities and selling them to their clients at a mark-up, this exemption retrospectively legitimized these contracts. The second exemption was to Article 96 Clause (e) of the Union Law that provided for the boards of directors of banks to determine the interest rates paid to depositors and charged to lenders. As Dubai Islamic Bank did not apply interest to any of its operations, this stipulation was clearly redundant.

Provisions for sharia governance are included under Articles 5 and 6 of the Federal Law of 1985. Article 5 which provides for the establishment of a Higher sharia Authority attached to the Ministry of Justice and Islamic Affairs was never implemented. This provision was subject to cabinet approval, which was not given, possibly because of lobbying by supporters of Islamic banking who resisted centralized control. Instead it was Article 6 which was implemented, as this provides for each Islamic bank having its own sharia supervisory authority comprising of at least three members. Article 6 provides that those nominated should be approved by the Higher Sharia Authority, but as none exists, this has never happened.

An alternative approach would have been for the Central Bank of the UAE to have its own sharia board, as is the case in Malaysia.[4] This might have been

4. Rodney Wilson, "*Sharia* Governance for Islamic Financial Institutions," *International Sharia*

more acceptable than having a federal ministry involved, especially one with little knowledge or capacity to deal with financial matters. Another explanation to resistance to centralized control might have been because it was being exercised from Abu Dhabi whereas Dubai Islamic Bank was, as its name suggests, based in Dubai, where financial institutions, whether Islamic or conventional, sought a high degree of autonomy. However, as Dubai Islamic Bank had branches in Abu Dhabi as well as other Emirates, this explanation does not stand up to scrutiny. Furthermore when Abu Dhabi Islamic Bank was opened in 1997, it was subject to the same regulatory provision, demonstrating that there is a level playing field for Islamic finance throughout the UAE.

Kuwait is the only other country in the GCC to have specific legislation pertaining to Islamic banking, but in its case, there was a very long lag between the time Islamic banking started in 1977 when the Kuwait Finance House was established and the addition in 2003 of a new section on Islamic banking to the banking law of 1968 (Section 10). The most significant provision relates to sharia governance. Under Article 93 of Section 10, each Islamic bank has to appoint an independent sharia board comprising at least three members. Where there are conflicts of opinion between sharia board members, these should be referred to the Fatwa Board of the Ministry of Awqaf and Islamic Affairs which is empowered to provide the definitive ruling. In practice, this has never happened, and the Strategic Plan of the Ministry of Awqaf and Islamic Affairs covering the 2006 to 2011 period contains no reference to Islamic banking.

Qatar and Bahrain have no specific laws governing Islamic banks, but both countries have special regulations, details of which can be found in the Qatar Central Bank's Instructions to Banks and in Bahrain Central Bank's Rulebook. In Qatar, Islamic banks have invested heavily in real estate for leasing through *ijara* contracts, which poses substantial risks, although the real estate sector in Doha has suffered less severe price declines than that of Dubai. Nevertheless, the Instructions to Banks specify that total investment by Islamic banks in real estate should not exceed 25 percent of the bank's capital and reserves and that the investment period should not exceed five years.[5] The Instructions to Banks in Qatar cover many areas of Islamic finance including the operations of Islamic subsidiaries of conventional banks, which has become the norm in Qatar. However, the Instructions are not clearly presented, and there is confusion over some issues such as number of sharia

Research Academy Journal of Islamic Finance, 1.1 (2009): 65.

5. Qatar Central Bank, *Instructions to Banks* (Doha, 2008), 153.

scholars to be appointed to each bank, with a minimum of two stipulated, but the Accounting and Auditing Organization for Islamic Financial Institutions, whose standards are recognized in Qatar, stipulates a minimum of three scholars.

The Central Bank of Bahrain's Rulebook contains the most comprehensive treatment of Islamic banking in the Gulf region, reflecting its status as an Islamic banking center hosting 26 institutions with assets worth over $26 billion. There are detailed rules governing the capital adequacy requirements, *murabaha*, *salam*, *istisna*, *musharaka*, *mudaraba* and *sukuk* including the treatment of credit, market and operational risk.[6] Detailed rules are also provided for profit sharing *mudaraba* investment accounts, including the treatment of profit equalization reserves that smooth the returns paid to time depositors, and investment risk reserves to mitigate possible losses. It is evident that there is much regulatory support for the Islamic banking sector in Bahrain, given its significance for the economy and employment in this small island nation. There is, of course, the question of whether effective regulation facilitates the growth of financial intermediation or is introduced in response to past financial crises. In the case of Bahrain's Islamic banking sector there has never been a crisis, hence the former positive proposition probably applies.

Saudi Arabia's Banking Control Law was introduced in 1966, 20 years before Al Rajhi Bank, the first Islamic bank in the Kingdom, was awarded a license. The law has never been revised to introduce provisions for Islamic banks, even though they have acquired major significance, with Al Rajhi having more branches than any other bank, and ranking third in terms of assets and deposits in Saudi Arabia. Under Article 10 of the Law, bank involvement in wholesale or retail trade including through imports or exports is prohibited, yet this is the basis of most *murabaha* transactions by Islamic banks such as Al Rajhi.[7] Similarly, there are minimal regulations for Islamic banking in Saudi Arabia even though the Monetary Agency had run 374 courses in the supervision and marketing of Islamic financial products attended by 6,300 people over the 2000-2007 period.[8] The only mention of Islamic finance is in the Regulations for Consumer Credit where it is stated that for Islamic products, documents for the purchase and sale of goods should conform to the requirements of the bank's sharia committee[9] and that a profit rate rather than a borrowing rate applies to all credit extended under Islamic contracts.[10]

---

6. Central Bank of Bahrain, *Rulebook* (Manama, 2010), CA-3
7. Saudi Arabia, "Banking Control Law" (Riyadh, 1966), Article 10.1
8. Governor of SAMA: 2007
9. Saudi Arabia, *Regulations for Consumer Credit* (Riyadh, 2008), 2.3.
10. Ibid., 5.3.

3. Market-driven Islamic Banking

The major attraction of Islamic banks from a client's perspective is that they are sharia-compliant, and therefore Muslim customers can undertake financial transactions with a clear conscience. Most Islamic banks in the GCC stress their Islamic ethos and values, not only in terms of avoiding *riba*, but by conveying a positive message about the *halal* nature of their financing methods. There is some concern that they could be accused of using religion for marketing purposes however, and in Saudi Arabia and Kuwait, the banks offering sharia-compliant financial services do not designate themselves as Islamic, hence the names Al Rajhi Bank and Kuwait Finance House (KFH). However, the term Islamic bank is used in Bahrain, Qatar and the UAE.

Although there has been much debate about whether modest interest receipts or charges actually constitute *riba*, or whether what is forbidden is usury, modern Islamic banks have succeeded in getting their message across that all interest transactions involve *riba*, and are therefore immoral.[11] In contrast, the merits of risk sharing are stressed, of bearing each other's burden in return for a proportion of any profits generated through a financial transaction. Hence, for example, with an investment *mudaraba* deposit a customer becomes a stakeholder and shares in the bank's profits, whereas savings accounts paying interest returns are related not to bank performance but rather to the monetary policy stance of the jurisdiction in which the deposits are placed. Furthermore, if the deposits are guaranteed there is no risk for the depositor, but then arguably no justification for a return either.

The first modern Islamic financial institutions in Pakistan and Egypt in the 1960s were organized as non-profit making credit unions which provided finance for rural communities with low incomes. In contrast, the emergence of Islamic banking in the GCC accompanied the oil boom of the 1970s, with the main focus being on providing financial services for affluent personal and business clients. The underlying philosophy was that Muslims who wished to use sharia-compliant financial services would want to have the same types of financial services as clients of commercial banks. In other words, the purposes for which the finance was used were the same, only the methods of financing were to be different. Hence Dubai Islamic Bank was established as a limited liability company, initially privately owned, but later to become a listed company on the Dubai Financial Market with the aim of paying dividends to its shareholders and producing capital gains on their investments.

Initially, institutions providing Islamic finance in the GCC focused on

11. Abdulkader Thomas, *Interest in Islamic Economics: Understanding riba* (Oxford: Routledge, 2006): 125-134.

commercial banking, especially import finance with *murabaha* whereby the bank would purchase goods from a foreign exporter and then sell them to a local distributor who would repay in installments, including a profit mark-up for the bank. In recent years, the use of *murabaha* has been widened to include consumer finance for retail clients, especially for the purchase of vehicles. Some Islamic banks such as KFH even have their own vehicle showrooms where customers can come and choose from a variety of makes. By bulk buying, KFH can save on purchase costs and pass on some of the discounts to its clients.

The marketing of retail financial products by Islamic banks in the GCC has become very professional and often is more focused than that of their conventional competitors. Dubai Islamic Bank, for example, offers an attractive range of tiered investment accounts for those with a minimum of $3,000 to deposit. For one month deposit, the profit rate paid was 3.3 percent during the third quarter of 2009 rising to 3.75 for one year deposits. For those with only $1,000 to deposit, Dubai Islamic Bank offers savings accounts paying a profit rate of 1.5 percent. These accounts are, of course, designated as Islamic, but neither the bank publicity nor the bank's financial statements specify what Islamic contract governs the deposit, whether *wakala* or *mudaraba*. It seems that clients are not concerned with such detail, and simply take the bank's sharia assurance on trust.

Much of the emphasis in retail financial product development has been on branding, with, for example, Dubai Islamic Bank offering Wajaha private banking services to high net worth clients. These services include personalized asset management services and private facilities in selected branches for conducting financial transactions including stock exchange dealings. Johara banking is provided exclusively for women at 10 branches of Dubai Islamic Bank with incentives to use these services including shopping vouchers and health club discounts. Al Rajhi Bank web-based service Al Mubasher enables clients to check account balances and make transfers and payments online.

4. State-directed Banking in Iran

In contrast to the customer-driven Islamic banking in the GCC, on the Iranian side of the Gulf the policies have been dictated by the government's economic priorities. Under Article 10 of Iran's Fourth Five-Year Development Plan, covering the period from 2005 to 2010, the allocation of banking facilities by sector and region is undertaken through cash subsidies which are approved at Cabinet level.[12] One

12. Central Bank of Iran, *Supervisory Policy Guidelines of the Banking System in 1388* (Tehran, 2009-10).

quarter of bank credit was to be allocated to agriculture under the Fourth Plan, 35 percent to manufacturing and mining, 20 percent to construction and housing, and 8 percent to exports. As almost half of Iran's GDP is accounted for by services, and only 10 percent by agriculture, 11 percent by industry and mining, and 5 percent by construction, the financing allocations in the Fourth Plan are clearly distorted.

Article 11 of the section dealing with credit policy in the Fourth Plan states that the banks are obliged to give priority in their lending to deprived and less-developed regions and technologically-advanced projects. While the former may be commendable from a social perspective, the article is contradictory, as high technology projects are unlikely to be located in such areas. Under Article 12, housing finance is solely for construction and not for mortgages on existing properties. This is unhelpful for the development of a housing market in Iran, and limits the return that investors can expect from housing or commercial property.

Such quotas and restrictions mean that potentially profitable projects may not get undertaken while resources are channeled to sectors and areas where returns may be low. The quotas are certain to result in an inefficient allocation of capital, with banks' autonomy to make financing decisions based on normal risk and return criteria severely curtailed. However, under Article 23, the Central Bank Guidelines encourage credit scoring, with banks urged to favor customers with good credit records and limiting credit to those who have not met their debt obligations by at least the amount of the outstanding debt.

Although the allocation of finance by the banks in Iran is state directed at the sector level, the economy is gradually coming under private rather than state control. The proportion of commercial bank assets accounted for by claims on the non-public sector increased from 47 percent in 2004-05 to over 54.5 percent by 2008-09.[13] Over the same period, the amount allocated to public corporations declined from 5 percent to a mere 1.3 percent. Deposits with the Central Bank increased from 7.7 percent to almost 10 percent, but this was largely because banks were required to hold more liquidity against contingencies due to the uncertain economic climate.

5. Liberalization of Banking in Iran and the Role of Private Banks

The public sector banks in Iran seem to be becoming more autonomous in their decision making, a development welcomed by the Central Bank which appears to recognize that there are efficiency gains from liberalization. In particular, the use of commercial criteria rather than political patronage is implicitly supported, although

13. Central Bank of Iran, *Annual Review*, 2008-9, 72.

the term political patronage is not, of course, used in Central Bank publications. Nevertheless, it is asserted that credit policies can affect sector growth rates. There was a reduction in direct controls over credit which meant the "free" allocation increased from 35 percent in 2004 to 75 percent in 2008.[14]

Although there has been no plan to privatize Iran's major commercial banks which have been under state ownership since 1979, there is no ideological objection to private banking by the authorities in Iran. The nationalization was simply driven by expediency, as without state support in the aftermath of the revolution, the banks would have become bankrupt. There was enormous capital flight in the late 1970s with a substantial run on bank deposits as upper and middle class Iranians, especially those influential under the Shah, left the country for a life in exile. Arguably the inefficiencies in the allocation of finance and the poor resultant returns was a result of government directives which would have applied regardless of whether the banks were under public or private ownership.

Giving the state-run commercial banks more autonomy is a necessary, though not sufficient, condition to improve their performance. One issue is the banking culture, which can be categorized in Iran as relationship banking, with long-term continuity in the relationships between the banks and their client. Relationship banking has the virtue of reducing contracting and monitoring costs, but the downside is that it can also result in cronyism and even corruption. Merely because the banks are in theory Islamic and are supposed to uphold Muslim religious values will not ensure that all employees behave honestly and responsibly, especially when effective enforcement mechanisms to reduce operational risk are absent. Bank Markazi, like other central banks, has a supervision department whose remit includes the prevention of financial crime, but its major concern is "about the fitness and propriety of the staff nominated by the banks for taking up posts of a managerial nature (assistant manager and above) in the banks' overseas branches"[15] and not the local staff. The worry is about the finance of illegal imports, evasion of taxes and money laundering by clients, and not the relationship of bank managers and clients.

In 2001, in response to lobbying by industry, there was a significant policy change in Iran permitting the establishment of private banks. Bank Eghtesad Novin (EN) was the first institution established. It is owned by a group of construction and industrial companies, including Behshahr, Behpak, and Novin, with Bank Melli,

14. Central Bank of Iran, *Economic Report*, 2008, 101.

15. Central Bank of Iran, Bank Supervision Department, 2010, http://www.cbi.ir/page/BanksSupervision_en.aspx

the largest state-owned bank together with the civil servants pension fund, having a minority stake. Given this ownership it is clear that the dividing line between state and private ownership is blurred in Iran. More important than the actual ownership was the ethos of EN Bank, the aim being to provide more modern and innovative banking services for bank clients in line with international standards, rather than having the bureaucratic form-filling approach of the state-owned commercial banks. EN Bank obtained a stock market listing in 2004 and by 2008 its assets exceeded $9.4 billion.

Parsian Bank, which was also established in 2001, has experienced even more rapid growth with its total assets worth almost $20 billion by 2009, making it the largest of the six private banks in Iran. This compares with total assets of just under $60 billion of Bank Melli, illustrating the increasing significance of the private banks, which now account for over 16 percent of total financing.[16] As on the Arab side of the Gulf, the private banks are focused on consumer finance, especially vehicle and housing funding. This contrasts with the state-owned commercial banks that are mainly involved in corporate finance, particularly import finance. The private banks are aiming to attract personal customers by offering an attractive range of accounts, and encouraging those with salaries to arrange direct transfers to their current accounts. In marketing terms, the focus is on middle class and more affluent customers. The majority of Iranians, and virtually all of the poorer classes, do not use banks, most household payments being in cash.

6. The Islamic Credentials of Iran's Banking System

In traditional Islamic societies markets, including credit markets, are overseen by the *hisba*, a moral enforcement agency to ensure fairness and justice, usually controlled by the state. Religious guidance is provided by the *muhtasib*, a scholar versed in *fiqh*. There was no attempt to establish such an institutional framework in Iran, either during the Islamic revolution or subsequently. The Central Bank of Iran conducts monetary and supervisory policy in the same manner as any other equivalent body internationally, although the terminology used conforms to that of Islamic finance. There is a stress on form, but in reality there is little substantial difference with conventional monetary policy.

The Monetary and Credit Council of Iran's Central Bank determines the profit rates paid for commercial bank financing, raising the rate to control inflation or reducing it to stimulate the demand for finance. As inflation is a continuing

16. Central Bank of Iran, *Economic Report*, 2008, 72.

problem in Iran, with the rate in 2009 exceeding 18 percent, monetary tightening has been the norm, partly to counteract the stimulus effects from high levels of current government spending, especially on subsidies. The other major instruments of monetary policy in Iran include credit ceilings, the reserve requirements ratio, open market operations involving so-called participation papers and open deposit accounts with the Central Bank. These operate in much the same way as on the Arab side of the Gulf, the only difference being that instead of referring to interest rates, the participation papers and the open deposits pay profit rates, but as the Central Bank is a financial regulator, not a business focused on profit, it is unclear what the profit rate actually represents.

Table 1 shows the types of Islamic financing provided by the different categories of banks in Iran. Farsi terms are used; *gharz-al-hasaneh* being what is transliterated in Arabic as *qard hasan*, an interest-free loan. Banks can levy an arrangement fee and a management charge to cover the administrative costs of such loans, but they must not earn a surplus, as this would represent *riba*. Not surprisingly little *gharz-al-hasaneh* is provided by the private banks in Iran. *Mozarebeh* (*mudaraba* in Arabic) is more widely offered by the private banks, a contract whereby the bank advances funds to a business in return for a share in its profits. Partnership contracts (*musharaka* in Arabic) are even more popular, whereby the bank and the business both invest in a new venture and share the profits according to a pre-determined ratio.

Table 1: Islamic Financing Facilities in Iran, %

	Commercial banks	Specialized banks	Private banks
Gharz-al-hasaneh	4.8	2.3	0.7
Mozarebeh	4.9	0.6	18.0
Forward transactions	4.4	2.0	0.0
Partnerships	13.8	11.7	42.1
Joaleh	6.0	1.2	2.2
Installment sale	47.2	71.8	11.2
Direct investment	0.9	0.1	1.0
Other	18.0	10.3	24.8

Source: Central Bank of Iran, 2010.

Commercial banks use forward transactions (*salam*) for financing; this refers to a contract whereby the financier pays in full in advance for a commodity, usually agricultural output, to be supplied at a future date. The advances can be used by farmers to cover the costs of seeds and fertilizers, as well as paying their workers. *Joaleh* (*wakala* in Arabic) is an amount of money advanced to an agent for a specific investment. The agent is paid a management fee but the investment and any returns remain the property of the bank. Of greater significance are installment sales (*ijara wa iqtina* in Arabic) whereby the bank purchases equipment or vehicles on behalf of a client, with the client then paying rent for its use and making repayments over a three-year period after which ownership will be transferred to the client. This is the most important method of financing by the state-owned banks in Iran, especially by specialized institutions such as the Bank of Industry and Mining, Bank Keshavarzi and Bank Maskan. For the private banks, partnership financing appears to be more significant, possibly because the expected returns are higher reflecting the risks involved.

7. Islamic Banking Facilities in the GCC

The methods of funding used by Islamic banks in the GCC are similar to those used in Iran, although there is considerable variation between institutions and it would be incorrect to generalize about the GCC or even within particular countries. For Al Rajhi, the largest Islamic bank in the GCC and the largest in the world with a stock market listing, installment sales are even more significant than with the state-owned banks in Iran, accounting for 60 percent of total financing in the quarter ending March 31, 2010. *Mutajara* refers to commodity *murabaha*, a facility that enables the client to receive a cash advance. Under this type of financing, the bank purchases a commodity on behalf of a client and resells it to the client who repays by deferred installments, including a premium, as with *murabaha* trading transactions. The bank appoints an agent to purchase the commodity from the client, with the proceeds from the sale being deposited in the client's account. The client and indeed the bank never take physical delivery of the commodity, but they have temporary legal title to make the transaction sharia compliant. Many sharia scholars object to such transactions, and the *Fiqh* Academy of the Organization of the Islamic Conference (OIC) issued a fatwa condemning the practice at a meeting in Sharjah in May 2009, but it still continues.

Table 2. Al Rajhi Bank Financing

	March 2009 SR million	March 2010 SR million	March 2009 %	March 2010 %
Mutajara	31,628	31,177	28	27
Installment sale	65,784	70,214	58	60
Istisnaa	901	800	1	1
Murabaha	14,227	14,394	12	12
Visa credit cards	558	548	1	0
Total	113,099	117,133	100	100

Source: Al Rajhi Bank, Interim Consolidated Financial Statement, Riyadh, March 31, 2010.

An analysis of the financing facilities provided by Kuwait Finance House (KFH), the second largest Islamic bank in the GCC, is provided in Table 3. The receivables, which accounted for over 45 percent of total financing in 2009, refer to the installments on *murabaha* financing which can extend to over one year. Leasing accounts for 11.4 percent of total financing, which in the case of KFH does not involve installment sale, as the equipment or other assets remain the property of the bank until sold to a third party at the end of the period. KFH has over KD1 billion of investments in traded and private equity as well as in *sukuk* securities, and in addition a property portfolio and investments in affiliates. Such exposure to market risk raises regulatory issues, but the assets are sufficiently diversified not to cause major concern.

Table 3: Kuwait Finance House Asset Maturity, KD million

	3 months	3 – 6 months	6 – 12 months	Over 1 year	Total
Cash and bank balances	440	5			445
International *murabaha*	1,257				1,257
Receivables	1,219	1,056	946	1,868	5,090
Trading properties	29	39	4	55	126
Leasing	269	236	272	510	1,288
Investments	67	39	55	882	1,042
Investment in associates				411	411
Property investment				506	506

Other assets	94	72	122	234	522
Premises				602	602
Total	3,376	1,447	1,400	5,068	11,291

Source: Kuwait Finance House, Annual Report, December 2009.

8. The Overseas Expansion of Islamic Banks

Islamic banking has become a global industry with its hub in the Gulf. Rather than being a destination for foreign investment in financial services, within the sharia-compliant segment, the Gulf has become a source of investment. What seems to have arisen is a new phenomenon, an Islamic mode of capital formation that presents an alternative to the western interest-based system. It is becoming possible to delineate an Islamic form of capitalism with its own unique characteristics, where spiritual rather than material values determine the agenda.[17] Capitalism arguably best thrives under competition, which not only applies to that between Islamic capitalism and other forms such as Anglo-Saxon, Russian or even Chinese capitalism, but also to different strands within the Islamic World, especially the ideas and concepts emanating from Iran versus those coming from the countries of the GCC. Of course, Iran is the centre for Shia Islam, which has its own Jafari School of Islamic jurisprudence, whereas the GCC, and Saudi Arabia in particular, is the center for Sunni Islam, including the Hanbali school of *fiqh*.

It would be a mistake, nevertheless, to view the overseas expansion of Islamic banking as part of a struggle for worldwide influence and supremacy of Shia versus Sunni Islam. Firstly, in Islamic finance there are no distinctive Shia and Sunni approaches; indeed insofar as there are differences they are most pronounced between the Shafii, a Sunni school which predominates in South East Asia, and the other three Sunni schools. In particular, the Shafii School permits trading in debt instruments, whereas this is not allowed in the GCC, or indeed Iran. The differences between the GCC and Iran in the way Islamic finance is organized and regulated largely reflect historical factors and perceptions of the role of the state.

Furthermore, and most importantly, the aims of overseas banking expansion are very different for Iran and the GCC. Bank Melli has had two branches in London since 1967, long before the Islamic Revolution, one being in the City, its business mainly involving trade finance, whereas the other branch is in Kensington, its remit being to serve affluent Iranians, visiting or semi permanently resident in London,

17. Rodney Wilson, *Islam et Capitalisme Reconsideres*, Maghreb-Machrek, no. 187 (2006): 29-44.

including during the reign of the Shah, many of his entourage. Bank Melli's most significant overseas operations in recent years have been in the UAE, where it has seven branches, its local headquarters being in Deira, Dubai. As much of Iran's imports pass through Dubai, the major business is trade finance, especially of supplies coming from Asia. In other words, the rationale for the presence of Iranian banks overseas is primarily to serve the country's internal business requirements and it is unrelated to the Islamic credentials of the banks.

Iran has long been subject to US sanctions dating from the Tehran Embassy hostage crisis of 1979. More recently, sanctions have been tightened because of Iran's nuclear enrichment program. So far the sanctions have had little impact on Iran's overseas bank branches. The Security Council Resolution SC/9948 on sanctions passed on June 9, 2010 calls upon states "to take appropriate measures that prohibit the opening of new Iranian bank branches or offices abroad if there is reason to suspect they might be aiding Iran's nuclear or missile programs."[18] It also calls on states "to exercise vigilance over transactions involving Iranian banks, including the Central Bank of Iran, to ensure that those transactions do not aid Tehran's nuclear and missile programs." It is unlikely that this will affect the activities of Bank Melli or other Iranian banks in Europe or the GCC, not least because any financial connections with enriching uranium or missile development will be difficult to prove.

On the GCC side of the Gulf, the expansion of Islamic banking overseas has been prompted by three factors. Firstly, the limited size of the domestic markets has meant that further branch expansion and the attraction of more business has become increasingly challenging. Secondly, the successful Islamic retail banking model can be exported to other countries where there are significant Muslim populations potentially receptive to the services offered. Thirdly, there is a demand for asset management and treasury services that can best be provided from international financial centers such as London. Furthermore, by operating in such markets, Islamic financial institutions can acquire investment banking skills which they currently lack such as the ability to arrange initial public offerings and advise on mergers and acquisitions.

KFH was the first GCC-based Islamic Bank to expand abroad when it established the Kuveyt Türk Participation Bank in 1989 of which it owns 62 percent, with a further 9 percent being owned by the Kuwait Social Security Fund. The remaining minority stake is held by the Islamic Development Bank and Turkish investors. Over the last two decades, the bank has expanded throughout Turkey with a network of 113 branches compared with 34 in Kuwait. Kuveyt Türk provides a full range of Islamic deposit and financing facilities for personal and

18. Reuters, "Iran Dismisses UN Sanctions Draft," May 19, 2010.

small business clients, but it also has the capacity to provide larger scale finance including aircraft leasing to Turkish Airlines. More recently, KFH has expanded into Malaysia where it has nine branches and the Kuala Lumpur regional office also overseas new ventures by the bank in Singapore and Australia.

Al Rajhi Bank has an even greater presence in Malaysia with 19 branches. Like KFH, it replicates the range of services it provides in its home location. Pragmatism has governed its sharia approval processes, as the sharia board in Kuala Lumpur comprises one Saudi scholar who serves on the home sharia board in Riyadh and three Malaysians, two of whom studied in Saudi Arabia. A similar sharia governance system has been adopted for Dubai Islamic Bank's operation in Pakistan which already has 14 branches with a further 20 openings planned. Operating since 2006, it has attracted business from many Pakistanis working in Dubai who are already clients of the bank and want to use its facilities in their home country.

Qatar Islamic Bank has adopted a different strategy, as rather than establishing retail networks overseas, it has opened three investment banking operations – European Finance House in London, Arab Finance House in Beirut, and Asia Finance House in Kuala Lumpur. It already has an investment banking subsidiary in Doha, QInvest, which is regulated by the Qatar Financial Center. The major focus to date has been on asset management, including private equity and real estate investment. Services are provided for Qatari citizens of high net worth and Doha-based corporate clients rather than retail services for the British Muslim community. European Finance House is the largest of the four Islamic investment banks in London, all of which are owned by GCC-based institutions. Islamic Bank of Britain, the retail institution that has attracted over 50,000 British Muslims to open accounts, is part Qatari-owned.

Conclusion

In terms of spreading the message about Islamic finance, GCC-based institutions appear to have been much more successful than their Iranian counterparts. In the GCC, Islamic finance is viewed as a business opportunity rather than being politically driven, and the aim increasingly is to reach a global market rather than be inwardly focused. The GCC-based Islamic banks have attracted considerable media coverage, most of it favorable, whereas in the case of Iran much of the press coverage has been concerned with the effects or possible effects of sanctions. Islamic banking is one non-energy related activity where the GCC has a comparative and, increasingly, a competitive advantage. The future looks promising, as links with the West and other parts of the Muslim World have developed. In contrast, the prospects for Islamic finance in Iran seem much more uncertain and will be inevitably tied to political developments and the sustainability of the Islamic revolution which many question.

References

Bank Melli. 2007: *Annual report*, Tehran.

Central Bank of Bahrain. 2010. *Rulebook*, Manama.

Central Bank of the Islamic Republic of Iran. 2008-9. *Annual review.*

Central Bank of Iran. 2010. Bank supervision department. http://www.cbi.ir/page/BanksSupervision_en.aspx

Central Bank of the Islamic Republic of Iran. 2008. *Economic report and balance sheet.*

Central Bank of the Islamic Republic of Iran. 2009/2010. *Economic trends*, 57.2.

Central Bank of the Islamic Republic of Iran. 1983. *The law for usury (interest) free banking*. Tehran.

Central Bank of the Islamic Republic of Iran. 2009-10. *Supervisory policy guidelines of the banking system in 1388*. Tehran.

Governor of the Saudi Arabian Monetary Agency. 2007. *Speech to the symposium on Islamic banking prudential standards*. Institute of Banking, Riyadh.

Qatar Central Bank. 2008. *Instructions to banks*. Doha.

Reuters. 2010. Iran dismisses UN sanctions draft. May 19.

Saudi Arabia. 1966. *Banking control law*. Riyadh.

Saudi Arabia. 2008. *Regulations for consumer credit*. Riyadh.

Thomas, Abdulkader (ed.). 2006. *Interest in Islamic economics: Understanding riba*, Oxford: Routledge.

UAE Federal Law 6, 1985. *Islamic banks, financial institutions and investment companies*, Abu Dhabi.

UAE Union Law 10, 1980. *The Central Bank, monetary system and the organization of banking*, Abu Dhabi.

Wilson, Rodney. 1998. The contribution of Muhammad Baqir Al-Sadr to contemporary Islamic economic thought. *Journal of Islamic Studies*, 9.1: 46-59.

Wilson, Rodney. 2006. Islam et Capitalisme Reconsidérés. *Maghreb-Machrek*, no. 187 : 29-44.

Wilson, Rodney. 2009. *Sharia* governance for Islamic financial institutions. *International Sharia Research Academy Journal of Islamic Finance,* 1.1: 59-75.

10

Gulf Sovereign Wealth Funds in International Comparison

Eckart Woertz

Introduction

When the first of today's sovereign wealth funds (SWF), the Kuwait Investment Authority (KIA) was established in 1953, the term itself was unknown and its founders would have probably been astonished by its stellar rise in the first decade of the 21st century. Kuwait was a reclusive desert state where oil had been found in 1936, but production only started in earnest after World War II. Even with oil prices at around $2 a barrel at that time, the inflows were substantial and could not be accommodated by the very basic Kuwaiti economy, which relied at the time on livestock breeding, trade and pearl fishing and had been severely hit by the Japanese invention of artificial pearl production in the 1930s and the ravaging worldwide economic depression.

One of the goals of the KIA, therefore, was a transformation of the country's dormant capital in the ground into capital above the ground by storing it on international capital markets and in bank accounts, with the possibility to balance volatile oil revenues or to put it to use in the gradual development of its economy at a future point in time. This linkage with national development and the preservation of oil wealth for future generations has been a model for other sovereign wealth funds that are based on commodity exports such as the Abu Dhabi Investment Authority (ADIA, est. 1976) and the Norwegian Pension Fund (est. 1990) as well as for Saudi Arabia, where the central bank (SAMA, est. 1952) has been undertaking the management of non-reserve foreign assets of the country. It is important to keep this dimension in mind when speaking about SWFs, as all too often there is a Western bias in the existing literature that regards them either as a threat or just a potential client for investment products.

While the nascence of commodity-based SWFs has been necessarily tied to the history of oil discovery and production in the respective countries, SWFs in Asia have been linked to the export-led growth model that was initially championed by Japan, South Korea and Singapore and was later adopted by China and others. This growth model led to sizable current account surpluses in the respective Asian countries and coincided with the inception of SWFs in the region, which dates to the 1970s and 1980s in Singapore, with a second wave in recent years when South Korea and China entered the fray.

The term 'sovereign wealth fund' was first coined by Andrew Rozanov in an article in the Central Banking Journal in 2005 and has gained widespread usage since then against the background of growing global imbalances.[1] There are two major reasons why SWFs are all of a sudden perceived as such a challenge: a) the fact that they are state owned and might use investments to leverage political objectives and b) that their assets have grown rapidly and they have become a force to reckon with in international markets. However, it needs to be noted that their combined assets of about $3.9 trillion are still much smaller than what international mutual funds, pension funds and insurance companies command (see Table 1).

Table 1: Global Assets under Management according to Fund Type

Fund Type	Assets under Management in $ trillion in 2008
Pension Funds	24
Mutual Funds	18.9
Insurance Funds	18.7
SWFs	3.9
Private Equity	2.5
Hedge Funds	1.5
Exchange Trade Funds (ETFs)	0.9

Source: IFSL Research, Fund Management 2009, London, October 2009

This means that SWFs not only have considerable differences in their asset

1. Andrew Rozanov, "Who Holds the Wealth of Nations?" *Central Banking Journal* XV, no. 4 (May 2005): 52-57.

allocation based on different development policies, but that they are also shaped by their local politics and institutional arrangements that need to be considered carefully and in a non-ideological fashion: the Western way of differentiating between "good" and purely economic investments and potentially "bad" and politically motivated investments by SWFs may be questioned after the recent spate of market failures and massive government interventions. It also does not hold up against the West's own history of state-led mercantilist development phases.

This chapter analyzes the nascence of SWFs against the backdrop of their respective home countries, their political systems and economic structures. It then takes a specific look at Gulf SWFs, how they differ from other SWFs, and what their future investment strategies may look like.

1. Liability-based Approach to Sovereign Wealth Fund Classification

The common trait of SWFs is that they are pools of assets held by states, but different from traditional reserve management by central banks or public pension funds. However, if central banks hold currency reserves well beyond what would be necessary to guarantee the stability of local currency, i.e. if short-term liabilities of up to one year are covered by reserves (Guidotti-Greenspan rule), one can arguably classify substantial parts of such central bank assets as sovereign wealth, too. This is the case with China, Japan, Hong Kong's Monetary Authority (HKMA) and Korea Investment Corporation (KIC), which all hold funds well beyond reserve requirements without differentiating between them and categorizing them separately. In recent years, there has been a trend to set such central bank funds aside in newly-established SWFs (e.g. China, Russia) and earmark them for long-term investments that are not confined to the traditional fixed income investment universe of central banks. Some disagreement exists whether SWFs should also include funds that invest predominantly in domestic assets like Singapore's Temasek, Khazanah of Malaysia, SASAC of China, Samruk of Kazakhstan or Investment Corporation of Dubai (ICD). But there is a good argument to be made to count them as SWFs as well because in many ways they function as typical SWFs and often they also hold substantial foreign holdings, like Temasek's stake in Thai telecom company Shin Corp. In fact, Temasek is usually included in most accounts as a typical and early example of a SWF.[2]

2. For a discussion of a suitable SWF definition that argues for an inclusive definition and against the more narrow definitions by the US Treasury and the IMF that generally exclude central bank assets and predominantly domestic investments, see John Nugée, "The Growing Role of Sovereign

While it makes sense to apply a broad definition of SWFs to grasp the phenomenon of increasing wealth that is at the discretion of states, particularly in emerging markets, it is also important to stress the vast differences that exist between them. All of them vary in terms of size and policy objectives and thus have different investment horizons, risk/return profiles and asset allocation strategies. All of them are also influenced by the politics of their homeland and their history and thus have different institutional structures and modes of governance with differing levels of transparency and accessibility. The most important difference, however, is the source of funding; one can roughly distinguish between two types of SWFs: Those which derive their wealth from commodity exports (e.g., Gulf States, Russia) and those that derive their wealth from sterilizing foreign exchange inflows of their local manufacturing exporters (e.g., China, South East Asia).

Andrew Rozanov has proposed a liability-based approach to SWFs that analyzes how their source of funds and their intended usage is instrumental in defining their major characteristics.[3] While a commodity fund essentially represents equity-financed assets that give the owning state considerable discretion, the non-commodity funds are debt-based. Their foreign exchange accumulation was attained by issuing debt in local currency that constitutes an important liability. Every dollar the Chinese Investment Corporation (CIC) holds, for example, was financed by the central bank, which has bought it from a local exporter by issuing renminbi debt and this liability has to be served on the other side. The central bank does not only need to roughly pay 4 percent interest on it, it also needs to take a continuous renminbi appreciation into account, as its local currency is under constant revaluation pressure due to China's burgeoning current account surplus.[4] This conservative estimate easily adds up to a 9 percent hurdle rate, a performance task that its foreign assets need to achieve – pretty much impossible under the conditions of current low interest rates and sluggish equity markets. The ill-fated multi-billion investments in Blackstone and Morgan Stanley of the CIC actually missed such a hurdle rate by a wide margin as they noted more than 50 percent below their purchasing price after the market corrections in 2008.

Wealth Funds," State Street, *Sovereign Wealth Funds. Assessing the Impact*, Vision III, Issue 2 (March 2008): 4-5.

3. Andrew Rozanov, "A Liability-Based Approach to Sovereign Wealth," *Central Banking Journal* XVIII, no. 3 (February 2008).
4. Ibid.

The second liability Rozanov focuses on is the actual usage of funds; here he differentiates between four types of funds and their respective liabilities:

Contingent liability funds, mainly stabilization funds that are supposed to smooth out budget revenues and expenditures thus preventing boom-bust cycles and the occurrence of Dutch disease phenomena. As they try to manage market volatility of commodity prices and export earnings, such funds are oriented towards safety, liquidity and nominal returns in foreign currency, not unlike the investment objectives of central bank reserve management (e.g. Russian oil stabilization fund).

Fixed liability funds have been set up to meet a fixed liability at a future point in time (e.g. expected pension shortfalls 20-30 years from now). The closer the day of the targeted liability approaches, the more risk averse such funds will become and will prefer, for example, fixed income over equities and shorter over longer maturities (e.g. French Pension Reserve).

Mixed liability funds resemble an endowment for future generations and constitute a mixture of fixed and open-ended liabilities. On the one hand, they are obliged to make fixed payments to the budget under a "fiscal" or "spending rule." On the other hand, they are essentially open-ended and do not have a targeted terminal value. Thus, they do not face the growing investment constraints of maturing fixed liability funds, but are more limited than a fixed liability fund at its inception as they have to cater to their ongoing payment obligation. Examples would be the Pension Fund of Norway or the Reserve Fund of Russia.

Open-ended liability funds are investment authorities and corporations without explicitly defined contractual obligations. Without formal spending rules and clearly defined liability targets, they can take a long-term view and show great discretion in asset allocation and a larger risk tolerance. The investment authorities of Abu Dhabi and Kuwait (ADIA, KIA) would be cases in point. While the first three types of SWFs mentioned above can use the practices of central banks, pension funds and endowments as respective role models, open-ended funds are essentially a unique kind. In countries with maturing and peaking oil production, where capital income instead of oil income is projected to finance fiscal expenditure in the near future, the respective SWFs increasingly acquire the characteristics of an endowment-type mixed liability fund.

The classification of SWFs according to their funding type (equity/commodity-based and debt/non-commodity based) and their liability structures (contingent, fixed, mixed, open-ended) serves as an important analysis tool for the very different SWFs operating worldwide.

2. The Role of Institutions, Political Frameworks and Economic Structures

Another important influence on the characteristics of a SWF naturally is the political and institutional framework in which it operates. Who is the sovereign and to which constituency is he accountable via which procedures? Whether it is a monarch (e.g. UAE), a ruling party (e.g. China) or a parliamentary democracy (e.g. Norway) can make a considerable difference in the institutional set-ups and modes of governance. Economic structures, development strategies, international relations and geopolitical questions can equally influence long-term asset allocation.

Sovereignty can be defined as the right to make laws and exert power over a territory, its people and its resources. This notion of internal sovereignty is linked with external sovereignty towards other states and mutual non-interference in internal affairs as first acknowledged in the Peace of Westphalia 1648. The evolution of the term has been closely associated with the development of modern territorial states, which asserted supreme authority, unrestrained by religious institutions, legislative bodies or customary law. While sovereignty was perceived as absolute when the term was first coined by Jean Bodin (1530-1596), it was not regarded as limitless, but restrained by natural law. Out of this caveat certain protection rights of the private sphere developed (e.g. human rights, personal and physical integrity, due course and property rights), while the various theories of social contract that followed after Bodin (e.g. Hobbes, Rousseau, Locke) took the concept and moved it from a divine right to "the people." This naturally raised the question who "the people" are and via which representation their will should be exerted. The notion that every grown up is "the people" and allowed to vote regardless of material wealth, social rank and gender, is a relatively new one and only became widespread in the 20th century. It is also not generalized as there are other notions of legitimacy as well such as monarchical hereditary systems or totalitarian rule.

Historically, states have at times violated their supposed restraint by constitutional rights and natural law – sovereignty is "the power to decide the state of exception" as the notorious saying of Carl Schmitt (1888-1985) goes – but overall the growth of sovereign state power in modern times has been accompanied by power limiting notions of accountability and checks and balances. One would expect that the asset allocation of a SWF is influenced by such political processes and overarching economic development goals. Thus, the different political frameworks and economic structures of the various home countries of SWFs carry major implications. One can broadly differentiate between three different kinds of political frameworks for SWFs:

- Commodity-based rentier states: Varying degrees of rent dependence subject to oil reserves and population size, limited participation

- Mercantilist growth regimes: Authoritarian rule and export-led development strategies
- Parliamentary democracies/industrialized countries: Public scrutiny and diversified economic structure

These are only archetypes for sure, hybrid forms are widespread and the categorizations can be debatable. South Korea is a parliamentary democracy and at the same time it follows a mercantilist export-led growth strategy and shows some institutional characteristics from its autocratic past. Similarly, Russia is formally a parliamentary democracy though its degree of checks and balances has been disputed in the recent past. Norway is a parliamentary democracy, but has avoided rentier state structures as oil was found at a time when it had already reached a considerable development level, and part of the raison d'être of the Norwegian Pension Fund is to avoid an excessive reliance on rents and spread their usage out over time. Although Russia is heavily reliant on income from oil and gas, this dependence is not as high compared to its population size as in the case of the Arab Gulf countries. In other commodity-based countries like Iran, Venezuela or Kazakhstan, the role of oil on a per capita basis is equally smaller and even the Arab Gulf States themselves have been orienting themselves for quite some time now towards building up productive capacities in order to reduce the reliance on external rents and provide jobs for a rapidly growing population. On the political level, their state apparatuses are not as autonomous as the rentier state theory has postulated either, but they have opened themselves up to timid forms of participation and the constitutional process.[5]

3. Commodity-based Rentier and Semi-rentier States

Commodity-based SWFs belong to the oldest known SWFs in the world as it was the state in relatively underdeveloped nations that first received royalty payments of International Oil Companies (IOCs) and then gradually took over the administration of the oil industry via nationalization in the 1970s. Allocation considerations and policies of commodity-based SWFs are different from those of SWFs in the mercantilist growth regimes, where asset allocation is often a function of industrial policies and an undervalued exchange rate. For commodity-based SWFs, risk adjusted performance and capital preservation is much more

5. Michael Herb, *All in the Family : Absolutism, Revolution, and Democracy in the Middle Eastern Monarchies*, Suny Series in Middle Eastern Studies (Albany: State University of New York Press, 1999).

important. The unwritten social contract of the rentier state is forfeiting of political participation against welfare distribution – no taxation and no representation. The state is relatively autonomous from society as the oil wealth accrues to it via the oil companies it owns. While in a production state it is the economy that supports the state via tax payments, in the allocative rentier state it is the state that supports the economy via redistribution of oil wealth. A decline in oil revenues due to falling prices or decreasing production in aging fields, therefore, immediately threatens regime stability. Hence, it is an explicit strategy of SWFs in the Arab Gulf to increasingly rely on capital income from financial investments in the face of decreasing production profiles and use oil income for investments that can help in strategic diversification of their economies.

This is especially true for countries where oil production actually has peaked already like Oman and Bahrain. Naturally, the sense of urgency about non-oil-based income is much more developed in such countries. While their relatively small SWFs cannot be expected to provide sufficient capital income for their growing population, it is safe to assume that such funds are part and parcel of a general diversification strategy that tries to develop new economic activities beyond energy, such as finance, tourism and manufacturing. Like Egypt, Yemen, and Syria, they can be termed semi-rentier states, as their reliance on external rents (e. g., aid money, canal fees, and oil exports) can be only partial because of the size of the population and the size of oil production, which is in many cases declining. Their investment horizon, therefore, is supposedly shorter than those of countries with large oil reserves and production rates that are not yet declining. Such funds have liability profiles that are much farther out into the future than in the case of Bahrain and Oman.

The inclusionary capacity of rentier states does not only vary with oil revenue but also with population size. While in smaller states like Qatar, the UAE and Kuwait redistribution of oil rent is still capable of generating sufficient amounts of social cohesion, this is decidedly less so in states with a larger population like Iraq and Iran and Saudi Arabia. Iraq is in a special situation as it is war-torn and its oil industry ravaged. Even in the case of a reinvigoration, it will need to rely on economic activity beyond oil to provide jobs and income for its large youth bulge population.[6] While Iran has witnessed a remarkable decline in fertility rates from 6.6 children per woman in the 1980s to 2.1 children now, it still needs to accommodate its large youth cohorts that were born 20 years ago. Its populist government is

6. Leonard Binder (ed.), *Rebuilding Devastated Economies in the Middle East* (Palgrave Macmillan, 2007).

presiding over a state-centered economy including banks and companies owned by the Revolutionary Guards to "Bonyads," which are religious foundations that undertake widespread economic activities and report directly to the Supreme Leader Ayatollah Khamenei. The populist government faces vast liabilities as subsidies are widespread. Iran needs to import about a third of its gasoline because of a lack of refining capacity and has tried to overcome this shortage by new large-scale projects for refineries.[7] A large part of the Oil Stabilization Fund has been loaned to domestic development projects inside the country, and President Mahmoud Ahmadinejad's government authorized the withdrawal of about $17 billion of an estimated total of $23-25 billion.[8] In fact, Iran is under great pressure to generate jobs and revenue streams beyond oil production.

Saudi Arabia has also embarked on a widespread diversification drive to create jobs for its growing youth population. The plans range from creating up to 2 million jobs in tourism until 2020 to the building of six specialized economic cities in Rabigh, Al Jizan and some other cities. Although these plans are still in their infancy and it is not clear yet how successful their implementation will be, such projects need funding and the state needs to be able to step in, in case the vagaries of markets and the drying up of finance prevent more market-based solutions. In fact, the Saudi government has already announced its commitment to fund infrastructure and development projects in a counter cyclical and expansive 2009 budget, as international project finance is more difficult to obtain. To finance the fiscal stimulus, it has repatriated $50 billion of its foreign assets in 2009.[9] Furthermore, the Saudi state has felt compelled to intervene in the economy on an ad-hoc basis on numerous occasions in order to guarantee social peace and the ruling bargain of the rentier state. Because of burgeoning inflation during the boom years, it has raised subsidies for petrol and food and hiked wages in the public sector. Furthermore, it has also released zero-interest loan facilities for needy segments of the population. Given the Saudi pursuit of interventionist polices and its efforts to meet the needs of a larger population, there is a preference for conservative fixed income investments at SAMA, a strategy that

7. Recently the government has announced that near self-sufficiency has been achieved amidst continuing doubts of experts. Najmeh Bozorgmehr, Javier Blas, "Iran to Lift Petrol Output as Sanctions Hit," *Financial Times*, September 9, 2010.

8. The Iranian central bank does not disclose the size of the fund. "Iran Feels Pinch of Oil Price Fall," *Financial Times*, October 22, 2008, http://www.ft.com/cms/s/0/852fac38-a05f-11dd-80a0-000077b07658.html .

9. Simon Williams, "Gulf Economics after the Storm," *HSBC Research Note*, October 5, 2009; John Sfakianakis, "A Confident Budget!" *Saudi British Bank (SABB) Research Note*, December 24, 2009.

has served it well during the current financial crisis. Only an estimated 20 percent of its assets is invested in more sophisticated fixed income and equities. Recently, a relatively modest SWF, Sanabil Al Saudia, was established with a capital of $5.3 billion, though it is not clear yet whether its strategy will be geared more toward portfolio investments or whether it will eye strategic FDI as well.

Smaller Gulf countries like Kuwait and UAE are in a more comfortable position than Saudi Arabia as their oil wealth is larger in comparison to the small numbers of their local population. Not surprisingly, their SWFs were established much earlier and they have a tradition of investing in more sophisticated products and equities, which is still uncommon for many Asian central banks/SWFs or SAMA. With an estimated share of equity investments of 60 percent and more, they have been hard hit by the global financial crisis. The Qatar Investment Authority (QIA) is a relative newcomer to the game as it was founded only in 2005. It has enjoyed inflows from the flourishing gas industry in the country which in turn is an outcome of the development of this sector since the current ruler Shaikh Hamad bin Khalifa Al-Thani took over power in 1995. Other commodity-based SWFs like the Libyan Investment Authority (LIA) or the Russian National Welfare Fund are also relatively new entities and indicate that high oil prices of recent years have led to currency reserves of oil exporters well beyond the necessary coverage of short-term liabilities. This has opened up the possibility of creating SWFs with a more yield and risk oriented approach. However, after the slump in oil prices since the summer of 2008, some of the currency reserves had to be mobilized to defend local currency or shore up capital in domestic equity markets. Therefore, it remains to be seen whether current account surpluses and SWF assets in oil-exporting countries will take the steep growth trajectory forecast until the summer of 2008. In fact, many oil-exporting countries faced budget deficits after the steep oil price corrections in the second half of 2008 and were forced to take recourse to savings and/or debt issuance in 2009. The threshold price for a balanced budget thereby varied considerably from country to country. It ranged from below $40 per barrel of Brent in the case of Qatar and the UAE to over $90 in the case of Iran. Saudi Arabia and Kuwait made ends meet with a more modest threshold price of around $50, while Bahrain, Oman and Russia were hovering at and above $70.[10]

Thus, there are considerable differences between the SWFs of the Gulf region. A very large Abu Dhabi Investment Authority (ADIA, now ca. $400-600 billion) is likely to have different goals and opportunities from Bahrain's Mumtalakat ($14

---

10. Institute of International Finance (IIF), *Regional Report Gulf Cooperation Council Countries*, Washington D. C., December 8, 2008.

billion). While Saudi Arabia still largely manages its foreign investments via its central bank (SAMA) and has responsibility for a very large population, Kuwait has one of the oldest incorporated SWFs of the world, with considerable investment know-how. On the other hand, KIA is under a completely different supervision compared to ADIA, because Kuwait has a pretty active and at times demanding parliament which the UAE does not have. And finally, some of the newer funds like Dubai International Capital or Istithmar are heavily debt-financed and leveraged – rather than constituting sovereign wealth, they are a sovereign liability that becomes increasingly discernible in the wake of the current financial crisis.

4. Mercantilist Growth Regimes and Industrialized Parliamentary Democracies

SWFs in Asia are very different from the commodity-based SWFs in rentier and semi-rentier states in terms of funding source, liability profile, history and political framework. On the surface, non-commodity SWFs in Asia follow a less politicized investment approach and are under less public scrutiny than the Norwegian Pension Fund due to their more authoritarian forms of government. But the allocation policies of SWFs in China and other Asian countries are strongly influenced by the mercantilist export-led growth strategies of these countries. To a certain extent, their foreign asset accumulation is a function of this strategy, and profit maximization of these assets can be subordinated to an undervaluation of the exchange rate and the build-up of a capital stock that is associated with the export-led growth model. To put it bluntly: In the event of a financial meltdown, China would still have its industries, though producing then below capacity, but the oil countries would have sold their past wealth for paper. The Asian foreign exchange reserves stem from a sterilization of export proceeds; they have a liability in domestic currency standing against them which results in a considerable hurdle rate as seen above. To be profitable, a foreign asset held by the Chinese central bank not only needs to earn the interest rate of the domestic currency liability that is standing against it, but also a possible appreciation of the domestic currency. This is a crucial difference from the GCC funds, which accrue directly to the state and the oil companies it owns and mostly stay offshore. As GCC overseas assets do not stem from a sterilization, they constitute equity with no strings attached and the motivation of long-term risk adjusted returns and capital preservation is arguably more prominent than in the case of Asian SWFs.

The first proper SWF in Asia was Singapore's Temasek established in 1974. It has considerable investments in the domestic market, while the Government of Singapore Investment Corporation (GIC), which was founded in 1990, aims predominantly at international markets. The Korea Investment Corporation was founded in 2005. Japan and China have chosen to manage their surpluses via their respective central banks. However, China recently decided to transfer $200 billion to the newly-established China Investment Corporation (CIC), which is supposed to target potentially higher-yielding equity investments instead of US treasuries and agency bonds. But after ill-fated investments in Blackstone and Morgan Stanley and its takeover of the Central Hujin Investment Corporation, it has turned to a number of domestic investments and it is not clear yet which strategy it will follow in the future.

Although less publicized, industrialized parliamentary democracies have a considerable number of SWFs with the Pension Fund of Norway being the most well-known. This fund is clearly influenced by the parliamentary democracy of Norway and its value system. It has to publish its asset allocation in a transparent manner, allocate part of its revenues to the government, and comply with ethical investment restrictions. Investments in the arms industry or those which have harmful environmental effects or violate labor rights are off limits to the fund, and on several occasions it had to divest for these reasons (e.g. Wal Mart, Raytheon).

SWFs in industrialized parliamentary democracies in some cases will have to contribute to pension shortfalls in a not too distant future and therefore they have a mixed or fixed liability profile, not an open-ended one like most of the GCC SWFs. Thus, their investment horizon cannot be as long-term and their risk tolerance is lower. The recently-established French Strategic Investment Fund is a case in point as its mandate is to invest in national companies in order to prevent possible and potentially unwanted takeovers by foreign institutions. It thus has a very clear and unapologetic political mandate, a trait that the Western governments have been wont to criticize in the case of Asian and Middle Eastern SWFs.

Table 2: Worldwide Sovereign Wealth Funds and Non Reserve Assets of Central Banks, 2009

Name	Home Country	Founded	Source of Funds (besides reinvested profits)	Liability Type	Assets under management in billion $	Linaburg-Maduell Transparency Index*
Rentier States						
Abu Dhabi Investment Authority (ADIA)	UAE	1976	Oil	Open-ended	627	3

Mubadala	UAE	2002	Oil	Open-ended	13.3	10
International Petroleum Investment Company (IPIC)	UAE	1984	Oil	Open-ended	14	n/a
Abu Dhabi Investment Council (ADIC)	UAE	2007	Oil	Open-ended	n/a	n/a
Saudi Arabia Monetary Agency (SAMA), non reserve assets	Saudi	1952	Oil	Open-ended, Mixed	415	2
Sanabil Al Saudia (owned by PIF)	Saudi	2008	Oil	Open-ended	n/a	n/a
Kuwait Investment Authority (KIA)	Kuwait	1953	Oil	Open-ended	202.8	6
Qatar Investment Authority (QIA)	Qatar	2005	Oil and Gas	Open-ended	65	5
Libyan Investment Authority	Libya	2006	Oil	Open-ended	70	2
Brunei Investment Authority	Brunei	1983	Oil	Open-ended	30	1
Middle East SWF with Domestic Development Orientation and Pension Funds						
Public Investment Fund (PIF)	Saudi	1971	Oil		5.3	3
General Organization for Social Security (GOSI)	Saudi	1969	Oil	Mixed	n/a	n/a
Saudi Industrial Development Fund	Saudi	1974	Oil		n/a	n/a
Agricultural Bank	Saudi	1964	Oil		n/a	n/a
Saudi Credit Bank	Saudi	1971	Oil		n/a	n/a
Real Estate Development Fund	Saudi	1974	Oil		n/a	n/a
Arab Fund for Economic and Social Development	Arab League Countries, Seat in Kuwait	1974	Oil , various		n/a	n/a

Semi-Rentier States						
Revenue Regulation Fund	Algeria	2000	Oil	Mixed, Contingent	54.8	1
Mumtalakat	Bahrain	2006	Oil	Mixed	9.1	8
State General Stabilization Fund (SGSF)	Oman	1980	Oil	Mixed	8.2	1
FEM	Venezuela	1998	Oil	Mixed, Contingent	0.8	1
National Welfare Fund, incl. oil stabilization fund	Russia	2004	Oil and Gas	Mixed, Contingent	142.5	5
Oil Stabilization Fund	Iran	1999	Oil	Mixed, Contingent	23	1
State Oil Fund	Azerbaijan	1999	Oil	Mixed	14.9	10
Kazakhstan National Fund	Kazakhstan	2000	Oil and Gas	Mixed	38	6
Excess Crude Account	Nigeria	2004	Oil	Contingent	0.5	1
Commodity Related/ Others						
Pula fund	Botswana	1993	Diamonds		6.9	1
Social and Economic Stabilization Fund	Chile	1985	Copper		21.8	10
Istithmar Global	UAE (Dubai)	Restructured 2007	Oil, debt	Open ended	n/a	n/a
Istithmar Real Estate	UAE (Dubai)	2007	Oil, debt	Open ended	n/a	n/a
Investment Corporation of Dubai	UAE, (Dubai)	2006	Oil, debt	Open ended	19.6	4
Dubai International Capital	UAE (Dubai)	2003-4	Oil, debt	Open ended	n/a	n/a
Ras Al Khaima Investment Corporation	UAE	2005	Debt	Open-ended	1.2	3
Heritage and Stabilization Fund	Trinidad Tobago	2000	Oil		2.9	5
Timor-Lease Petroleum Fund	East Timor	2005	Oil		6.3	6

Mercantilist Growth Regimes						
China Investment Corporation (CIC)	China	2007	Excess Reserves	Open ended	332.4	6
China SAFE Investment Company	China	1997	Other	Open ended	347.1	2
Hong Kong Monetary Authority, Investment Portfolio	Hong Kong	1993	Excess Reserves	Open ended	227.6	8
Temasek	Singapore	1974	Excess Reserves	Open ended	133	10
Government of Singapore Investment Corporation (GIC)	Singapore	1981	Excess Reserves	Open ended	247.5	6
Taiwan National Stabilization Fund	Taiwan	2000	Postal Savings, loans		n/a	n/a
Government Pension Fund	Thailand	1997	Budget Surpluses, Payroll Taxes		n/a	n/a
Korea Investment Corporation	South Korea	2005	Excess Reserves		30.3	9
Khazanah Nasional	Malaysia	1993	Debt		25	4
Industrialized Parliamentary Democracies						
Government Pension Fund- Global	Norway	1990	Oil	Mixed	443	10
Government Petroleum Insurance Fund	Norway	1986	Oil	Mixed	n/a	n/a
Australian Future Fund	Australia	2004	Budget Surpluses, Sale of Telstra	Mixed	59.1	9
Alaska Permanent Fund	US	1976	Oil		35.5	10
National Pensions Reserve Fund	Ireland	2001	Other	Fixed	33	10
Alberta Heritage Savings Trust Fund	Canada	1976	Oil		13.8	9

New Mexico State Investment Council	US	1958	Other		12.9	9
Superannuation Fund	New Zealand	2003	Other		12.1	10
Permanent Wyoming Mineral Trust Fund	US	1974	Minerals		3.6	9
Strategic Investment Fund	France	2008			28	n/a

Source: SWF Institute (as of September 2010)
* 10 marks the highest, 1 the lowest rank of transparency

Note: For consistency purposes, the numbers of the SWF Institute have been chosen, but estimates of SWF assets vary considerable by source. Brad Setser and Rachel Ziemba, for example, have a much lower estimate of ADIA's assets under management and the Iranian Oil Stabilization Fund has faced withdrawals as mentioned and most likely does not hold $23 billion any more.

5. GCC SWFs and their Investment Strategies

5.1 Abu Dhabi Investment Authority

Abu Dhabi Investment Authority (ADIA) is a passive portfolio investor; its declared investment strategy is not to acquire more than five percent of a particular company and to avoid the disclosure obligations that come with it. It also refrains from actively influencing the management of respective companies. Its investment horizon is decidedly long-term, as the liability profile of its assets presumably will not increase several decades out into the future as oil production is not expected to decrease anytime soon.[11] Only at a later stage will the state need to increasingly rely on capital gains from the fund to finance state expenditure such as pensions and infrastructure investments.

ADIA has a high equity exposure of over 60 percent and additionally invests in alternative assets such as hedge funds, private equity and real estate. According to a rare insight ADIA has given into its investment strategy, equities of developed countries comprise 45-55 percent, emerging markets equities 8-12 percent, small cap equities 1-4 percent, government bonds 12-18 percent, non-government

11. According to *BP Statistical Review of World Energy*, the reserve to production ratio is 89.7 years, although this ratio unrealistically assumes a flat production curve that falls to zero at the end of the period, while in reality an earlier peak and a subsequent stretched out fall is more likely.

bonds 4-8 percent, alternative investments 5-10 percent, real estate 5-10 percent, private equity 2-8 percent, infrastructure 0-4 percent and cash 0-5 percent. [12] Its investments are spread across the globe with an overweight in more risky emerging markets, where 15-25 percent of assets are invested on average. In an interview with German magazine *Handelsblatt*, the late head of ADIA Shaikh Ahmed bin Zayed Al-Nahyan said that between 35 and 50 percent of ADIA's assets had been invested in the US, 25-35 percent in Europe and around 10 to 20 percent in Asia.[13]

The risk-tolerant long-term investment approach has led to large losses for ADIA in the wake of the global financial crisis. It has lost about 40 percent of its capital stock in 2008 without taking new inflows into consideration.[14] According to sources, ADIA has shifted increasingly to index funds since 2007-08 after active money managers have failed to generate alpha and returns above benchmarks, while incurring higher management fees.

Estimates of ADIA's assets under management vary greatly. A widely quoted research note by Stephen Jen of Morgan Stanley put it at $875 billion in 2007.[15] This estimate almost certainly was too high even before the financial crisis; Setser/Ziemba put ADIA's assets at $453 billion at the end of 2007 and at only $328 billion at the end of 2008 after heavy losses were incurred.[16] The latter number marks a conservative lower end of estimates that are currently in the market. The Sovereign Wealth Fund Institute quoted in Table 2 sticks to a considerably higher number of $627 billion. Even if the market recovery since March 2009 is taken into consideration, this marks an optimistic estimate.

According to a SWF transparency ranking of the Washington-based Peterson Institute, ADIA fared very poorly and took the last rank, while the SWFs of Norway and New Zealand were the most transparent and published quarterly reports with detailed asset allocation and profit/loss statements. Until recently, ADIA had only its address on its website which consisted of exactly one page. Now this has changed, and more meaningful information about the institution and its investment process

12. "Inside the Abu Dhabi Investment Authority," *Business Week*, June 6, 2008; Thomas Atkins, "Abu Dhabi's ADIA to Slash Hedge Fund Investments," *Arabian Business*, June 8, 2008, available at: http://www.arabianbusiness.com/521421?tmpl=print&page .

13. "Scheich Ahmed Bin Zayed Al-Nahyan: Öffentliche Aufmerksamkeit gehört nicht zu unserer Strategie," *Handelsblatt*, January 11, 2010.

14. Brad Setser, Rachel Ziemba, "GCC Sovereign Wealth Funds Reversal of Fortune," (*Council on Foreign Relations Working Paper*,) New York, January 2009.

15. Jen Stephen, "How Big Could Sovereign Wealth Funds Be by 2015?" (*Morgan Stanley Research Note*,) March 3, 2007.

16. Brad Setser, Rachel Ziemba, "GCC Sovereign Wealth Funds,"21.

has been added. ADIA also hired the US public relations firm Burson Marsteller to improve its image and alleviate fears in countries it wants to invest in about the lack of transparency and the motivation of its investments. ADIA also took part in the SWF initiative International Working Group (IWG) of the IMF, which it chaired together with Singapore's Temasek. The initiative, which led to the declaration of the Santiago Principles and the Kuwait Declaration in Kuwait City in April 2009, aims to ensure transparency and implement appropriate governance and accountability arrangements for SWF investments while at the same time maintaining an open and stable investment environment.[17]

5.2 Kuwait Investment Authority

Kuwait Investment Authority (KIA) is a portfolio investor like ADIA. Its funds are split into the Fund for Future Generations and the General Reserve Fund (GRF). Like ADIA, it has a high equity exposure of an estimated 60 percent KIA invests according to the international GDP weights of its investment destinations, but like ADIA it has been overweighing emerging markets,[18] notably in Asia where it has opened an office in China.[19] Like ADIA, its assets have lost a lot of their value in 2008, about 36 percent according to estimates by Setser/Ziemba. The Peterson ranking deems KIA the most transparent among Gulf SWFs because it is subjected to an independent and regular audit and it presents an annual report to Kuwait's parliament and cabinet.[20] Of the 3 points KIA achieves on the scoreboard of the Peterson paper, 0.5 points are for the provision of annual and semi-annual statements of its accounts which have to be reported to the Kuwait parliament and the Council of Ministers, 0.25 points for a declaration about the size of the fund, and 2 points for the fact that KIA is subjected to an independent and regular audit. As Kuwait has the most democratic institutional set-up in the Gulf region with a very vocal parliament, KIA is under a comparably high amount of public scrutiny. KIA provides the Kuwait parliament, through the State Audit Bureau, with a detailed report concerning all aspects of its activities every six months.[21]

---

17. Sven Behrendt, "The Santiago Principles of the International Working Group of SWFs: Blue Print of a 12-point Action Plan," Carnegie Middle East Center, Beirut 2009.
18. See KIA website, http://www.kia.gov.kw/En/Pages/default.aspx
19. "Wall Street Journal Examines KIA," Zawya, August 27, 2007, available at: http://www.zawya.com/printstory.cfm?storyid=ZAWYA20070827114242&l=114200070827
20. M. Edwin, "A Scoreboard for Sovereign Wealth Funds," Peterson Institute for International Economies, Washington 2007, 5-15.
21. See KIA website, http://www.kia.gov.kw/En/About_KIA/Pages/default.aspx

5.3 Qatar Investment Authority

Qatar Investment Authority (QIA) is a latecomer on the Gulf SWF investment scene. It was founded only in 2005 after the development of Qatar's gas reserves had led to increasing wealth in the country. Its assets are estimated at $65 billion. Like ADIA and KIA, it has a high equity exposure, but also holds large strategic stakes besides portfolio investments. It is relatively overweighed in Europe, where it has engaged in a number of high-profile deals such as London Stock Exchange, Barclays, Four Seasons Healthcare and J. Sainsbury.[22] It has also used leverage and shown a penchant for trophy assets. Like its counterparts, QIA has suffered steep losses of about 41 percent in 2008, according to Setser/Ziemba's estimates.

5.4 Saudi Arabia Monetary Agency

Saudi Arabia Monetary Agency (SAMA) is not a SWF in the strict sense and is closer to a conservative central bank. It manages the government reserves and its non-reserve foreign assets. Of all GCC SWFs, SAMA has performed by far the best in 2008 as it follows a conservative asset allocation in bonds and bank deposits with a preference for liquidity. According to Setser/Ziemba estimates, 80 percent of SAMA's assets are bonds and dollar-denominated. Given the low equity exposure, which is about 20 percent, SAMA's losses in 2008 have been low compared to the other funds and are estimated to be just about 12 percent. The liability profile of SAMA is more short term than ADIA, KIA, QIA because Saudi Arabia has a larger population. SAMA has withdrawn about $50 billion of its foreign assets in 2009 in order to fund budget shortfalls in the wake of the global financial crisis, oil price fall and production cuts.[23]

5.5 Saudi Arabian Investment Company

Saudi Arabian Investment Company (Sanabel) is a new state-owned fund with a capital of $5.3 billion. It has not really taken off yet, but is supposed to invest in financial securities, capital assets, real estate, and foreign currencies. It seeks to invest mainly in developed markets in Europe, the US and Japan and aims to carry out various investment projects through to 2020. Saudi Arabia aims to use it as a

22. Megan Davies, "QIA Learns from Its Mistakes," Reuters, July 7, 2009, available at http://blogs.reuters.com/reuters-dealzone/2009/07/07/qia-learns-from-its-mistakes/ and QIA website, http://www.qia.qa/QIA/ .
23. Daliah Merzaban, "Saudi Sells Assets to Cover Budget Shortfalls," Business Maktoob, May 31, 2009, available at: http://business.maktoob.com/20090000004339/Saudi_sells_assets_to_cover_budget_shortfalls/Article.htm .

bridge to connect the Saudi economy with international companies in technology transfer and marketing.[24]

5.6 Mubadala

Mubadala is the private equity and strategic investment arm of the Abu Dhabi government, founded in 2002 under the chairmanship of Shaikh Mohammed bin Zayed Al-Nahyan, the Crown Prince of Abu Dhabi. Its assets under management are approximately $13.3 billion.[25] It focuses on long-term investments that potentially offer high yields and can contribute to diversification of the domestic economy of the UAE via technology transfer and joint ventures. Mubadala has been investing in various sectors such as energy, aerospace, real estate, automotives, semi-conductors, aluminum and healthcare (e.g. Dolphin Energy, Masdar, Ferrari, AMD, Carlyle group, Emirates Aluminum). Recently, it published its first annual report which was hailed as a significant step towards more transparency and has opened for the company new avenues to raise financing such as bond issuance.[26] It also has a high transparency rating of 10 in the ranking of the SWF Institute (see Table 2). Mubadala has lost around 22 percent of its assets in the recent market turmoils.

5.7 International Petroleum Investment Company

International Petroleum Investment Company (IPIC) is a state corporation formed by the Abu Dhabi government in 1984 and chaired by Shaikh Mansour bin Zayed Al-Nahyan. Like Mubadala, IPIC is a long-term equity investor that focuses on strategic stakes in oil-related companies such as petrochemical industries and refineries. Recently, it ventured beyond this narrow field and acquired stakes in other companies such as a 10 percent stake in Daimler via its subsidiary Al Aabar, which makes it the largest shareholder in the global car brand. Its investment portfolio exceeds $14 billion.[27] IPIC also owns 65 percent of Borealis, a European petrochemical company. It owns the company jointly with Austrian OMV in which it holds, in turn, 17.6 percent which further increases its controlling stake of Borealis. The Borealis investment is an interesting example of how an international investment is used to contribute to economic diversification at home, as it is the joint

24. "Saudi Investments Abroad Valued at SR1.4 Trillion," AME Info, August 11, 2008, available at http://www.ameinfo.com/165902.html

25. See Sovereign Wealth Fund Institute website, http://www.swfinstitute.org/fund/mubadala.php

26. Wayne Arnold, "Mubadala Issues First Annual Report," *The National*, April 23, 2009, available at: http://www.thenational.ae/article/20090423/BUSINESS/704239941/1005

27. See IPIC website, http://www.ipic.ae/en/home/index.aspx

venture partner in the Abu Dhabi-based petrochemical company Borouge, which was founded in 1998 as a 50-50 joint venture between the Abu Dhabi National Oil Company (ADNOC) and Borealis.

5.8 Abu Dhabi Investment Council

Abu Dhabi Investment Council (ADIC) is the most recent Sovereign Wealth Fund of Abu Dhabi and was founded in 2006. About 30 percent of Abu Dhabi's ongoing surplus resources accrue to it with ADIA receiving the other 70 percent.[28] Besides international investments such as the purchase of the Chrysler Building in New York, ADIC holds stakes in two large state-owned banks: Abu Dhabi Commercial Bank and the National Bank of Abu Dhabi. It thus has a stronger focus on domestic investments than ADIA, which invests mostly internationally.[29]

5.9 Mumtalakat Holding Company (Bahrain) and the State General Reserve Fund (Oman)

Mumtalakat and the State General Reserve Fund are investment arms of the Kingdom of Bahrain and the Sultanate of Oman, respectively, with a capital of $9.1 billion and $8.2 billion. Each of them manages investments of its government reserves. They are smaller than the SWFs of their oil-rich neighbors and more geared towards the domestic market and its development. Yet they are in the process of diversifying their portfolios. Bahrain's Mumtalakat holds foreign stakes in various sectors in US, Europe and Asia, including in financial services and commodities, while the Omani fund owns a majority equity stake in Bulgarian Corporate Commercial Bank.[30]

5.10 Istithmar, Dubai International Capital, RAK Investment Authority

Istithmar, Dubai International Capital (DIC) and the Ras Al Khaimah Investment Authority (RAKIA) are newcomers in the Gulf SWF universe and were only founded in recent years. The Dubai investment companies are highly leveraged and have purportedly financed their investments with a debt share of up to 80 percent and have performed badly in the wake of the global financial crisis. Essentially they are financed via the capital account and debt, not via oil wealth. As they constitute

28. See SWFs institute website, http://www.swfinstitute.org/fund/adia.php
29. See ADIC website, http://www.adcouncil.ae/AboutUs/InvestmentStrategy/tabid/63/Default.aspx
30. "Bulgaria Corpbank Says Sells 30 pct to Omani Fund," Reuters, July 27, 2009, available at http://www.reuters.com/article/rbssBanks/idUSLR50175820090127

a sovereign liability, it is debatable whether they should be classified as SWFs. Dubai International Capital, which is overweighed in Europe,[31] is owned not by the government but by the Dubai ruler and could therefore be classified as a private company, although this is a moot distinction given the unison of government and ruler in an absolute monarchy. Istithmar, on the other hand, is an investment vehicle of Dubai World, which is owned by the Dubai government.[32]

RAKIA is the investment arm of Ras Al Khaimah government with capital worth of $1.2 billion. It has used a considerable amount of leverage and is invested in the local economy of Ras Al Khaimah such as in the production of tiles and generic drugs.[33] It has also a proven penchant for more exotic investment destinations such as mines and supermarkets in Congo and has announced plans to invest $2 billion in Georgia over the next five years.[34]

6. SWF and other Forms of Sovereign Wealth: State-owned Enterprises

State-owned Enterprises (SoE) constitute a third kind of sovereign wealth besides central bank reserves and SWFs. Large parts of the GCC economies are owned by the state. Stock markets are dominated by a few big companies, which have the state as a majority shareholder, while most of the larger private enterprises are family-owned and not listed. The same is true for the biggest state companies, namely the oil sector. Thus the largest 20 or so companies in each of the GCC countries are not listed at all (e.g. Saudi Aramco and other national oil companies, Dubai Holding, Alba, Dubal, Emirates Airline, ADIA, KIA and other investment bodies).[35] On the other hand, among the listed companies, the largest 10 companies in each country make up between 50 percent and 80 percent of market capitalization. In most of the bigger companies of the GCC, the respective state holds a majority stake (e.g. around 70 percent each in Sabic, Saudi Telecom, Saudi Electricity, Emirates Bank). In others, it holds a substantial minority position (e.g. 30 percent in Emaar). At the

31. See DIC website (DIC annual review of 2008): http://www.dubaiic.com/media-files/2009/10/29/20091029_DIC-Annual-Review-2008.pdf

32. "Istithmar World named Best Private Equity House by Banker Middle East," AME info FZ LLC, June 18, 2008, available at: http://www.ameinfo.com/160844.html

33. See SWFs Institute website, http://www.swfinstitute.org/fund/rak.php

34. "RAK Will Invest $2b in Georgia," *Gulf News*, February 19, 2009, available at: http://gulfnews.com/business/investment/rak-will-invest-2b-in-georgia-1.52455

35. OECD, "Ownership Structures in MENA Countries: Listed Companies, Sate-Owned, Family Enterprises and some Policy Implications," Working Paper 2005, available at http://www.oecd.org/dataoecd/26/2/35402110.pdf

same time, the hydrocarbon sector, which on average accounts for 40 percent of the nominal GDP of GCC countries, is not even listed.

The national oil companies are not only the most important companies for the GCC economies; they also belong to the "most valuable" category internationally. Financial Times in collaboration with McKinsey has identified Saudi Aramco as the most valuable company worldwide with an estimated value of $781 billion; Kuwait Petroleum Corporation comes fifth on the same list with an estimated value of $378 billion.[36] It has been argued that increased privatization on the one hand and going public of private family enterprises on the other would lead to broader markets and higher free floats, which would be beneficial for the further development of GCC stock markets. While the oil sector would certainly offer quality shares, it is highly unlikely that GCC governments would forego control of a resource they regard as strategic.

SABIC is one of the earliest and most quoted examples of strategic diversification of Gulf economies into petrochemicals, which was emulated later by Abu Dhabi-based Borouge and others. SABIC was founded in 1976 against the advice of many naysayers in the consultancy community who argued that it would not be successful as at that time petrochemical plants were usually close to the final markets in industrial countries rather than close to the feedstock sources. Over the years, SABIC has developed into a global player in the petrochemical business and has grown by acquisitions in developed markets as the acquisitions of GE Plastics, UK-based Huntsman Petrochemicals and the petrochemical division of Dutch DSM show.

DUBAL and Qatar Steel are other examples of GCC diversification into heavy industries. Both companies have invested internationally in recent years to secure their feedstock supply needs of alumina and iron ore, respectively. In the field of telecommunication, companies like Etisalat or Zain have acquired international mobile licenses in West Africa, Pakistan and the Middle East, while Dubai-based Emaar has tried to position itself as a global real estate brand, and Dubai Ports World has developed into an international logistics provider by buying ports all over the world.

TAQA is another example of a strategically-oriented state-owned company. It is controlled by the Government of Abu Dhabi and was founded in 2005. Its assets are estimated to be worth more than $23.4 billion.[37] As a global player in the energy sector, it has investments in power generation, water desalination, oil and gas, renewable

36. "Private vs. Public," *Financial Times*, December 14, 2006, available at http://www.ft.com/cms/s/965bc3fc-8b9e-11db-a61f-0000779e2340.html

37. See TAQA website, http://www.taqa.ae/en/abouttaqa.html .

energies, and even mining and metals. It constitutes an overseas investment vehicle expanding across the Gulf, Middle East, North Africa, Europe, Asia, and the United States. It holds majority stakes in assets that provide about 85 percent of Abu Dhabi's power generation and 90 percent of its water desalination capacity.

Table 3: Strategic GCC Companies with Foreign Investment Interests

Company	Industry	Founded	State Ownership %	FDI
Saudi Basic Industries (SABIC)	Petrochemicals	1976	70	GE Plastics (US), Huntsman Petrochemicals (UK), DSM (NL), projects in China
Qatar Steel (QASCO)	Steel	1974	70	Sphere Investments (Mauritania)
Abu Dhabi Energy (Taqa)	Utilities, Energy	2005	75.1	Canadian oil companies, oil licenses in Libya, power stations in Morocco
Emaar	Real estate	1997	32	MENA, India, John Laings (USA)
Dubai Ports World	Logistics	1999	80	Ports all over the world
Dubai Aluminum	Aluminum	1979	100	Alumina smelters in Guinea and Orissa/ India
Borealis/ Borouge	Petrochemicals	1998	64	JV with OMV
Etisalat	Telecom	1976	100	Mobile licenses in West Africa and Pakistan
Zain	Telecom	1983	24.4	Mobile licenses in the Middle East, Sudan and Morocco

7. From SWFs to Strategic Global Companies?

The large losses that GCC SWFs incurred in the second half of 2008, however, have raised the question whether concentration on international portfolio investments is wise and whether the development of real assets at home could be an alternative worth contemplating. With the exception of SAMA, which had a conservative portfolio of bonds, ADIA, KIA and QIA suffered heavy losses with their equity-centered portfolios. Giacomo Luciani has argued that it would be advisable to invest more funds domestically and enable local champions by pooling assets and competencies.

Such focused companies would have the potential to be internationally competitive and grow by foreign acquisitions as well.[38] As it is the declared policy of the GCC states to foster a growing role for the private sector, such local champions would ideally emerge by development of private sector companies and not by favoring state-owned enterprises or acquiring stakes in private companies by SWFs, which would be nationalization of private companies in a hidden fashion.

Instead of investing predominantly in foreign markets via SWFs, GCC states could instead put more of their money into endowments and national development banks, which in turn could acquire shares in domestic private companies and lend money to them. Semi-autonomous social services (e.g. education, health care, pensions) financed by endowments could contribute to a more efficient and decentralized economy, and such institutions could provide necessary capital for the expansion, specialization and professionalization of private family businesses that often have conglomerate-like and non-transparent corporate structures. The state could thus help in the modernization of the Gulf private sector and its adaptation to international markets standards and competition, while SWFs would gradually lose importance at the expense of such endowments and national development banks as tools of national development.

While the logic of this argument is compelling, it needs to be taken into consideration that GCC stock markets have lost even more than stock markets in the OECD countries in 2008 and that the absorption capacities for meaningful and sustainable investment projects in the GCC are limited, given the hydrocarbon-centered economies, lack of skilled human resources, and other structural shortcomings. White elephant projects and a real estate bust in the wake of the recent oil boom are striking reminders of this dilemma. Thus, a domestic investment strategy should not be regarded as an insurance policy against capital losses such as have occurred in the case of international assets of SWFs, rather it would be an integration of the SWF assets in development and diversification drives at the national level, and success would largely depend on whether such policies bear more fruit than investments on international capital markets.

Conclusion

Sovereign wealth funds (SWFs) have attracted the attention of investment professionals and politicians in recent years as global imbalances in the international

38. Giacomo Luciani, "Promises and Pitfalls of Sovereign Funds," *GRC Commentary*, March 25, 2008 and "Encouraging Strategic International Investment," *GRC Commentary*, April 17, 2008.

financial system and the growing economic power of China and oil exporters have changed the global balance of power. Many accounts of SWFs have a slightly "Western bias" as they tend to regard these funds either as a threat or a potential client for investment products. However, SWFs are interwoven with the domestic development models of their owners, i.e. sovereign governments and their respective liability profiles. Their investment policies might shift with changing structures in the local economies (e.g. diversification, increasing role of domestic global players, growing role for private companies), changing fortunes in the international financial markets (e.g. current financial turmoil) and new socio-economic challenges, and changing asset liabilities (e.g. demographics, infrastructure expansion).

These differences are also obvious in the case of the GCC countries, where large SWFs with open liability profiles and considerable risk tolerance and equity exposure (ADIA, KIA) exist alongside conservative central bank management of assets (SAMA). Higher liquidity preference in the latter case stems from a potential need to mobilize assets in a relatively short period of time to finance development projects for a larger population in case of financial crisis or volatility of oil revenues. Such mixed liability profiles apply even more to countries where oil production is past its peak and where SWFs will be needed to finance diversification efforts in the foreseeable future (Oman, Bahrain). Finally, some of the leveraged funds that were founded in recent years cannot be classified as sovereign wealth due to their debt-financed nature (e.g. Istithmar, Dubai International Capital).

Beside portfolio investments in Western securities markets, strategic foreign investments of GCC countries are gaining prominence. Ranging from proper foreign direct investment and the acquisition of majority stakes to huge portfolio investments running into billions of dollars, they help in the diversification and reorientation of the domestic GCC economies. In comparison to the last oil boom of the 1970s, such strategic foreign investments have clearly increased. As a novelty, they target Asia as well, albeit coming from a low statistical base. SWFs are not appropriate vehicles for such strategic foreign investments, rather new private equity-like funds (e.g. Mubadala, IPIC) or state-owned enterprises (e.g. SABIC, DPW) seem to be. As it is a declared goal of the GCC countries to give the private sector a larger role, and as the latter's family-owned enterprises are often in need of capital and expertise for international expansion, new ways of national development might be contemplated in the future that could foster private sector development via endowment funds and national development banks. SWFs in the Gulf region might therefore gradually lose importance over time at the expense of such investment vehicles.

11

How Competitive are Gulf Economies?*

Kenneth Wilson

Introduction

Recently, the United Arab Emirates (UAE) federal government launched its UAE Vision 2021 & UAE Government Strategy 2011-2013, which identifies seven Strategic Priorities including "Competitive Knowledge Economy."[1] This is the most recent example of a formal statement by a Gulf State that it is focusing on the knowledge economy and international competitiveness. The Competitive Knowledge Economy Strategic Priority combines two rather complex and not well-understood concepts: international competitiveness and knowledge economy. This paper considers questions related to the international competitiveness of Gulf economies. In addition, attention is paid to the role that innovation and knowledge economy fundamentals play in impacting the international competitiveness of Gulf States. Indeed it is the premise of this paper that a lack of innovation and entrepreneurship on the one hand, combined with inadequate knowledge economy fundamentals on the other hand, are important constraints retarding the international competitiveness of Gulf States. Therefore, the paper tackles the issue of how to build a stronger more vibrant private sector in the Gulf economies by focusing attention upon key fundamental driving forces

* Maha Korttom provided valuable research assistance in preparing this paper. An earlier version was presented at the Al Jisr Workshop in Dubai, on June 6, 2010. The helpful comments and feedback from workshop participants are acknowledged, though all errors are my responsibility.

1. http://www.uaecabinet.ae/English/Documents/PMO%20StrategyDocEngFinV2.pdf

behind the international competitiveness of the most innovative countries in the world, namely knowledge economy fundamentals and innovation ecosystem competitiveness enablers.

Part of the interest in international competitiveness emanates from the desire of hydrocarbon-dependent Gulf States, particularly the Kingdom of Saudi Arabia (KSA), UAE, Qatar and Oman to build more diversified economies. A recent example of this desire is the Abu Dhabi Economic Vision 2030 document which identifies 12 sectors that Abu Dhabi wishes to diversify into. Unlike Dubai which is 90 percent diversified away from hydrocarbons, the Abu Dhabi economy is currently 66 percent hydrocarbon-based. Fluctuating oil prices and recognition of the narrowness of its economic base have led Abu Dhabi to develop a coherent strategy which identifies the key sectors that it wishes to move into. Some of these are totally new, such as aerospace and aviation. Mubadala, the sovereign wealth fund that has been given the responsibility to lead Abu Dhabi's diversification strategy, has entered into some major joint ventures with impressive international knowledge-based manufacturing enterprises such as GlobalFoundries Inc., the world's third largest semi-conductor foundry, in a bid to realize its diversification vision. Linked to the diversification strategy is a belief that diversified economies are more internationally competitive because they are more able to ride out commodity price fluctuations. Norway and Australia are used as examples of diversified commodity-based economies to illustrate the point.

Discussion of a lack of international competitiveness presupposes that an uncompetitive economy is the outcome of an uncompetitive industrial structure and that this is a bad thing in the same way that an uncompetitive firm – or an uncompetitive racing car or an uncompetitive athlete – is undesirable.[2] However, it is not precisely clear what 'competitiveness' means for a national economy.[3] It is also in some ways an unfortunate term, as it suggests that nations are competing like firms chasing market share or athletes competing for medals and that one nation doing better economically means that others are doing worse. In reality, of course, the Gulf countries benefit when there is stronger economic growth in the rest of the

2. J. Hawkins, "The Concept of Competitiveness," Treasury Working Paper, 2006-02, Australian Treasury, Canberra, April 2006.

3. Krugman (1994, 1996) criticizes the analogy, noting that economies are much more self-contained than companies. Also, that unlike uncompetitive companies, a country cannot go out of business. Furthermore, a national economy is substantially more diverse and complex than even a multinational conglomerate. See P. Krugman, "Competitiveness: a Dangerous Obsession," *Foreign Affairs* (March/April 1994): 28-44; and P. Krugman, "A Country is not a Company," *Harvard Business Review* (January-February 1996): 40-51.

world, particularly when there is an increase in the demand for hydrocarbons, which boosts the oil and gas revenues they receive.

When considering the issue of the competitiveness of Gulf economies and the firms and sectors they comprise, it is worth noting that we are dealing with a very heterogeneous group of countries. Table 1 contains some basic economic and social indicators for each of the six Gulf States that comprise the Gulf Cooperation Council (GCC) to illustrate this point. KSA dwarfs the other Gulf States in many ways, but particularly with respect to population.[4] Qatar and Bahrain have tiny populations for nation states and are not much bigger than the size of a regional city in many countries of the world. Dependency on non-nationals, particularly in non-public enterprise, is greatest in the UAE and Qatar but still substantial in Kuwait and Bahrain. Oman and KSA are the least dependent upon non-nationals, but neither would be able to run their economies successfully without substantial input from non-national labor. Literacy rates are low by world standards for such rich countries. This is partly because many non-national workers have only the most basic education. Table 1 also points to the enormous income inequality between the Gulf States and when one takes into account the huge wealth dispersion in countries like KSA and UAE, it is clear that there are many poor nationals in Gulf countries with limited human capital, a fact that may surprise readers not familiar with the Gulf. However, this means that Gulf States seeking to build competitive knowledge-based economies and societies face considerable challenges.

Table 1: Economic and Social Indicators for Gulf States

Country	Population[a] (millions) Year 2008	Nationals[b] (%)	Literacy[b] (%)	Labor Force[b] (millions)	Per Capita GDP PPP[a] (USD) Year 2008	Public Debt[b] (% of GDP)
Bahrain	1.1	68.1	86.5	0.6	19.8	86.5
Kuwait	2.5	53.7	93.3	2.04	59.4	8.1
Oman	2.9	80.5	81.4	0.97	20.9	4.5

4. It should be noted that the compilation of tables of economic and social indicators for Gulf States is not straightforward and quite problematic for several reasons including the use of different standards by different statistical agencies, often the lack of a single reliable source within a country and inconsistencies between them. This is particularly true of population data.

Qatar	1.4	10.1c	94.7c	1.3c	69.3	15.7
KSA	24.8	80.9	78.8	6.92	19.2	22.9
UAE	4.8	26.1	77.9	3.15	53.4	54

a Source: GCC Website- GCC countries main Statistics-year 2008 available at http://www.gcc-sg.org/eng/index.php?action=GCC
b Source: The CIA World Factbook (last update August 3, 2010) at https://www.cia.gov/library/publications/the-world-factbook
c Source: Qatar Statistics Authority-Population Structure at http://www.qsa.gov.qa/eng/Population Structure.htm & Qatar-Bulletin-Labour-Force-Sample-Survey-2009 & Qatar Information Exchange

This paper is structured as follows: following this brief introduction, Section 1 introduces a taxonomy of competitiveness so that we have a clearer understanding of how to answer the question: "How competitive are Gulf economies?" Section 1 introduces a range of measures of competitiveness and provides a summary of the latest WEF findings on competitiveness drivers for each of the six Gulf States. Section 2 then takes a closer look at two of the biggest constraints on the international competitiveness of Gulf economies, namely the lack of innovation and entrepreneurship on the one hand, and the inadequate knowledge economy fundamentals currently experienced by Gulf States on the other hand. Section 3 provides some policy implications and a simple competitiveness uplift strategy for Gulf States that focuses upon innovation, entrepreneurship and the knowledge economy.

1. What Is Competitiveness?

International benchmarking analysis of competitiveness is popular. Such benchmarking is useful because it allows policy makers to identify gaps in international competitiveness that require remedial policy intervention, but also strengths for leverage. Two of the more popular international competitiveness benchmark indicators are the Global Competitiveness Index (GCI) produced by the World Economic Forum (WEF) and the Doing Business Index (DBI) produced by the World Bank. Table 2 compares benchmark data for each Gulf country for these two indexes.

According to the GCI, Qatar and UAE are internationally competitive at rank positions 22 and 23, respectively. KSA also ranks quite well at 28, while Bahrain, Kuwait and Oman are less internationally competitive. With respect to the DBI, KSA and Bahrain are internationally competitive at rank position 13 and 20, respectively, while UAE and Qatar rank quite reasonably, though Kuwait and Oman are not internationally competitive.

Aggregate indicators such as GCI and DBI are interesting, but they are not able to tell us in a detailed or disaggregated sense about international competitiveness drivers or characteristics unless we disentangle them and also have a clearer definition and understanding of the concept of competitiveness.

Table 2: International Competitiveness Benchmarks for Gulf Countries

Global Competitiveness Index (World Economic Forum), 134 Countries		Doing Business Index (World Bank), 183 Countries	
Rank	Country	Rank	Country
22	Qatar	13	KSA
23	UAE	20	Bahrain
28	KSA	33	UAE
38	Bahrain	39	Qatar
39	Kuwait	61	Kuwait
41	Oman	65	Oman

Source: The Global Competitiveness Report available at http://www.weforum.org/pdf/GCR09/GCR20092010fullreport.pdf; Doing Business Index available at http://www.doingbusiness.org/economyrankings

Therefore, before we consider some disaggregated international competitiveness benchmark indicators, we discuss briefly what international competitiveness means. To help answer the question: what is competitiveness, a simple taxonomy of competitiveness suggested by Hawkins (2006) is introduced.[5] Hawkins classifies competitiveness into four concepts, termed 'internal market competitiveness,' 'external price competitiveness,' 'external cost competitiveness' and 'measures of competitiveness based on growth fundamentals.' Hawkins' taxonomy is helpful up to a point. However, it is not always straightforward to identify simple and tractable measures of one or the other measures of competitiveness identified by Hawkins. These difficulties force us to focus upon indicators of internal market competition and indicators of growth competitiveness, since these are more readily available.

5. Hawkins, "The Concept of Competitiveness."

1.1 Internal Market Competitiveness

Perfectly competitive markets generally perform more efficiently than monopolies.[6] Economies where most markets have many producers competing for sales are likely to be more dynamic. Even small economies can have many competitors in their markets if they are open to competitors from outside their borders — by having low or no tariffs or no other barriers to trade.

Governments can encourage competition in several ways. First, they can avoid favoritism in their own purchases. Second, they can avoid protecting dominant firms by using legislation to encourage new entrants and by not allowing unnecessary monopolies.[7] The Gulf States lag the rest of the world in terms of their current state of competition policies and consumer protection policies, and indeed there is very little intra-brand competition within each Gulf State with brand monopoly rights being common. Improvements in this aspect of competitiveness can be thought of as the economy keeps moving towards and/or shifting out the production possibility frontier. However, there is little evidence of improvement in this respect in the Gulf currently, something that is emphasized further Later.

Internal or domestic market competitiveness relates to the domestic rules, regulations and conditions that influence resource allocation and pricing. Economic theory tells us that, except in certain rare cases, competitive markets generally perform better than oligopolies and monopolies, particularly with respect to pricing. Moreover, competitive markets tend to be more dynamic and innovative. There are many things that governments can do to encourage domestic competition and avoid the emergence of monopoly and rent-seeking behavior. It is often difficult to measure internal market competitiveness, however, the annual Executive Opinion Survey conducted by the WEF provides us with some insight into just how internally competitive each of the Gulf States are.

Table 3 provides information on the Gulf States' rankings compared to a total of 134 countries globally against a number of indicators of domestic or internal market competition. The table is constructed using information extracted from WEF's The Global Competitiveness Report 2009-2010. WEF uses hard data and survey data to determine cross-country rankings on a range of economically important factors covering such things as: public institutions; infrastructure; the

6. Some 'natural monopolies' are an exception. Sometimes a combination of high fixed and low marginal costs means that a project would only be undertaken by a monopoly.

7. A natural monopoly may be better in public ownership than private, but it might be possible to introduce elements of competition to some parts of its operations.

macro economy; education and training; market efficiency; and innovation. From the long list of indicators that the WEF produces, we have chosen a sample that captures and reflects some dimensions of internal market competitiveness in the Gulf States. Although not definitive, nor complete, Table 3, nevertheless, provides some useful insights into the extent, or lack, of internal market competitiveness in each Gulf State.

The first set of indicators listed in Table 3 (variables 1.01 to 1.17) focus upon institutions, the legal framework, and firm behavior that facilitate internal market making and market transactions. Here we see that there is considerable diversity between the Gulf States. Generally speaking Oman, UAE and Qatar are quite internationally competitive across these indicators, just ahead of KSA and substantially ahead of Bahrain and Kuwait. If we look at indicators of 'markets in action' (variables 6.01 to 6.03), we see that UAE and Qatar are internationally competitive and well ahead of the remaining Gulf States with Kuwait again ranked last behind its Gulf neighbors. Turning to indicators of market dynamism (variables 6.06 to 6.13), we see a more uneven picture. In some respects, UAE, Qatar, Oman, Bahrain and KSA are quite competitive and only Kuwait is well below international competitiveness standards.

The overall impression from Table 3 is that, although there is some unevenness across internal market indicators, generally speaking UAE and Qatar are quite internationally competitive with respect to internal market competitiveness. Oman is not far behind, but comfortably ahead of Bahrain and KSA, but Kuwait lags substantially and cannot be considered internationally competitive in this regard.

Table 3: Gulf Countries' Ranking among 134 Countries

WEF variable #	Indicator	Bahrain	Kuwait	KSA	Oman	Qatar	UAE
1.01	Property Rights	32	45	37	26	16	34
1.05	Judicial independence	36	48	34	29	10	32
1.06	Favoritism in decisions of government officials	55	61	19	14	6	11

1.08	Burden of Government regulation	32	115	20	7	10	6
1.09	Efficiency of legal framework in settling disputes	79	38	58	19	5	9
1.16	Ethical behavior of firms	26	55	35	23	29	19
1.17	Strength of auditing and reporting standards	33	65	53	45	28	31
6.01	Intensity of local competition	51	45	37	59	14	9
6.02	Extent of market dominance	46	56	37	79	6	16
6.03	Effectiveness of anti-monopoly policy	44	97	41	48	39	29
6.06	Number of procedures to start a business	46	111	46	46	26	60
6.07	Time required to start a business	23	92	31	38	9	49
6.09	Prevalence of trade barriers	16	72	37	26	5	7
6.13	Burden of customs procedures	12	94	30	22	44	3

Source: World Economic Forum (2009) The Global Competitiveness Report 2009-2010.

1.2 External Price Competitiveness

A firm will be uncompetitive in a market if its price is well above that charged by its rivals for a similar product and it makes few sales. An analogous approach is used to measure external price competitiveness for national economies.

Measuring external price competitiveness in international markets requires converting domestic prices into a common currency so they can be compared. An example is the annual exercise conducted by *The Economist* magazine in compiling its 'Big Mac' index.[8] *The Economist* converts the local price of a Big Mac hamburger, chosen because Big Macs are basically the same all over the world, into US dollars. Unfortunately, *The Economist* does not collect data on Big Macs for all Gulf States. According to the latest data published on Oanda.com (for Big Macs purchased on 16 July 2009), a Big Mac in KSA cost $2.92 compared to a cost of $3.57 in the US. The cheapest Big Macs are in Hong Kong (China) at $1.70 and the most expensive are in Norway at $6.42.

If we assume that Big Macs are roughly the same price in other Gulf States as they are in KSA, then we are able to conclude that, based on the Big Mac index, the Gulf States are reasonably competitive in the global market for Big Macs, certainly more competitive than the US and Norway. However, this is not particularly helpful since Big Macs are not traded internationally. But, as Hawkins points out, in principle the same exercise can be undertaken for a range of traded goods and these can be weighted appropriately to derive an index of overall external price competitiveness.[9] Abstracting from transport costs and taxes, if global markets are competitive then the price of the same good should be the same all around the world provided the good is traded.

A milder version of the same argument noted by Hawkins is the long-established idea of 'purchasing power parity'.[10] This suggests that either domestic prices (in a world of fixed exchange rates) or exchange rates (if they are floating) will adjust to keep the real exchange rate stable. Purchasing power parity does not hold in the short term, but many studies find it seems to hold in the longer term. Typically, the 'half-life' of fluctuations in the real exchange rate is around 3-5 years.[11] This would imply that if real exchange rates are a valid measure of competitiveness, any loss of competitiveness is self-correcting.

---

8. The index has been calculated since 1986. Parsley and Wei (2003) provide a more technical analysis. See D. Parsley and S.J. Wei, "A Prism into the PPP Puzzles: the Microfoundations of Big Mac Real Exchange Rates," National Bureau of Economic Research Working Papers, no. 10074, November 2003.

9. Hawkins, "The Concept of Competitiveness."

10. The term 'purchasing power parity' was first used by Cassel (1922) in discussing the setting of new gold standard parities after World War I, but Angell (1926) traces the basic idea back over a century earlier. See G. Cassel, *Money and Foreign Exchange after* 1914 (London: Constable & Co., 1922) and J. Angell *The Theory of International Prices: History, Criticism and Restatement* (Cambridge: Harvard University Press, 1926).

11. See, for example, A. Taylor, "A Century of Purchasing Power Parity," Review of Economics and Statistics 84 (2002): 139-50; and the survey by Rogoff in K. Rogoff, "The Purcahsing Power Parity Puzzle," *Journal of Economic Literature* XXXIV, no. 2 (June 1996).

Hawkins also points out that another complication of using real exchange rates as a measure of international competitiveness is that prices should conceptually be adjusted for quality changes, but this is hard to do in practice.[12] A company improving the quality of its goods may have rising prices but this would be a reflection of greater competitiveness, not a sign of declining competitiveness. Something analogous may happen with economies. The real exchange rate tends to rise in economies which are innovative and successful, making their price competitiveness appear worse. For these reasons, we will focus upon other indicators and aspects of international competitiveness in assessing how Gulf States perform, relatively to each other and the rest of the world.

1.3 External Cost Competitiveness

A variant of the external price competitiveness proposition is to compare costs between countries, which can vary even if the law of one price holds. The largest business cost, and the one most commonly compared internationally, is (unit) labor costs.[13] Although the United States Bureau of Labor Statistics undertakes a comparison of costs in manufacturing across 17 countries, none are from the Gulf region. In principle, a comparison could be done for 'unit labor costs,' the ratio of wages to productivity. But given the difficulties involved in getting internationally consistent data on the levels of both wages and productivity, measures of this ratio may be quite unreliable. Unfortunately there are no reliable data on relative labor costs or on productivity for the Gulf States, and so we are unable to perform this comparison.

1.4 Competitiveness Measures Based on Growth Fundamentals

Another concept of competitiveness, and the one most relevant to the purpose of this paper, is that an economy is competitive if it does things that are likely to encourage economic growth. Moreover, it is likely to be more competitive if it has innovative and entrepreneurial enterprises that form part of a strong knowledge economy. There are many aspects to, or drivers of, growth competitiveness. WEF has been looking at growth competitiveness for more than two decades and has over time refined its ideas and measurement approaches to develop a method for comparing the international growth competitiveness of countries. WEF defines competitiveness as "the set of institutions, policies, and factors that determine the

12. Hawkins, "The Concept of Competitiveness."

13. The next most commonly compared cost is taxation. However, with respect to taxation, the Gulf States experience a competitive advantage. Although there are differences between them with respect to taxation and government charges, they are very low by international standards.

level of productivity of a country."[14] Although WEF recognizes that the determinants of competitiveness are many and complex, it nevertheless has developed a GCI that captures the open-ended, complex and multi-faceted nature of growth and groups them into 12 pillars of competitiveness:

1. Institutions (the legal and administrative framework)
2. Infrastructure (the transport, logistics, power, telecommunications and other networks)
3. Macroeconomic stability (the underlying macroeconomic fundamentals)
4. Health and primary education (basic health status and education)
5. Higher education and training (secondary, and tertiary enrolments and quality)
6. Goods market efficiency (rules affecting the ease of doing business)
7. Labor market efficiency (flexibility and incentive regime)
8. Financial market sophistication (efficiency, availability and access)
9. Technological readiness (ICT, access to global knowledge)
10. Market size (opportunities for increasing returns)
11. Business sophistication (networks, clusters and sophistication)
12. Innovation (R&D, intellectual property protection, venture capital)

Table 4 is constructed using data taken from WEF's *The Global Competitiveness Report 2009-2010*. Again without being definitive, Table 4 provides us with valuable insights into how well the Gulf States perform in a global benchmarking exercise aimed at identifying important drivers of international growth competitiveness. To help the discussion, we have chosen indicators that may be grouped into five broad areas that are strongly linked to growth competitiveness: infrastructure;[15] the macro economy; education; technological readiness; and innovation. Table 4 contains rankings on four indicators (2.01 to 2.08) related to infrastructure in the Gulf States. There are considerable differences between Gulf States with respect to their relative abilities to access the increasing returns from networks associated with good infrastructure. Clearly, UAE and Qatar are internationally competitive. Except for telephone lines, Oman is also reasonably competitive as is Bahrain except for the quality of electricity supply. Next comes KSA and finally Kuwait which lacks internationally competitive infrastructure.

---

14. WEF, *The Global Competitiveness Report 2009-2010* (Palgrave Macmillan, 2009), 4.

15. The importance of the network effects flowing from good infrastructure are often overlooked in analyses of growth competitiveness, but these should not be understated. See J. Squalli and K. Wilson, "Openness and Access," *Applied Economics* 41, no. 3 (February 2009) and J. Squalli, K. Wilson and S. Hugo, "An Analysis of Growth Competitiveness," *International Review of Applied Economics* 22, no. 1 (January 2008) for evidence.

Table 4: Rank Position of Gulf Countries among 134 Countries in Terms of Drivers of International Growth Competitiveness in the UAE

WEF variable #	Indicator	Bahrain	Kuwait	KSA	Oman	Qatar	UAE
2.01	Quality of overall infrastructure	26	44	32	22	47	11
2.05	Quality of air transport infrastructure	22	58	51	52	12	3
2.07	Quality of electricity supply	70	80	33	29	25	16
2.08	Telephone lines	45	67	71	86	42	35
3.01	Government budget balance	12	5	3	20	11	7
3.02	National savings rate	21	3	9	11	6	16
3.03	Inflation rate	17	90	81	107	116	98
3.05	Government debt	51	7	24	2	5	77
4.09	Quality of primary education	50	88	71	54	7	19
5.01	Secondary enrollment	18	56	45	60	15	50
5.02	Tertiary enrollment	67	89	72	77	93	81
5.03	Quality of the educational system	40	81	60	54	10	20
5.04	Quality of math & science education	54	89	76	71	3	20
9.01	Availability of latest technologies	28	55	43	59	25	8

9.02	Firm-level technology absorption	59	42	40	60	19	4
9.03	Laws relating to ICT	28	99	45	36	40	10
12.01	Capacity for innovation	58	85	31	87	109	39
12.02	Quality of scientific research institutions	112	83	37	63	32	53
12.03	Company spending on R&D	87	100	34	62	64	30
12.04	University-industry collaboration in R&D	101	99	37	53	38	39
12.07	Utility Patents	90	30	45	40	46	38

Source: World Economic Forum (2009) The Global Competitiveness Report 2009-2010.

Turning to macro economy indicators (3.01 to 3.05), it is clear that all the Gulf States are internationally competitive except for inflation rates (though here the published data used for these rankings are now out of date – the inflation problem of the Gulf States has largely disappeared now), and only Bahrain has a public debt level considerably worse than other Gulf States, largely because it does not have access to the hydrocarbon revenues enjoyed by the others. The large public debt of the UAE is perceived to be less of a sovereign risk than its rank position may indicate. The UAE's public debt is linked to the debt-financed economic diversification strategy of Dubai. However, since Abu Dhabi and its sovereign wealth funds effectively stand behind Dubai, the country risk that such a large public debt may indicate is largely mitigated.

With respect to education (4.09 to 5.04) Kuwait, KSA and Oman are not internationally competitive and lag the other Gulf States considerably. Bahrain and UAE perform reasonably except for tertiary enrolment, while Qatar is internationally competitive except for tertiary enrolment performance. In fact, with respect to tertiary enrolment none of the Gulf States is internationally competitive. This is one of the rare occasions where there is a common problem across the Gulf, though it manifests itself differently in each Gulf State. Part of the problem relates to the lack of incentives for many young Gulf men, in particular, to graduate high school and continue with their tertiary education since many of them have access to relatively high paying public sector work, particularly in the defense and police forces. This indicator highlights the single biggest challenge faced by the Gulf States in trying to build a competitive knowledge economy using their own nationals.

With respect to technological readiness (9.01 to 9.03), UAE and Qatar are internationally competitive. The other four Gulf States lag, but the gap is not so great. Unlike other growth competitiveness areas, technology readiness is not a major constraint on the international competitiveness of Gulf States.

Turning to innovation (12.01 to 12.07), we note that this is the one broad area where all Gulf States are not internationally competitive across all indicators, though the relative position of each Gulf State differs. KSA, UAE and Qatar perform relatively better than Oman, Bahrain and Kuwait, which are not internationally competitive with respect to innovation. Because of the importance of innovation to building a knowledge economy, we will take a closer look at innovation.

In summary, the evidence contained in Table 4 is clear. In terms of growth competitiveness, UAE and Qatar are quite internationally competitive in infrastructure, macro economy and technological readiness while the other Gulf States generally are considerably less so. However, in the areas of education and innovation, two key drivers of the knowledge economy and enablers of economic diversification, none of the Gulf States are internationally competitive.

International benchmarking of countries according to a range of economic and social indicators is becoming increasingly popular, and there is no shortage of sources to turn to in order to illustrate a point. For example, Legatum Institute now publishes an annual Prosperity Index (PI). According to Legatum, "the purpose of the Prosperity Index is to encourage policy makers, scholars, the media, and the interested public to take a holistic view of prosperity and understand how it is created."[16] Unlike the WEF GCI, the intellectual pedigree of the PI is less well established; however, there are similarities between GCI and PI. Whereas GCI identifies 12 pillars of international competitiveness, PI is made up of nine "building blocks of prosperity":

1. Economic fundamentals
2. Entrepreneurship and innovation
3. Democratic institutions
4. Education
5. Health
6. Safety and security
7. Governance
8. Personal freedom
9. Social capital.

16. Legatum Institute, *The 2009 Legatum Prosperity Index* (London: Legatum Institute, 2009), 1.

Unfortunately, Legatum produces PI for only three Gulf countries currently: Kuwait, KSA and UAE. Table 5 provides PI rankings for each of these Gulf States and also provides the rank position for each of the nine sub-index "building blocks." The UAE is ranked above Kuwait and KSA. For the sake of the current discussion, the most important rankings relate to economic fundamentals, entrepreneurialism and innovation, education and governance. Not surprisingly, these sub-index rankings under PI are similar to the indicators produced by WEF and discussed earlier. Currently, no Gulf State performs well but Kuwait and KSA lag the UAE considerably.

Table 5: Prosperity Index Ranking for Gulf Countries among 104 Countries

Overall Rank	Country	Economic Fundamentals	Entrepreneurship & Innovation	Democratic Institutions	Education	Health	Safety & Security	Governance	Personal Freedom	Social Capital
47	UAE	38	44	98	47	29	18	39	72	77
52	Kuwait	62	71	83	33	33	24	44	87	79
81	KSA	44	81	101	56	42	56	67	98	43
	Average rank									
	Strong rank									
	Weak rank									

Source: The 2009 Legatum Prosperity Index available at http://www.prosperity.com/rankings.aspx

2. Innovation and the Knowledge Economy

The previous discussion demonstrates that some Gulf States are not internationally competitive with respect to internal market competition and important economic growth fundamentals. In this section, we take a closer look at one area of particular challenge and concern, namely the lack of international competitiveness emanating from inadequacies in terms of innovation and entrepreneurialism and the resulting challenges faced by Gulf States in building a knowledge-based economy and society.

The accumulation of knowledge through scientific research and its application to productive activity lies at the heart of the impressive economic growth records of western developed economies and emerging and transition economies. It is the accumulation of knowledge, rather than the accumulation of physical capital and the exploitation of natural resources, that is the engine of long-run economic growth. Knowledge accumulation results from research and development (R&D). It is important to note that even though the Gulf States lag considerably the leading knowledge-based economies in terms of knowledge economy fundamentals, they have been able over the past several decades to improve their position from a historically weak base.

2.1 The Economic and Other Benefits of Research and Development Investment

There is extensive international evidence that demonstrates the economic benefits that result from investment in R&D. Essentially, the economic benefits fall under two categories: 1) the direct economic benefits associated with building the knowledge economy that result in productivity growth in knowledge-based industries; and 2) the indirect, or spillover, economic benefits that flow across the economy from building the knowledge economy. There are several types of spillovers: (i) knowledge spillovers; (ii) market spillovers; and (iii) network spillovers.[17]

Productivity growth occurs in firms and industries involved directly in the knowledge economy. Knowledge-based economies are characterized by four key components:

- Extensive entrepreneurship
- Well educated and highly skilled population
- Excellent information and communication infrastructure, and
- Dynamic innovation system comprising extensive R&D

Economists and other social scientists have demonstrated that the R&D activities of private business enterprises generate widespread benefits enjoyed by consumers and society at large. As a result, the overall economic value to society often exceeds the economic benefits enjoyed by innovating businesses as a result of their research efforts. This excess of the social rate of return over the private rate of return enjoyed by innovating firms is described by economists as a positive spillover or externality. These spillovers imply that private businesses will invest less than is socially desirable in research, with the result that some desirable projects will not be

17. A. Jaffe, *Economic Analysis of Research Spillovers Implications for the Advanced Technology Program*, Brandeis University, National Bureau of Economic, 1996, 1.

undertaken, and others will be delayed or occur on a scale smaller than is socially desirable.[18]

Knowledge spillovers occur because of the public goods nature of knowledge. Knowledge, once created, can be used by others freely and without appropriate compensation for its creator or the desires of its inventor to limit use. Market spillovers occur when innovation leads to both improved quality and lower prices for new products. There may be unintended benefits beyond the purpose of the original innovation. Network spillovers arise when an improvement in one area of commerce or industry spills over into a complementary area. For instance, improvements in computer operating systems enable faster and more attractive computer games to be developed.

Often these spillovers involve universities and business enterprises. There is often a mutual benefit that flows between industrial R&D on the one hand and university research on the other. There is strong international evidence that university research encourages industrial R&D in close proximity to a university. There is also evidence of significant spillovers from university research and 'high technology' innovations in industries and sectors upstream or downstream from a particular R&D activity.

According to Dowrick, there are at least six additional benefits that can be linked to R&D:[19]

- Increasing the stock of useful knowledge
- Training skilled graduates
- Creating new scientific instrumentation and methodologies
- Forming networks and stimulating social interaction
- Increasing the capacity for scientific and technological problem-solving
- Creating new firms

It is not possible to build a knowledge-based economy without investment in R&D. That is why all the knowledge-based economies in the world fund research in universities, either in the form of direct block grants, or in the form of competitive funds via national funding bodies, similar to the National Science Foundation in the US. Such R&D funding may be in conjunction with industry, but often it is independent of commercial partnerships. There is a long tradition in knowledge-based

18. Ibid., 2.
19. Steve Dowrick, *A Review of the Evidence on Science, R&D and Productivity,* Australian Department of Education, Science and Training, 2003, 10.

economies of government support for science and technology research, from prizes to current systems of direct and competitive funding of research. Today there is also an increased awareness in the value of social sciences and humanities – appreciating that what we think, how we live, and how we interact with each other and the world around us provides for a healthier community, more competitive businesses, and better government.[20] In all knowledge-based economies, governments play a major funding role. For instance in the US, the federal government provides more than 60 percent of university research expenditures.[21]

To illustrate the extent to which knowledge-based economies invest in R&D, it is possible to consider what percentage of a country's Gross Domestic Product (GDP) is invested in R&D. Figure 1 provides data on the percentage of GDP spent on R&D for a broad sample of countries provided by OECD. There is considerable dispersion from below 0.5 percent for Mexico to above 3.5 percent for Sweden. However, the OECD average is 2.26 percent of GDP on R&D. Unfortunately there are no reliable data for any Gulf State. Importantly, Qatar has announced that it plans to spend 2.8 percent of GDP on R&D going forward. No similar announcements have been made by other Gulf States. Expenditure of GDP on R&D is likely to be below 0.3 percent in each Gulf State except KSA where it is likely to be about 0.5 percent. Currently, the Gulf States lag dramatically behind OECD countries in terms of R&D investment expenditure.

Figure 1: Gross Domestic Expenditure on R&D as a Percentage of GDP

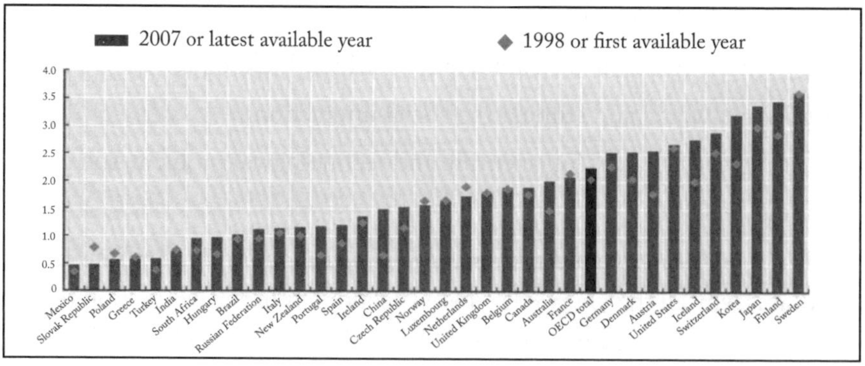

Source: OECD in Figures-2009

20. Social Sciences and Humanities Research Council (SSHRC), *Framing our Direction*. 2010, available at: http://www.sshrc.ca/site/about-crsh/publications/framing_our_direction_e.pdf, 2.
21. National Science Foundation.Science & Engineering Indicators 2008. Available at http://www.nsf.gov/statistics/seind08/

The National Innovation System

According to Cutler, innovation is the conversion of knowledge and ideas into a benefit.[22] The benefit may be in the form of new or improved products, processes or services. The benefit may be for commercial use or the public good. Innovation may be described as 'creating value by doing things differently'; or 'doing something in a novel way'. In other words, it is 'good ideas put to work'. Moreover, innovation:

- is a process of continuously generating and applying new ideas
- complements and facilitates the knowledge creation and application process
- is one of the key drivers of economic growth
- is essential to the competitiveness and sustainability of an economy

Therefore, innovation is a dynamic, evolving and learning process. There are three highly interdependent components within an innovation system:

- Knowledge production (the origination of new knowledge and ideas)
- Knowledge application (the deployment of knowledge and ideas in the real world)
- Knowledge diffusion (the absorption of this applied knowledge and its adaptation in use)

The innovation process may be represented graphically, following Cutler (2008).

Figure 2: The Systemic Elements of the Innovation Process

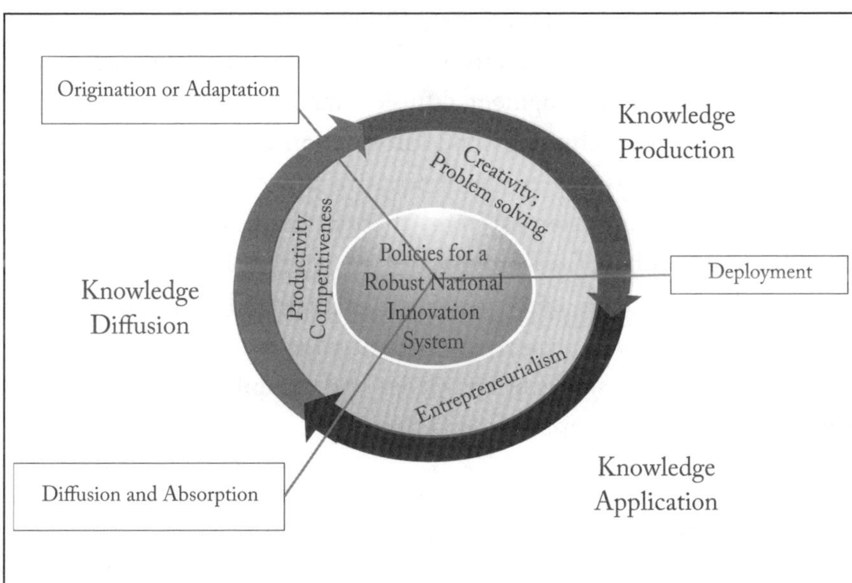

22. T. Cutler, *Venturous Australia* (Melbourne: Cutler & Co, Melbourne), 2008.

Innovation is the result of numerous interactions between key organizations and groups in the economy including universities, government, firms and other institutions, which together form an innovation system. The national innovation system consists of the flows and relationships which exist among industry, government and universities in the development of science and technology.

The simple virtuous innovation cycle approach presented by Cutler is a very useful way to look at innovation. However, in reality it is likely to contain many non-linearities and feedback effects. The link between knowledge and innovation is far from straightforward. Innovation does not occur in isolation but emerges from an innovation system characterized by innovative firms, often small and medium sized enterprises (SMEs), often working with government and universities as R&D partners. This has led to the Triple Helix model of innovation[23] with the university as the SME founder via leveraging off its intellectual property assets generated from research; industry as the incubator through companies that subsequently spin off, and governments as the venture capitalist bearing the risk of commercialization.

Irrespective of how innovation occurs, it is clear that innovation does not occur in a vacuum. That is, innovative business enterprises interact with the public and private sector, including universities and Higher Education Institutions (HEIs). Therefore, the National Innovation System (NIS) may be thought of as embracing all important economic, social, political, organizational, institutional and other factors that influence the development, diffusion and use of innovation.[24]

NIS is the flow of technology and information among people, enterprises and institutions which is key to the innovative process on the national level. According to the innovation system theory, innovation and technology development are results of a complex set of relationships among actors in the system, which includes enterprises, universities and government research institutes.[25] In summary:

- Innovation is built on stocks of knowledge and capability, and the information flows of the innovation capital around these

---

23. H. Etzkowitz, "Innovation in Innovation: The Triple Helix of University – Industry – Government Relations," *Social Sciences Information* 42, no. 3 (September 2003): 293-337.
24. J. Fagerberg, D. Mowery, and R. Nelson, *The Oxford Handbook of Innovation* (Oxford University Press, 2005), 182.
25. R. Nelson, (ed.) *National Innovation Systems. A Comparative Analysis* (New York/Oxford:Oxford University Press, 1993).

- Innovation Policy is a central part of economic policy
- A successful NIS invests in each innovation stock component as well as in the flows and linkages between them
- A NIS incorporates regional (RIS) and sectoral (SIS) clusters of activity; and
- Within a globalized economy, a NIS also needs to be positioned within a global innovation ecosystem.

More recently, innovations systems have moved to more open platforms. According to Chesbrough, 'open innovation' embraces the commercialization of external as well as internal ideas by firms using outside pathways to market new products, processes or services.[26]

Further evidence on just how far the Gulf States lag the most innovative economies is provided by the Economist Intelligence Unit, which has created an Innovation Index to rank countries. According to the Economist Intelligence Unit, "Innovation is described as the application of knowledge in a novel way, primarily for economic benefit. Companies deem it vitally important as a competitive tool. Government policymakers see it as essential for economic growth."[27] To rank countries, the Economist Intelligence Unit distinguishes between innovation output and innovation inputs. Innovation output is measured by patents granted by the three major government patent offices: European Patent Office; Japanese Patent Office and US Patent and Trademark Office. By contrast, innovation inputs include direct drivers of innovation such as R&D expenditures, quality of research infrastructure, education and skills of the workforce, ICT infrastructure and broadband penetration. Indirect drivers of innovation such as the political environment, market opportunities, economic policy environment, and the regulatory environment are also included in the innovation inputs measure.

Table 6: Innovation Index Rank for Gulf Countries among 82 Countries

Country	2002-2006	2004-2008	2009-2013	Change from 2004-08 to 2009-13
Bahrain	50	60	56	4

26. H. Chesbrough, "Open Innovation: The New Imperative for Creating and Profiting from Technology," Harvard Business School, Cambridge Ma., 2003.
27. The Economist Intelligence Unit Limited, *A New Ranking of the World's Most Innovative Countries*, 2009. Available at http://graphics.eiu.com/PDF/Cisco_Innovation_Methodology.pdf , 2.

Kuwait	35	37	36	1
Oman	N/A	N/A	N/A	N/A
Qatar	57	51	53	-2
Saudi Arabia	41	42	37	5
UAE	43	40	44	-4

Source: The Economist Intelligence Unit Limited, A New Ranking of the World's Most Innovative Countries, 2009. Available at http://graphics.eiu.com/PDF/Cisco_Innovation_Methodology.pdf

Note: N/A means not available

The Economist Intelligence Unit is forecasting a fall of four places in both Qatar's and UAE's rank position on the Innovation Index in the period 2009-2013. Knowledge production is a key part of the national innovation system. In contrast to the indicators published by WEF, Kuwait does better than the other Gulf States on the Innovation Index, but still lags the most innovative countries in the world substantially.

An alternative set of international benchmark data are provided by INSEAD, which produces a Global Innovation Index for 130 countries.[28] The rank positions for the six Gulf States according to INSEAD's Global Innovation Index are as follows: UAE (24), Kuwait (33), Qatar (35), Bahrain (40), KSA (54) and Oman (65).

It is interesting that UAE and Qatar are ranked considerably better by INSEAD than by the Economist Intelligence Unit, while KSA performs better according to the Economist Intelligence Unit compared to GCI. These apparent contradictions between these two innovation indexes highlight the care that must be taken when using such international benchmark indicators. The differences in methodology used to construct each index provide only a partial explanation. Equally important is the rapid rate of change that is occurring in the Gulf States as they move to build more knowledge-based economies and societies. This combined with questions about the quality of data available to measure elements of the benchmark indicators, means that care must be taken when using such international benchmark data. Notwithstanding these caveats, the various international benchmark data discussed above indicate that currently the Gulf States, generally, are not internationally competitive with respect to innovation.

28. See http://www.globalinnovationindex.org/gii/main/reports/2009-10/FullReport_09-10.pdf.

2.3 The Role of University Research in the Knowledge Economy and National Innovation System

The essential contribution of knowledge to economic competitiveness and social welfare is widely recognized. Critical in the early stages of the development of an innovations system is the key role played by a country's universities. Such recognition has increased the attention to the role of universities and HEIs in the production and dissemination of knowledge. To increase the universities' contribution to development through the production and distribution of knowledge, universities in developing countries need to transform themselves into 'developmental universities.' To achieve this, other participants, such as industry and government, must also be prepared to take on new responsibilities.[29]

Universities and HEIs are a major force in shaping the country's knowledge power and innovative capacity. They accept the responsibilities which this brings and, in return, ask that governments, and civil society in general, should recognize their responsibility to enable universities and HEIs to secure the resources which will permit them to fulfill their mission not just well, but with excellence and in a way which allows them to compete with the higher education systems of other countries.[30] According to the European University Association, there are four ways that universities may contribute to building the knowledge economy and enhancing innovation.[31]

a. Linking higher education and research

The provision of research-based education at all levels is a particular strength of leading universities. Institutions offering research-based higher education should ensure that a research component is included and developed in all cycles thus allowing students to acquire research experience and encouraging an interest in research as a possible career. This also applies in relation to the acquisition of a broad range of transferable skills that should be included not only at the doctoral level but in curricula at all levels, thus promoting a new generation of leaders able to integrate multiple perspectives and be responsive to the needs of rapidly changing labor markets.

29. J. Sutz, *The Role of Universities in Knowledge Production, Science & Innovation Policy: Aid for Higher Education,* 2005, 1. Available from: http://www.scidev.net/en/science-and-innovation-policy/aid-for-higher-education/policy-briefs/the-role-of-universities-in-knowledge-production-.html [Accessed: Apr 1, 2010].

30. European University Association, Lisbon Declaration Europe's Universities beyond 2010: Diversity with a Common Purpose, The European University Association, 2007, 7.

31. Ibid., 4.

b. Embedding high quality doctoral programs in universities

Original research has to remain the main component of all doctorates. Furthermore, recognizing that the attractiveness of a future career in research and professorial appointments are determined largely at the doctoral stage, universities need to engage actively with national research councils and other funding agencies to improve the conditions of the financing of doctoral candidates and programs, and the future career development of researchers in both academic and non-academic sectors.

c. Developing institutional strategies for research

Universities should work to strengthen further their institutional research strategies with a view to introducing strategic management approaches. These will reinforce the pooling of research expertise within the university. The increased costs of research (including scientific infrastructure) will intensify the need to identify priorities.

d. Promoting innovation capacity

Universities should increasingly seek to enhance their research and improve their innovation capacities by further developing partnerships with external partners, by professionalizing their processes of knowledge transfer, and by looking for synergy between international, regional, and national research policy initiatives.

So how well resourced and equipped are universities in the Gulf to contribute to their national innovation systems? Are there any research-intensive universities in the Gulf that are internationally competitive? How well placed are the Gulf States to leverage their universities to help build an internationally competitive innovation system and knowledge base? These are difficult questions to answer due to data limitations. However, one imperfect approach is to look at the university rankings provided by the Times Higher Education Supplement and Shanghai Jiaotong University, two well-known league tables.[32] For this exercise, let us make the generous assumption that a rank position of 500 or better is consistent with being internationally competitive. Turning to the more research demanding and comprehensive Shanghai Jiaotong (ARWU) 2010 ranking list, only two universities from the Gulf make the top 500: King Saud University in KSA makes the 301-400 group while King Fahd University of Petroleum & Minerals is ranked in the 401-500 group. On the Times Higher Education ranking list, King Saud University is ranked 247, King Fahd University is ranked 266, and United Arab Emirates University (UAE) is ranked 374. There are no other universities from the Gulf

32. See http://www.timeshighereducation.co.uk/, and http://www.arwu.org/, respectively.

States in the top 500 of either list. That is, only three universities from the Gulf may be considered as internationally competitive according to the Times Higher Education list and only two may be considered as internationally competitive using the Shanghai Jiaotong ranks. What this means is that there is very little scope currently for Gulf States to become more internationally competitive with respect to innovation and knowledge fundamentals. Of course, the initiatives in KSA with respect to King Abdulla University of Science and Technology, in Qatar via the Qatar Foundation with its six branch campuses of US universities, and in Abu Dhabi with respect to Masdar Institute, Khalifa University of Science Technology and Research, New York University and the Sorbonne should help grow the research base in these countries, but they are each at the very early stages of development and are very much experiments associated with using the brands of well-known international universities. To have any significant impact, clearly what is needed is a much bigger investment in the research capacity of all national universities in each Gulf State, in addition to attempts to pick winners by partnering with famous brands.

2.4 The Knowledge Economy

Knowledge possesses unusual properties. Unlike other resources, knowledge is not depleted when shared, and once it is made public others cannot easily be excluded from its use. Moreover, the stock of knowledge is often enlarged, rather than depleted, by extensive use.[33] Knowledge breeds more knowledge.

As was noted earlier, to build a knowledge-based economy and society requires the development of innovation and a NIS. There are three interdependent components of a NIS: 1) Knowledge Production; 2) Knowledge Application; and 3) Knowledge Diffusion. These components involve extensive participation of university researchers. Without a strong university research base, it is impossible to have a successful innovation system.

"A knowledge-driven economy is one in which the generation and exploitation of knowledge play the predominant part in the creation of wealth."[34] Economic prosperity depends upon knowledge creation and learning.

Knowledge economy is a term that refers either to an economy of knowledge focused on the production and management of knowledge in the frame of

---

33. Dowrick, *A Review of the Evidence on Science, R&D and Productivity*, 1.
34. United Kingdom Department of Trade & Industry, Secretary of State for Trade and Industry 1998, "Our Competitive Future: Building the Knowledge Economy," Vol.CM 4176, London, 1998.

economic constraints, or to a knowledge-based economy. In the second meaning, more frequently used, it refers to the use of knowledge technologies (such as knowledge engineering and knowledge management) to produce economic benefits. The essential difference is that in a knowledge economy, knowledge is a product, in a knowledge-based economy, knowledge is a tool.[35] Knowledge includes "know-what"; "know-why"; "know-who"; "know-when"; and "know-where."[36]

According to the Organization for Economic Cooperation and Development (OECD), the term "Knowledge-based Economy" results from a fuller recognition of the role of knowledge and technology in economic growth. Knowledge, as embodied in human beings (as "human capital") and in technology, has always been central to economic development. But only over the last few years has its relative importance been recognized, just as that importance is growing. The OECD member countries' economies are more strongly dependent on the production, distribution and use of knowledge than ever before. Output and employment are expanding fastest in high-technology industries, such as computers, electronics and aerospace. In the past decade, the high-technology share of OECD manufacturing production and exports has more than doubled, to reach 20-25 per cent. Knowledge-intensive service sectors, such as education, communications and information, are growing even faster. Indeed, it is estimated that more than 50 per cent of Gross Domestic Product (GDP) in the major OECD economies is now knowledge-based.[37]

The knowledge economy recognizes that an organization's intellectual capital is embodied in its employees' knowledge, brain power and its processes. The ability to improve these processes continuously is a source of competitive advantage. Since the process by which research affects the larger society is often complex and sometimes unpredictable, no single indicator of this impact can capture the full value of the research. Hence, one key challenge is to conceptualize and assess how research improves and enriches the daily lives of individuals, groups and communities. This expands from counting journal articles and books to expanding outcomes which help to change thinking and behavior in everyday life.[38]

35. P. Drucker, *The Age of Discontinuity: Guidelines to Our Changing Society* (New Jersey: Harper & Row, 1992 Reprint), Ch. 12.

36. D. Norris, Mason, J. Robson 2003, "A Revolution in Knowledge Sharing," *Educase Review* 38, no. 5:17.

37. Organization for Economic Co-operation and Development 1996, *The Knowledge-Based Economy*. Paris, .9

38. Social Sciences and Humanities Research Council (SSHRC), *Framing our Direction*, 12.

2.5 Measuring the Knowledge Economy

In order to measure the knowledge economy, the World Bank Institute has developed the Knowledge Economy Index, using its Knowledge Assessment Methodology. According to the World Bank Institute, the Knowledge Economy Index is composed of four pillars:

Pillar 1: Economic and Institutional Regime

The country's economic and institutional regime must provide incentives for the efficient use of existing and new knowledge and the flourishing of entrepreneurship.

Pillar 2: Education and Skills

The country's people need education and skills that enable them to create and share, and to use it well.

Pillar 3: ICT Infrastructure

A dynamic information infrastructure is needed to facilitate the effective communication, dissemination, and processing of information.

Pillar 4: Innovation System

The country's innovation system - firms, research centers, universities, think tanks, consultants, and other organizations - must be capable of tapping the growing stock of global knowledge, assimilating and adapting it to local needs, and creating new technology.

The World Bank Institute has calculated the Knowledge Economy Index (KEI) and Knowledge Index (KI) for 146 countries. KEI includes all four pillars, whereas, KI comprises Pillars 2 to 4. KEI takes into account whether the environment is conducive for knowledge to be used effectively for economic development and is calculated based on the average of the normalized scores of a country on all four pillars. The KI measures a country's ability to generate, adopt and diffuse knowledge and is a simple average of the normalized scores of a country on the key variables in the three pillars (Education, Innovation and ICT).

Table 7 summarizes the rank position for the Gulf States. None of the Gulf States is ranked particularly well on KEI and KI. UAE and Qatar are ranked reasonably well in terms of ICT. In contrast to the Economist Intelligence Unit Innovation Index, Kuwait is ranked considerably below UAE and Qatar on innovation and only just above Oman, Bahrain and KSA. Table 7 is useful in drawing attention to the extent to which the Gulf States lag internationally competitive countries in terms of innovation and knowledge economy fundamentals.

Table 7: Rank of Gulf Countries among 146 Countries with Regard to Knowledge Economy

Country	Knowledge Economy Index (KEI)	Knowledge Index (KI)	Pillar 1: Economic Incentive Regime	Pillar 2: Education	Pillar 3: ICT	Pillar 4: Innovation
Bahrain	49	56	48	60	40	80
Kuwait	52	59	51	76	46	70
Oman	66	79	40	86	76	71
Qatar	44	45	42	67	27	48
Saudi Arabia	68	73	58	80	52	86
UAE	45	44	47	79	21	46

Source: The Knowledge Assessment Methodology (KAM) 2009 rankings for 146 countries, The World Bank Institute, available at: http://info.worldbank.org/etools/kam2/KAM_page5.asp

3. Policy Implications and Concluding Remarks

This paper has focused attention on the extent to which Gulf States are currently not internationally competitive. In particular, evidence has been presented that identifies the extent to which Gulf States lag in terms of internal market competitiveness and growth competitiveness. It was noted that, although there is some unevenness across internal market indicators, generally speaking UAE and Qatar are quite internationally competitive with respect to internal market competitiveness and Oman is not far behind, but comfortably ahead of Bahrain and KSA. However, Kuwait lags substantially and cannot be considered internationally competitive in this regard.

In terms of growth competitiveness, UAE and Qatar are quite internationally competitive in infrastructure, macro economy and technological readiness while the other Gulf States generally are not. However, in the areas of education and innovation, two key drivers of the knowledge economy and enablers of economic diversification, none of the Gulf States are internationally competitive.

Several important factors that constrain the international growth competitiveness of Gulf States have been identified. In particular, the generally inadequate state of the education systems, the lack of national innovation systems, the lack of internationally competitive universities and the lack of entrepreneurship were identified as key impediments although the Gulf States vary in terms of the degree to which they are not internationally competitive. The lack of internal market competitiveness compounds the challenges faced by several Gulf States.

In knowledge-based economies, there exists a regulatory framework of property rights and institutions that encourages and enhances entrepreneurial activity. Furthermore, knowledge-based economies have high literacy rates and excellent primary and secondary school systems and large high quality higher education systems including research-based universities. In addition, knowledge-based economies possess dynamic information infrastructure that facilitate the effective communication, dissemination and processing of information. Finally, knowledge-based economies possess extensive innovation systems that comprise research centers, research-based universities and think tanks capable of tapping the growing stock of global knowledge, assimilating and adapting it to local needs and creating new technology.[39] From the evidence presented here there is not a single Gulf State that presently gets near this description.

As IKED notes,[40] governments all around the world today recognize that one of their core policy responsibilities is to contribute to putting in place the conditions for building and using knowledge to sustain long-term growth, in recognition that:

- Knowledge may add critically to the performance of all other production factors
- Knowledge has become important for the competitiveness of basically all sectors and industries, even for those which used to be dependent on low labor costs and mature standardized technology
- Markets left to themselves will not on their own manage to put in place the conditions that are required for success in knowledge creation and use – so governments have a key role to play.

39. World Bank Institute, *The Knowledge Assessment Methodology (KAM) 2009 Rankings for 146 Countries* , 2009, 5, available at http://info.worldbank.org/etools/kam2/KAM_page5.asp
40. IKED, *Towards Innovation Policy in Abu Dhabi*, General Secretariat of the Abu Dhabi Executive Council, May 2010.

To overcome their lack of international competitiveness, particularly with respect to knowledge economy drivers, there are many things that each Gulf State must do. Although the recipe will vary from one Gulf State to another, there are several generalized reforms that represent a generic uplift strategy to help improve the international competitiveness of the Gulf States:

- Reform their education systems to move away from rote learning to creative thinking pedagogy and help develop entrepreneurial spirit and risk taking behavior
- Develop national innovation systems by investing in knowledge production (increase competitive research funding for universities), knowledge application (expand university-industry research collaboration), and knowledge diffusion (expand venture capital and improve intellectual property protection)
- Increase substantially their percentage GDP expenditure on Research and Development
- Increase the block funding for basic research at universities (the award of research grants not on a competitive basis) for the following important reasons. The need to:

  - forge a strong link between teaching and learning on the one hand, and research, on the other, in core disciplines within these institutions
  - facilitate undergraduate research skill and capacity building
  - allow laboratory-based research and desk-based scholarship to occur
  - recruit and retain the very best faculty available; and
  - enable the delivery of University mission-based research outcomes
- Establish a national research foundation in each Gulf State modeled on the best international research funding foundations in the world similar to the National Science Foundation in the US in order to: provide funding support on a competitive basis to researchers at the universities of each Gulf State; help build national innovation systems; help promote research activity in private and public universities, colleges, centers, institutes and companies, by individuals or teams of researchers; help build a knowledge-based economy and knowledge society; provide research leadership; enhance the development process; and raise the international ranking of the Gulf State with regard to research, innovation, patents and knowledge economy.
- Issue a Gulf Cooperation Council decision approved by all Gulf States for the establishment of a 'National Portfolio' (fund) for the funding of scientific research activities on a competitive basis through the National Research Foundations established in Gulf States;

- Establish a ministry of innovation and research in each Gulf State
- Set regulations and policies that govern and promote research and innovation in each country
- Encourage university joint research with the private sector's institutions
- Diversify the economies of each Gulf State coherently and in complementary ways
- Adjust their incentive systems to encourage their nationals to participate in higher education and become knowledge workers, particularly in productive sectors
- Link their education systems much more closely to the workforce needs of the productive sectors, particularly knowledge-based sectors

The ability of the Gulf States to move their economies towards a stronger knowledge base is easier said than done. However, most Gulf States possess sufficient resources to facilitate this shift. It remains to be seen if there is sufficient political will across the Gulf to implement the necessary reforms and incentives. One thing is clear from the survey presented here, in order for the Gulf States to increase their international competitiveness they will each need to improve their knowledge economy fundamentals. Importantly, it is possible to improve the international competitiveness of the Gulf States with the implementation of suitable knowledge economy uplift strategies in each Gulf State.

Bibliography

Angell, J. *The Theory of International Prices: History, Criticism and Restatement.* Harvard University Press, 1926.

ARWU. *Academic Ranking of World Universities-2010.* Available at http://www.arwu.org/index.jsp

Chesbrough, H. *Open Innovation: The New Imperative for Creating and Profiting from Technology.* Harvard Business School, Cambridge Ma., 2003.

Cutler, T. *Venturous Australia.* Melbourne, Australia: Cutler & Co, 2008.

Cassel, G. *Money and Foreign Exchange after 1914.* London: Constable and Co., 1992.

Dowrick, S. *A Review of the Evidence on Science, R&D and Productivity.* Australian Department of Education, Science and Training, 2003.

Drucker, P. T*he Age of Discontinuity: Guidelines to Our Changing Society.* Ch. 12. New Jersey: Harper & Row, 1992, Reprint.

Etzkowitz, H. "Innovation in Innovation: The Triple Helix of University - Industry - Government Relations." *Social Sciences Information* 42, no. 3 (September 2003): 293-337.

European University Association. *Lisbon Declaration Europe's Universities beyond 2010: Diversity with a Common Purpose.* The European University Association, 2007.

Fagerberg, J., D. Mowery, and R. Nelson, *The Oxford Handbook of Innovation.* Oxford University Press, 2005.

Hawkins, J. "The Concept of Competitiveness," Treasury Working Paper, 2006-02, Australian Treasury, Canberra, April 2006.

IKED. *Towards Innovation Policy in Abu Dhabi.* General Secretariat of the Abu Dhabi Executive Council, May 2010.

Insead. *Global Innovation Index Report 2009-2010.* Insead, 2010.

Jaffe, A. *Economic Analysis of Research Spillovers Implications for the Advanced Technology Program.* Brandeis University, National Bureau of Economic, 1996.

Krugman, P. "Competitiveness: a Dangerous Obsession." *Foreign Affairs* (March/April 1994): 28-44.

Krugman, P. "A Country is not a Company." *Harvard Business Review* (January-February 1996): 40-51.

Legatum Institute. *The 2009 Legatum Prosperity Index*. Legatum Institute, London, UK, 2009.

National Science Foundation.*Science & Engineering Indicators 2008*. Available at http://www.nsf.gov/statistics/seind08/

Nelson, R. (ed.) *National Innovation Systems. A Comparative Analysis.* New York/ Oxford: Oxford University Press, 1993.

Norris,D.,J.Mason, R. Robson. 2003."A Revolution in Knowledge Sharing." *Educase Review* 38, no. 5 (2003):14-26.

Organization for Economic Co-operation and Development. *The Knowledge-Based Economy*. Paris, 1996, p.9.

Organization for Economic Cooperation and Development. *Going for Growth 2006: Economic Policy Reform*, Paris, 2006.

Organization for Economic Cooperation and Development. *OECD in Figures 2009*. OECD Observer, 2009.

Parsley, D. and S-J. Wei. *A Prism into the PPP Puzzles: the Microfoundations of Big Mac Real Exchange Rates*. National Bureau of Economic Research working papers, no. 10074, November 2003.

Rogoff, K. "The Purchasing Power Parity Puzzle." *Journal of Economic Literature* XXXIV, no. 2 (June 1996): 647-68.

Squalli, J., K. Wilson and S. Hugo. "An Analysis of Growth Competitiveness." *International Review of Applied Economics* 22, no. 1 (January 2008): 105-125.

Squalli, J and K. Wilson. "Openness and Access." *Applied Economics* 41, no. 3 (February 2009): 363-379.

Social Sciences and Humanities Research Council (SSHRC). *Framing our Direction*. 2010. Available at: http://www.sshrc.ca/site/about-crsh/publications/framing_our_direction_e.pdf

Sutz, J. The Role of Universities in Knowledge Production, Science & Innovation Policy: Aid for Higher Education. 2005. Available at: http://www.scidev.net/en/science-and-innovation-policy/aid-for-higher-education/policy-briefs/the-role-of-universities-in-knowledge-production-.html [Accessed April 1, 2010].

Taylor, A. "A Century of Purchasing Power Parity." *Review of Economics and Statistics* 84 (2002): 139-50.

The Economist Intelligence Unit Limited. *A New Ranking of the World's Most*

Innovative Countries, 2009. Available at http://graphics.eiu.com/PDF/Cisco_Innovation_Methodology.pdf

UAE Cabinet. *UAE Government Strategy 2011-2013.* 2010. Available at: http://www.uaecabinet.ae/English/UAEStrategy/Pages/UAEGovtStrategy2011-2013.aspx

United Kingdom Department of Trade & Industry, Secretary of State for Trade and Industry 1998. *Our Competitive Future: Building the Knowledge Economy.* Vol. CM 4176, London, 1998.

World Bank Institute. *The Knowledge Assessment Methodology (KAM) 2009 Rankings for 146 Countries 2009.* Available at http://info.worldbank.org/etools/kam2/KAM_page5.asp

World Economic Forum. *The Global Competitiveness Report 2009-2010.* Palgrave Macmillan, 2009.

About the Contributors

Randa Alami is a development economist specializing in the Middle East, and currently a Teaching Fellow, School of Oriental and African Studies, London University. She has also worked as a Research Fellow at the Oxford Institute for Energy Studies and UNCTAD, and been a consultant to DFID, ESCWA and others. She holds a Ph.D. in Economics from London University.

Elias El-Achkar is Director of Research and Statistics at the Association of Banks in Lebanon and has taught Banking and Finance at major universities in Lebanon. He is a graduate of Leeds University and has presented academic and policy research in international conferences and seminars.

Michael P. Grifferty is President of the Gulf Bond and Sukuk Association (GBSA), an organization he helped to found in 2009 and that represents fixed income market participants in the Arabian Gulf. Previously, he had been a US Treasury sovereign debt and markets advisor, where he advised over 40 countries and regional organizations. Prior to his international career, he worked for Government Finance Associates, advising US state and local governments and public authorities. He has degrees from New York University and Georgetown University in public finance and international relations, respectively.

Gabriela Lippe-Holst is a consultant in international business law with a focus on banking and capital markets law. During an international career, she has worked for major international institutions and financial services companies. She is admitted to the Swiss bar, was elected Young Leader by the American Swiss Foundation in 2005 and holds a master's degree in Law from the University of Neuchâtel.

Erwin Nierop is Senior Adviser at the European Central Bank (ECB) and Head Project Manager for Technical Assistance to the Gulf Cooperation Council, advising the latter on its monetary union initiatives. In a similar capacity, together with a team of consultants and ECB staff, he has also prepared a study on East African Monetary Union for the East African Community. Prior to joining ECB he worked at the Dutch central bank after completion of his studies in civil and international law.

Lamia A. Obay is Assistant Professor and Chair, Finance Department, College of Business Administration, Abu Dhabi University. She holds a Ph.D. in International Finance and Banking from the George Washington University, USA.

Mandagolathur Raghu is the head of research at Kuwait Financial Center (Markaz) and leads the strategic research initiative of Markaz with specific focus on asset allocation, capital market, quantitative finance, and volatility studies. He has obtained CFA Charter from the CFA Institute, USA and is a certified Financial Risk Manager (FRM) from the Global Association for Risk Professionals, USA.

Wassim Shahin is Dean of the School of Business and Professor of Business Economics at the Lebanese American University, Byblos, Lebanon and holds a Ph.D. from Indiana University, Bloomington, USA. He has authored, co-authored and edited three books, several monographs, and over 20 academic articles dealing with monetary policy, banking, exchange rates, budgetary politics and the application of economic methodology to hostage-taking activities. He is the founding editor of *Review of Middle East Economics and Finance* and serves on the editorial board of several academic journals.

Kenneth Wilson is Director of the National Research Foundation (NRF) of UAE. Prior to joining NRF, he was Professor of Economics and Director of the Economic & Policy Research Unit, Zayed University, UAE. Originally from Australia, Dr. Wilson has undertaken research in a wide range of applied economic areas and has published more than 50 refereed publications including books, book chapters and international peer reviewed journal articles on topics such as international competitiveness, contingent protection, dumping and anti-dumping, intra-industry trade, tourism economics, productivity and labor market issues. He received his Ph.D. from the University of Wisconsin-Milwaukee, USA.

Rodney Wilson is Director of the Islamic Finance Programme in Durham University. He currently chairs the academic committee of the Institute of Islamic Banking and Insurance in London and is acting as consultant to the Islamic Financial Services Board with respect to its Sharia Governance Guidelines. His previous consultancy experience included work for the Islamic Development Bank in Jeddah, the Ministry of Economy and Planning in Riyadh, and the Qatar Central Bank. From January until June 2009, he was a Visiting Professor at the Qatar Foundation's Faculty of Islamic Studies in Doha, and he returned there in 2010. He has also acted as Course Director for Euromoney Legal Training in various financial centers.

Eckart Woertz is a visiting fellow at Princeton University and Senior Research Fellow Associate at the Barcelona Centre for International Affairs (CIDOB). Formerly he was Director of Economic Studies at the Gulf Research Center (GRC) in Dubai, UAE. He has worked for financial services companies in Germany and the UAE and as a consultant for international and regional organizations such as UNCTAD, UNDP, and the Saudi Ministry of Economy and Planning. He holds a Ph.D. in Economics from Friedrich-Alexander University, Erlangen-Nuremberg.